COLLINS COBUILD

ENGLISH GUIDES
8: SPELLING

Jonathan Payne

THE UNIVERSITY
OF BIRMINGHAM

COLLINS
COBUILD

HarperCollins*Publishers*

HarperCollins Publishers
77-85 Fulham Palace Road
London W6 8JB

COBUILD is a trademark of William Collins Sons & Co Ltd

© HarperCollins Publishers Ltd 1995
First published 1995

10 9 8 7 6 5 4 3 2 1

All rights reserved. No part of this book may be reproduced, stored
in a retrieval system, or transmitted in any form or by any means,
electronic, mechanical, photocopying, recording or otherwise,
without the prior permission in writing of the Publisher.

ISBN 0 00 370950 7

Computer typeset by Tradespools Ltd, Frome, Somerset

Printed in Great Britain by HarperCollins Manufacturing, Glasgow

For Aidan Alexander Charles

Corpus Acknowledgements

We would like to acknowledge the assistance of the many hundreds
of individuals and companies who have kindly given permission for
copyright material to be used in The Bank of English. The written
sources include many national and regional newspapers in Britain and
overseas; magazine and periodical publishers; and book publishers in
Britain, the United States, and Australia. Extensive spoken data has
been provided by radio and television broadcasting companies; research
workers at many universities and other institutions; and numerous
individual contributors. We are grateful to them all.

The COBUILD Series

Founding Editor-in-Chief　　　John Sinclair

Editorial Team

Editorial Director　　　Gwyneth Fox

Series Editor　　　Jane Bradbury

Editor　　　Ramesh Krishnamurthy

Computer Staff　　　Tim Lane
　　　　　　　　　　Andrea Lewis

Secretarial Staff　　　Sue Crawley
　　　　　　　　　　Michelle Devereux

Publishing Manager　　　Debbie Seymour

HarperCollins*Publishers*
Gillian McNair

Acknowledgements

We would like to thank Annette Capel for her invaluable contribution to the early stages of this project, Susan Hunston and Deborah Orpin for their helpful comments on the text, and Geoff Barnbrook for his ideas on 'enough'.

Contents

Introduction	v
Glossary	vii
Chart of Sounds, Guide Words and Main Spelling Patterns	xi

1 The English Spelling System   1-58

1.1 A brief historical background	1-5
1.2 The rules of English spelling	6-11
1.3 American spellings	12-15
1.4 Apostrophes	16
1.5 Capital letters	17-18
1.6 Double consonants	19-22
1.7 Etymology – the history of words	23
1.8 Final **e**	24-25
1.9 Foreign words	26
1.10 Grammar	27-28
1.11 Greek spelling conventions	29
1.12 Hyphens	30
1.13 Latin spelling conventions	31
1.14 Meaning	32-34
1.15 Native spelling conventions	35-36
1.16 Plurals	37-39
1.17 Silent consonants	40-48
1.18 Sounds and spelling	49-52
1.19 Three letter rule	53
1.20 Vowel digraphs	54-55
1.21 Word formation	56-58

2 Sounds and their Spelling Patterns   59-179

2.1 The 24 main vowel sounds	**59-105**
2.2 'Schwa' (/ə/) in word endings	**106-116**
2.2.1 **-able** or **-ible**?	106-107
2.2.2 **-ant** or **-ent**?	108-110
2.2.3 **-er, -or,** or **-ar**?	111-115
2.2.4 **-al, -el, -il, -le, -ol,** or **-ul**?	116
2.3 The 24 main consonant sounds	**117-179**

3 Word Lists   180-303

Introduction

Most users of English have problems in spelling some words. This book will help you to learn and understand the principles of English spelling, and you will soon begin to recognize the spelling patterns and the groups of words which share the same pattern.

The **Glossary** (pages vii-x) contains a brief explanation of the technical terms used in this book.

The **Chart of Sounds, Guide Words, and Main Spelling Patterns** (pages xi-xvi) is a list of the main sounds used in English, represented by International Phonetic Alphabet (IPA) symbols, which are used in all COBUILD dictionaries and reference books and in many other publications.

But do not worry if you do not know the IPA symbols. For each sound in the Chart we also give a simple Guide Word, which you are likely to know how to pronounce, and the letters in the word which represent the sound are in bold face, for example the Guide Word for the sound /e/ is '**e**gg', and the Guide Word for the sound /ʃ/ is '**sh**ow'.

The Chart also lists the main spelling patterns for the sound when it occurs at the beginning of words, in the middle of words, and at the end of words (under the headings **Initial, Middle,** and **Final**), by giving an example word for each pattern. For example, the sound /e/ is usually spelled **e** when it occurs at the beginning of a word, as in '**e**gg', but can be spelled **e** or **ea** when it occurs in the middle of the word, as in 'b**e**st' and 'h**ea**d'. All the spelling patterns are shown in bold face letters. These spelling patterns are explained in more detail in Section 2 of this book, with many more example words.

The order in which the sounds are listed in the Chart is also very important, because the same order is used in Sections 2 and 3 of this book. The 24 main vowel sounds are listed before the 24 main consonant sounds. The vowel sounds commonly spelled with the letter **a** (/æ/, /eɪ/, /ɑː/, and /eəʳ/) come first, then the vowel sounds commonly spelled with **e, i, o,** and **u**. The last vowel sound is the weak vowel called 'schwa' /ə/. The consonant sounds are also listed according to the alphabetical order of the letters that are commonly used to spell them, so the first consonant sound is /b/ (commonly spelled **b**), then /k/ (usually spelled **c**), and so on, and the last consonant sound is /z/ (usually spelled **z**).

Section 1 (pages 1-58) contains 21 articles which give you general information about the English spelling system. See the **Contents** page.

If you want to know how to spell a particular sound, you will find detailed entries for all the main sounds of English in **Section 2**.

Each entry tells you how the sound is spelled when it occurs at the beginning of words, in the middle of words, and at the end of words (under the headings **Initial, Middle,** and **Final**, as in the Chart). Each spelling pattern will tell you, where possible, what type of words are involved (e.g. 'in Foreign words', or 'in words of Classical origin'), or what the rule is (e.g. 'after **l, m,** or **v**', or 'before a vowel sound'). Each pattern has a list of the words that share the pattern. If there are too many words to print them all, the list will end in three dots. If a list is introduced by 'in these words' and does not have three dots at the end, all the important words are in the list. At the end of the entry, you will find a section headed **Inflection and word formation**, which tells you about any changes in spelling when you add inflections or suffixes, and a section headed **Pronunciation**, which tells you any important variations in the normal pronunciation of the sound. The order of entries is the same as in the Chart. 2.1 (pages 59-105) deals with the 24 main vowel sounds. 2.2 (pages 106-116) explains in more detail the spelling patterns for the 24th vowel sound, /ə/, called 'schwa', when it occurs in the final syllable of a word. 'Schwa' is spelled in many different ways, and therefore causes spelling problems, especially when it occurs in word endings, because the endings often sound the same. 2.3 (pages 117-179) deals with the 24 main consonant sounds.

Section 3 (pages 180-303) is a list of over 25,000 words from the latest edition of the Collins COBUILD English Dictionary (1995). The problem with dictionaries is that you cannot look up a word if you do not know how to spell the beginning of the word. This section will help you, because the words are grouped according to their first two sounds. For example, you will find '**au**burn' and '**or**bit' in the same group, because they both begin with the sounds /ɔː**b**/. The order of the sounds is the same as in the Chart and in Section 2. Because all the important words with the same initial sound are listed together, you will also begin to understand the range of initial spelling patterns for that sound.

Words can be pronounced differently in different accents of English. In this book, we use the RP (or Received Pronunciation) accent of British English, which is a standard in the teaching of English throughout the world. When it is necessary in order to explain a spelling pattern, we also mention non-RP accents, especially GenAm (General American), which is also used as an international standard. One important feature of RP is that it is a **non-r accent**, which means that it is very difficult to know from the pronunciation whether a word has a letter **r** in the spelling or not. In Section 2, a small superscript **r** (/ʳ/) is used in the pronunciations to show that the /r/ sound is sometimes pronounced and sometimes not. In Section 3, however, because you will not hear an /r/ sound when you hear the word being pronounced in RP, we do not use superscript /ʳ/. For example, the words 'bah' and 'bar' will sound the same in RP, and are therefore listed together at /bɑː/.

Glossary

accent: the **sound system** that is used by a particular group of speakers of the same language to pronounce words. As well as using different sounds, different accents can use the same sounds in a different way. In a **non-r accent**, for example, /r/ only occurs before a vowel sound, whereas in an **r accent** it can occur before a consonant sound as well. The two most important accents of English for learners are **RP** and **GenAm**.

beginning: the first letter or first group of letters in a word, occurring in a number of different words. Thus 'summer' and 'summit' share the beginning **summ**. A **prefix** is a special type of beginning.

Classical spelling pattern: a spelling pattern which has come from Latin or Greek. The same pattern is sometimes pronounced differently in related English words. For example the pattern **ign** is pronounced /aɪn/ in 'resign', but /ɪgn/ in 'resignation', because of **stress shift**. Classical spelling patterns often show spelling conventions that are different from **Native spelling patterns**. For example, /k/ is spelled **ch** in Classical words (rather than **c** or **k**, as in Native words), and /ʃ/ is spelled **ti** (rather than **sh**).

Classical word: a word which includes a **Classical spelling pattern**. Many English words include both **Classical** and **Native** spelling patterns.

'closed r' vowel sound: one of the sounds /ɑː/, /ɜː/, or /ɔː/.

complex word: a word that has been formed by adding a **prefix** or a **suffix** to a simple word. For example, 'like' is a simple word, and 'unlike' and 'likely' are complex words.

compound word: a word that has been formed by combining **simple** or **complex** words, whether it is written as two words, separated by a space or a hyphen, or as a single word. For example 'alarm clock', 'deep-freeze', and 'fireman' are compound words.

consonant: one of the letters **b c d f g h j k l m n p q r s t v w x y z**. The letter **y** is sometimes a consonant, as in 'yes', and sometimes a vowel, as in 'by'. The sounds associated with these letters are called **consonant sounds**.

digraph: two letters that are used to represent a single sound. For example, the letters **gh** in the word 'graph' are a digraph, because they represent the single sound /f/.

'digraph' vowel sounds: one of the sounds /ɔɪ/ or /aʊ/, because they are always spelled with a vowel digraph such as **oi**, **oy**, or **ow**.

ending: the final letter or final group of letters in a word, occurring in a number of different words. Thus 'hammock' and 'paddock' share the ending **ock**. A **suffix** is a special type of ending.

Foreign spelling pattern: a spelling pattern which has come from a language other than English, Latin, or Greek.

Foreign word: a word which contains a **Foreign spelling pattern**. After Foreign words have come into English, the spelling tends to remain fixed, although the pronunciation may gradually change.

GenAm or General American: the **accent** of American English that is used as a standard in the teaching of English throughout the world. It is an **r accent**.

grammatical word: one of the very common words of English, such as articles, prepositions and auxiliary verbs, whose main function is to join together the **lexical words**. Grammatical words often have different spelling conventions to lexical words.

homophone: a word that has the same **pronunciation** as another word, but a different **spelling**. For example, 'right' is a homophone of 'write'. Homophones depend on **accent**: 'flawed' and 'floored' are homophones in **RP**, but not in **GenAm**, while 'very' and 'vary' are homophones in **GenAm**, but not in **RP**.

inflectional ending: a suffix that is added to a word in order to change its grammatical form. Inflectional endings include the verb endings -s, -ing, and -ed, the noun endings -s and -'s, and the adjective endings -er and -est. For example, in 'call – calls – calling – called', 'called' is a different grammatical form of the word 'call'.

lexical word: a word which has meanings and refers to things, ideas, or actions. Most nouns, adjectives, adverbs, and main verbs are lexical words. Some people call these words 'content' words.

'long' vowel: a single vowel letter when it has its 'long' pronunciation. For example, **a** in 'plane' (/eɪ/), **e** in 'scene' (/iː/), **i** in 'line' (/aɪ/), **o** in 'phone' (/oʊ/), and **u** in 'prune' (/uː/) or 'tune' (/juː/).

'long' vowel sound: one of the sounds /eɪ/, /iː/, /aɪ/, /oʊ/, /uː/ or /juː/.

nasal vowel sound: a vowel sound when it is pronounced partly through the nose, as in some words of French origin. For example, the /ɒ/ in 'encore' and 'restaurant' are nasal vowel sounds.

Native spelling pattern: a spelling pattern which reflects English pronunciation of about 500 years ago.

Native word: a word which includes a **Native spelling pattern** and has not been borrowed from another language.

non-r accent: an English accent, such as RP or Australian, in which r is pronounced only before a vowel sound. Before a consonant sound or at the end of a word, r is silent. For example, in RP 'red', 'port', and 'car' are pronounced /red/, /pɔːt/ and /kɑː/. See also **r accent**.

'open r' vowel sound: one of the sounds /eə/, /ɪə/, /aɪə/, /jʊə/, or /ʊə/.

prefix: a letter or group of letters added to the beginning of a word in order to make a new word with a different meaning. For example, the prefix **un-** can be added to the adjective 'likely' to form the adjective '**un**likely', which has the opposite meaning.

pronunciation: the spoken form of a word in a particular **accent**.

r accent: an English accent such as **GenAm** or Scottish, in which the letter r is always pronounced and is never a silent letter. For example in GenAm, 'red', 'port', and 'car' are pronounced /red/, /pɔːrt/ and /kɑːr/. See also **non-r accent**.

RP: an abbreviation for **Received Pronunciation**, the accent of British English that is used as a standard in the teaching of English throughout the world. It is a **non-r accent**. The pronunciations in all COBUILD books are given in RP.

'r' vowel sounds: one of the vowel sounds /ɑː/, /eə/, /ɜː/, /aɪə/, /ɔː/, /ʊə/, /aʊə/, /jʊə/ and /ə/, which occur very frequently in words followed by a silent r in RP. It is therefore convenient to consider that r forms part of the spelling of the vowel sound. However, when the r is followed by another vowel, it is pronounced. For example, -ear represents /eə/ in the word 'bear', but /eər/ in the word 'bearing'. Therefore, in Section 2 of this Guide, the sound represented by -ear is shown as /eəʳ/. Similarly, the other 'r' vowel sounds are shown as: /ɑːʳ/, /ɜːʳ/, /ɪəʳ/, /aɪəʳ/, /ɔːʳ/, /ʊəʳ/, /aʊəʳ/, /jʊəʳ/ and /əʳ/.

'short' vowel: a single vowel letter when it has its 'short' pronunciation: **a** in pat (/æ/), **e** in pet (/e/), **i** in pit (/ɪ/), **o** in pot (/ɒ/), **u** in put (/ʊ/) or putt (/ʌ/).

'short' vowel sound: one of the sounds /æ/, /e/, /ɪ/, /ɒ/, /ʊ/, or /ʌ/.

silent letter: a vowel or consonant in the spelling with no corresponding sound in the pronunciation: e.g. **k** is silent in 'knee', and **e** is silent in 'mile'. Silent letters often modify the pronunciation of other letters: e.g. 'taking' (/teɪkɪŋ/) plus silent l becomes 'talking' (/tɔːkɪŋ/); 'rag' (/ræg/) plus silent e becomes 'rage' (/reɪdʒ/).

simple word: a word that has not been formed from another English word.

single consonant: a consonant that is not next to another consonant. It is between two vowels, or at the beginning of a word, or at the end of a word.

single vowel: a vowel that is not next to another vowel in the same syllable.

sound system: the system of different sounds used to pronounce words. It can be compared to the **alphabet**, which is a system of letters used to spell words. **Accents** can have different sound systems. For example, the vowel sound used in 'bus' in RP does not exist in many accents from the North of England.

sound value: the main sound, or one of the main sounds, associated with a letter. For example, the letter **e** has the sound value /e/ in 'red' and the sound value /iː/ in 'legal'.

spelling: the written form of a word. This does not depend on **accent**. Apart from a few minor differences between American and British spelling conventions, English spelling is standard throughout the world.

spelling pattern: a letter or group of letters, especially one which occurs in a number of different words.

stress shift: a change in stress that often occurs between a word and a related word in English, particularly in **Classical words**. The same **spelling pattern** can have a different stress pattern, and this can affect the pronunciation considerably. For example, a vowel may be **short, long,** or **weak** in related words. Compare the pronunciation of **a** in 'photograph' (/ˈfoʊtəɡrɑːf/), 'photographic' (/ˌfoʊtəˈɡræfɪk/), and 'photographer' (/fəˈtɒɡrəfəʳ/).

suffix: a letter or a group of letters which are added to a word in order to make a new word with different grammar or with a different meaning, or to express the grammatical relationship between words. For example, the suffix **er** is added to the verb 'swim' to make the noun 'swimmer'. An **inflectional ending** is a kind of suffix. See also **ending**.

three letter rule: a feature of the English spelling system which means that **lexical words** always have at least three letters. One-syllable lexical words that do not have an initial consonant often have a double final consonant, e.g. 'inn' (hotel). One-syllable lexical words that do not have a final consonant often have a silent final **e**, e.g. 'bee' (insect). However, grammatical words often have less than three letters, e.g. 'in' (preposition) and 'be' (auxiliary verb).

vowel: one of the letters **a e i o u** or **y**. The letter **y** is sometimes a consonant, as in 'yes', and sometimes a vowel, as in 'by'. The sounds associated with these letters are called **vowel sounds**.

vowel digraph: two vowel letters used in spelling to represent a single vowel sound, such as **ea** in 'head' (/hed/), **oa** in 'boat' (/boʊt/) or **oi** in 'boil' (/bɔɪl/). Except for **oi** and **ou**, vowel digraphs usually represent a sound which is spelled with a single vowel in other words: e.g. /e/ is spelled **e** in 'bed', /oʊ/ is spelled **o** in 'voting'. Most vowel digraphs have more than one pronunciation: e.g. **ea** in 'head' (/hed/), 'bead' (/biːd/), and 'great' (/ɡreɪt/).

weak vowel sound: an indistinct vowel sound which occurs only in unstressed syllables, and is called 'schwa' (/ə/). For example, the initial vowel sound is weak in 'across', and the final vowel sound is weak in 'extra'.

Chart of Sounds, Guide Words and Main Spelling Patterns

Vowel Sounds:

Sound	Guide Word	Main Spelling Patterns		
		Initial	Middle	Final
/æ/	act	act	began	
/eɪ/	able	able aid eight	made again mayor veil	may they
/ɑːʳ/ /ɑː/	arm after	arm after	park father balm	far ma ah
/eəʳ/	air	air aerial	parent dairy concerto	care chair millionaire bear there
/e/	egg	egg	best head	
/iː/	equal	equal each	these mean been believe receive police	see sea the [unstressed = /i/: any we bikini movie abbey]
/ɜːʳ/	early	early urban ermine	person burn first pearl journey word	prefer occur chauffeur

Sound	Guide Word	Main Spelling Patterns		
		Initial	Middle	Final
/ɪəʳ/	ear	ear	hero	clear beer here pier
/ɪ/	it	it [unstressed: enough include]	his system build [unstressed: before crisis damage bicycle]	
/aɪ/	idea	idea	time right style seismic guide	sky dye alibi lie high
/aɪəʳ/ /aɪə/	iron science	iron	pirate diary science bias	fire tyre drier flyer
/ɒ/	odd	odd envelope	from quality because	
/oʊ/	open	open oak	most road soul bowl mauve	no know toe dough bureau
/ɔːʳ/ /ɔː/	order also	order also author awful	report court board award ball cause caught dawn bought	more for law roar your door
/ɔɪ/	oil	oil	point royal	boy

Sound	Guide Word	Main Spelling Patterns		
		Initial	Middle	Final
/ʊ/	book		book bush woman could	
/uː/	food	ooze	food group move truth juice jewel	crew too do you true
/ʊəʳ/	poor		jury bourgeois	insure poor tour
/aʊ/	out	out	found down	now
/aʊəʳ/	our	our hour		power sour
/ʌ/	up	up un-	but some country	
/juː/	use	use euphoria you	music neutral steward	due new view
/jʊəʳ/	during		during	cure
/ə/ /əʳ/	about other	about obey	advertising forward circuitous comfort colourful surprise company children family today support famous	other doctor beggar labour centre nature camera messiah the

Consonant Sounds:

Sound	Guide Word	Main Spelling Patterns		
		Initial	Middle	Final
/b/	but	but	about rubber	club tube

/k/	can	can
		keep
		chemical
		(/kw/: quick)
			act
			market
			accuse
			wicked
			school
			mosquito
			(/ks/: next
			     accept
			(/kʃ/: luxury
			     action
			(/kw/: liquid)
				think
				like
				back
				public
				stomach
				antique
				(/ks/: climax
				     athletics)

/tʃ/	child	child	teacher butcher question actual	each catch
/d/	do	do	under sudden	find side called
/f/	for	for phone	after suffer elephant laughter	leaf stiff life graph cough
/g/	go	go guard ghost	again luggage (/gz/: example)	big vague (/gz/: bags)
/h/	have	have whole	ahead	
/dʒ/	just	just general	danger budget object education	large bridge

Sound	Guide Word	Main Spelling Patterns		
		Initial	Middle	Final
/l/	like	like	only bullet	hotel will while
/m/	more	more	among summer salmon plumber	from time bomb calm column
/n/	not	not knife gnaw	any annoy	in line sign
/ŋ/	sing		include	sing
/p/	put	put	company apple	shop hope
/r/	run	run rhyme wrong	from correct	
/s/	say	say city scene psychic	ask essay capacity discipline	across gas notice case waltz
/ʒ/	measure	genre	measure regime	barrage
/ʃ/	show	show chef schedule sugar	initial crucial mission pension ashamed machine assure insure conscience	bush creche

Sound	Guide Word	Main Spelling Patterns		
		Initial	Middle	Final
/t/	time	time	after better	want asked waste bat cigarette boycott
/θ/	thank	thank	nothing	both
/ð/	than	than	father	breathe with
/v/	very	very	over chivvy	have rev
/w/	was	was which	always (/kw/: frequent) (/gw/: language) (/sw/: persuade)	
/j/	yes	yes (/juː/: use eulogy)	behaviour lawyer (/jə/: document)	
/z/	zone	zone	visit magazine dizzy	days lose amaze quiz buzz

1 The English Spelling System

1.1 A brief historical background

Where words come from

Languages are always changing. Most of the modern languages of Europe, for example, have developed from a single language spoken in the area now occupied by Iran and Iraq and labelled by linguists as 'Indo-European'. This language gave rise to various families of languages: the Germanic languages (including English, German, Dutch, and Danish), the Hellenic languages (including Greek), the Italic languages (including Latin, Italian, Spanish, Portuguese, and French) and the Celtic languages (including Breton, Gaelic, and Welsh).

Individual words, and other features of the Indo-European language, have developed in very different ways in different languages. The pronunciation of the word for '100', for example, changed so much that it became *hund* in Germanic, *hecat* in Hellenic, *cent* in Italic, and *cet* in Celtic.

Where modern English words come from

Very few modern English words have been invented spontaneously. Some words have developed from words that existed in older forms of English, such as the word 'hundred', which has developed from Germanic *hund*. Many words, though, have been borrowed from other languages, such as 'century' (100 years) from Latin *centuria* and 'hectogramme' (100 grammes) from Greek *hecaton* and *gramma*. Because English has borrowed so many words from other languages, there are often several different words available for expressing a particular idea, such as that of '100' here. It can also be seen that the origin of words has an important influence on how they are spelled, because they may be borrowed in their original form from languages with different spelling rules. The sound /s/ is always spelled **s-** at the beginning of Native words, such as 'send', and its past tense 'sent', so that the **c-** spelling in 'century' is characteristic of a word of Latin origin.

Native words, Classical words, and Foreign words

Although many words can be traced back to Indo-European, the recent history of a word is much more important from the spelling point of view. Native words like 'hundred' have developed in English, and are originally spoken words which have subsequently been written down according to spelling conventions which reflected English pronunciation at the time. Foreign words and words of Classical origin (which can be further subdivided into words of Latin origin and words of Greek origin) like 'century', by contrast, have usually been borrowed in their written form, and therefore their spelling reflects different conventions from those of Native words.

Pronunciation and spelling

In the case of Native words, for centuries there were no fixed conventions for representing sounds with letters. People spelled the same word differently on different occasions: there was no 'correct spelling'. Here are some of the ways in which the word 'enough' has been spelled since the 14th century:

| *inoch* | *ynogh* | *enogh* | *ynowh* | *inowhe* | *ynowghe* |
| *ynought* | *enoff* | *inoffe* | *enufe* | *enuff* | *inuff* |

Some of these spellings seem to imply different pronunciations, such as the final **ch** in *inoch*, compared with the final **ff** in *enuff*, while others probably imply different conventions for representing the same sounds, such as the choice between initial **y** or **i**, and between **gh** and **ch**.

With words of Classical or Foreign origin, the spelling pattern in the language of origin is usually reproduced in English. The word 'idea', for example, is spelled in English in the same way that it is in Latin, which in turn is connected to the original form of the word in Ancient Greek: *ιδέα*. In English this word is pronounced /aɪdiːə/. In Italian and Spanish, the word 'idea' is spelled the same way as in English, but the pronunciation has not changed much from the way the word was pronounced in Greek and Latin: /idea/. Similarly, the Norwegian word 'ski' is pronounced /ʃiː/. English has borrowed the written form, but the pronunciation has changed to /skiː/ to conform to English conventions.

Standardizing Native spellings

Starting 500 years ago, there was a gradual standardization of the spelling of Native words. This started with the invention of printing: from the 15th century onwards the written forms of words became more important, and spelling tended not to change with accent. At the time of Shakespeare, it was still possible to spell many words in more than one way. But for the last 200 years spelling has been standardized and *enough*, for example, has been accepted as the correct spelling, and other spellings such as *inuff* have been regarded as mistakes.

Although 'enough', like a few other common words, retains an inconsistent spelling pattern, this standardization has been broadly consistent. In most words, for example, the sound /f/ is spelled **ff** after a short vowel: e.g. 'cliff', 'off', 'stiff', and 'stuff'.

Historical spelling

Inconsistency in spelling is partly explained by the fact that the spelling of most Native words has been standardized not according to their current pronunciation, but according to the way in which they were pronounced many hundreds of years ago. English spelling, that is, has always been out of date. As with words of Classical origin, the spelling has come to show the history of the word. This is connected with the influence of Johnson's Dictionary of 1755, which generally favoured conservative spellings over more recent spellings which reflected pronunciation more closely. The choice of the spelling pattern *enough* rather than *inuff* did not depend on the most recent pronunciation, but on the fact that the word used to end in the same sound that is spelled **ch** in the Scottish word *loch* and the German word *Nacht*. (This sound also occurred in 'night', which was pronounced like the Scottish word *nicht*, and in many other words which now have **gh** in the spelling.)

Sound changes

Spelling is based on a historical pronunciation rather than a current pronunciation because of the considerable changes in English pronunciation which have been occurring since the 15th century. At the same time as printing was beginning to fix spellings which reflected a particular pronunciation, that pronunciation was changing. Originally, the English pronunciation of long vowel sounds was similar to that of other European languages, and Latin letters provided a standard way of representing these sounds in different languages. 'Idea' would have been pronounced with an **i** as in 'machine', and an **e** as in 'fete' – as it still is in Italian, for example, where similar sound changes did not occur.

The English Spelling System

Conventions

Changes in pronunciation after the early 15th century are not reflected in spelling. Current English pronunciation has to be linked to this spelling by means of conventions which account for the changes in pronunciation after 1400. The letter **i**, for instance, as well as representing /ɪ/ (e.g. in 'political'), now also represents /aɪ/ (e.g. in 'polite'), and the letter **e**, as well as representing /e/ (e.g. in 'premise'), now also represents /iː/ (e.g. in 'premium').

Implications

The adoption of a historical spelling system has had three important implications for English:

1. English spelling is not dependent on any particular accent.

As the accents of English have changed, the conventions linking each of them to the spelling system have also changed, but the spelling system itself has remained more or less the same. This is an important feature of the written form of a language which is spoken by 350 million people around the world with a large variety of different accents, and is a major means of communication for many more. Apart from a few minor differences in American and British conventions, English words are spelled the same throughout the world, however they are pronounced. If we still changed our spelling to reflect our pronunciation, written communication would be much more difficult. When spelling reflects the accent of the writer more closely than standard orthography, as is the case with Chaucer, or with the spelling adopted by Scots poets such as Robert Burns, it becomes more difficult to read. When there is a standard written form of the language, it is possible for speakers of mutually unintelligible dialects to communicate in writing, as is the case, for example, in Modern China.

2. English spelling reveals features of words which have been lost in the pronunciation.

There is a general tendency for the pronunciation of words to simplify over time. Sounds can disappear, and words which used to be pronounced differently can begin to sound the same. For example, the **k** in 'knight' was originally pronounced, so that it sounded different from 'night'.

Because the context of written language is necessarily more restricted than that of spoken language, there are many words such as this in English, which are distinguished in writing but not in speech: these words are often called **homophones**. If you want to know more about these words, see Collins COBUILD English Guides 6: Homophones.

The regular past tense inflectional ending -**ed** used to be pronounced as a separate syllable. This is no longer the case in most words, but the spelling -**ed** remains an important grammatical marker, whether it is pronounced /**t**/ as in 'grasp**ed**', /**d**/ as in 'harm**ed**' or /ɪd/ as in 'wait**ed**'.

3. English spelling conventions for Native words reflect a historical English sound system.

For more information about these conventions, see the articles on 'Double consonants', 'Final **e**', 'Native spelling conventions', and 'Vowel digraphs'.

1.2 The rules of English spelling

A. Conventions for representing the sounds of English

The purpose of this section is to give an overview of the way in which English spelling represents English sounds, and to introduce the main rules. More detailed information about the individual sounds and spelling patterns will be found in Section 2.

The alphabet

English is written using the following alphabet of 26 letters:

a b c d e f g h i j k l m n o p q r s t u v w x y z

There is a capital letter equivalent to each of these:

A B C D E F G H I J K L M N O P Q R S T U V W X Y Z

Capital letters are used at the beginning of a sentence, at the beginning of proper names, and in some abbreviations. For more details, see the article on 'Capital letters'.

The vowel letters are:

a e i o u

Note: **y** can be a vowel letter or a consonant letter.

The consonant letters are:

b c d f g h j k l m n p q r s t v w x z

Vowels

There are many different vowel sounds in English. The exact number varies according to the particular accent of a particular speaker. For this book we have selected the most common sounds used in RP, and this includes 24 vowel sounds.

However, the English alphabet has only 6 vowel letters (including **y**). The English spelling system uses a range of different conventions for overcoming this shortage of letters. These conventions affect not just the way in which the vowel sound itself is spelled, but also the spelling of the other sounds around it.

1. 'Short' vowel sounds:

In a closed syllable (that is, a syllable that has been closed by a consonant sound), the sounds /æ/, /e/, /ɪ/, /ɒ/, and /ʌ/ are usually spelled with a single vowel letter, **a**, **e**, **i**, **o**, and **u** respectively. The short vowel /ʊ/ is more commonly spelled **oo**, although it is spelled **u** in some words.

This means that, in Native words at least, the vowel letter will be followed by at least one consonant letter at the end of a word (e.g. '**ba**nk', '**ba**t', '**bu**t', '**i**tch', and '**pu**t') and at least two consonant letters in the middle of a word (e.g. '**lo**ttery', '**plu**cking', and '**ri**ches').

Unstressed /ɪ/ is usually spelled **e-** or **i-** at the beginning of a word (e.g. '**e**nough', '**e**xpected', '**i**mportant', and '**i**nvolve').

2. 'Long' vowel sounds:

In an open syllable (that is, a syllable that has not been closed by a consonant sound), the sounds /eɪ/, /i:/, /aɪ/, /oʊ/, and /ju:/ are usually spelled with a single vowel letter, **a**, **e**, **i**, **o**, and **u** respectively. The long vowel /u:/ is more commonly spelled **oo**, although it is spelled **u** in some words.

This means that the vowel letter will not be followed by a consonant letter (e.g. '**go**', '**he**', '**me**n**u**', '**ra**di**o**', and '**wh**y'), or will be followed by a single consonant letter before another vowel letter (e.g. '**cri**sis', '**fi**nance', '**fu**ture', '**la**bour', '**lo**cal', '**o**pen', '**ru**de', and '**u**nion').

Long vowel sounds are also often represented by a vowel digraph (e.g. 'ag**ai**n', 'appr**oa**ch', 'b**ee**n', 'iss**ue**', 'j**ew**el', 'm**ay**or', 'n**eu**tral', 'n**ew**', 'n**ow**', 's**ay**', and 's**ee**').

Unstressed /i:/ (/i/) is usually spelled **y** at the end of a word (e.g. 'an**y**', 'onl**y**', and 'ver**y**').

3. 'Closed r' vowel sounds:

The vowel sounds /ɑ:/, /ɜ:/, and /ɔ:/ are usually spelled with a single vowel letter, in a syllable closed by **r**. This means that the vowel letter will be followed by **r** at the end of a word (e.g. 'bl**ur**', 'f**ar**', 'h**er**', '**or**', and 'st**ir**'), and by **r** and at least one other consonant letter in the middle of a word (e.g. 'f**ir**st', 'f**or**ce', 'p**ar**ty', 'rep**or**t', 's**er**vice', 'th**ir**ty', and 't**ur**n').

4. 'Open r' vowel sounds:

The vowel sounds /eə/, /ɪə/, /aɪə/, /ʊə/, and /jʊə/ are usually spelled with a single vowel letter in an open syllable (that is, a syllable which has not been closed by a consonant), when the next consonant is **r**. This means that the vowel letter will be followed by a single **r**

The English Spelling System

before another vowel letter (e.g. '**du**ring', 'envi**ro**nment', 'expe**ri**ence', '**fire**', '**here**', '**pare**nt', '**share**', and '**sure**'), or by a vowel digraph followed by an **r** (e.g. '**air**', '**bear**d', '**dair**y', '**steer**', '**tear**', and '**tour**').

Note: '*r' vowel sounds:* (1) Because the vowel sounds /ɑ:/, /eə/, /ɜ:/, /ɪə/, /aɪə/, /ɔ:/, /ʊə/, /aʊə/, /jʊə/, and /ə/ so frequently occur in words with a silent **r**, it is convenient to consider that **r** forms part of the spelling of the vowel sound. For example, in the word 'bear', the vowel sound /eə/ is represented by '-ear'. In the word 'bearing', however, because the next sound is a vowel, the sound represented by 'ear' is not /eə/ but /eər/. (2) For this reason, in Section 2 of this Guide, the sound represented by '-ear' is shown as /eə^r/, that is with a small superscript /^{r}/, which means that it is pronounced /eər/ before a vowel sound, and /eə/ otherwise. Similarly, the other 'r' vowel sounds are shown as: /ɑ:^{r}/, /ɜ:^{r}/, /ɪə^r/, /aɪə^r/, /ɔ:^{r}/, /ʊə^r/, /aʊə^r/, /jʊə^r/, and /ə^r/. (3) The superscript /^{r}/ represents a sound which is always pronounced in an **r** accent, such as GenAm. (4) In cases where there is no **r** in the spelling, the vowel sounds are shown without the superscript /^{r}/. For example, the vowel sound in 'father' is shown as /ɑ:/.

5. 'Digraph' vowel sounds:

The vowel sounds /ɔɪ/ and /aʊ/ are always spelled with a vowel digraph (e.g. 'ab**ou**t', 'b**oy**', 'd**ow**n', 'n**ow**', 'p**oi**nt', and 'r**oy**al').

6. Weak vowel sounds:

Weak vowel sounds only occur in unstressed syllables. Their sound /ə/ is spelled in many different ways. However, it is usually spelled **a** when it is the first sound in a word (e.g. '**a**bout', '**a**ccording', and '**a**cross'), and is often followed by -**r** at the end of words (e.g. 'afte**r**', 'labou**r**', and 'othe**r**').

Unstressed /ɪ/ and /i:/ are sometimes considered to be weak vowels. In this Guide, they are treated as variants of /ɪ/ and /i:/.

Consonants

There are 24 different consonant sounds in English, and 21 consonant letters. There is not, therefore, the same shortage of letters that occurs with vowels, although the way in which a consonant sound is spelled is commonly influenced by other sounds around it.

1. 'Simple' consonants:

The consonant sounds /**b**/, /**d**/, /**g**/, /**h**/, /**l**/, /**m**/, /**n**/, /**p**/, /**r**/, /**t**/, /**w**/ and /**j**/ can be described as 'simple' because they are commonly represented by the same letter in all words, regardless of context.

e.g. /l/ – life, old, real; /p/ – company, put, up.

Most of these letters (except **h**, **w**, and **y**) can be doubled in some positions (e.g. **nn** in 'begi**nn**ing'). In some words, many of these letters are accompanied by silent letters (e.g. silent **g** with **n** in 'si**gn**', silent **k** with **n** in '**kn**ife', silent **p** with **n** in '**pn**eumonia'). For more details, see the articles on 'Double consonants' and 'Silent consonants'.

2. 'Complex' consonants:

The consonant sounds /k/, /tʃ/, /f/, /dʒ/, /ŋ/, /s/, /ʒ/, /ʃ/, /θ/, /ð/, /v/, and /z/ are generally not represented by the same letter in all contexts. Most of them are represented by different letters in different words. Also, many of them can be represented by digraphs rather than single letters.

e.g. /f/ – **f**rom, gra**ph**, rou**gh**; /dʒ/ – a**dj**ust, e**dg**e, e**d**ucation, **g**em, **j**ob.

Consonant digraphs do not double, and the only single letters that can be doubled are **f** (when it spells /f/), **s** (when it spells /s/) and **z** (when it spells /z/).

Full details of the various spelling patterns for each sound are given in Section 2.

B. Conventions for putting letters together

There are a number of restrictions which limit the way in which letters can be combined to spell words, many of which reflect the characteristics of the spoken language. There is a tendency for vowels and consonants to alternate, and it is unusual to find more than two vowel letters, or more than two consonant letters together.

Vowel combinations

1. Digraphs:

The usual reason for putting vowel letters together is to represent an individual vowel sound as a vowel digraph (e.g. **ea** spells /iː/ in 'm**ea**n', **oa** spells /oʊ/ in 'r**oa**d', **oe** spells /oʊ/ in 't**oe**', and **oo** spells /ʊ/ in 'g**oo**d'). As a general guideline, we can say that vowel digraphs are much more common in short Native words than in long words of Classical origin.

2. Sounds:

Less commonly, two vowel sounds can occur together in separate syllables in a word:

area	guardian	reality	union
create	liaison	society	...

In general, this is more common in words of Classical origin than in Native words.

Consonant combinations

1. Sounds:

It is more common to have two consonant sounds together than two vowel sounds:

and	from	still	world
between	only	think	...

It is also possible to have more than two consonant sounds together, but this is rare. At the beginning of a word, for example, the first of three consonant sounds must be /s/, always spelled **s-**:

scrape   **spl**endid   **str**ing   ...

2. Silent Consonants:

Not all consonant letters represent sounds. A number of silent consonant letters occur in English words:

com**b**	**g**host	**p**neumonia	**w**rong
deb**t**	**k**now	si**g**n	...

For more details, see the article on 'Silent consonants'.

3. Digraphs:

The following digraphs (all including the letter **h**) are used to represent individual consonant sounds:

e.g. **ch** spells /tʃ/ in '**mu**ch', **gh** spells /f/ in 'rou**gh**', **ph** spells /f/ in '**ph**one', **sh** spells /ʃ/ in '**sh**ould', and **th** spells /θ/ in '**th**ink'.

For more details, see the entries for these sounds in Section 2.

4. Double consonants:

Another way in which consonant letters are combined is to produce double consonants:

e.g. **bb** in 'rubber', **cc** in 'account', **dd** in 'add', **ff** in 'office', **gg** in 'bigger', **ll** in 'will', **mm** in 'co**mm**on', **nn** in 'a**nn**ounce', **pp** in 'su**pp**ort', **rr** in 'cu**rr**ent', **ss** in 'pre**ss**', **tt** in 'li**tt**le', and **zz** in 'pu**zz**le'.

For more details, see the article on 'Double consonants'.

Vowel and consonant combinations

The following sequences of up to four letters can be used to represent individual vowel sounds:

e.g. **aigh** spells /eɪ/ in 'str**aigh**t', **al** spells /ɑː/ in 'p**al**m', **augh** spells /ɔː/ in 'c**augh**t', **eigh** spells /eɪ/ in '**eigh**t', **ig** spells /aɪ/ in 's**ig**n', **igh** spells /aɪ/ in 'r**igh**t', **ough** spells /ɔː/ in 'th**ough**t', and **oul** spells /ʊ/ in 'w**oul**d'.

Individual letters

The use of certain letters has a particularly strong influence on what letter comes next:

Single -**a**, -**i**, and -**u** only come at the end of Foreign words and proper nouns. In Native words they are usually followed by another letter (e.g. 'd**ue**', 's**ay**', and 't**ie**').

j and **v** are always followed by a vowel and **j** is only found at the beginning of a syllable:

con**j**ure	p**yj**amas	gi**v**ing	**v**oice
join	...	ne**v**er	...

q is always followed by **u**, and is usually pronounced /**kw**/, but sometimes /**k**/:

queen	**qu**iet	**qu**ay	**qu**iche
quick	...	**qu**eue	...

For more details, see the entries in Section 2.

1.3 American spellings

There are a few minor differences between American and British spellings, but they are not normally related to differences in pronunciation.

History

Noah Webster's 'An American Dictionary of the English Language', published in 1828, incorporated several spellings which differed from those found in Samuel Johnson's 'Dictionary of the English Language', published in 1755. Webster was concerned to establish the independence of American English from British English to mirror the independence of America from Britain. This was a popular objective, and the dictionary was a bestseller. Webster's spellings were based on American usage, rather than being conscious 'reforms'.

Before this, there had been greater variability of spelling on both sides of the Atlantic, so that, for example, both 'labor' and 'labour' were possible in America <u>and</u> Britain. But the establishment of 'labor' as a specifically American spelling coincided with its decline as an acceptable spelling in Britain.

The main function of these differences remains that of marking a text as American rather than British. These differences are important, as an American spelling may be regarded as a mistake by a British reader, and a British spelling as a mistake by an American reader.

-or for -our

Most of the 30 or so nouns which are spelled with a final unstressed **-our** in British English are usually spelled **-or** in American English:

arb**or**	demean**or**	hum**or**	savi**or**
ard**or**	endeav**or**	lab**or**	sav**or**
arm**or**	fav**or**	neighb**or**	splend**or**
behavi**or**	ferv**or**	od**or**	succ**or**
cand**or**	flav**or**	parl**or**	tum**or**
clam**or**	glam**or**	ranc**or**	vap**or**
clang**or**	harb**or**	rig**or**	vig**or**
col**or**	hon**or**	rum**or**	

However, some of these words can be spelled **-our** in American English as well. This is particularly true of 'glam**our**' and 'savi**our**'.

American spellings

-er for -re

Words which are spelled with a final unstressed **-re** following a consonant in British English are usually spelled **-er** in American English:

caliber	luster	saber	specter
center	maneuver	saltpeter	theater
fiber	meager	scepter	...
liter	meter	sepulcher	
louver	reconnoiter	somber	

These words are spelled with **-re** in both British English and American English:

| acre | genre | massacre | ogre |
| cadre | lucre | mediocre | timbre |

Doubling of l

The rules for doubling **l** are more consistent in American English than in British English.

a) **l** is not doubled at the end of an unstressed syllable before an ending beginning with a vowel:

e.g. jewel – jeweler; travel – traveled; travel – traveling; wool – woolen.

Note: The British English spellings are 'jeweller', 'travelled', 'travelling', and 'woollen'.

b) **l** is more frequently doubled in a stressed syllable:

| appall | enroll | install | ... |
| distill | fulfill | skillful | |

Note: (1) The British English spellings are 'appal', 'distil', 'enrol', 'fulfil', and 'skilful'. (2) But 'install' in British English spelling as well. (3) In both American and British English, single l in 'expel', 'repel', and 'until'.

-ise and -ize

Words which can be spelled either **-ize** or **-ise** in British English are always spelled **-ize** in American English:

apologize	emphasize	recognize	...
authorize	minimize	specialize	
characterize	organize	stabilize	

The English Spelling System

The following words are spelled -ise in both British English and American English:

advertise	comprise	excise	rise
advise	compromise	exercise	supervise
arise	despise	franchise	surmise
chastise	devise	improvise	surprise
circumcise	disguise	revise	televise

Note: In American English spelling, -yze in 'analyze', 'breathalyze', and 'paralyze', which are spelled -yse in British English.

e for ae and oe

Some words are spelled ae or oe in British English, representing the sound /e/ or /i:/, but are usually spelled e in American English:

anemic	estrogen	hemophilia	orthopedic
anesthetist	feces	hemorrhage	pediatrician
diarrhea	fetus	hemorrhoids	pedophile
esophagus	gynecology	leukemia	
esthetic	hemoglobin	maneuver	

Note: In British English spelling, 'anaemic', 'anaesthetist', 'diarrhoea', 'oesophagus', and so on.

These words are often spelled ae or oe in British English, or sometimes e, but are always spelled e in American English:

encyclopedia	homeopathy	medieval	peony
eon	hyena	paleontology	primeval

Some words are spelled ae or oe in both British English and American English:

aegis	aerobic	onomatopoeia	phoenix
aerial	Caesarean	paean	

Words spelled ae or oe in British English that are not pronounced /e/ or /i:/ are usually spelled ae or oe in American English as well:

canoe	Gaelic	paella
coerce	maelstrom	reggae
does	maestro	...

American spellings

Other distinctive American spellings

American	British	American	British
analog	analogue	molt	moult
ax	axe	naught	nought
catalog	catalogue	pajamas	pyjamas
check	cheque	plow	plough
curb	kerb	practise	practice
defense	defence	pretense	pretence
disk	disc	program	programme
distention	distention	skeptic	sceptic
draft	draught	smolder	smoulder
glycerin	glycerine	tire	tyre
gray	grey	vise	vice
license	licence	worshiped	worshipped
mold	mould	worshiping	worshipping

Note: With many of these words, the American spelling also occurs in British English, but with a more restricted meaning. The use of 'disk' and 'program' in British English, for example, is restricted to the world of computers. In all other contexts, these words are spelled 'disc' and 'programme'. In American English, 'disk' and 'program' are used for all meanings. The reverse happens in the case of 'vise', which is only used for the tool in American English. Both varieties of English use the spelling 'vice' for a moral failing or a criminal activity.

1.4 Apostrophes

The apostrophe has three main functions in English:

1. It is added to nouns and some pronouns before adding an **s**, to produce the possessive form:

e.g. my friend's house ... children's games ... one's self-esteem.

When a plural noun already ends in -s, the apostrophe is added without **s**:

e.g. their parents' activities ... friends' houses.

Note: (1) There is no apostrophe in the possessive pronouns 'yours', 'hers', 'ours' and 'theirs'. (2) There is no apostrophe in the possessive determiner 'its', meaning 'belonging to it'. (3) The form **it's** is the contraction of '**it has**' or '**it is**' (see below).

2. It is used to show that one or more letters are missing in some common words or combinations of words, mainly in contractions of 'am', 'are', 'had', 'has', 'have', 'is', 'not', 'shall', 'will', and 'would':

e.g. I'm, he'd, she's, aren't, I'll, shan't.

3. An apostrophe is also used to indicate that the first two numbers of a year or decade are missing: e.g. 'the '68 campaign' means 'the campaign of 1968 (or 1868, or 1768, etc)'. The apostrophe in **o'clock** is a historical feature: originally, it was a contraction of '**of the clock**'.

It is occasionally used in plural forms of letters of the alphabet, numbers, and other words which do not normally have a plural form:

e.g. His grades were all **A's** ... He was in his **40's** ... How many **l's** are there in 'parallel'?

1.5 Capital letters

Starting with a capital letter

When a word is used as the first word in a sentence, the first word in a piece of direct speech, the first word in a line of poetry, or the first word of the name of a book, film, or play, it must begin with a capital letter.

Names

Proper nouns, that is nouns which are the names of unique things, are written with initial capital letters. These can include people and their titles, organizations, books, films, plays, addresses, countries and other place names, days, months, festivals, and famous events:

e.g. Mummy; Picasso; President Clinton; Dr. Helen Perkins; Birmingham University; Volkswagen; Price Waterhouse; British Airways; Lord of the Flies; Star Wars; The Merchant of Venice; Curzon Street; Berry Head, Brixham, Devon; Westminster Abbey; Germany; India; Monday; December; Christmas; The Gulf War.

Note: (1) When there are several words in a proper noun, short common words like 'of', 'the', and 'and' are usually written with small letters, unless they are the first word: e.g. 'Gone with the Wind', 'Death and the Maiden', 'William the Conqueror', and 'A Passage to India'. (2) When these words are used with a more general meaning, they may be written with small letters: e.g. 'mummy', 'university', and 'war'.

Products

When the names of organizations or individuals are used to refer to things which they have made or done, the capital letter is retained:

e.g. a Volkswagen; a Picasso.

Associated adjectives and nouns

Nationality words and other words which are associated with names of people and places also retain the capital letter of the original name:

e.g. a Brummie (a person from Birmingham); Californian wine; French cheese; a Frenchman; a German; Kafkaesque; a Londoner; Shakespearean; Victorian.

Note: If a word has lost its connection with the original name and has acquired a more general meaning, it may be written with a small letter:

e.g. bohemian (originally from 'Bohemia'); lesbian (originally from 'Lesbos'); sadist (originally from 'de Sade').

The English Spelling System

The personal pronoun 'I'

In English, this is always written with a capital letter.

Optional capitals

The names of the four seasons, the four points of the compass, and decades can be written either with a capital letter or with a small letter:

e.g. from the North – from the north; in the Spring – in the spring; the Nineties – the nineties.

God

Nouns which refer to God are always written with capital letters:

e.g. the Almighty; the Lord; the Merciful.

Note: Some people also write pronouns which refer to God with capital letters: e.g. 'He', 'Thou', and 'Your'. This is becoming less common.

1.6 Double consonants

In Modern English, **double consonants** within words are pronounced in exactly the same way as **single consonants**. Therefore, it can be difficult to remember whether a letter should be doubled or not in a particular word, and this is the cause of many spelling mistakes in English. In Section 2 of this Guide, information is given at each consonant sound about the circumstances in which the spelling involves a double letter, with a list of the common words that are spelled with double consonants.

Frequency

Single consonants are more common than double consonants, so if you are not sure, it is likely that a consonant will be single.

History

There are two principal, and unrelated, reasons for the occurrence of double consonants within English words.

Native doubling

English spelling conventions reflect a sound system that has changed considerably. Like Modern Italian, English used to have a system of double consonants which had twice the duration of single consonants. A single consonant would always form a syllable with the vowel that followed, but the duration of a double consonant would be shared between two syllables. In the word 'mating', for example, the two syllables would have been 'ma' and 'ting'. 'Ma' was an 'open syllable', as it did not have a final consonant. In the word 'matting', the two syllables would have been 'mat' and 'ting'. The first syllable was 'closed' as it had a final consonant. 'Mating' had a long **a** and a short **t**, while 'matting' had a short **a** and a long **t**.

Two important changes have occurred in the English sound system since these conventions were established. Firstly, the long **a** sound has changed considerably (to /eɪ/), so that it is very different in quality from short **a** (/æ/). Secondly, double consonants within words now have the same duration as single consonants, so there is no difference in the pronunciation of **t** and **tt** in 'city' and 'witty'.

If we start with the word 'mat' and wish to add the ending **-ing**, in order to keep the first syllable 'closed' and the vowel short, it is necessary to double the final **t**, to produce 'mat+ting' rather than 'ma+ting'. This is the origin of doubling before suffixes that begin with a vowel.

There are many words which have been formed in this way in English where either the original base word is no longer current in English (such as in 'gid**d**y') or the ending is no longer a suffix (such as -le). Such words are listed in the **Middle** section of the appropriate consonant entry in Section 2.

Doubling is also an important feature in the forming of new words, so information about when you have to double the final consonant before adding suffixes is included in the **Inflection and word formation** section of the appropriate consonant entry in Section 2.

Classical doubling

The Latin prefixes *ad-*, *con-*, *in-*, *ob-*, and *sub-* are a major source of double consonants in English words which come directly from Latin or from Latin through French. The prefix *ad-*, for example, when added to a Latin word which began with *d*, would produce a double consonant. These double consonants have been retained in English in words like 'a**dd**ict', 'a**dd**ress', and 'a**dd**uce'.

In the case of *ad-*, however, double consonants were not only produced when a word began with *d*. When a word began with a different consonant, the *d* in *ad-* would change to 'assimilate' to the following consonant, so *ad-* followed by *b* would become *abb-*, *ad-* followed by *c* would become *acc-*, and so on. This is the reason for the double consonants in 'a**bb**reviate', 'a**cc**use', 'a**ff**ect', 'a**gg**ressive', 'a**ll**eviate', 'a**nn**ounce', 'a**rr**est', and 'a**tt**empt', for example. A similar process occurred with other Latin prefixes, and gives rise to a large number of double letters at the beginning of English words:

ad-	a**bb**-, a**cc**-, a**dd**-, a**ff**-, a**gg**-, a**ll**-, a**mm**-, a**nn**-, a**pp**-, a**rr**-, a**ss**-, a**tt**-
con-	co**ll**-, co**mm**-, co**nn**-, co**rr**-
ex-	e**ff**-
in-	i**ll**-, i**mm**-, i**nn**-, i**rr**-
ob-	o**cc**-, o**ff**-, o**pp**-
sub-	su**cc**-, su**ff**-, su**gg**-, su**pp**-, su**rr**-

In Section 2, these double letters are presented in the **Middle** section of the appropriate consonant entries, as spelling patterns of frequent occurrence at the beginning of words.

Consonants with double forms

These consonant letters can be doubled:

b d f g l m n p r s t z

c can be doubled in the patterns **acc-**, **occ-**, and **succ-** at the beginning of words:

ac**c**use	oc**c**asion	suc**c**our
ac**c**ess	oc**c**upy	suc**c**eed
...	...	...

The remaining consonant letters are never doubled:

h j k q v w x y

Note: (1) **v** can be doubled only in a few colloquial words: e.g. 'bovver', 'civvy', 'navvy', 'revved', and 'savvy'. (2) **k** can be doubled in some Foreign words: e.g. 'Nikkei average' and 'chicken tikka'.

Double consonants and word position

Initial

Double consonants do not normally occur initially in English words (but note the Foreign word 'llama').

Middle

Native doubling: In some words, double consonants mark the preceding vowel as short. For example, compare 'latter' (/l**æ**tə^r/) with 'later' (/l**e**ɪtə^r/). Such double consonants occur only after a single vowel letter, and most commonly before the endings **-ed**, **-en**, **-er**, **-est**, **-ing**, **-le**, and **-y**:

fu**nn**y	li**tt**le	su**dd**en	we**dd**ing
ho**tt**est	ru**gg**ed	su**mm**er	...

The endings which cause doubling are not the same for every letter. Thus, **-ow** produces doubling in **l** (e.g. 'yellow') and **r** (e.g. 'narrow'), but not in **d** (e.g. 'shadow' and 'widow'). The endings which cause a particular letter to be doubled are listed in the **Middle** section of the appropriate consonant entry in Section 2.

This system of 'Native doubling' is still operational in the language, so that when a suffix that begins with a vowel is added to a word which finishes in a single vowel followed by a single consonant, the consonant is usually doubled. If the final syllable is not stressed, it is only doubled under certain circumstances. More details and any exceptions can be found in the **Inflection and word formation** section for the appropriate consonant in Section 2.

Classical doubling: Double consonants occur after the first syllable of many words of Classical origin which begin with the letters **a-**, **co-**, **e-**, **i-**, **o-**, and **su-**:

abbreviate	...	...	oppose
accuse	college	illicit	...
affect	command	immaterial	succour
aggressive	connect	innate	sufficient
alleviate	correct	irritate	suggest
announce	...	...	suppose
arrest	effect	occasion	surrender
attempt	effort	office	...

Classical doubling is no longer an active process in the language.

Complex doubling: Double letters can occur when one part of a word ends in a particular letter and the next part of the word begins with the same letter:

bookkeeper	dumbbell	midday	unnatural
dissatisfied	ennoble	overrun	...

Foreign doubling: Double letters occur in some Foreign words: e.g. 'guerrilla' and 'pizza'.

Final

Double consonants occur in two main ways:

1. Some consonants are usually doubled when they occur in a stressed syllable after a single vowel: e.g. **f** in 'doff' and 'stiff'; **l** in 'fill', 'full', and 'roll'; **s** in 'mass' and 'miss'; and **z** in 'buzz' and 'jazz'.

Note: (1) In British English, **-ll** does not usually occur at the end of words of more than one syllable: e.g. 'annul', 'appal', 'canal', 'enrol', 'fulfil', 'repel', and 'until'. (2) In American English, **-ll** does occur in 'appall', 'enroll', and 'fulfill'; but not in 'annul', 'canal', 'repel', and 'until'.

2. In a small number of lexical words that begin with vowels, the consonant is doubled because of the three letter rule: e.g. 'a**dd**', 'e**bb**', 'e**gg**', 'i**nn**', and 'o**dd**'. For more details, see the article on the 'Three letter rule'.

1.7 Etymology – the history of words

Etymology is the history of words. Words change over time: neither their use nor their form is fixed. Meaning, grammatical behaviour, pronunciation, and written form can all change.

Knowing how a word used to be pronounced may not help us to know how it is pronounced now. In Shakespeare's day, 'prove' used to rhyme with 'love', but this is no longer the case. Similarly, knowing what a word used to mean does not necessarily help us to know what it means now. The word 'consider' is derived from the Latin word *sidus, sideris* meaning 'star', and originally referred to astrological speculation, but it has no such meaning now. While meanings, grammatical behaviour, and pronunciation have changed, the spelling of words has generally remained fixed.

In many cases, some knowledge of the origin of a word can help us to work out how to spell it. **Silent consonants**, for example, are usually connected with the history of words. The **s** in 'isle' has come from the Latin word *insula*, and is also found in the English words 'insulate' and 'isolate', which come from the same source.

When several spelling patterns seem possible, choosing the correct one can be helped by some knowledge of etymology. You might think that someone who writes a play should be a 'playwriter' or a 'playwrite'. However, the old word for a craftsman who produces skilled work is a 'wright', as in 'wheelwright' and 'shipwright', which gives us 'playwright'.

The spelling of unstressed syllables can also be helped by knowledge of the history of words. For example, in Latin, **-io(n)** was added to the past participles of verbs to produce abstract nouns meaning 'an action or state', while **-or** was added to produce nouns meaning 'a person who does an action'. For this reason, many English words which end in **-or** can be related to other words which end in **-ion**:

e.g. direct**or** – direct**ion**; edit**or** – edit**ion**; profess**or** – profess**ion**; sect**or** – sect**ion**.

More broadly, it is helpful in spelling a word to know whether it is a **Native** word, or whether it is of **Classical** or **Foreign** origin. If 'consider' were of Native origin it would be spelled **dd** like 'bi**dd**er', because Native words spelled **ider** are pronounced differently, with /aɪ/, as in 'ins**ider**', 'sp**ider**', and 'w**ider**'.

1.8 Final e

In Modern English, final **e** is not normally sounded. It does not indicate a new syllable in the way that, for example, final **a** or final **y** does: compare 'engine' /<u>e</u>ndʒɪn/ and 'babe' /b<u>eɪ</u>b/ with 'angina' /ændʒ<u>aɪ</u>nə/ and 'baby' /b<u>eɪ</u>bi/.

History

English words used to have different endings according to the way in which they were used in a sentence, in a similar way to Latin. Gradually, however, there was a simplification in the system of endings, so that most words ended in -e, which had been generally pronounced as a weak vowel sound /ə/.

As this ending was the same in all words, it no longer had any function in the spoken language, and therefore was not pronounced at all. So, for example, both the words *hatte* and *hate* would have had one syllable only. The only significant difference in the pronunciation of these words was in the length of the vowel (see the article on 'Double consonants'), which was short in *hatte* and long in *hate*. In time, the spelling of *hatte* was simplified to 'hat'. In the spelling 'hate', the final **e** marks 'hate' as having a longer vowel sound than 'hat'.

Functions

1. The main function of final **e** remains that of marking the preceding vowel letter as having its 'long' pronunciation: e.g. 'bit' /bɪt/ (short **i**) and 'bite' /baɪt/ (long **i**).

2. After a single **s** at the end of a word, final **e** can indicate that the **s** is not an inflectional ending: compare 'laps' and 'lapse' (both pronounced /læps/), and 'rays' and 'raise' (both pronounced /reɪz/). This occurs after another consonant letter, or after two vowel letters:

collapse	sense	...	increase
corpse	tense	because	loose
false	universe	cheese	noise
pulse	worse	house	praise

Note: After a single vowel letter, **s** is doubled: e.g. 'across', 'class', 'less', and 'miss'.

3. Final **e** is also found after **z** when preceded by two vowel letters:

| breeze | gauze | seize | snooze |
| frieze | ooze | sneeze | ... |

4. After **c** and **g**, final **e** indicates that these letters have the pronunciations /s/ and /dʒ/ respectively: compare 'ra**g**' and 'ra**ge**', 'ri**ck**' and 'ri**ce**', 'ba**g**' and 'ba**dge**'.

5. Final **e** is always necessary after **v**:

behave	grieve	have	sieve
give	halve	persuasive	...

Note: This makes it difficult to know whether the previous vowel is 'long' or 'short': e.g. 'live' can be pronounced /lɪv/ (verb) or /laɪv/ (adjective).

6. Final **e** occurs after /ʌ/ spelled **o** followed by **m** or **n** in some very common words:

become	done	none	some
come	everyone	one	...

Final e does represent a sound in a few words:

1. In grammatical words:

e.g. be, he, me, we, ye.

2. In words of Foreign origin:

Aborigine	epitome	machete	reveille
acme	facsimile	minestrone	simile
andante	finale	pianoforte	sub judice
anemone	hyperbole	posse	ukulele
catastrophe	karaoke	psyche	vigilante
coyote	karate	recipe	...

3. After **l**:

able	double	people	table
available	example	possible	trouble
couple	middle	single	...

4. After **r**, mainly in British English:

acre	genre	massacre	metre
centre	litre	meagre	theatre
fibre	manoeuvre	mediocre	...

Note: The American spellings are 'center', 'fiber', 'liter', 'maneuver', 'meager', 'meter', and 'theater'.

1.9 Foreign words

There is a basic difference between words whose spelling reflects an English pronunciation of 500 years ago (when most English spelling conventions were established) and words whose spelling has been borrowed from other languages, and therefore entered English as written forms.

Words which have been borrowed from European languages which are written with a Latin alphabet, such as French, German, and Italian, tend not to have been respelled:

ennui	guerrilla	pizza	yacht
garage	kitsch	ski	...

While the pronunciation of these words has changed over time to become more 'English', the non-English features of their spelling remain.

Words which have been borrowed from languages which do not use a Latin alphabet are often transliterated in ways which distinguish them from Native words:

anorak	igloo	karaoke	okra
coypu	kaftan	manioc	...

The number of words which have come from Greek and Latin is so great that many of the Classical spelling patterns are as important as Native conventions. See the separate articles on 'Greek spelling conventions' and 'Latin spelling conventions'.

1.10 Grammar

Although English does not have an extensive set of inflectional endings, it is often the case that a spelling pattern is linked to a grammatical word class. This is sometimes not reflected in the pronunciation.

Endings

1. The most obvious way in which spelling gives grammatical information is by means of suffixes and inflectional endings that are added to words: **-s** is used for the plurals of nouns and the third person singular of the present tense of verbs, and **-ed** is used for past tenses and past participles, for example. However, the same ending can be pronounced very differently in different words: e.g. **-ed** is pronounced /ɪd/ in 'unit**ed**', /d/ in 'call**ed**', and /t/ in 'ask**ed**'.

2. Suffixes which can give a clear indication of word class include noun endings such as **-ation**, **-er**, **-ist**, and **-ness**, and adjective endings such as **-al**, **-ic**, **-less**, and **-ous**:

artist	endless	information	organization
basic	famous	leader	political
darkness	hopeless	manager	socialist
economic	illness	national	various

3. Often two different endings can have the same pronunciation: e.g. **-nous** in 'muti**nous**' sounds the same as **-ness** in 'empti**ness**', but the spelling shows that the first is an adjective ending, and the second is a noun ending.

4. Similarly, when /s/ at the end of a word is not an inflectional ending, it is often spelled **-se** or **-ss**. For example, 'laps' is the plural of 'lap', but the final silent **e** in 'lapse' shows that it is not connected to 'lap'. When /ks/ occurs at the end of a word, the single letter **x** can be used in the same way: compare 'la**cks**' ('lack' with the inflectional ending **-s**) and 'la**x**'.

Other features

Spelling patterns can indicate word class to a greater or lesser extent. For example, the three modal auxiliary verbs 'c**ould**', 'w**ould**' and 'sh**ould**' are linked by spelling and pronunciation, as are the personal pronouns 'm**e**', 'h**e**', 'sh**e**' and 'w**e**', but the pronouns 'y**ou**' /juː/ and 'th**ou**' /ðaʊ/ are only linked by spelling. There are important differences between the spelling patterns of **grammatical words** and **lexical words**. Also, many of the conventions which affect the spelling of Native words do not apply to grammatical words: articles, pronouns, and prepositions can have fewer than three letters, and can end in single vowel letters or single -s, for example.

Spelling, grammar, and pronunciation

It is sometimes not just the spelling, but the relationship between spelling and pronunciation which reflects word class. There are a number of words of Classical origin, for example, which have a different pronunciation according to their word class. As a noun and adjective, for example, 'present' is pronounced /**prez°nt**/, but as a verb the pronunciation changes to /**prɪzent**/.

The pronunciation of some Native patterns can also reflect word class. For example, **ough** represents /ɔː/ in the irregular verb past tenses '**bought**' and '**thought**', /ɒf/ in the nouns '**cough**' and 'tr**ough**', /oʊ/ in the conjunctions 'alth**ough**' and 'th**ough**', /uː/ in the preposition 'thr**ough**', /aʊ/ in the nouns 'b**ough**' and 'pl**ough**', /ʌf/ in the adjectives '**rough**' and '**tough**', and is weak (/ə/) in 'thor**ough**' and 'bor**ough**'.

Note: The American spelling of 'pl**ough**' is 'pl**ow**'.

1.11 Greek spelling conventions

Many technical words which are used in science and other academic disciplines, and also many everyday words, are of Greek origin. The conventions used for writing these words in English are based on the way they were spelled in late Latin, which may differ from the way in which similar words are spelled in other languages.

/f/ is usually spelled **ph**:

| em**ph**asis | **ph**ilosophy | **ph**ysical | triumph |
| **ph**ase | **ph**otogra**ph** | telep**h**one | ... |

/k/ is often spelled **ch**:

| **ch**aracter | monar**ch** | s**ch**eme | te**ch**nology |
| **ch**emical | **sch**edule | stoma**ch** | ... |

Note: This spelling pattern is also found for the English pronunciation of the Scots word 'lo**ch**'.

/ɪ/ and /aɪ/ are often spelled **y** before consonants:

| anal**y**st | ps**y**chological | s**y**mptom | t**y**pe |
| Ol**y**mpic | st**y**le | s**y**stem | ... |

/juː/ is often spelled **eu**:

| **eu**calyptus | n**eu**rotic | pharmac**eu**tical | therap**eu**tic |
| **eu**phoria | n**eu**tron | ps**eu**do | ... |

n, **s**, and **t** are sometimes preceded by a silent **p-** at the beginning of words:

| **p**neumatic | **p**salm | **p**seudonym | **p**terodactyl |
| **p**neumonia | **p**sephologist | **p**sychology | ... |

Note: (1) Silent letters also occur in '**g**nome', '**m**nemonic', and 'paradi**g**m'. (2) But in 'paradigmatic', the **g** is pronounced.

1.12 Hyphens

When two or more words combine to produce a new word, there are three ways in which the resulting compound word can be written:

1. as a single word: e.g. court + house = **courthouse**

2. as individual words: e.g. alarm + clock = **alarm clock**

3. with a hyphen: e.g. make + up = **make-up**

It can be difficult to know which of these ways is correct in a particular case, and if you are not certain, it is a good idea to check in a COBUILD dictionary. There are some general guidelines about when a hyphen is appropriate in a compound word:

1. When the compound word is used as a modifier (that is, before a noun):

e.g. a **brand-new** uniform; a **stained-glass** window.

2. When the second word ends in **-ed** or **-ing**, or is an irregular past participle:

e.g. the absent-**minded** professor; political muck-**raking**; a has-**been**; jerry-**built** houses; water-**borne** diseases.

3. In nouns which are associated with phrasal verbs:

e.g. a **hanger-on**; a **slip-up**; a **try-out**.

4. In numbers from 21 to 99, and in fractions:

e.g. **thirty-five**; one hundred and **eighty-nine**; **three-fifths**.

5. When one of the words consists of a single capital letter:

e.g. **T-shirt**; **U-turn**; **X-ray**.

6. In these compounds:

great-uncle (and other words with '**great**' for members of a family)
son-in-law (and other words with '**in-law**' for relatives by marriage)
half-price (and most other compounds with '**half**')
self-esteem (and most other compounds with '**self**')

7. Hyphens are sometimes used after prefixes, especially after **ex-** and **non-**, before a capital letter or a number, or to avoid double vowel letters:

e.g. **ex**-wife; **non**-violent; anti-British; neo-Classical; post-**1945**; co-operate; pre-empt.

1.13 Latin spelling conventions

A very large number of English words come from Latin, either directly or through French. There are a number of distinct spelling conventions which occur in words of Latin origin:

/s/ is often spelled **c** before **e, i,** or **y**:

| cell | circumstance | medicine | tendency |
| centre | city | privacy | ... |

/dʒ/ is often spelled **g** before **e, i,** or **y**:

| agent | giant | imagine | prodigy |
| general | gyrate | original | ... |

/ʃ/ is spelled **ti, ci,** or **ssi** in the middle of words:

| action | discussion | official | social |
| commission | national | profession | ... |

After the first vowel of words of Latin origin, double letters often occur:

| access | commotion | illicit | suggest |
| collect | effort | opposite | ... |

For more details, see the section on 'Classical doubling' in the article on 'Double consonants'.

The English Spelling System

1.14 Meaning

Spelling patterns can be shared by words which have similar meanings. The beginning may be the same, as in '**lead**', '**lead**er', and '**lead**ership' (all connected with '**lead**ing'). The ending may be the same, as in 'ge**ology**', 'physi**ology**', and 'bi**ology**' (all referring to areas of scientific study). Sometimes, the same pattern can appear in different places in related words, as in 'gramo**phone**' and '**phone**tics' (both connected with 'sound').

Native words

In Native words, when the same spelling pattern appears in words that are related, it usually has the same pronunciation. The pattern **lead** is pronounced /li:d/ in 'lead', 'leader' and 'leadership', and also when combined with 'ring' to form 'ringleader'.

If **lead** has a different pronunciation, this shows that the words are not related. 'Leaded' /ledɪd/ and 'leaden' /ledᵊn/ are related to 'lead' /led/ meaning a heavy metal.

This reflects the normal method of word formation in English. Complex words are formed by adding affixes to existing English words. Compound words are formed by combining existing English words. In both cases, the pronunciation of the basic English word remains the same. In complex words, the basic word will also retain its stress: e.g. in 'lead', 'leader', and 'leadership'. In compound words, even though one of the words may lose its stress, it will still retain its vowel quality. Thus, 'lead' in 'ringleader', though it is not stressed, is still pronounced /li:d/.

Classical words

In words of Classical origin, the same spelling pattern may have different pronunciations in related words. For example, 'acid' is pronounced /æsɪd/ but 'acidic' is pronounced /əsɪdɪk/. 'Compose' is pronounced /kəmpoʊz/, but 'composition' is pronounced /kɒmpəzɪʃn/. Similarly, the spelling pattern **graph** is pronounced differently in 'photographic' and 'photographer'.

One reason is that words of Classical origin are formed from elements which are not necessarily recognizable English words. The word 'acid', for example, is a complex word in origin, consisting of the Latin root *ac* meaning 'sharp' (also found in '**ac**ute') and the adjectival ending -*id* (also found in 'sol**id**'). Unlike 'lead', however, 'ac' does not have an independent meaning in English. In English, 'acid' is a simple word which happens to have two syllables, and its meaning belongs to both syllables equally. For this reason, the stress is more flexible, and English words of Classical origin generally have different stress patterns according to their endings: e.g. 'atom – atomic', 'colony – colonial', 'editor – editorial', 'inform – information'.

Even when their endings are not different, related words of Classical origin can have a different stress pattern. This is because nouns and adjectives are frequently stressed on the first syllable, while verbs are usually stressed on the second syllable: e.g. 'present' (noun and adjective) – 'present' (verb); 'subject' (noun and adjective) – 'subject' (verb).

The important implication of stress shift for spelling is that in these words the different stress pattern means that there is a different pattern of strong and weak vowel sounds. There is a very strong tendency for the unstressed syllables of words of Classical origin to be pronounced with a **weak vowel sound** (/ə/). This makes it difficult to know which vowel to use in the spelling, if words are considered in isolation. We might be unsure, for example, of how to spell the final syllable of 'editor': is it **-er** like 'writ**er**', **-or** like 'direct**or**', or **-ar** like 'begg**ar**'? By considering the spelling of the related word 'edit**or**ial', the doubt is resolved. Similarly, if we are unsure about the spelling of the second vowel in 'photographic', the related word 'photographer' provides the answer.

In relating the spelling of these words of Classical origin to current English pronunciation, it is important to remember that Classical spelling patterns have never resulted from English pronunciation. Words of Classical origin came into the language in written form, and were then pronounced. There are so many words of Classical origin in English that strong conventions exist connecting Latin spelling with English pronunciation, but we cannot expect to derive Latin spellings from English pronunciations.

One of the most significant features of the English spelling system is that the Classical spelling patterns have not been reformed to make them compatible with native conventions. Therefore it is a considerable help in English spelling to be aware of common Classical spelling patterns and how they are pronounced in different words, and to be able to make the link between words such as 're**sign**' and **'sign**ature', 'miso**gyn**ist' and '**gyn**aecology', or 'Anglo**phile**' and '**phil**anthropy'. Some of these are listed below.

The English Spelling System

Some common Classical spelling patterns in English words:

Classical Pattern	Meaning	English words
ac	sharp	**ac**id **ac**rid **ac**ute
ana	back	**ana**chronism **ana**gram **ana**logy **ana**lyst
ann or *enn*	year	**ann**iversary **ann**ual cent**enn**ial mill**enn**ium per**enn**ial
arch	chief	an**arch**y **arch**bishop **arch**etype hier**arch**y mon**arch**
bio	life	antibiotics **bio**graphy **bio**psy **bio**sphere sym**bio**sis
chron	time	ana**chron**ism **chron**ic **chron**icle syn**chron**ize
crypt	hidden	**crypt** **crypt**ic **crypt**o-
cycl	round	bi**cycl**e **cycl**e **cycl**ical **cycl**one en**cycl**opedia
derm	skin	**derm**atologist epi**derm**is hypo**derm**ic taxi**derm**ist
duc	lead	con**duc**t e**duc**ation intro**duc**e pro**duc**e re**duc**tion
dyna	power	**dyna**mic **dyna**mo **dyna**sty
dys	bad	**dys**entery **dys**lexic **dys**pepsia **dys**trophy
eu	well, good	**eu**genics **eu**phemism **eu**phoria **eu**thanasia
fact	make, do	arte**fact** **fact**or **fact**ory manu**fact**ure satis**fact**ion
form	shape, realization	**form**ula in**form**ation re**form** uni**form**
gen	productive	**gen**e **gen**erate **gen**eration **gen**esis **gen**etic **gen**ital
gen	type, high class, race	**gen**der **gen**eral **gen**erous **gen**ocide **gen**re **gen**tle **gen**uine
gram	something written or drawn	ana**gram** dia**gram** **gram**mar **gram**matical pro**gram**me tele**gram**
gyn	woman	andro**gyn**ous **gyn**aecologist miso**gyn**y
hydr	water	de**hydr**ation **hydr**aulic **hydr**oelectric **hydr**ofoil
hyper	over, too much	**hyper**active **hyper**bole **hyper**tension
hypo	under	**hypo**dermic **hypo**thermia **hypo**thesis
iatr	heal	ger**iatr**ic ped**iatr**ician psych**iatr**ist
idio	distinctive	**idio**m **idio**syncrasy **idio**t
itis	disease	arthr**itis** cyst**itis** tonsill**itis**
log	study, system	astro**log**y ideo**log**ical techno**log**y
log	speak, word	apo**log**y dia**log**ue epi**log**ue pro**log**ue
man	hand	**man**age **man**icure **man**ipulate **man**ual **man**ufacture **man**uscript
man	obsession	**man**ia **man**ic
onym	name	acr**onym** an**onym**ous pseud**onym** syn**onym**ous
osis	illness	neur**osis** psych**osis** scler**osis** thromb**osis**
path	suffer	anti**path**y a**path**y em**path**y homeo**path**y **path**etic **path**ology **path**os sym**path**y
phon	sound	caco**phon**y micro**phon**e **phon**e **phon**etics sym**phon**y
phys	nature	**phys**ical **phys**iognomy **phys**iology
poly	many	**poly**gamous **poly**gamy **poly**glot **poly**math **poly**technic
popul	people	**popul**ar **popul**ation
pos	place, put forward	im**pos**e op**pos**e **pos**ition **pos**itive pur**pos**e
psych	mind	**psych**iatry **psych**ic **psych**ology
rupt	break	bank**rupt** cor**rupt** dis**rupt** e**rupt** inter**rupt** **rupt**ure
rh or *rrh*	flow	cata**rrh** dia**rrh**oea haemo**rrh**age **rh**eumatism **rh**ythm
scop	observe	horo**scop**e micro**scop**ic tele**scop**e
sign	mark	de**sign**ate de**sign**er in**sign**ia **sign**al **sign**ature **sign**ificant
stella	star	con**stella**tion **stella**r
sy	together	**sy**mmetry **sy**mpathy **sy**mphony **sy**ntax **sy**nthesis **sy**stem
tele	distant	**tele**phone **tele**phonist **tele**vision **tele**x
tend	lean towards	at**tend** in**tend** pre**tend** **tend**ency
vis	see	in**vis**ible re**vis**e super**vis**e tele**vis**ion **vis**ion **vis**it **vis**ual

1.15 Native spelling conventions

'Native' words are words whose spelling conventions reflect English pronunciation of 500 years ago. Here are some of the main characteristics of Native spelling conventions:

Single **-a**, **-i**, **-o**, and **-u** do not normally occur at the end of **lexical words**. They sometimes occur at the end of **grammatical words**, and **Foreign** or **Classical** words:

a	so	...	menu
do	to	alibi	radio
I	who	drama	...

Stressed vowel sounds at the end of words were long, as they were in open syllables, while unstressed vowel sounds were always short. One way of distinguishing stressed sounds from unstressed sounds was to use more than one letter for the stressed sounds, to indicate that the vowel was long and therefore stressed. As grammatical words were typically unstressed, they were generally spelled with a single final vowel letter: compare the grammatical words 'b**e**', 'h**e**', and 'w**e**' with the lexical words 'agr**ee**', 'b**ee**', 'fr**ee**', and 's**ee**'.

Single **-e** occurs very commonly at the end of words, but is not normally sounded. It has a number of functions, the most important of which is to show that the preceding vowel is long:

| bite | house | make | state |
| five | life | place | ... |

Note: Final **e** is sounded in some words of Foreign or Classical origin: e.g. 'epitome', 'karaoke', and 'ukulele'.

For more details, see the article on 'Final **e**'.

Vowel sounds are often spelled by **vowel digraphs**:

ab**ou**t	g**oo**d	h**ou**se	s**ai**d
ag**ai**n	gr**ea**t	p**au**se	s**ou**th
each	gr**ou**p	r**ea**dy	...

For more details, see the article on 'Vowel digraphs'.

Short vowels are not usually followed by **single consonants** in the middle of words: compare 'forbi**dd**en' (a Native word) with 'consi**d**er' (a word of Classical origin).

Single **j**, **q**, **v**, and **z** do not normally occur at the end of words.

The English Spelling System

Final single **s** is normally used for the plural of nouns and the third person singular present tense of verbs. In other cases, final /**s**/ is spelled **ss** or **se**:

cross	grass	release
glimpse	miss	...

Single **c** does not occur at the end of words of one syllable: compare 'bloc' (a Foreign word) with 'block' (a Native word).

gh is usually silent in the middle of words and at the end of words:

although	might	sigh	through
bough	night	though	weigh
height	right	thought	...

gh spells /**f**/ in these words:

cough	laugh	tough
enough	rough	trough

k is silent before **n** at the beginning of a word:

knack	knife	know	knuckle
knee	knight	knowledge	...

Lexical words have at least three letters. For more details, see the article on the 'Three letter rule'.

Note: We can recognize words which originated as abbreviations because, like Foreign words, they do not follow Native spelling conventions: e.g. 'ad' breaks the 'three letter rule', 'rev' breaks the convention that **v** does not occur at the end of words, and 'hi-fi' breaks the convention that words do not end in **i**.

1.16 Plurals

You usually form the plural of English nouns by adding **-s**:

e.g. day – day**s**; force – force**s**; hour – hour**s**; member – member**s**; month – month**s**; photo – photo**s**; pound – pound**s**; thing – thing**s**; year – year**s**.

When a noun ends in **-sh**, **-ch** (pronounced /tʃ/), **-ss**, **-x**, or **-s**, you add **-es**:

e.g. bonus – bonus**es**; branch – branch**es**; bus – bus**es**; business – business**es**; clash – clash**es**; class – class**es**; dish – dish**es**; gas – gas**es**; loss – loss**es**; match – match**es**; tax – tax**es**.

When a noun ends in **-ch** (pronounced /k/), you add **-s**:

e.g. epoch – epoch**s**; eunuch – eunuch**s**; monarch – monarch**s**; patriarch – patriarch**s**; stomach – stomach**s**.

When a noun ends in a consonant followed by **-y**, you form the plural with **-ies**:

e.g. authority – authorit**ies**; country – countr**ies**; party – part**ies**.

When a noun ends in a vowel followed by **-y**, you add **-s**:

e.g. attorney – attorney**s**; boy – boy**s**; day – day**s**; guy – guy**s**; key – key**s**; play – play**s**; ray – ray**s**; toy – toy**s**; way – way**s**.

For these nouns which end in single **-f** or **-fe**, you form the plural with **-ves**:

calf – cal**ves**; elf – el**ves**; half – hal**ves**; knife – kni**ves**; leaf – lea**ves**; life – li**ves**; loaf – loa**ves**; scarf – scar**ves**; sheaf – shea**ves**; shelf – shel**ves**; thief – thie**ves**; wharf – whar**ves**; wife – wi**ves**; wolf – wol**ves**.

For other nouns which end in **-f** or **-fe**, you add **-s**:

e.g. aperitif – aperitif**s**; belief – belief**s**; brief – brief**s**; chef – chef**s**; chief – chief**s**; dwarf – dwarf**s**; gulf – gulf**s**; handkerchief – handkerchief**s**; motif – motif**s**; proof – proof**s**; reef – reef**s**; relief – relief**s**; roof – roof**s**; safe – safe**s**; serf – serf**s**; waif – waif**s**.

Note: The plural of 'hoof' can be either 'hoofs' or 'hooves'.

For these nouns which end in **-o**, you add **-es**:

buffalo – buffalo**es**; cargo – cargo**es**; echo – echo**es**; embargo – embargo**es**; fresco – fresco**es**; grotto – grotto**es**; halo – halo**es**; hero – hero**es**; innuendo – innuendo**es**; mango – mango**es**; memento – memento**es**; mosquito – mosquito**es**; motto – motto**es**; negro – negro**es**; no – no**es**; potato – potato**es**; tomato – tomato**es**; torpedo – torpedo**es**; veto – veto**es**; volcano – volcano**es**.

For other nouns which end in -o, you add -s:

e.g. auto – autos; casino – casinos; demo – demos; disco – discos; embryo – embryos; eskimo – eskimos; ghetto – ghettos; kilo – kilos; memo – memos; photo – photos; portfolio – portfolios; radio – radios; ratio – ratios; scenario – scenarios; stereo – stereos; studio – studios; taboo – taboos; tornado – tornados; video – videos.

Note: (1) The noun 'quiz' doubles its final z in the plural: 'quizzes'. (2) An apostrophe is sometimes used before -s in the case of numbers and letters of the alphabet, but this is becoming less common: e.g. 'the 40's and 50's' and 'two C's and a D'.

Foreign plurals

In some nouns of French origin, there is no difference in spelling between the singular and plural forms, but there is a change in the pronunciation. In these nouns of French origin, the final s is silent in the singular, but pronounced /z/ in the plural:

bourgeois	chassis	faux pas	precis
chamois	corps	patois	rendezvous

In these nouns of French origin, a silent -x is added in the plural:

bureau – bureaux; chateau – chateaux; gateau – gateaux; plateau – plateaux; tableau – tableaux.

Note: (1) Some people pronounce the final x as /z/. (2) The spellings 'bureaus', 'plateaus, and 'tableaus' are also used.

Most nouns from other languages are treated like Native nouns, and you can add -s or -es for the plural following Native rules, or use expressions that avoid the need for a plural:

e.g. 'two chicken tikkas'; 'four glasses of Beaujolais'.

Note: These Italian nouns are sometimes given their original plural forms, but also have -s forms: tempo – tempi (or tempos); virtuoso – virtuosi (or virtuosos).

Classical plurals

English nouns of Classical origin have plurals which are formed according to Classical rules. However, most of them are technical or formal, and in informal situations they can be used with a regular -s or -es plural form, following the rules for Native nouns. Only commonly used Classical plural forms are given here. For other nouns, you will need to look in a COBUILD dictionary.

Plurals

These nouns ending in **-us** have plurals ending in **-i**:

focus – foci; nucleus – nuclei; radius – radii; stimulus – stimuli.

These nouns ending in **-um** have plurals ending in **-a**:

aquarium – aquaria; memorandum – memoranda; referendum – referenda; spectrum – spectra; stratum – strata.

Most nouns ending in **-is** have plurals ending in **-es**:

e.g. analysis – analyses; axis – axes; basis – bases; crisis – crises; diagnosis – diagnoses; hypothesis – hypotheses; neurosis – neuroses; parenthesis – parentheses; thesis – theses.

Some nouns ending in **-a** add **-e** for the plural:

e.g. larva – larvae; vertebra – vertebrae.

Note: 'amoeba', 'antenna', 'formula', and 'nebula' have plurals in **-e**, but are commonly used with regular plurals in **-s** in most contexts.

A few nouns have other ways of forming their plurals:

e.g. appendix – appendices; automaton – automata; corpus – corpora; criterion – criteria; genus – genera; index – indices; matrix – matrices; phenomenon – phenomena; vortex – vortices.

Note: Some of these nouns can also have regular plurals ending in **-s** or **-es**: e.g. 'appendixes', 'automatons', 'indexes', and 'vortexes'.

1.17 Silent consonants

A large number of English words have **silent consonants**. This means that there is a consonant letter in the spelling, but it is not sounded. The silent consonant is usually associated with another consonant letter which is sounded, for example silent **k-** often comes before **n** at the beginning of words like 'knee' and 'know'. In Section 2, words spelled with silent consonants are given in the entry for the sounded consonant. So you will find '**kn**ee' and '**kn**ow' at the spelling pattern **kn** in the entry for /**n**/, because that is the consonant that you will hear, and you may not realize that there is a silent **k** in the spelling.

Note that there is a difference between silent consonants and consonant letters which combine to form digraphs and 'multi-graphs' which have their own unique sound. For example, **sh** is a digraph because it represents the sound /ʃ/ and neither **s** by itself nor **h** by itself usually represents this sound. So neither **s** nor **h** can be called 'silent'. But in the word 'de**b**t', the t by itself usually represents the sound /t/, so the **b** is a silent consonant letter.

History

Silent consonants occur for different reasons. Often the pronunciation of a word has changed without a change in spelling. The **gh** in words like 'ni**gh**t' and 'si**gh**' represents a sound that has disappeared from most accents of English, although it can still be heard in Scots 'lo**ch**'. '**Kn**ee' and '**kn**ow' used to be pronounced /kn/ (as in the German word *Knabe*). Over time, the English pronunciation has simplified to /n/, but the spelling has not changed. The process of simplifying pronunciations continues: the **d** in 'han**d**kerchief' is now not always sounded. This is an important feature of silent consonants: they are not silent for all speakers. Also they are not necessarily silent in all contexts: **g** is silent in 'paradi**g**m', but is sounded in 'paradi**g**matic'.

The spelling patterns of **Foreign words** are not usually changed when the words come into English, so they may contain consonant letters that were silent in the original language. This is particularly common in words borrowed from French: the **t** at the end of 'debu**t**', the **d** and **x** in 'Gran**d** Pri**x**', and the **z** and **s** in 'rende**z**vou**s**'. In other cases, the consonant letters in the Foreign word may represent a combination of sounds which does not occur in English. This occurs frequently in words which have come from Greek: the **pn** at the beginning of '**pn**eumonia', the **ps** in '**ps**ychology', and the **gn** in '**gn**ome'.

Sometimes silent consonants have been added to Native words: l was added to 'could' in the 16th century because of the pattern in 'shou**l**d' and 'wou**l**d'. And **b** was added to 'doubt' in the 15th century to show its connection with the Latin verb *dubitare*.

Function

English spelling is not simply a system for representing pronunciation. The way in which words are spelled can reflect whether they are of Native, Classical or Foreign origin: the same sound /ʃ/ is spelled differently in 'fi**sh**ing' (Native), 'fi**ss**ion' (Classical), and 'fi**ch**e' (French). The spelling can also indicate whether words are **lexical words** ('eye', 'inn', 'bee') or **grammatical words** ('I', 'in', 'be'), what other words they are related to ('**seri**al' is related to '**seri**es'; 'cereal' is not), and whether the text is British ('col**ou**r') or American ('col**o**r').

In writing, silent consonants can distinguish between words which sound the same. 'The **knight** approached' cannot be confused with 'The **night** approached' in the written language. In some cases, silent consonants have been added to words to distinguish them from similar words of different meaning. Thus **c** was added to 'scent' 200 years ago to distinguish it from the verb past tense 'sent'.

Silent consonants can show the links between English words: the **b** in 'de**b**t' links it with 'de**b**it'; the silent **g** in 'si**g**n' is related to the sounded **g** in 'si**g**nal'; the **l** in 'could', 'should', and 'would' shows that they are all in the same grammatical class.

Silent consonants can show the history of words: their etymology. This is not necessarily a good guide to their current meaning, because the meaning of words can change in very unpredictable ways over time. But it can help to relate words of similar origin in different languages: the silent **s** in 'i**s**le' and 'i**s**land' originates in the Latin word *insula* (which is also the source for 'in**s**ulate' and 'i**s**olate'), and the same **s** also appears (and is sounded) in the German word *Insel* and the Italian word *isola*.

Silent consonants can indicate something about the sound value of other letters in a word. Although **gh** is silent in 'fi**gh**t', it indicates that 'fight' is not pronounced the same as 'fit'.

The English Spelling System

Silent b:

Silent **b** occurs before final **t** in these words:

de**b**t	dou**b**t	su**b**tle

Silent **b** occurs after **m** in these words:

aplom**b**	com**b**	lam**b**	succum**b**
bom**b**	crum**b**	lim**b**	thum**b**
catacom**b**	dum**b**	num**b**	tom**b**
clim**b**	honeycom**b**	plum**b**	wom**b**

Note: (1) Silent **b** remains silent when most suffixes are added: e.g. clim**b** – clim**b**s – clim**b**ing – clim**b**ed – clim**b**er. (2) **b** is not silent in 'clamber'.

Silent c:

Silent **c** occurs only in 'indict'.

Note: When /s/ or /ʃ/ are spelled **sc**, the **c** might be considered to be silent:

corpuscle	muscle	...	fascism
discipline	scene	conscious	luscious
fascinate	science	crescendo	...

Silent ch:

Silent **ch** occurs only in these words:

fuchsia	schism	yacht

Silent d:

Silent **d** occurs after **n** and before another consonant, especially in the pattern -**and**- :

frien**d**ship	han**d**kerchief	soun**d**track	win**d**mill
gran**d**father	lan**d**scape	We**d**nesday	...

Silent g:

Silent **g** occurs before **n** in these words:

gnarled	...	dei**g**n	mali**g**n
gnash	ali**g**n	desi**g**n	physio**g**nomy
gnat	assi**g**n	ensi**g**n	rei**g**n
gnaw	beni**g**n	fei**g**n	resi**g**n
gnome	campai**g**n	forei**g**n	si**g**n
gnostic	consi**g**n	impu**g**n	soverei**g**n

Silent **g** occurs before **m** in these words:

diaphra**g**m	paradi**g**m	phle**g**m

Silent consonants

Note: Silent **g** becomes pronounced after suffixes have been added in these words: 'assignation', 'malignant', 'paradigmatic', 'phlegmatic', 'resignation', 'signal'.

Silent h:

Silent **h** occurs in these words:

heir	ghetto	rhythm	Jehovah
honest	ghost	shepherd	loofah
honour	ghostly	silhouette	myrrh
hour	ghoul	spaghetti	oh
...	haemorrhage	vehicle	ooh
annihilate	khaki	...	pariah
burgher	rhapsody	ah	pharaoh
cirrhosis	rhetoric	Allah	purdah
diarrhoea	rheumatic	blah	Shah
exhibit	rhinoceros	catarrh	torah
forehead	rhododendron	cheetah	verandah
ghastly	rhubarb	eh	yeah
gherkin	rhyme	huh	

Note: (1) In American English, silent **h** also occurs in 'herb' and 'humble'. (2) **h** also forms part of the digraphs **ch**, **gh**, **ph**, **sh** and **th**.

Silent **h** occurs after **w** in these words:

whack	when	while	whirl
whale	whence	whilst	whisk
wharf	whenever	whim	whisky
what	where	whimper	whisper
whatever	whether	whine	whistle
wheat	which	whingeing	white
wheel	whiff	whip	why

Note: Most speakers of American English, and some speakers of British English, pronounce the beginning of these words /**hw**/.

Silent k:

Silent **k** occurs before **n** in these words:

knack	kneel	knight	knot
knave	knew	knit	know
knead	knickers	knob	knowledge
knee	knife	knock	knuckle

The English Spelling System

Silent l:

Silent l occurs before **d**, **f** and **v**, **k**, and **m** in these words:

could	half	talk	balm
should	halves	walk	calm
would	...	yolk	palm
...	chalk	...	psalm
calf	folk	almond	qualm
calves	stalk	alms	salmon

Note: (1) l in 'alms' is not silent in American English. (2) Silent l in 'colonel'. (3) Silent l in 'solder' in American English.

Silent n:

Silent n occurs after **m** in these words:

autumn	condemn	hymn
column	damn	solemn

Note: (1) Silent **n** becomes pronounced when a suffix beginning with a vowel is added to a word ending in -mn: e.g. 'autumnal', 'columnar', 'condemnation', 'damnation', 'hymnal', 'solemnity'. (2) Some people do not pronounce the **n** in 'columnist'. (3) Before inflectional endings, silent **n** remains silent: e.g. 'condemning' and 'damned'.

Silent p:

Silent **p** occurs before **n** or **s** in these words of Greek origin:

pneumatic	psalm	psychiatrist	psychology
pneumonia	pseudonym	psychic	psychotic

Silent **p** also occurs in these words:

corps	cupboard	raspberry
coup	peepbo	receipt

Silent r:

In RP, and in other **non-r accents**, silent r usually follows these vowel sounds before a consonant, before silent **e**, and at the end of a word: /ɑː/, /eə/, /ɜː/, /ɪə/, /aɪə/, /ɔː/, /ʊə/, /aʊə/, and /jʊə/. See the appropriate entries in Section 2 for details.

Note: *'r' vowel sounds:* (1) Because the vowel sounds /ɑː/, /eə/, /ɜː/, /ɪə/, /aɪə/, /ɔː/, /ʊə/, /aʊə/, /jʊə/, and /ə/ so frequently occur in words with a silent r, it is convenient to consider that r forms part of the spelling of the vowel sound. For example, in the word 'bear', the vowel sound /eə/ is represented by '-ear'. In the word 'bearing', however, because the next sound is a vowel, the sound represented by 'ear' is not /eə/ but /eər/. (2) For this reason, in Section 2

Silent consonants

of this Guide, the sound represented by '-ear' is shown as /eə^r/, that is with a small superscript /^{r}/, which means that it is pronounced /eər/ before a vowel sound, and /eə/ otherwise. Similarly the other 'r' vowel sounds are shown as: /ɑː^r/, /ɜː^r/, /ɪə^r/, /aɪə^r/, /ɔː^r/, /ʊə^r/, /aʊə^r/, /jʊə^r/, and /ə^r/. (3) The superscript /^{r}/ represents a sound which is always pronounced in an **r accent**, such as GenAm. (4) In cases where there is no r in the spelling, the vowel sounds are shown without the superscript /^{r}/. For example, the vowel sound in 'father' is shown as /ɑː/.

Silent r is also common after a **weak vowel sound**. In GenAm, and in other **r accents**, r is always pronounced.

Silent r occurs before a consonant:

according	further	north	third
airtight	government	order	turn
certain	hard	part	university
course	heard	person	western
early	important	report	work
force	journalism	sort	world
former	large	start	...

Silent r occurs before silent e followed by a consonant:

awareness	entirely	offered	shareholders
careful	forecast	requirements	therefore
considered	merely	retirement	...

Note: the silent r in 'iron'.

Silent r occurs after /ɑː/ and /ɜː/:

car	per	sir	incur
far	prefer	stir	recur
star	refer	...	slur
...	...	blur	spur
her	fir	fur	...

Silent r occurs after /ɔː/:

abhor	decor	matador	nor
condor	for	mentor	or
corridor	guarantor	metaphor	...

Silent r occurs after vowel digraphs:

air	door	oar	their
appear	four	our	weir
beer	hair	poor	year
clear	heir	roar	your
deer	hour	stair	...

Silent **r** occurs in many words after **weak vowel sounds**:

after	later	other	rapper
director	major	particular	visitor
labour	nuclear	popular	...

Silent **r** is spelled **rr** in these words:

burr	err	whirr

Silent **r** is spelled **re**, with a silent **e**, after /eə/, /ɪə/, /aɪə/, and /jʊə/:

aware	square	acquire	assure
bare	...	desire	cure
care	atmosphere	empire	mature
prepare	here	entire	obscure
rare	interfere	fire	pure
share	mere	require	secure
software	severe	wire	sure
spare	...	...	...

Silent **r** is also spelled **re** in many words after **u** pronounced /ə/:

failure	measure	pressure
figure	nature	structure
future	picture	...

Note: (1) Also spelled **re** sometimes after /ɔː/: e.g. 'before', 'more', 'score', 'store' and 'therefore'. (2) Also spelled **re** in these words: 'are', 'there', 'were', and 'where'. (3) Silent **r** is spelled **rre** in 'bizarre'. (4) Silent final **r** is doubled after /ɑː/ or /ɜː/ and before **-ed** or **-ing**: e.g. 'star – starring – starred; occur – occurring – occurred'. (5) **r** is pronounced before suffixes beginning with a vowel, except in the case of **-ed**, where the **e** is silent.

Silent s:

Silent **s** occurs mainly in words of French origin:

aisle	chamois	debris	précis
apropos	chassis	faux pas	vis-à-vis
bourgeois	corps	patois	viscount

Silent t:

Silent **t** occurs in:

often	soften

Silent **t** occurs in the endings **-sten** and **-stle**:

castle	hasten	listen	whistle
fasten	jostle	rustle	...

Silent consonants

Silent t occurs in these words of French origin:

argot	chalet	haricot	ricochet
ballet	crochet	nougat	sachet
beret	croissant	parquet	sorbet
bidet	debut	penchant	tarot
bouquet	denouement	pierrot	valet
buffet	depot	rapport	vol-au-vent
cabaret	duvet	rapprochement	
cachet	gourmet	restaurant	

Note: When s is added to a word ending in -nt, the t usually becomes silent: 'patients' sounds the same as 'patience'.

Silent w:

Silent w occurs before h or r in these words:

who	...	wrench	writ
whoever	wrack	wrest	write
whole	wrangle	wrestle	writhe
wholesale	wrap	wretch	written
wholesome	wrath	wretched	wrong
whom	wreath	wriggle	wrote
whooping cough	wreathe	wring	wrought
whore	wreck	wrinkled	wrung
whose	wren	wrist	wry

Silent w also occurs in these words:

answer	knowledge	sword	twosome
answerphone	lawyer	two	unanswerable

Silent w at the end of a word is always a part of a vowel digraph, aw, ew, or ow:

gnaw	...	...	low
law	few	allow	now
paw	knew	below	show
raw	new	how	tomorrow
saw	view	know	...

Silent x:

Silent x occurs at the end of words of French origin:

bureaux	faux pas	Grand Prix	tableaux
chateaux	gateaux	pas de deux	...

The English Spelling System

Words with silent letters near the beginning

Words with a silent letter in their first three letters are difficult to locate in a dictionary:

aisle	guild	knuckle	where
almond	guile	mnemonic	which
alms	guillotine	order	while
arm	guilt	our	white
asthma	guinea	palm	who
balk	guise	pneumatic	whole
balm	guitar	pneumonia	whom
calf	half	psalm	whore
calm	heir	psephology	whose
chalk	her	pseudonym	why
colonel	honest	psychiatrist	world
debt	honour	psychic	wraith
exhaust	hour	psychology	wrangle
exhibit	iron	qualm	wrap
exhilarate	island	rhapsody	wrath
exhort	isle	rhetoric	wreak
first	isthmus	rheumatism	wreath
folk	khaki	rhinoceros	wreck
ghastly	knack	rhododendron	wren
gherkin	knave	rhombus	wrench
ghetto	knead	rhubarb	wrest
ghost	knee	rhyme	wrestle
ghoul	kneel	rhythm	wretch
gnarled	knell	salmon	wretched
gnash	knickers	schism	wriggle
gnat	knick-knacks	sign	wring
gnaw	knife	stalk	wrinkle
gnome	knight	subtle	wrist
gnu	knit	sword	writ
guarantee	knob	two	write
guard	knock	victuals	wrought
guerrilla	knoll	walk	wry
guess	knot	Wednesday	yacht
guest	know	what	yolk
guide	knowledge	when	

1.18 Sounds and spelling

The underlying principle of an alphabetic writing system is that each sound in the language is represented by one letter. But although it uses an alphabet, the English writing system does not represent each sound in current English pronunciation by one letter.

Insufficient letters

In most accents of spoken English there are more than 40 different sounds: thus it is not possible for each sound to have a single letter which corresponds to it in every context. One of the ways in which written English deals with this is to use the same letter to represent different sounds. For example, the letter **a** alone can regularly represent eight different sounds, as in these words:

matting mating marring Mary   mall majestic   many manage

/mætɪŋ/ /meɪtɪŋ/ /mɑːrɪŋ/ /meəri/ /mɔːl/ /mədʒestɪk/ /meni/ /mænɪdʒ/

Another way in which an alphabet of 26 letters can be used to represent more than 40 sounds is to use a combination of letters to represent a particular sound. For example, whereas /s/ is represented by **s** in 'sow', and /h/ is represented by **h** in 'hat', the combination of letters **sh** is used to represent /ʃ/ in 'show'. Where two letters combine in this way, they form a 'digraph'.

Inconsistency

However, for historical reasons, the English spelling system is even more complicated. Most English sounds are represented by more than one letter or combination of letters: in fact, well over 100 different spelling patterns are used to represent the 40 or so individual sounds in English. For example, /ʃ/ is not only spelled **sh** in 'show', but also spelled **s** in 'sugar', **ssi** in 'mission', **ti** in 'nation', **ch** in 'parachute', and **ci** in 'facial'.

Many of the spelling patterns can be used for more than one of the sounds: as well as representing /ʃ/ in 'parachute', for example, **ch** represents /tʃ/ in 'change' and /k/ in 'character', and as mentioned earlier, the single letter **a** can represent eight different sounds.

This means that the number of ways of spelling any particular sound can be quite large. The main problem for the speller, then, is not just that sounds are not represented on a one sound for one letter basis, but that sounds are represented inconsistently in different words.

The English Spelling System

Occasionally a single letter represents a combination of sounds, for example **x** represents /k/ + /s/, or a sound in the pronunciation is not represented in the spelling, such as the /w/ in 'one'.

Silent letters and digraphs

This inconsistency in the writing system is also reflected in the number of silent letters which occur in English words:

autum**n**	**k**now	sig**n**	**w**rite
deb**t**	pa**l**m	**w**ho	...

A distinction can be made between single letters which represent sounds, single letters which do not represent sounds ('silent' letters), and letters which represent sounds in combination with other letters ('digraphs').

The sound /n/ is normally represented by **n**, as in 'next' and 'man'. In the words 'know' and 'sign', the sound /n/ is still represented by **n**, but there is an additional 'silent' letter in the spellings, **k** and **g** respectively. The sound /f/ is represented by **ph** in many words of Greek origin, but as neither **p** nor **h** is used on its own to represent /f/, **ph** is clearly a 'digraph'.

In practice, the distinction between silent letters and digraphs is not always a clear one. The sound /dʒ/, for example, is often spelled **g** in words such as 'general' and 'page', so that there are certain English speech sounds which have more than one element phonetically, for example /dʒ/, /tʃ/, /eɪ/, and so on.

Relating sounds and spelling

There can, therefore, be considerable difficulties in relating the sound and spelling of English words. For 500 years, the systems of spelling and pronunciation developed separately. In moving from the spoken language to the written language, or vice versa, it is necessary to translate from one system into another. Particular problems arise when a term in one system corresponds to more than one term in the other. In moving between spoken and written English, there are, as mentioned earlier in this article, eight possible pronunciations of **a**, and five possible spellings of /ʃ/.

Spelling and context

In deciding on how to spell the sound /ʃ/, it is important to know what the context of the sound is. This is because the probability of each of the five ways of spelling /ʃ/ varies greatly according to where it appears in the word, and what the letters and sounds are which precede it and follow it. At the beginning or at the end of a word, for example, apart from a few words which begin with s-, such as 'sure' and 'sugar', **sh** is the only possibility. In the middle of 'abolition' this sound is spelled **ti**, but when the sound occurs at the end of a word it is spelled **-sh** again, as in 'aboli**sh**'. Although all the patterns are possible in the middle of words, **ssi** can only occur after a short vowel (as in 'pa**ssi**on'), and **ci** and **ti** usually occur after a long vowel (as in 'na**ti**on'); **ci** and **ti** are both common before final **-al** but **ssi** never occurs in this position; **ssi** and **ti** are both common before final **-on**, but **ci** is very rare (as in 'suspi**ci**on'). When **sh** occurs in the middle of words, this is normally in Native words and before a Native suffix such as **-ing** or **-ed**. So we can see that spellings are determined not only on a sound-by-sound basis, but sometimes also by considering sequences of letters which represent sequences of sounds in particular contexts.

Spelling and pronunciation

Although the use of an alphabet makes us think that letters will relate to sounds, it is of course quite possible to have a writing system that identifies words without reference to their pronunciation. In the writing systems of languages such as Ancient Egyptian and Modern Chinese, the written form of a word depends on its meaning rather than its sound and must be learned separately from its pronunciation.

There are certain features of the spelling of English words which seem to reflect meaning rather than sound. For example, the vowels in 'photograph' and 'photography' are spelled the same, even though they are different sounds. This kind of feature has led to the suggestion that schoolchildren should learn English spelling on a 'whole word' basis, in the same way that Chinese schoolchildren have to learn to write.

But notice that the spelling of both 'photograph' and 'photography' remain closely related to their English pronunciation. The consonants are spelled the same and pronounced the same in both words. The only vowel sound that is spelled in more than one way is /ə/, which has no predominant spelling pattern: its two most common spellings in the middle of words are, in fact, **a** and **o**. /oʊ/ is regularly spelled **o** followed by a single consonant and another vowel, while /ɒ/ is regularly spelled **o** followed by more than one consonant in the middle of words.

The English Spelling System

Spelling sounds

The English spelling system originally reflected pronunciation more closely, and there remains a strong relationship between the internal structure of the spoken word and that of the written word, so that although it is not usually possible to predict the spelling only from the sequence of sounds, there will often be a considerable correlation between the two. Most English sounds can only be represented in a limited number of ways in spelling, and this choice is often further limited by factors such as the way in which the other sounds in the word are spelled, the origin of the word, the meaning of the word, and the grammatical function of the word, all of which can considerably affect the probability of particular patterns. For this reason, it remains a useful exercise to relate individual sounds to the way in which they are spelled in different words. Section 2 of this Guide deals with spelling in this way.

Finding words

However sophisticated the rules are for English spelling, and however many different factors are taken into account, there will always be a number of exceptions. It will never be possible to correctly predict the spelling of every English word. For this reason, Section 3 of this Guide contains a list of all the most useful words in English, to enable you to check their spelling pattern. If you know the first few letters of a word, it is a simple matter to find it in a conventional dictionary. If you are not sure of the spelling of the first syllable, it can be more difficult. For this reason, the list is arranged according to sound: words which begin with the same two or three sounds will be found together.

1.19 Three letter rule

It is an important convention of English spelling that **lexical words** have at least three letters:

Compare: 'inn' (noun)   with   'in' (preposition)
           'lie' (verb)   with   'by' (preposition)
           'bee' (noun)   with   'be' (auxiliary verb)
           'see' (verb)   with   'he' (pronoun)
           'toe' (noun)   with   'to' (preposition)

One syllable **lexical words** which begin or end in a vowel sound, and would otherwise have only two letters therefore display one of these features:

Double consonants	e.g. **add ebb egg inn odd** ...
Final silent **e**	e.g. **foe lie owe** ...
Vowel digraphs	e.g. **out sea see** ...
Final **w** or **y**	e.g. **pay sew sow** ...
Silent letters	e.g. **know nigh two** ...

Words with one or two letters are usually **grammatical words**:

at	do	in	to
be	he	me	us
by	I	on	...

A few two letter words originated as **Foreign words** or **abbreviations**:

e.g. ad (abbreviation); pi (Greek).

The only important exceptions to this rule are 'go' (which has a clear grammatical function in the 'going to' future of verbs) and 'ox'. In American English, 'ax' (compare British English 'axe') is a further exception.

1.20 Vowel digraphs

A major source of difficulty in English spelling is the use of two letters for a single vowel sound, such as **ea** in 'head', **oa** in 'boat', and **oi** in 'boil'.

These vowel digraphs are used in Modern English:

ai or ay	said, say
au or aw	pause, saw
ea	head, mean
ee	see, week
ei or ey	grey, vein
eu or ew	neutral, new
ie	chief, friend

oa	abroad, road
oe	shoe, toe
oi or oy	enjoy, point
oo	good, too
ou or ow	know, out
ue	guess, true
ui or uy	buy, fruit

It will be noticed that, with the exception of **ee** and **oi**, they can be used for representing a number of different sounds.

In general, -**ai**, -**au**, -**ei**, -**eu**, -**oa**, -**oi**, and -**ou** are not used at the end of **Native** words, whereas -**ay**, -**aw**, -**ey**, -**ew**, -**oy**, and -**ow** are usual. The one major exception is 'you'.

History

English, like most European languages, is written using the Latin alphabet, which only has 5 vowel letters. This is due to the fact that Latin, like modern Spanish, had only 5 different vowel sounds. English has always had more than 5 vowel sounds, and combinations of vowel letters have always been used to represent some of the sounds.

Current inconsistency

If particular digraphs were used consistently for particular sounds (as is the case in German, for example) there would not be a problem. But because the pronunciation of words has changed in different ways without a corresponding change in spelling, there are now a large number of inconsistencies. Most vowel digraphs are now used to represent a number of different sounds. For example, **ea** can be used to represent /eɪ/ in 'great', /ɑː/ in 'heart', /eə/ in 'bear', /e/ in 'head', /iː/ in 'read', /ɜː/ in 'earth', and /ɪə/ in 'near'.

All these sounds are spelled with a single vowel letter in other words, so that from the point of view of representing unusual sounds, **ea** is clearly redundant. In fact, there are only two vowel sounds, /aʊ/ in

Vowel digraphs

'r**ou**nd' and /ɔɪ/ in 'p**oi**nt', which can only be written by using vowel digraphs (**ou** and **oi** respectively).

In this Guide, vowel digraphs are treated as representations of a particular sound value: 'great' will be found in the entry for /eɪ/ with words spelled **a** such as 'late' and 'place', as well as words in which this sound is spelled differently, such as **ai** in 'aid', **ei** in 'rein', **e** in 'elite', **ae** in 'Gaelic', and **au** in 'gauge'.

Vowel digraphs tend to be found frequently in Native words, especially in words of one syllable, and also in some words which have come into the language from French. This reflects the fact that both English and French have always had a more complex vowel system than Latin. Vowel digraphs are therefore naturally much less common in words of Classical origin.

It is a general feature of vowel digraphs that, with the exception of endings, they are not so likely to represent a weak vowel sound as are single vowels.

1.21 Word formation

As well as knowing how basic words are spelled, it is important to be aware of the spelling conventions involved in the building of **complex words** and **compound words**.

Adding to the beginning of words

1. The basic principle is that you do not add or take away any letters when you add a prefix or combine two words:

e.g. mis- + spell = mis**s**pell; head + dress = hea**dd**ress.

A hyphen is sometimes used in order to avoid a sequence of vowel letters which might be interpreted as a vowel digraph:

e.g. co- + operate = co-operate; pre- + eminent = pre-eminent.

2. Some Latin prefixes change their final consonant according to the following consonant:

e.g. in- + formal = informal; in- + legal = illegal; in- + moral = immoral; in- + possible = impossible; in- + relevant = irrelevant.

As we see, this can often result in double consonants. For more details, see the section on 'Classical doubling' in the article on 'Double consonants'.

Adding to the end of words

1. Native word formation:

Letters sometimes need to be added or taken away when suffixes and inflectional endings are added. The spelling has to change because otherwise the 'word + suffix' combination would produce a sequence of letters that indicated a different pronunciation:

e.g. 'note – not**ing** – not**able**' and 'regret – regre**tt**ing – regre**tt**able'.

2. Classical word formation:

With the exception of final silent **e**, which is usually dropped, letters are not generally added or taken away when suffixes are added. But the pronunciation, and particularly the stress pattern, often changes:

e.g. 'acid – acid**ic**', 'cone – con**ical**', and 'relate – rel**ative**'.

Words with final silent e

The silent **e** is generally omitted before a suffix that begins with a vowel, or before a final **y**: e.g. 'compare – compar**able**', 'cone – con**ical**', 'ease – eas**y**', and 'live – liv**ing**'. This applies both to Native and Classical word formation.

Word formation

Exceptions:

1. In words which end in **-ce** or **-ge** the **e** shows that the pronunciation of **c** is /s/ and of **g** is /dʒ/. As **c** before **a** would be pronounced /k/, and **g** before **a** would be pronounced /g/, the **e** in **-ce** and **-ge** is retained before **-able**, in keeping with the principle of Native word formation mentioned above:

e.g. 'knowledg**e**able', 'manag**e**able', and 'notic**e**able'.

Note: (1) **e** is retained for the same reason before **-ous** in 'advantag**e**ous', 'courag**e**ous', and 'outrag**e**ous', and before **-ing** in 'singe – sing**e**ing', 'swinge – swing**e**ing', and 'whinge – whing**e**ing'. (2) 'ag**e**ing' is more common than 'aging', but only 'ageism' is possible.

2. In words which end in **-ee**, **-oe**, or **-ye**, final **e** is retained before all suffixes:

e.g. agree – agrees – agre**e**ing – agreed – agre**e**able – agre**e**ment.

Note: But **-ee** + **-ed** becomes **-eed** in 'agreed'.

3. In words which end in **-ie**, you replace **-ie** with **-y** before **-ing**:

e.g. 'die – d**y**ing' (cf. 'dye – dy**e**ing'), 'lie – l**y**ing', and 'tie – t**y**ing'.

Note: (1) Words ending in **-ue** keep the **e** before **-y**: 'blu**e**y', 'cliqu**e**y', and 'glu**e**y'. (2) A few other words keep their final silent **e** before a suffix that begins with a vowel, or **-y**: 'acr**e**age', 'cag**e**y', 'dic**e**y', 'mat**e**y', 'mil**e**age', and 'pric**e**y'.

4. In a number of words, especially words to which **-able** is being added, it is a matter of choice whether the final **e** is omitted:

e.g. 'blam**able**' or 'blam**e**able', 'lik**able**' or 'lik**e**able', 'mov**able**' or 'mov**e**able', 'rat**able**' or 'rat**e**able', 'siz**able**' or 'siz**e**able', 'unmistak**able**' or 'unmistak**e**able', and 'unshak**able**' or 'unshak**e**able'.

Note: Also 'nosy' or 'nosey' and 'routing' or 'rout**e**ing'.

Before a suffix that begins with a consonant, final silent **e** is generally retained:

e.g. 'lik**e**ly', 'lik**e**ness', and 'lik**e**wise'.

Exception:

Some adverbs do not have the final **e** of the related adjective:

e.g. 'due – duly', 'gentle – gently', 'probable – probably', 'simple – simply', 'true – truly', and 'whole – wholly'.

Note: (1) Final **e** is also omitted in 'awe – awful' and 'nine – ninth'. (2) Final **e** is commonly omitted in 'judge – judg**ment**', but 'judg**e**ment' is also used.

The English Spelling System

Words which end in -y

After a consonant letter, **-y** is generally changed to **-i** before suffixes which do not begin with **i**:

e.g. 'rely – rel**i**es – rel**i**ed – rel**i**able – rel**i**ant', but 'rel**y**ing'; 'happy – happ**i**er – happ**i**est – happ**i**ly – happ**i**ness', but 'happ**y**ish'.

Note: A few one syllable adjectives tend to keep the **-y** before suffixes that begin with a consonant: e.g. 'dry – dryness – dryly or drily'.

After a vowel, when it is a part of a vowel digraph, **-y** does not change:

e.g. play – plays – playing – played – player – playful – unplayable.

Words which end in a single consonant

1. Native conventions:

When a word ends in a single consonant after a single vowel, the consonant is often doubled before a suffix or inflectional ending that begins with a vowel, or before a **-y**:

e.g. 'fat – fa**tt**er – fa**tt**est – fa**tt**en – fa**tt**y' and 'stop – sto**pp**ing – sto**pp**ed – sto**pp**able – sto**pp**age'.

Note: (1) If the final syllable of the word is unstressed, the consonant is not doubled unless it is **l**: e.g. 'benefit – benefiting – benefited', 'fidget – fidgeting – fidgeted', but 'travel – trave**ll**ing – trave**ll**ed'. (2) In American English, **l** is not doubled: 'traveling – traveled'. (3) The consonant is sometimes doubled in an unstressed final syllable: 'handicap – handica**pp**ing – handica**pp**ed', 'kidnap – kidna**pp**ing – kidna**pp**ed – kidna**pp**er', and 'worship – worshi**pp**ing – worshi**pp**ed – worshi**pp**er'. (4) In American English, 'worshiping – worshiped'. (5) **l** is not doubled in 'parallel – paralleling – paralleled'.

2. Classical conventions:

Many Classical endings, such as **-ic**, **-ist**, and **-ity** do not produce doubling:

e.g. 'atom – atomic', 'human – humanity', 'symbol – symbolic', 'violin – violinist'.

Adding -s

Final **s** is required for noun plurals and the third person singular of the present tense of verbs. In either case the principles are largely the same. See also the article on 'Plurals'.

2.1 The 24 main vowel sounds

/æ/	act

This sound is very easy to spell. It is nearly always spelled **a**.

Initial

/æ/ is usually spelled **a**:

absolute	add	animal	average
act	angry	apple	...

Note: (1) **i** in 'imp**a**sse' and 'ing**e**nue', which are of French origin. (2) In some non-RP accents, **au** in '**au**nt' and '**au**ntie'.

Middle

/æ/ is usually spelled **a**:

began	can	have	stand
black	exact	marry	...

Note: (1) **ai** in 'pl**ai**d' and 'pl**ai**t'. (2) **i** in 'f**i**n de siècle', 'l**i**ngerie', 'mer**i**ngue', 'p**i**nce-nez', and 't**i**mbre', and **ei** in 'rev**ei**lle', which are all of French origin. (3) In GenAm, **al** in 'c**al**f', 'c**al**fskin', 'c**al**ve', 'h**al**f', 'h**al**fway', and 'h**al**ve'. (4) In some non-RP accents, **au** in 'l**au**gh', 'l**au**ghable', 'l**au**ghingly', and 'l**au**ghter'.

Final

/æ/ does not usually occur at the end of words in English.

Note: **-ah** at the end of the exclamations '**pah**' and (in some non-RP accents) '**bah**'.

The 24 main vowel sounds

/eɪ/	able

This sound is spelled **a** in most words. There are a number of common words in which it is spelled **ai** (usually in the middle of the word) or **ay** (usually at the end of the word). The other spelling patterns are not very common.

Initial

/eɪ/ is usually spelled **a**:

able	age	ape	atheist
ace	alias	aphid	aviator
ache	ancient	apron	...

/eɪ/ is spelled **ai** in these words:

aid	aide-memoire	aileron	aim
aide	AIDS	ailing	aimless
aide-de-camp	ail	ailment	ain't

/eɪ/ is spelled **eigh** in these words relating to the number 8:

| eight | eighteenth | eightieth |
| eighteen | eighth | eighty |

Note: (1) **e** in 'ecru' and 'ecu', and **é** in 'élan' and 'épée', which are all of French origin. (2) **eh** in the exclamation 'eh'. (3) /eɪ/ is the sound when you say the letter **A** or abbreviations such as 'ABC', 'RAF', and 'USA'. (4) /eɪ/ is the initial sound when you say the letter **H** or abbreviations such as 'HIV', 'VHF', and 'GBH'.

Middle

/eɪ/ is usually spelled **a**:

bacon	case	mason	state
basin	face	place	take
came	late	same	...

/eɪ/ is spelled **ai**, especially before **l** or **n**:

available	tail	main	faith
daily	trail	plain	liaise
detail	...	rain	praise
fail	again	saint	raid
gaily	brain	train	renaissance
mail	chain	...	waist
rail	complain	afraid	wait
sail	gain	claim	...

Note: (1) **aig** in 'arr**aig**n', 'arr**aig**nment', and 'camp**aig**n'. (2) **aigh** in 'str**aigh**t', 'str**aigh**ten', and 'str**aigh**tforward'.

/eɪ/ is spelled **ay** before a vowel sound in these words:

b**ay**onet	m**ay**o	m**ay**or	r**ay**on
cr**ay**on	m**ay**onnaise	m**ay**oress	

Note: **ay** in 'alw**ay**s' and 'm**ay**be', and in compounds of words that end in -**ay**: e.g. 'betr**ay**al', 'brickl**ay**er', 'd**ay**time', 'Mal**ay**sian', 'p**ay**ment', 'spr**ay**er', and 'w**ay**ward'.

/eɪ/ is spelled **ei** in these words:

abs**ei**l	f**ei**nt	ob**ei**sance	surv**ei**llance
b**ei**ge	g**ei**sha	r**ei**n	v**ei**l
c**ei**lidh	h**ei**nous	sh**ei**kh	v**ei**n
chow m**ei**n	inv**ei**gle	sk**ei**n	

Note: (1) **eig** in 'd**eig**n', 'f**eig**n', and 'r**eig**n'. (2) **eigh** in 'fr**eigh**t', 'n**eigh**bour', and 'w**eigh**t'. (3) **ea** in 'br**ea**k', 'gr**ea**t', and 'st**ea**k'. (4) **e** in 'cr**e**pe', 'f**e**te' ('fête' in American English), 's**e**ance', and 's**ue**de, and **é** in 'pièce de résistance', which are all of French origin. (5) **e** in 'd**e**ification', 'd**e**ify', 'd**e**ity', 'nucl**e**ic acid', and 'spontan**e**ity'. (6) **ey** in 'ab**ey**ance' and 'conv**ey**ance'. (7) **ae** in 'G**ae**lic' and 'm**ae**lstrom', **ao** in 'g**ao**l', and **au** in 'g**au**ge'.

Final

/eɪ/ is usually spelled **ay**:

b**ay**	m**ay**	pl**ay**	st**ay**
d**ay**	ok**ay**	r**ay**	w**ay**
ess**ay**	p**ay**	s**ay**	...

/eɪ/ is spelled **ey** in these words:

conv**ey**	gr**ey**	pr**ey**	th**ey**
disob**ey**	h**ey**	purv**ey**	wh**ey**
f**ey**	ob**ey**	surv**ey**	

Note: (1) **ae** in 'regg**ae**', 'sund**ae**', and 'vertebr**ae**'. (2) **eigh** in 'inv**eigh**', 'n**eigh**', 'sl**eigh**', and 'w**eigh**'. (3) **ait** in 'tr**ait**'. (4) **ea** in 'y**ea**'. (5) /eɪ/ is spelled in various other ways in words of French origin: e.g. **é** in 'attach**é**', 'caf**é**', 'fianc**é**', 'pât**é**', 'souffl**é**', 'touch**é**', **ée** in 'ép**ée**', 'fianc**ée**', 'n**ée**', and 'toup**ée**'; **er** in 'croupi**er**', 'foy**er**', and 'meti**er**'; **et** in 'bouqu**et**', 'cabar**et**', 'duv**et**', 'gourm**et**', and 'sorb**et**'; **ais** in 'cor angl**ais**'; **ez** in 'pince-n**ez**'. (6) As words of French origin become accepted in English, they often lose their accents, so **é** and **ée** become **e** and **ee** : e.g. 'appliqu**e**', 'crudit**es**', 'matin**ee**', 'pur**ee**', 'soir**ee**', and 'toup**ee**', and in GenAm 'repart**ee**'. (7) **e** or **é** in other words of Foreign origin: e.g. 'al dent**e**', 'padr**e**', 'pianofort**e**', 'sak**é**', and 'segu**e**'.

The 24 main vowel sounds

/ɑːʳ/	**ar**m
/ɑː/	**a**fter

The main problem is whether there is an **r** in the spelling or not. More words are spelled **ar** than **a**. The other spellings are fairly rare. When **ar** is not at the end of a word, it is followed by a consonant letter. In GenAm, /ɑː/ is pronounced the same as /ɒ/, so also see the spelling patterns for /ɒ/.

Initial

/ɑːʳ/ is usually spelled **ar**:

arch	**ar**gument	**ar**senal	**ar**ticle
archive	**ar**m	**ar**t	...

/ɑː/ is spelled **a** in these words:

aft	**a**fter	**a**nswer	**a**sk

Note: (1) **au** in '**au**nt' and '**au**ntie'. (2) **à** in '**à** la' and '**à** la carte', which are of French origin. (3) **ah** in '**ah**'. (4) **al** in '**al**mond' and '**al**ms'.

Middle

/ɑːʳ/ is usually spelled **ar**:

al**ar**m	d**ar**k	l**ar**ge	p**ar**liament
ap**ar**t	f**ar**m	m**ar**k	st**ar**t
b**ar**k	g**ar**den	m**ar**ket	y**ar**d
c**ar**d	h**ar**d	p**ar**k	...

Note: (1) **ear** in 'h**ear**t' and 'h**ear**th'. (2) **er** in 'cl**er**k', 'd**er**by', and 's**er**geant'. (3) **ir** in 'savo**ir**-faire', which is of French origin.

/ɑː/ is commonly spelled **a**:

adv**a**nce	comm**a**nd	gl**a**ss	pl**a**nt
b**a**sket	cr**a**ft	gr**a**nt	r**a**ther
br**a**nch	d**a**nce	gr**a**ph	reprim**a**nd
c**a**st	dem**a**nd	gr**a**ss	s**a**mple
c**a**stle	dis**a**ster	l**a**st	sl**a**nder
ch**a**nce	ex**a**mple	p**a**ss	st**a**ff
cl**a**sp	f**a**st	p**a**st	v**a**st
cl**a**ss	f**a**ther	p**a**th	...

/ɑːʳ/ is spelled **al** before **f**, **m**, or **v** in these words:

b**al**m	c**al**m	h**al**f	p**al**m
beh**al**f	c**al**ve	h**al**ve	ps**al**m
c**al**f	emb**al**m	nap**al**m	qu**al**m

Note: (1) **au** in 'dr**au**ght', 'dr**au**ghtsman', 'l**au**gh'. (2) **i** in 'bourgeo**i**sie', 'co**i**ffed', 'co**i**ffure', 'co**i**ffured', 'so**i**gnee' and 'so**i**ree', and (in GenAm) 'cro**i**ssant', and **ie** in 'jo**ie** de vivre', which are all of French origin.

Final

/ɑːʳ/ is spelled **ar** in these words:

b**ar**	f**ar**	j**ar**	rad**ar**
c**ar**	guit**ar**	m**ar**	st**ar**

Note: (1) **aar** in 'baz**aar**', a Foreign word. (2) **ard** in 'boulev**ard**', **arre** in 'biz**arre**', **arrh** in 'cat**arrh**', **ir** in 'abatto**ir**', 'boudo**ir**', 'memo**ir**', 'reservo**ir**', **ire** in 'aide-memo**ire**', 'conservato**ire**', and 'reperto**ire**', which are all of French origin.

/ɑː/ is spelled **a** in these words:

br**a**	la-di-d**a**	p**a**	t**a**
gag**a**	m**a**	qu**a**	
h**a**	mam**a**	sp**a**	

/ɑː/ is spelled **ah** in these words:

ah	bl**ah**	h**ah**
b**ah**	dood**ah**	

Note: **as** in 'faux p**as**', **at** in 'coup d'et**at**' and 'hors de comb**at**', **id** in 'sang fro**id**', **is** in 'bourgeo**is**', 'chamo**is**', and 'pato**is**', which are all of French origin.

Inflection and word formation

Final **r** is doubled before a suffix that begins with a vowel, such as **-ing** or **-ed**:

e.g. star – starring – starred.

Pronunciation

Words that are pronounced /ɑː/ in RP, and do not have an **r** in their spelling, are usually pronounced /æ/ in GenAm and in the North of England. Note that the **a** in 'father' is pronounced /ɑː/ in most accents.

If a word is spelled **ar**, the **r** is silent in RP, unless the next sound is a vowel sound.

The 24 main vowel sounds

/eəʳ/	air

In most words, this sound is spelled **ar**, usually followed by a vowel letter. At the end of a word, the vowel letter is usually silent **e**. In a small number of common words, it is spelled **air** or **ear**. It is spelled **ere** in two very common words: 'there' and 'where'. The other spelling patterns are not very common. In most words beginning with this sound, it is spelled **air-**.

Initial

/eəʳ/ is usually spelled **air**:

air	aircraft	airmail	airwaves
airbag	airgun	airplane	airy
airborne	airlift	airport	...

/eəʳ/ is spelled **aer** in these words:

aerate	aerobics	aeronautics
aerial	aerodrome	aeroplane
aerobatics	aerodynamic	aerospace

Note: (1) **ar** in 'area' and 'Aryan'. (2) **er** in 'ere' and 'ersatz'. (3) **eyr** in 'eyrie'. (4) **heir** in 'heir' and 'heirloom'.

Middle

/eəʳ/ is usually spelled **ar**:

careful	parent	scarcely	wary
malaria	primarily	various	...

/eəʳ/ is spelled **air** in these words:

cairn	dairy	fairy	prairie
clairvoyant	fairway	laird	

/eəʳ/ is spelled **er** in these Foreign words:

bolero	concierge	scherzo
concerto	recherché	sombrero

Final

/eəʳ/ is usually spelled **are**:

aware	compare	prepare	share
bare	dare	rare	square
care	declare	scare	...

/eə_r/ is spelled **air** in these words:

affair	despair	hair	pair
chair	fair	impair	repair
debonair	flair	lair	stair

/eə_r/ is spelled **aire** in these words of French origin:

billion**aire**	extraordin**aire**	questionn**aire**
concession**aire**	laissez-f**aire**	savoir-f**aire**
doctrin**aire**	million**aire**	solit**aire**

/eə_r/ is spelled **ear** in these words:

bear	forswear	swear	underwear
forebear	pear	tear	wear

/eə_r/ is spelled **ere** in these words:

| compere | premiere | there | where |

Note: (1) **ère** or **ere** in 'ampère' or 'ampere'. (2) **eir** in 'their'. (3) **ayer** in 'prayer'. (4) **ayor** in 'mayor'.

Inflection and word formation

Final silent **e** is dropped before suffixes that begin with a vowel, such as **-ing** and **-ed**:

e.g. share – sharing – shared.

Note: rare + ify = rare**fy**

Pronunciation

/eə_r/ is always spelled with an **r**. In RP, this **r** is silent, unless the next sound is a vowel sound.

Words with /eə_r/ in RP are usually pronounced /er/ or /ær/ in GenAm. This means that 'vary' sounds the same as 'very' in GenAm.

The 24 main vowel sounds

/e/	egg

In most words, this sound is spelled **e**. There are some common words in which it is spelled **ea**. There are not many words with other spelling patterns, but some of the words are very common ones, like 'again', 'any', 'friend', 'many', 'said', and 'says'.

Initial

/e/ is spelled **e**:

education	egg	end	extra
effort	else	every	...

Note: **a** in 'any' and 'ate'.

Middle

/e/ is usually spelled **e**:

best	less	set	west
general	men	them	when
get	never	very	yes
help	next	well	yesterday
left	second	went	...

/e/ is spelled **ea** in many Native words:

bread	head	leather	spread
breakfast	health	meadow	steady
breath	heather	meant	sweat
dead	heaven	measure	thread
deaf	heavy	peasant	threat
dealt	instead	pleasant	treasure
death	jealous	pleasure	wealth
dread	lead	ready	weapon
feather	leapt	realm	...

Note: (1) **a** in 'many' and 'necessarily'. (2) **ae** in 'haemorrhage' and 'haemorrhoid'. (3) **ai** in 'again', 'against', and 'said'. (4) **ay** in 'says'. (5) **ei** in 'heifer' and 'leisure'. (6) **eo** in 'jeopardy' and 'leopard'. (7) **ie** in 'friend'. (8) **u** in 'burial' and 'bury'. (9) Note the spelling 'lieutenant' for /**left**en**ə**nt/.

Final

/e/ does not occur at the end of words in English.

/iː/ equal

This sound is most commonly spelled **e**, and is usually followed by a single consonant letter. At the end of a word, the consonant letter is followed by a final silent **e**. In most other words the sound is spelled **ea** or **ee**. Other spelling patterns are fairly rare, except when the unstressed version of this sound (/i/) occurs at the end of a word.

Initial

/iː/ is usually spelled **e**:

ecological	equal	evening	evolution
economic	even	evil	…

/iː/ is spelled **ea** in these words:

each	ease	Easter	eaves
eager	easel	easy	
eagle	east	eat	

Note: (1) **ae** in 'aegis' and 'aesthetic'. (2) **ee** in 'eel'. (3) **ei** in 'either'. (4) **oe** in 'oesophagus' and 'oestrogen'. (5) /iː/ is the sound when you say the letter **E** or abbreviations such as 'e.g.', 'REM', and 'GCSE'.

Middle

/iː/ is usually spelled **e**:

being	immediate	previous	secret
create	legal	recent	these
extreme	metre	scene	…

/iː/ is spelled **ea** or **ee**, especially in Native words of one syllable:

appeal	peace	been	screen
beach	reach	cheese	seem
clean	reason	deep	speech
disease	reveal	feel	steel
heat	speak	fifteen	succeed
ideal	teacher	fleet	teeth
league	treaty	keep	week
mean	…	need	…

/iː/ is spelled **ie** in these words:

achieve	field	liege	shield
Aries	fiend	niece	shriek
believe	frieze	piece	siege
brief	grief	priest	thief
chief	grievance	relief	wield
diesel	hygiene	retrieve	yield

/iː/ is spelled **ei**, usually after **c**, in these words:

ceiling	deceive	...	protein
conceit	perceive	caffeine	seize
conceive	receipts	counterfeit	
deceit	receive	neither	

/iː/ is spelled **i**, especially in words of Foreign origin:

antique	litre	police	submarine
chic	machine	regime	unique
kilo	motif	routine	...

Note: (1) **ae** in 'anaesthetist'. (2) **eo** in 'people'. (3) **ey** in 'geyser'. (4) **oe** in 'amoeba', 'foetus', and 'phoenix'.

Final

Stressed syllables:

/iː/ is usually spelled **ee**:

agree	free	referee	spree
bee	glee	refugee	trainee
decree	guarantee	see	tree
employee	knee	settee	...

/iː/ is spelled **ea** in these words:

| flea | plea | tea |
| pea | sea | |

/iː/ is the stressed pronunciation or 'strong form' of these grammatical words spelled with a final **e**:

| be | me | the |
| he | she | we |

Note: (1) **ay** in 'quay'. (2) **ey** in 'key'. (3) **i** in 'ennui' and 'ski', which are both of Foreign origin. (4) **ie** in 'bourgeoisie', **is** in 'vis-à-vis', and **ix** in 'Grand Prix', which are all of French origin.

Unstressed syllables:

The unstressed version of this sound, when it occurs at the end of a word, is often represented by /i/, as it is shortened. In most words this is spelled **y**, which is never used for stressed /iː/.

/i/ is usually spelled **y**:

any	company	family	party
body	country	happy	very
city	daddy	only	...

/iː/ equal

/i/ is spelled **e** in the unstressed pronunciation or 'weak form' of the grammatical words 'be', 'he', 'me', 'she', 'the', and 'we', and in some words of Foreign or Classical origin:

Aborigine	catastrophe	karaoke	reveille
acme	coyote	karate	simile
acne	epitome	machete	sub judice
andante	facsimile	minestrone	syncope
anemone	finale	pianoforte	ukulele
ante	furore	posse	vigilante
apostrophe	hyperbole	psyche	...
bona fide	kamikaze	recipe	

/i/ is spelled **i** in some words of Foreign or Classical origin:

bikini	graffiti	pastrami	tutti-frutti
broccoli	Jacuzzi	ravioli	vermicelli
chilli	khaki	salami	virtuosi
cognoscenti	kiwi	scampi	yeti
deli	macaroni	semi	yogi
fait accompli	muesli	timpani	zucchini

/i/ is spelled **ie** in shortened forms of English personal names, in some informal words and slang forms, and in some words of Foreign origin:

Archie	...	cookie	bourgeoisie
Bertie	auntie	freebie	calorie
Chrissie	birdie	junkie	eyrie
Debbie	bogie	movie	genie
Freddie	boogie	nightie	lingerie
Jackie	bookie	stymie	menagerie
Lizzie	budgie	yuppie	prairie
Maggie	cabbie	...	zombie
Ronnie	commie	bonhomie	...

/i/ is spelled **ey** in these words, which are mostly nouns:

abbey	dicey	journey	pricey
alley	donkey	kidney	storey
attorney	galley	lackey	trolley
barley	gulley	medley	turkey
bogey	hockey	money	valley
cagey	honey	monkey	volley
chimney	jersey	parley	whiskey
cockney	jockey	phoney	...

Note: (1) **ea** in 'guinea'. (2) **ee** in 'coffee' and 'jubilee'. (3) **ois** in 'chamois'. (4) **ae** in 'larvae' and 'minutiae'. (5) **i** in 'fungi', 'modus operandi' and 'modus vivendi'. (6) **is** in 'précis'. (7) 'whiskey' is the Irish and American spelling. (8) 'storey' is the British spelling; the American spelling is 'story'.

Inflection and word formation

Final **e** is only dropped before an ending beginning with **e**:

e.g. agree – agree**s** – agre**eing** – agre**ed**.

The plural of 'Grand Prix' is either 'Grands Prix' or 'Grand Prix'.

Final **-y** generally changes to **-i** before all suffixes, except those which begin with **i**:

e.g. likely – likel**ier** – likel**iest** – likel**ihood**; lobby – lobb**ies** – lobb**ied** but 'lobb**ying**' and 'lobb**yist**'.

Note: (1) **-y** does not change to **-i** in 'lad**yship**'. (2) **-y** does not change to **-i** in compounds: e.g. 'an**y**body', 'bod**y**guard', 'clerg**y**man', 'ever**y**thing', and 'pigg**y**bank'. (3) Words ending in **-y** change **-y** to **-i** and add **-es** (not **-s**) for the plural forms of nouns and the third person singular present tense forms of verbs.

Words ending in **-ie** drop **-e** before a suffix beginning with **e**:

e.g. birdi**ed**, boogi**ed**.

Note: but 'boogi**eing**' or 'boog**ying**'.

Nouns which end in **-i** generally form their plural with **s**:

e.g. bikini – bikini**s**; deli – deli**s**; yogi – yogi**s**.

Note: but 'chilli' – 'chill**ies**'.

ey does not change before suffixes:

e.g. journ**ey** – journ**eys** – journ**eyed** – journ**eying**.

Pronunciation

Final unstressed /i/ is sometimes pronounced like /ɪ/.

/ɜːʳ/	early

In most words, this sound is spelled **er**, and in many other words it is spelled **ur**. In some very common words, it is spelled **ir**, **or**, or **ear**. In the middle of a word, these patterns are always followed by a consonant letter.

Initial

/ɜːʳ/ is spelled **ear** in these words:

earl	**ear**n	**ear**th
early	**ear**nest	**ear**then

/ɜːʳ/ is spelled **ur** in these words:

urban	**ur**chin	**ur**gent
urbane	**ur**ge	**ur**n

/ɜːʳ/ is spelled **er** in these words:

er	**er**gonomics	**er**mine	**er**stwhile

Note: **ir** in 'irk' and 'irksome'.

Middle

/ɜːʳ/ is most commonly spelled **er**:

al**er**t	conc**er**n	em**er**gency	t**er**m
c**er**tain	cons**er**ve	p**er**son	univ**er**sity
comm**er**cial	det**er**mined	s**er**vice	...

/ɜːʳ/ is often spelled **ur**:

b**ur**st	h**ur**t	p**ur**pose	Th**ur**sday
ch**ur**ch	m**ur**der	ret**ur**n	t**ur**n
f**ur**niture	n**ur**se	s**ur**face	...

/ɜːʳ/ is often spelled **ir**:

b**ir**d	d**ir**t	g**ir**l	th**ir**teen
c**ir**cle	f**ir**m	sh**ir**t	v**ir**tual
conf**ir**m	f**ir**st	th**ir**d	...

/ɜːʳ/ is spelled **ear** in these words:

d**ear**th	h**ear**se	p**ear**l	s**ear**ch
h**ear**d	l**ear**n	reh**ear**se	y**ear**n

/ɜːʳ/ is spelled **our** in these words:

adj**our**n	c**our**teous	j**our**nal	sc**our**ge
b**our**bon	c**our**tesy	j**our**ney	

/ɜːʳ/ is spelled **or** in these words, after **w**:

| word | worm | worship | worth |
| work | worse | worst | worthy |

Note: (1) **or** also in 'attorney' and 'whorl'. (2) /ɜː/ is very rare: **eu** in 'masseuse', **oeu** in 'hors d'oeuvre', and **olo** in 'colonel', all of French origin.

Final

/ɜːʳ/ is spelled **er** in these words:

aver	deter	infer	prefer
confer	er	inter	refer
defer	her	per	transfer

Note: (1) **rr** in 'err' because of the 'Three letter rule'. (2) final silent **e** in 'were'.

/ɜːʳ/ is spelled **ur** in these words:

blur	fur	recur
concur	incur	slur
demur	occur	spur

Note: **urr** in 'burr' and 'purr'.

/ɜːʳ/ is spelled **eur** in these words, which are all of French origin:

agent provocateur	de rigueur	masseur	restaurateur
amateur	entrepreneur	poseur	saboteur
chauffeur	hauteur	raconteur	voyeur
connoisseur	liqueur	rapporteur	

Note: (1) **ir** in 'fir', 'sir', and 'stir'. (2) **irr** in 'whirr', which is also spelled 'whir'. (3) Very few words end in /ɜː/, which is spelled **-eu** in 'cordon bleu' and 'milieu', and **-eux** in 'pas de deux', which are of French origin; and **-uh** (in some non-RP accents) in 'huh'.

Inflection and word formation

Final **r** is doubled before a suffix beginning with a vowel, such as **-ing** or **-ed**:

e.g. blurred, concurred, concurrent, deterred, stirring.

Pronunciation

The **r** in all the words above is silent in RP, unless it is followed by a vowel. In many Scottish accents, words pronounced /ɜːʳ/ in RP are pronounced /er/, /ɪr/, or /ʌr/.

/ɪə^r/ ear

Although this sound is spelled **er** (followed by a vowel letter) in more words, it is spelled **ear** in most of the very common words. In a few common words, it is spelled **eer**. The other spelling patterns are fairly rare.

Initial

/ɪə^r/ is spelled **ear** in these words related to '**ear**':

earache	earlobe	earphone	earring
eardrum	earmark	earpiece	earshot
earful	earmuffs	earplug	earwig

Note: (1) **eer** in 'eerie' and 'eerily'. (2) **er** in 'era'. (3) **eyr** in 'eyrie'.

Middle

/ɪə^r/ is usually spelled **er**, especially in polysyllabic words of Classical origin:

arterial	exterior	material	series
bacteria	hero	period	serious
deteriorate	inferior	query	...

Note: (1) **ear** in 'beard', 'bleary', 'dreary', and 'weary'. (2) **eir** in 'madeira' and 'weird'. (3) **ir** in 'delirious', 'delirium', 'kirsch', 'nirvana', and 'tiramisu'. (4) **ier** in 'fierce' and 'pierce'.

Final

/ɪə^r/ is most commonly spelled **ear**, usually in monosyllabic Native words:

appear	fear	near	tear
clear	gear	rear	year
dear	hear	spear	...

/ɪə^r/ is often spelled **eer**:

beer	engineer	queer	veer
career	jeer	sheer	veneer
cheer	peer	sneer	volunteer
deer	pioneer	steer	...

/ɪəʳ/ is spelled **ere** in these words, mostly polysyllabic words of Classical origin:

ad**here**	cashm**ere**	insinc**ere**	rev**ere**
atmosph**ere**	coh**ere**	interf**ere**	sev**ere**
aust**ere**	hemisph**ere**	m**ere**	sinc**ere**
biosph**ere**	h**ere**	persev**ere**	sph**ere**

/ɪəʳ/ is spelled **ier** in these words:

brigad**ier**	caval**ier**	front**ier**	t**ier**
cash**ier**	chandel**ier**	p**ier**	

Note: (1) **ir** in 'am**ir**', 'em**ir**', 'nad**ir**', and 'souven**ir**', all words of Foreign origin. (2) **eir** in 'w**eir**'.

Inflection and word formation

Final **e** is dropped before suffixes that begin with a vowel, such as **-ing** and **-ed**:

e.g. adhere – adheres – adhering – adhered.

Final **r** is not doubled, e.g. 'appearing' and 'revered'.

/ɪ/ it

Stressed syllables:

In most words, the stressed sound is spelled **i**. There are a number of words in which it is spelled **y**. Five very common words have different spelling patterns: **e** in 'English' and 'pretty', **o** in 'women', and **u** in 'business' and 'busy'.

Initial

/ɪ/ is usually spelled **i**:

if	index	interest	is
image	industry	international	issue
in	influence	interview	it
income	information	into	...

Note: **e** in 'England' and 'English'.

Middle

/ɪ/ is usually spelled **i**:

big	little	since	until
children	live	six	which
did	military	still	will
give	million	thing	with
his	minister	think	...

/ɪ/ is spelled **y** in these words of Greek origin:

analytic	gypsy	myth	symphony
crystal	hymn	physical	symptom
cyclical	hypocrite	physics	synagogue
cylinder	hysterectomy	physiology	syndicate
cynical	idyllic	pyramid	syndrome
cynicism	lymph	rhythm	synod
cystic	lynch	sybil	synthesis
dynasty	lyrics	syllable	syphilis
eucalyptus	myriad	symbol	syrup
gym	mystery	symmetry	system
gymnast	mystic	sympathy	typical

/ɪ/ is spelled **ui** in these words:

build	guild	guillemot	guilt
built	guilder	guillotine	guinea

Note: (1) **e** in 'pretty'. (2) **ee** in 'been' and 'breeches'. (3) **ie** in 'sieve'. (4) **o** in 'women'. (5) **u** in 'business' and 'busy'.

Final

/ɪ/ does not occur at the end of English words.

Unstressed syllables:

In unstressed syllables, **e** is a very common spelling pattern as well as **i**, so the main problem is deciding whether the spelling is **e** or **i**.

Initial

Guidelines:

(1) /ɪ/ followed by /**m**/ or /**n**/ is more commonly spelled **i**. (2) /ɪ/ followed by other sounds is more commonly spelled **e**. (3) **l** and **m** are doubled more often after **i** than after **e**, before a vowel sound: e.g. 'illicit' but 'elicit'. (4) When the word means '**not** something', the spelling is always **i**: e.g. 'illegal' and 'illicit'. (5) When the word means '**in** something', the spelling is always **i**: e.g. 'inside' and 'instead'.

/ɪ/ is commonly spelled **e**:

economy	enjoy	establish	expenses
edition	enough	estate	experience
effect	ensure	event	explain
effectively	entire	exact	explode
elected	environment	example	expression
election	equipment	except	extended
emerge	equivalent	exchange	extent
emotional	escape	executive	extreme
employee	especially	existence	extremely
encourage	essential	expect	...

/ɪ/ is commonly spelled **i**:

ignore	include	inquiry	internal
illegal	including	inside	invasion
imagine	indeed	insist	investment
immediately	industrial	insisted	investors
important	infection	instead	involve
impose	inflation	insurance	involved
impossible	initial	intelligent	involvement
impression	initially	intended	Islamic
improve	initiative	interior	...

Note: (1) **e** or **i** in 'enquire', 'inquire'. (2) 'ensure' and 'insure' have different meanings.

/ɪ/   it

Middle

/ɪ/ is spelled **e**, **i**, **a**, or **y** before a consonant:

before	crisis	...	hypocrisy
between	discover	average	hysteria
correspondent	economic	damage	hysterical
decision	feeling	language	labyrinth
latest	minister	temperate	paralysis
predict	office	village	physician
reports	public	...	presbyterian
united	service	analysis	pyjamas
wallet	university	anonymous	syringe
women	without	anything	vinyl
...	worship	bicycle	...

Note: (1) **e** is common in beginnings such as **be-**, **de-**, **pre-**, and **re-**, and in endings such as **-ed**, **-est**, **-et**, and **-let**. (2) **i** is common in beginnings such as **dis-**, and in endings such as **-ic**, **-ing**, **-ish**, **-ism**, **-ist**, and **-ship**. (3) **a** is common mainly in the endings **-age** and **-ate**. (4) **y** occurs mainly in words of Greek origin.

/ɪ/ is spelled **e** or **i** before a vowel:

area	...	radio	serious
really	period	senior	...

Final

/ɪ/ does not occur at the end of English words.

Pronunciation

/ə/ is often an alternative for /ɪ/ in an unstressed syllable before a consonant.

The 24 main vowel sounds

/aɪ/	idea

In most words, this sound is spelled **i** when it is not final, and **y** or **ie** when it is final. In some very common words, it is spelled **igh**. In some less common words, it is spelled **y** in the middle of a word. The other patterns are fairly rare.

Initial

/aɪ/ is usually spelled **i**:

ice	identity	iota	isotope
icing	ideology	Irish	item
icon	idle	irony	itinerary
icy	idol	island	ivory
idea	iodine	isobar	ivy
idealist	ion	isolated	...

Note: (1) **is** in 'island' and 'isle'. (2) **ei** in 'eiderdown', 'eisteddfod', and 'either'. (3) **eye** in 'eye'. (4) **aye** in 'aye'. (5) **ais** in 'aisle'. (6) /aɪ/ is the sound when you say the letter **I** or abbreviations such as 'ID', 'DIY', or 'FBI'.

Middle

/aɪ/ is usually spelled **i**:

advice	fine	nice	time
behind	five	nine	trial
child	Friday	outside	twice
crime	kind	price	unite
crisis	life	prime	vice
decide	like	private	violence
despite	likely	provide	while
diet	line	quite	white
drive	live	rise	wide
exercise	mike	side	wife
final	mile	size	wine
financial	mind	society	write
find	minute	strike	...

/aɪ/ is spelled **igh** before **t** in these words:

alight	fight	light	right
blight	flight	might	sight
bright	fright	night	slight
delight	knight	plight	tight

/aɪ/ is spelled **y** in these words of Greek origin:

analyse	encyclopedia	hypothetical	style
asylum	gynaecologist	psyche	stylish
bystander	hybrid	psychic	thyme
cyanide	hydraulic	psychical	thyroid
cycle	hydro	psycho	type
cyclone	hydrogen	psychology	typewriter
cypress	hygiene	psychotherapist	typhoid
dehydration	hype	psychotic	tyrant
dynamics	hyper	python	tyre
dynamo	hypothesis	rhyme	

/aɪ/ is spelled **ei** in these words:

Alzheimer	Fahrenheit	kaleidoscope	rottweiler
apartheid	feisty	neither	seismic

Note: **eigh** in 'height' and 'sleight of hand'.

/aɪ/ is spelled **ui** after **g** in these words of French origin:

beguile	guidance	guile
disguise	guide	guise

Note: (1) **ae** in 'maestro'. (2) **oy** in 'coyote'.

Final

/aɪ/ is usually spelled **y**:

ally	flyby	pigsty	spy
apply	fry	ply	standby
awry	hereby	preoccupy	sty
by	imply	prophesy	supply
comply	July	pry	thereby
cry	lullaby	rely	thy
decry	multiply	reply	try
deny	my	shy	whereby
dry	nearby	sky	why
espy	occupy	sly	wry
fly	outcry	spry	...

Note: Many verbs end in **-ify**, such as 'clarify' and 'rectify'.

/aɪ/ is spelled **ye** in these words:

bye	goodbye	stye
dye	rye	

/aɪ/ is spelled **i** in some words of Classical or Foreign origin:

alibi	cacti	loci	rabbi
alkali	decree nisi	narcissi	radii
a posteriori	fungi	nuclei	stimuli
a priori	lapis lazuli	pi	

Note: (1) The personal pronoun 'I'. (2) **i** in 'hi'.

/aɪ/ is spelled **ie** in these words:

bel**ie**	magp**ie**	underl**ie**
d**ie**	p**ie**	unt**ie**
l**ie**	t**ie**	v**ie**

/aɪ/ is spelled **igh** in these words:

h**igh**   n**igh**   s**igh**   th**igh**

Note: (1) **ae** in words of Latin origin such as 'alg**ae**', 'curriculum vit**ae**', and 'dramatis person**ae**'. (2) **uy** in 'b**uy**' and 'g**uy**'. (3) **ai** in the Japanese word 'bons**ai**'.

Inflection and word formation

Final -**y** changes to -**i** before a suffix is added, unless the suffix begins with an **i**:

e.g. rely – rel**i**es – rel**i**ed – rel**i**able – rel**i**ant, but 'rely**i**ng'; try – tr**i**es – tr**i**ed – tr**i**al but 'try**i**ng'.

Note: (1) after changing **y** to **i**, you add **es** (not **s**) for the plural form of nouns and the third person singular form of verbs. (2) The plural of 'lay-by' is 'lay-bys'. (3) The comparative of the adjective 'dry' is 'drier' or 'dryer', and the related nouns are 'dryer' or 'drier', and 'dryness'. (4) The comparative and superlative of the adjective 'shy' are 'shyer' and 'shyest', the related adverb is 'shyly' and the related noun is 'shyness'. (5) The adjectives 'sly' and 'wry' have the related adverbs 'slyly' and 'wryly'.

Final **ie** changes to **y** before -**ing**:

e.g. d**ie** – d**ie**s – d**ie**d but 'd**y**ing'; t**ie** – t**ie**s – t**ie**d but 't**y**ing'.

Final **ye** does not change before -**ing**:

e.g. d**ye** – d**ye**s – d**ye**ing – d**ye**d.

Final **i** does not change before -**s**:

e.g. alib**is**, alkal**is**, bonsa**is**, rabb**is**.

| /aɪəʳ/ | iron |
| /aɪə/ | science |

In most words, this sound is spelled **ir**, which is nearly always followed by a vowel letter. At the end of a word, this vowel letter is a silent **e**.

Initial

/aɪəʳ/ is very rare at the beginning of words. It is spelled **ir** in 'iron' (where r is silent), 'iris', and 'irony'.

Note: (1) Final silent **e** in 'ire'. (2) /aɪə/ is spelled **io** in 'iodine', 'ion', and 'ionizer', which are all of Greek origin.

Middle

/aɪəʳ/ is usually spelled **ir**:

chiropractic	environs	pirate	siren
environment	firing	spiral	...

Note: (1) There is often a silent **e** after the **r**: e.g. 'entirely', 'hireling', 'requirement', 'tiresome'. (2) **yr** in 'tyrant'.

/aɪəʳ/ is spelled **iar** or **ier** in these words of Classical origin:

diarrhoea	diary	hierarchy	hieroglyphic

Note: **oyeur** in 'voyeuristic'.

/aɪə/ is spelled **ia**, **ya**, or **ie**:

alliance	biased	hyacinth	verifiable
anxiety	cyanide	science	...

Note: **ihi** in 'annihilate'.

Final

/aɪəʳ/ is usually spelled **ire**:

admire	entire	inquire	tire
desire	expire	inspire	umpire
dire	fire	require	wire
empire	hire	satire	...

/aɪəʳ/ is spelled **yre** in these words:

byre	lyre	pyre	tyre

/aɪəʳ/ is spelled **ier** or **yer** when **-er** is added to words that end in **-y**:

amplif**ier**	modif**ier**	suppl**ier**	fl**yer**
dr**ier**	occup**ier**	...	...
fl**ier**	qualif**ier**	dr**yer**	

Note: (1) 'd**ye**' becomes 'd**yer**', and 'h**igh**' becomes 'h**igher**'. (2) **iar** in 'br**iar**', 'fr**iar**', and 'l**iar**', **ior** in 'pr**ior**', and **ir** in 'cho**ir**'. (3) /aɪə/ is rare at the end of words. It is spelled **aya** in 'pap**aya**', **ia** in 'v**ia**', and **iah** in 'mess**iah**' and 'par**iah**'.

Inflection and word formation

Final silent **e** is dropped before a suffix beginning with a vowel:

e.g. desir**able**, fir**ing**, requir**ing**, retir**al**, wir**ing**.

Note: but not in 'enti**re**ty'.

Pronunciation

In RP, the **r** is silent in 'iron', so 'iron' and 'ion' sound the same.

/ɒ/ odd

In most words, this sound is spelled **o**. It is spelled **a** after **qu** or **w**. The other patterns are fairly rare.

Initial

/ɒ/ is usually spelled **o**:

obvious	**o**dd	**o**peration	**o**pposition
October	**o**n	**o**pportunity	...

Note: **ho** in '**ho**nest' and '**ho**nour' ('**ho**nor' in American English).

/ɒ/ is pronounced with a nasal sound and spelled **en** in these words of French origin:

double **en**tendre	**en**nui	**en**tente	**en**trepreneur
encore	**en** route	**en**tourage	
enfant	**en**semble	**en**trée	

Middle

/ɒ/ is usually spelled **o**:

b**o**dy	g**o**t	n**o**t	pr**o**blem
d**o**n	l**o**ng	p**o**licy	t**o**p
fr**o**m	l**o**t	p**o**ssible	...

Note: **ow** in 'kn**ow**ledge'.

/ɒ/ is spelled **a** after **qu**:

equ**a**lity	qu**a**lity	qu**a**rrel	squ**a**lid
qu**a**d	qu**a**ndary	qu**a**rry	squ**a**lor
qu**a**druple	qu**a**ntity	qu**a**sh	squ**a**nder
qu**a**ff	qu**a**ntum	squ**a**bble	squ**a**sh
qu**a**lify	qu**a**rantine	squ**a**d	squ**a**t

/ɒ/ is spelled **a** after **w**:

sw**a**b	...	w**a**llow	w**a**rren
sw**a**llow	w**a**d	w**a**lly	w**a**rrior
sw**a**mp	w**a**ddle	w**a**n	w**a**s
sw**a**n	w**a**ffle	w**a**nd	w**a**sh
sw**a**p	w**a**ft	w**a**nder	w**a**sp
sw**a**shbuckle	w**a**llaby	w**a**nt	w**a**tch
sw**a**stika	w**a**llet	w**a**nton	w**a**tt
sw**a**t	w**a**llop	w**a**rrant	...

Note: (1) **a** after **wh** in 'wh**a**t'. (2) **o** after **w** in 'w**o**bble', 'w**o**k', 'w**o**nky', 'w**o**p', 'w**o**tcher', and 'w**o**z'. (3) **o** after **wh** in 'wh**o**pper'.

/ɒ/ is also spelled **a** in these words:

blancmange	scallop	wrath	yacht

Note: the **a** in these words is pronounced /ɑː/ in GenAm.

/ɒ/ is spelled **au** in these words:

bec**au**se	c**au**liflower	l**au**reate	s**au**sage
bure**au**cracy	hydr**au**lic	l**au**rel	

Note: the **au** in these words is pronounced /ɔː/ in GenAm.

Final

/ɒ/ does not occur at the end of Native words.

Note: /ɒ/ pronounced with a nasal sound at the end of French words is spelled **amps** in 'aide-de-c**amps**', **ant** in 'croiss**ant**', 'en pass**ant**', 'pench**ant**', and 'restaur**ant**', **emps** in 'contret**emps**', **ent** in 'denouem**ent**' and 'rapprochem**ent**', and **on** in 'chiff**on**' and 'sal**on**'.

Pronunciation

/ɒ/ in RP is usually pronounced /ɑː/ in GenAm.

/oʊ/ open

In most words, this sound is spelled **o**. In the middle of words, it is often spelled **oa**. At the end of words, it is often spelled **ow**. The other spelling patterns are fairly rare.

Initial

/oʊ/ is usually spelled **o**:

oasis	odour	omen	opium
obesity	ogle	onerous	opus
oboe	ogre	only	oval
ocean	oh	onus	over
ochre	okay	opal	ovum
ode	old	opaque	ozone
odious	omega	open	...

/oʊ/ is spelled **oa** in these words:

oaf	oak	oat	oath

Note: (1) **ow** in 'owe' and 'own'. (2) **au** in 'au fait', 'au pair', and 'aubergine', **eau** in 'eau de cologne', **hau** in 'haute cuisine' and 'hauteur', which are all of French origin. (3) /oʊ/ is the sound when you say the letter **O** or abbreviations such as 'OK', 'SOS', or 'UFO'.

Middle

/oʊ/ is usually spelled **o**:

almost	control	most	told
both	home	soviet	whole
close	local	those	...

/oʊ/ is spelled **oa** in these words, which are mostly Native words:

approach	coax	goatee	roach
bemoan	cockroach	groan	road
bloated	croak	hoax	roam
boast	encroach	load	roast
boat	float	loaf	shoal
charcoal	foal	loan	soak
cloak	foam	loathe	soap
coach	gloat	moan	stoat
coal	goad	moat	throat
coast	goal	poach	toad
coat	goat	reproach	toast

85

The 24 main vowel sounds

/oʊ/ is spelled **ou** in these words:

b**ou**lder	m**ou**ld	p**ou**ltry	sm**ou**lder
b**ou**quet	m**ou**lt	sh**ou**lder	s**ou**l

Note: (1) **ow** in 'b**ow**l', 'gr**ow**n', 'gr**ow**th' and 'kn**ow**n'. (2) **oo** in 'br**oo**ch'. (3) **eo** in 'y**eo**man'. (4) **au** in 'ch**au**ffeur', 'ch**au**vinist', 'f**au**x pas', 'g**au**che', 'm**au**ve', and 's**au**te' (or 's**au**té'), and **eau** in 'nouv**eau**-riche', which are all of French origin.

Final

/oʊ/ is usually spelled **o**:

ag**o**	fiasc**o**	negr**o**	sopran**o**
als**o**	ghett**o**	n**o**	stere**o**
audi**o**	g**o**	phot**o**	studi**o**
aut**o**	hell**o**	pian**o**	tobacc**o**
buffal**o**	her**o**	pol**o**	tomat**o**
carg**o**	jumb**o**	portfoli**o**	torped**o**
casin**o**	log**o**	potat**o**	tri**o**
dem**o**	mach**o**	pr**o**	vet**o**
disc**o**	manifest**o**	radi**o**	vide**o**
ech**o**	mem**o**	rati**o**	volcan**o**
eg**o**	metr**o**	scenari**o**	zer**o**
embarg**o**	micr**o**	s**o**	...
embry**o**	mott**o**	sol**o**	

Note: In general, except for a few very common short words ('ago', 'also', 'go', 'no', and 'so'), these words are of Classical origin ('echo', 'hero'), of Foreign origin ('macho', 'piano'), or are shortened forms ('demo', 'disco').

/oʊ/ is often spelled **ow**, mostly in Native words:

arr**ow**	fl**ow**	mell**ow**	sorr**ow**
barr**ow**	foll**ow**	morr**ow**	sparr**ow**
bell**ow**	gl**ow**	narr**ow**	swall**ow**
bel**ow**	gr**ow**	pill**ow**	thr**ow**
bl**ow**	hall**ow**	rainb**ow**	tomorr**ow**
borr**ow**	harr**ow**	r**ow**	t**ow**
b**ow**	holl**ow**	shad**ow**	wid**ow**
bungal**ow**	kn**ow**	shall**ow**	will**ow**
elb**ow**	l**ow**	sh**ow**	wind**ow**
farr**ow**	marr**ow**	sl**ow**	yell**ow**
fell**ow**	mead**ow**	sn**ow**	...

Note: Final silent **e** in '**owe**'.

/oʊ/ is spelled **oe** in these words:

al**oe**	f**oe**	ob**oe**	t**oe**
d**oe**	h**oe**	r**oe**	w**oe**
fl**oe**	mistlet**oe**	sl**oe**	

Note: (1) **ough** in 'although', 'dough', 'though'. (2) **eau** in 'bureau', 'chateau', 'nouveau', 'plateau', and 'tableau', **os** in 'à propos', and **ot** in 'argot' and 'haricot', which are all of French origin.

Inflection and word formation

These words ending in **-o** have **-es** in their plural forms or third person singular present tense forms:

buffaloes	frescoes	mementoes	toes
cargoes	goes	mosquitoes	tomatoes
desperadoes	grottoes	mottoes	torpedoes
dominoes	haloes	negroes	vetoes
echoes	heroes	noes	volcanoes
embargoes	innuendoes	peccadilloes	
flamingoes	mangoes	potatoes	

Other words ending in **-o** add **s**:

e.g. pianos, studios, videos.

Final silent **e** is dropped by '**owe**' before **-ed** and **-ing**:

e.g. owed, owing.

Final silent **e** is dropped by words ending in **-oe** before **-ed** but not before **-ing**:

e.g. hoed, tiptoed, hoeing, tiptoeing.

The 24 main vowel sounds

| /ɔːr/ | order |
| /ɔː/ | also |

The main problem is whether there is an **r** in the spelling or not: **or** (or **ore** at the end of a word) is the most common pattern, but **a** (before **l**) and **au** (or **aw** at the end of a word) are also common patterns. A few very common words have some of the rarer patterns, such as '**door**', 'th**ough**t', and '**your**'.

Initial

/ɔːr/ is usually spelled **or**:

or	**or**chestra	**or**dinary	**or**ient
oral	**or**deal	**or**e	**or**thodox
orbit	**or**der	**or**ganize	...

Note: (1) **oar** in '**oar**'. (2) **aur** in '**aur**a' and '**aur**al'. (3) **hors** in '**hors** d'oeuvre' and '**hors** de combat', which are of French origin.

/ɔː/ is spelled **a** before **l**:

| **a**lmost | **a**lso | **a**lternative | **a**lways |
| **a**lready | **a**lter | **a**lthough | ... |

/ɔː/ is sometimes spelled **au**:

| **au**ction | **au**dio | **au**thority | **au**tumn |
| **au**dience | **au**thor | **au**tomatic | ... |

Note: (1) **aw** in '**aw**e', '**aw**ful', '**aw**kward', and '**aw**ning'. (2) **ough** in '**ough**t'.

Middle

/ɔːr/ is usually spelled **or**:

ab**or**tion	en**or**mous	imp**or**t	rep**or**t
acc**or**ding	exp**or**t	imp**or**tant	sh**or**t
aff**or**d	f**or**ce	l**or**d	s**or**t
airp**or**t	f**or**m	m**or**ning	sp**or**t
b**or**der	f**or**mer	m**or**tgage	st**or**m
b**or**n	f**or**mula	n**or**mal	st**or**y
b**or**ne	f**or**th	n**or**th	supp**or**t
c**or**n	f**or**tune	perf**or**m	T**or**y
c**or**ner	f**or**ty	p**or**t	transp**or**t
c**or**poration	h**or**de	rec**or**d	...
div**or**ce	h**or**se	ref**or**m	

/ɔːʳ/ is spelled **our** in these words:

c**our**se	disc**our**se	g**our**d	s**our**ce
c**our**t	f**our**teen	interc**our**se	
c**our**tesan	f**our**th	res**our**ce	

/ɔːʳ/ is spelled **oar** in these words:

ab**oar**d	b**oar**der	h**oar**d	h**oar**y
b**oar**d	c**oar**se	h**oar**se	upr**oar**ious

/ɔːʳ/ is spelled **ar** after **w** or **qu**:

aw**ar**d	thw**ar**t	w**ar**lock	...
bulw**ar**k	tow**ar**ds	w**ar**m	head**quar**ters
dw**ar**f	untow**ar**d	w**ar**n	**quar**t
lukew**ar**m	w**ar**bler	w**ar**p	**quar**ter
rew**ar**d	w**ar**d	w**ar**ship	**quar**tet
sw**ar**m	w**ar**den	w**ar**t	**quar**tz
sw**ar**thy	w**ar**drobe	w**ar**thog	...

/ɔːʳ/ is spelled **aur** in these words of Classical origin:

baccal**aur**eate	brontos**aur**us	T**aur**us	thes**aur**us

/ɔː/ is spelled **a** before **l** or **ll**:

b**a**ld	f**a**ll	h**a**ll	t**a**ll
b**a**ll	f**a**lse	s**a**lt	w**a**ll
c**a**ll	g**a**ll	sm**a**ll	...

Note: the **l** is silent before **k** in 'balk', 'chalk', 'stalk', 'talk', and 'walk'.

/ɔː/ is sometimes spelled **au**:

ass**au**lt	c**au**tious	fr**au**d	r**au**cous
b**au**lk	exh**au**sted	l**au**nch	s**au**ce
c**au**se	f**au**lt	p**au**se	...

/ɔː/ is spelled **augh** before **t** in these words:

c**augh**t	fr**augh**t	n**augh**t	sl**augh**ter
d**augh**ter	h**augh**ty	n**augh**ty	stepd**augh**ter
distr**augh**t	mansl**augh**ter	onsl**augh**t	t**augh**t

/ɔː/ is spelled **aw** in these words, often before **l** or **n**:

b**aw**l	dr**aw**l	l**aw**yer	spr**aw**l
br**aw**n	dr**aw**n	pr**aw**n	squ**aw**k
cr**aw**l	h**aw**k	sh**aw**l	tr**aw**l
d**aw**n	l**aw**n	sp**aw**n	y**aw**n

/ɔː/ is spelled **ough** before **t** in these irregular past tenses of verbs:

b**ough**t	f**ough**t	th**ough**t
br**ough**t	s**ough**t	wr**ough**t

Note: also in the number 'nought'.

Final

/ɔː^r/ is usually spelled **ore**:

adore	explore	shore	tore
before	more	store	wore
bore	score	swore	...

/ɔː^r/ is spelled **or** in some words:

abhor	decor	matador	nor
condor	for	mentor	or
corridor	guarantor	metaphor	...

Note: (1) Silent **ps** and **t** in '**corps**' and '**rapport**', which are of French origin. (2) **ar** in '**war**'. (3) **aur** in '**centaur**' and '**dinosaur**'. (4) **oar** in '**oar**', '**soar**', and '**uproar**'. (5) **oor** in '**door**', '**floor**', and '**poor**'. (6) **our** in '**four**', '**tour**', and '**your**'.

/ɔː/ is spelled **aw** in these words:

caw	gnaw	law	saw
claw	guffaw	maw	squaw
coleslaw	haw	paw	straw
draw	jackdaw	raw	thaw
flaw	jaw	rickshaw	yaw

Inflection and word formation

Final silent **e** is dropped before a suffix beginning with a vowel:

e.g. bore – boring; store – storage.

Note: '**awful**' is irregular, but '**awesome**' is regular.

Final **r** is doubled after a single vowel:

e.g. abhor – abhorred; war – warring.

Pronunciation

These words are often pronounced /ɔːr/ (that is, with an /r/ in the pronunciation) in **non-r accents**, but do not have an **r** in the spelling:

e.g. cawing, clawing, drawing, gnawing, pawing, sawing, thawing, withdrawal, yawing.

In GenAm, the **ar** in '**quarrel**', '**quarry**', '**warrant**', and '**warren**' is pronounced /ɔːr/.

/ɔɪ/ oil

This sound is spelled **oi** before a consonant, and **oy** before a vowel or at the end of a word.

Initial

/ɔɪ/ is usually spelled **oi**:

oik	**oi**lfield	**oi**lskins	**oi**ntment
oil	**oi**lman	**oi**ly	...

Note: **oy** in '**oy**ster'.

Middle

/ɔɪ/ is spelled **oi** before a consonant:

app**oi**nt	expl**oi**t	paran**oi**d	tabl**oi**d
av**oi**d	f**oi**l	p**oi**gnant	thyr**oi**d
b**oi**l	gr**oi**n	p**oi**nt	t**oi**let
b**oi**ler	h**oi**st	p**oi**se	turm**oi**l
ch**oi**ce	j**oi**n	p**oi**son	turqu**oi**se
c**oi**l	j**oi**nt	s**oi**l	v**oi**ce
c**oi**n	m**oi**st	sp**oi**l	v**oi**d
dev**oi**d	n**oi**se	ster**oi**d	...

Note: **oy** before a consonant in '**boy**cott' and 'gar**goy**le'.

/ɔɪ/ is spelled **oy** before a vowel:

anno**y**ing	do**y**en	fo**y**er	so**y**a
buo**y**ant	emplo**y**ee	lo**y**al	vo**y**age
clairvo**y**ance	flambo**y**ant	ro**y**al	...

Note: **awy** in '**lawy**er'.

Final

/ɔɪ/ is spelled **oy**:

ah**oy**	conv**oy**	destr**oy**	pl**oy**
all**oy**	cordur**oy**	empl**oy**	tann**oy**
ann**oy**	c**oy**	enj**oy**	t**oy**
b**oy**	dec**oy**	env**oy**	vicer**oy**
bu**oy**	depl**oy**	j**oy**	...

Note: **oi** in 'h**oi** poll**oi**'.

Inflection and word formation

Words ending in **-oy** do not change when suffixes are added:

e.g. b**oy**friend, b**oy**s, destr**oy**ed, empl**oy**ees, enj**oy**ing, unempl**oy**ment.

The 24 main vowel sounds

/ʊ/	book

This sound has two common spelling patterns, **oo** and **u**. In three very common words, the pattern is **oul**: '**cou**ld', '**shou**ld', and '**wou**ld'.

Initial

/ʊ/ is rare at the beginning of a word. It is spelled **oo** in '**oo**mph' and '**oo**ps'.

Middle

/ʊ/ is spelled **oo**, usually before **k** or **d**:

brook	nook	misunderstood	mushroom
cook	rookie	woodland	poof
cookie	took	...	whoopee
hookah	...	foot	whoosh
lookout	good	gooseberry	wool
mistook	hoodwink	hooray	...

/ʊ/ is spelled **u**, usually before **ll**, **l**, or **sh**, in these words:

bull	...	bushel	butcher
bullet	bulwark	cushion	guru
bullion	fulfil	push	Muslim
bully	fulsome	...	ombudsman
full	pulpit	adjutant	pudding
pull	...	Buddhist	put
pulley	ambush	buffet	sugar

Note: This pattern occurs in a large number of adjectives ending in **-ful** such as 'beautiful' and 'wonderful', and adverbs ending in **-fully** such as 'faithfully' and 'peacefully'.

/ʊ/ is spelled **o** in these words:

bosom	wolf	wolves	woman

Note: (1) **ou** followed by silent **l** in the modal auxiliary verbs 'could', 'should', and 'would'. (2) **ou** followed by **r** in 'courier' and 'entourage'. (3) **o** and silent **r** in 'worsted'.

Final

/ʊ/ does not occur at the end of English words.

Pronunciation

/ʊ/ in RP is pronounced /**u:**/ in many Scottish accents.

/**u:**/ food

This sound has two common spelling patterns, **oo** (mainly in Native words) and **u** (mainly in words of Classical origin). **ew** is fairly common at the end of words, and **ou** occurs mainly in words of French origin.

Initial

/**u:**/ is not common at the beginning of words. It is spelled **oo** in these words:

o**o**dles	o**o**h	o**o**ps	o**o**ze

Note: **ou** in these words of Foreign origin: '**ou**tré' and '**ou**zo'.

Middle

/**u:**/ is usually spelled **oo**, mainly in monosyllabic Native words:

aftern**oo**n	c**oo**l	p**oo**l	s**oo**n
ball**oo**n	d**oo**m	pr**oo**f	s**oo**the
bl**oo**m	f**oo**d	r**oo**f	sp**oo**n
b**oo**gie	f**oo**l	r**oo**m	st**oo**l
b**oo**m	gl**oo**m	r**oo**t	t**oo**l
b**oo**st	g**oo**se	sal**oo**n	t**oo**th
b**oo**t	l**oo**se	sch**oo**l	tr**oo**p
b**oo**th	m**oo**d	sh**oo**t	v**oo**d**oo**
cart**oo**n	m**oo**n	sm**oo**th	z**oo**m
ch**oo**se	n**oo**dles	sn**oo**ker	...

/**u:**/ is spelled **ou** in these words, which are mostly of French origin:

ac**ou**stic	c**ou**pon	n**ou**veau-riche	s**ou**venir
b**ou**doir	cr**ou**pier	rec**ou**p	t**ou**ché
b**ou**illon	d**ou**che	r**ou**ble	t**ou**pee
b**ou**levard	gh**ou**l	r**ou**ge	tr**ou**badour
b**ou**quet	g**ou**lash	r**ou**lette	tr**ou**sseau
b**ou**tique	gr**ou**p	r**ou**te	unc**ou**th
c**ou**gar	j**ou**le	r**ou**tine	w**ou**nd
c**ou**p	l**ou**vre	s**ou**fflé	
c**ou**pé	m**ou**sse	s**ou**p	

/**u:**/ is spelled **o** in these common words:

l**o**se	pr**o**ve	wh**o**m	w**o**mb
m**o**ve	t**o**mb	wh**o**se	

The 24 main vowel sounds

/**u:**/ is spelled **u**, usually after **j**, **l**, **r**, or **s**, mainly in polysyllabic words of Classical origin:

absolute	instrument	marsupial	superb
crucial	judiciary	recuperate	superior
crude	June	rule	supreme
include	junior	solution	truth
influence	lugubrious	super	...

/**u:**/ is spelled **u** in these words of Foreign origin:

chute	parachute	tutti-frutti	yakuza
duvet	scuba	tutu	zucchini

/**u:**/ is spelled **ui** in these words:

bruise	fruit	recruit	suit
cruise	juice	sluice	

Note: (1) **ew** in 'jewel', 'sewage', 'strewn', and in GenAm in 'lewd' and 'news'. (2) **ee** in 'leeward'.

Final

/**u:**/ is often spelled **ew**:

blew	drew	Jew	strew
brew	flew	screw	threw
chew	grew	shrew	yew
crew	Hebrew	slew	...

/**u:**/ is sometimes spelled **oo**:

bamboo	loo	tattoo	woo
boo	shampoo	too	zoo
cuckoo	taboo	voodoo	...

Note: (1) In GenAm, **ieu** in 'adieu' and 'lieu', both of French origin. (2) **o** in 'do', 'to', and 'who'. (3) **oe** in 'canoe' and 'shoe'. (4) **ooh** in 'ooh' and 'pooh'. (5) **ou** in 'bijou' and 'you'. (6) **ou** followed by a silent letter in 'coup' and 'rendezvous', both of French origin. (7) **ough** in 'through'. (8) **u** in 'déjà vu', 'flu', and 'Hindu'. (9) **ue** in 'blue', 'clue', 'fondue', 'sue', and 'true'. (10) **wo** in 'two'.

Inflection and word formation

Words ending in **-oe** keep the final silent **e** before suffixes beginning with a vowel:

e.g. can**oe**ing, can**oe**ist, sh**oe**ing.

Words ending in **-ue** drop the final silent **e** before suffixes beginning with a vowel:

e.g. bl**u**ish, gl**u**ing, tr**u**er, tr**u**est, tr**u**ism.

/u:/ food

Note: Final silent **e** is dropped before a consonant in 'tr**u**ly'.

The third person singular of the verb 'do' is '**do**es' (/dʌz/); the plural of the noun 'do' is '**do**s' (/du:z/).

Pronunciation

In GenAm, /u:/ is spelled **u**, **ui**, or **ew** after **d**, **n**, and **t** (as well as after **j**, **l**, **r**, and **s** as given for RP above):

d**u**al	prod**u**ce	...	n**ew**
d**ue**	sit**u**ation	n**ui**sance	n**ew**s
d**u**ne	st**u**dent	...	st**ew**ard
n**u**clear	t**u**ne	d**ew**	...

Note: also **eu** in 'n**eu**tral'.

The 24 main vowel sounds

/ʊəʳ/	poor

This sound is not very common in English, but has several spelling patterns. It is most commonly spelled **ur** (followed by a vowel letter) or **oor**, and **our** in words of French origin.

Initial

/ʊəʳ/ does not occur at the beginning of English words.

Middle

/ʊəʳ/ is spelled **ur**, usually after **j**, **r**, or **s**:

ass**ur**ance	j**ur**or	r**ur**al	s**ur**ety
inj**ur**ious	j**ur**y	s**ur**ely	...

/ʊəʳ/ is spelled **our** in these words of French origin:

b**our**geois	g**our**d	g**our**met
ent**our**age	g**our**mand	

Note: **uor** in 'fl**uor**escent' and 'fl**uor**ide'.

Final

/ʊəʳ/ is spelled **ure** in these words:

abj**ure**	ass**ure**	ins**ure**	s**ure**

/ʊəʳ/ is spelled **oor** in these words:

b**oor**	m**oor**	p**oor**	sp**oor**

/ʊəʳ/ is spelled **our** in these words, mostly of French origin:

det**our**	d**our**	t**our**	vel**our**

Pronunciation

Words with the sound /ʊəʳ/ are increasingly being pronounced /ɔːʳ/ in RP. In GenAm and Scots English, they are usually pronounced /ʊʳ/.

/aʊ/   out

In most words, this sound is spelled **ou** before a consonant, and **ow** before a vowel or at the end of a word.

Initial

/aʊ/ is spelled **ou** in these words:

ouch	**ou**nce	**ou**st	**ou**t

Note: (1) There are many compound words beginning with **out**-: e.g. '**out**break', '**out**come', '**out**line', '**out**look', '**out**put', '**out**side', and '**out**standing'. (2) **ow** in the exclamation '**ow**' and in '**ow**l'.

Middle

/aʊ/ is usually spelled **ou** before a consonant:

ab**ou**t	c**ou**ncil	h**ou**se	r**ou**nd
am**ou**nt	c**ou**nt	m**ou**ntain	s**ou**nd
ann**ou**nce	d**ou**bt	m**ou**th	s**ou**th
ar**ou**nd	f**ou**nd	p**ou**nd	th**ou**sand
b**ou**nd	gr**ou**nd	pr**ou**d	...

Note: **ough** in 'd**ough**ty' and 'dr**ough**t'.

/aʊ/ is spelled **ow**, usually followed by **n**, **l**, **d**, or a vowel, in these words:

br**ow**n	f**ow**l	p**ow**der	tr**ow**el
cl**ow**n	gr**ow**l	r**ow**dy	v**ow**el
cr**ow**n	h**ow**l	...	...
d**ow**n	j**ow**ls	all**ow**ed	br**ow**se
dr**ow**n	pr**ow**l	b**ow**el	d**ow**ry
fr**ow**n	sc**ow**l	c**ow**ard	d**ow**se
g**ow**n	...	d**ow**ager	dr**ow**sy
t**ow**n	ch**ow**der	h**ow**itzer	end**ow**ment
...	cr**ow**d	pr**ow**ess	k**ow**t**ow**
c**ow**l	d**ow**dy	t**ow**el	n**ow**t

Final

/aʊ/ is spelled **ow** in these words:

all**ow**	c**ow**	h**ow**	r**ow**
b**ow**	disav**ow**	n**ow**	s**ow**
br**ow**	end**ow**	pl**ow**	v**ow**
ch**ow**	highbr**ow**	pr**ow**	w**ow**

Note: (1) **ough** in 'b**ough**' and 'pl**ough**'. (2) **ou** in 'th**ou**'.

| /aʊəʳ/ | our |

In most words, this sound is spelled either **our** or **ower**.

Initial

/aʊəʳ/ is spelled **our** in these words:

our	ours	ourselves

Note: **hour** in 'hour', 'hourglass', 'hourly', and 'hours'.

Middle

/aʊəʳ/ is not common in the middle of a word. It is spelled **auer** in 'sauerkraut' (a German word), **owar** in 'coward', and **owr** in 'dowry'.

Final

/aʊəʳ/ is spelled **ower** in these words:

bower	empower	glower	shower
cower	flower	power	tower

/aʊəʳ/ is spelled **our** in these words:

devour	flour	sour
dour	scour	

Inflection and word formation

The final **r** is never doubled:

e.g. devouring, empowered.

Pronunciation

In RP, **our** is sometimes pronounced /ɑːʳ/. 'Dour' is also pronounced /dʊəʳ/, especially in Scotland.

/ʌ/ up

In most words, this sound is spelled **u**. It is often spelled **o** in the middle of a word before **m**, **n**, **th**, or **v**. The rarer pattern **ou** occurs in some very common words, such as 'c**ou**ple', 'd**ou**ble', 'en**ou**gh', 'r**ou**gh', 't**ou**ch', and 'y**ou**ng'.

Initial

/ʌ/ is usually spelled **u**:

ugly	**u**mpire	**u**p	**u**tmost
ulcer	**u**ncle	**u**pper	**u**tterly
ultimate	**u**nder	**u**s	...

Note: (1) There are many words beginning with the negative prefix **un-**: e.g. '**un**able', '**un**employment', '**un**expected', '**un**fortunate', '**un**likely', and '**un**usual'. (2) /ʌ/ is spelled **o** in '**o**nion', '**o**ther', and '**o**ven'.

Middle

/ʌ/ is usually spelled **u**:

b**u**dget	g**u**lf	n**u**mber	s**u**ch
b**u**t	h**u**ndred	pl**u**s	s**u**dden
cl**u**b	h**u**sband	prod**u**ct	s**u**mmer
c**u**p	j**u**dge	p**u**blic	s**u**mmit
c**u**t	j**u**st	res**u**lt	s**u**n
disc**u**ss	j**u**stice	r**u**n	th**u**s
dr**u**g	m**u**ch	st**u**dy	tr**u**st
f**u**nd	m**u**st	s**u**bject	...

/ʌ/ is spelled **o**, particularly before **m**, **n**, **th**, or **v**:

bec**o**me	fr**o**ntier	w**o**nder	d**o**ve
c**o**me	h**o**ney	...	gl**o**ve
c**o**mfort	M**o**nday	an**o**ther	g**o**vern
c**o**mpany	m**o**ney	br**o**ther	l**o**ve
inc**o**me	m**o**ngrel	d**o**th	rec**o**ver
s**o**me	m**o**nk	m**o**ther	sh**o**ve
s**o**mersault	m**o**nkey	n**o**thing	sh**o**vel
st**o**mach	m**o**nth	sm**o**ther	sl**o**venly
...	n**o**ne	...	...
am**o**ng	s**o**n	ab**o**ve	c**o**lour
c**o**njure	sp**o**nge	c**o**venant	d**o**st
c**o**nstable	t**o**n	c**o**ver	d**o**zen
d**o**ne	t**o**ngue	c**o**vet	w**o**rry
fr**o**nt	w**o**n	disc**o**ver	...

Note: (1) **oo** in 'blood' and 'flood'. (3) **oe** in 'does'. (3) **o** is pronounced /wʌ/ in 'once' and 'one'.

/ʌ/ is spelled **ou** in these words:

country	cousin	rough	tough
couple	double	southerly	trouble
couplet	encourage	southern	young
courage	enough	touch	

Note: **gh** is pronounced /f/ in 'enough', 'rough', and 'tough'.

Final

/ʌ/ does not occur at the end of English words.

Pronunciation

Words pronounced with the sound /ʌ/ in RP and GenAm are usually pronounced /ʊ/ in Northern British English.

/juː/ use

In most words, this sound is spelled **u**, or **ue** when it is at the end of a word. The pattern **ew** is also fairly common.

Initial

/**juː**/ is usually spelled **u**:

uniform	unique	universe	useful
unify	unit	university	usual
union	united	use	...

/**juː**/ is spelled **eu** in these words of Greek origin:

eucalyptus	eulogy	euphemism	eureka
eugenics	eunuch	euphoria	euthanasia

Note: (1) **you** in 'you', 'youth', and 'youthful'. (2) **yew** in 'yew'. (3) **yu** in 'Yule'. (4) **ewe** in 'ewe'. (5) /**juː**/ is the sound when you say the letter **U** or abbreviations such as 'UK', 'TUC' or 'VDU'.

Middle

/**juː**/ is usually spelled **u**:

accuse	future	nuclear	sexual
community	huge	popular	situation
computer	human	population	student
education	music	produce	...

Note: (1) also in the adjective 'minute' (/maɪnjuːt/). (2) **ui** in 'nuisance' and 'pursuit'.

/**juː**/ is spelled **eu** in these words, which are mainly of Greek origin:

deuce	neural	neutron	pseudo
feud	neuralgia	pharmaceuticals	pseudonym
feudal	neurological	pneumatic	Teutonic
hermeneutic	neutral	pneumonia	therapeutic

/**juː**/ is spelled **ew** in these words:

hewn	mews	pewter	steward
lewd	newt	skewer	

The 24 main vowel sounds

Final

/ju:/ is usually spelled **ue**:

arg**ue**	ens**ue**	reiss**ue**	subd**ue**
autoc**ue**	fond**ue**	resc**ue**	tiss**ue**
aven**ue**	h**ue**	resid**ue**	und**ue**
barbec**ue**	imb**ue**	retin**ue**	val**ue**
contin**ue**	iss**ue**	reven**ue**	ven**ue**
c**ue**	overd**ue**	rev**ue**	...
d**ue**	purs**ue**	stat**ue**	

Note: the spelling of '**queue**'.

/ju:/ is spelled **ew** in these words:

ask**ew**	h**ew**	n**ew**	sk**ew**
curf**ew**	kn**ew**	p**ew**	sp**ew**
curl**ew**	m**ew**	ph**ew**	st**ew**
d**ew**	mild**ew**	ren**ew**	wh**ew**
f**ew**	neph**ew**	sin**ew**	y**ew**

Note: (1) Final silent e in '**ewe**'. (2) **ieu** in '**adieu**' and '**lieu**', both of French origin. (3) **iew** in '**view**' and related words such as '**interview**', '**overview**', '**preview**', and '**review**'. (4) **u** in these words of Foreign origin: '**emu**', '**impromptu**', and '**menu**'. (5) **ut** in '**debut**'.

Inflection and word formation

Final silent **e** is dropped before a suffix beginning with a vowel:

e.g issue – iss**uing** – iss**ued**; subdue – subd**uing** – subd**ued**.

Note: (1) e is not dropped in '**cueing**'. (2) Both '**queueing**' or '**queuing**' are used. (3) e is dropped before a suffix beginning with a consonant in '**argue – argument**' and '**due – duly**'.

Pronunciation

In some of these words, usually after **t**, **d**, and **n**, the GenAm pronunciation is /u:/ (not /ju:/).

/jʊər/ during

In most words, this sound is spelled **ur** (followed by a vowel letter) or **ure** at the end of a word.

Initial

/jʊər/ is not common at the beginning of words. It is spelled **ur-** in '**ur**inary', '**ur**inate', and '**ur**ine'.

Note: **eur** in '**Eur**ope' and related words such as '**Eur**asian', '**Eur**o-', and '**Eur**opean'.

Middle

/jʊər/ is usually spelled **ur**:

b**ur**eau	d**ur**ing	l**ur**id	t**ur**een
c**ur**ious	f**ur**ious	m**ur**al	...

Note: (1) **eur** in 'h**eur**istic', 'n**eur**algia', 'n**eur**osis', and 'n**eur**otic'. (2) **uer** in 'p**uer**ile'.

Final

/jʊər/ is spelled **ure**:

all**ure**	end**ure**	man**ure**	proc**ure**
az**ure**	epic**ure**	mat**ure**	p**ure**
coiff**ure**	in**ure**	obsc**ure**	sec**ure**
c**ure**	l**ure**	ord**ure**	sinec**ure**
dem**ure**	manic**ure**	overt**ure**	...

Note: **eur** in 'liqu**eur**'.

Inflection and word formation

Final silent **e** is dropped before suffixes beginning with a vowel:

e.g. end**ure** – end**ur**ing – end**ur**ed – end**ur**ance – end**ur**able.

Pronunciation

The sound /jʊər/ is increasingly being pronounced /jɔːr/ in RP, and is usually pronounced /jʊr/ in GenAm and Scots English.

Note: The word 'your' is sometimes pronounced /jʊər/ in RP.

The 24 main vowel sounds

| /ə/ | about |
| /əʳ/ | other |

This sound is often called 'schwa'. The problem is that it can be spelled in a large number of different ways.

Initial

/ə/ is most frequently spelled **a**:

| about | ago | announce | away |
| according | among | around | ... |

/ə/ is also commonly spelled **o**:

| obey | occasion | omit | original |
| obtain | official | opposed | ... |

Note: **u** in 'upon'.

Middle

/əʳ/ is most frequently spelled **er**, but **ar**, **ir**, **or**, **our**, and **ur** are also common:

advertising	forward	comfort	...
government	...	information	Saturday
yesterday	circumference	...	surprise
...	...	colourful	...

/ə/ is most frequently spelled **a**, but **e**, **i**, **o**, and **u** are also common:

company	children	policy	...
important	president	...	industry
political	...	million	support
...	family	political	...

/ə/ is spelled **ou** before **s** in many common adjectives:

adventurous	enormous	jealous	serious
conscious	famous	nervous	tremendous
dangerous	generous	precious	...

Note: (1) also the noun 'moustache'. (2) **ou** followed by a silent **l** in the weak forms of 'could', 'should', and 'would'. (3) **ai** in 'certain', 'curtain', 'villain', and in the weak form of 'saint'. (4) **eo** in 'luncheon'. (5) **ia** in 'parliament'. (6) **oi** in 'porpoise' and 'tortoise'.

Note: (1) A related word with a different stress pattern will often help you to identify the spelling of /ə/ in a particular word. For example, the /e/ in 'presidential' tells you that the /ə/ in 'president' is also spelled **e**. (2) /ə/ is spelled in different ways in words with similar endings. For example 'afford**a**ble' but 'cred**i**ble', 'differ**e**nt' but 'import**a**nt'. See Section 2.2 for more details.

Final

/ər/ is commonly spelled **er**, **or**, **ar**, **our**, **re**, and **ure**:

aft**er**	mot**or**	arm**our**	cent**re**
lead**er**	...	behavi**our**	lit**re**
moth**er**	burgl**ar**	col**our**	manoeuv**re**
numb**er**	doll**ar**	fav**our**	theat**re**
...	gramm**ar**	hon**our**	...
act**or**	particul**ar**	hum**our**	cult**ure**
err**or**	simil**ar**	lab**our**	press**ure**
maj**or**	...	...	...

Note: (1) **our** in British spelling is usually **or** in American spelling: e.g. 'armor', 'behavior', 'color', 'favor'. (2) **re** in British spelling is usually **er** in American spelling: e.g. 'center', 'liter', and 'theater'. (3) Words ending in /ər/ can be difficult to spell correctly. See Section 2.2 for more details.

/ə/ is usually spelled **a**, and occurs mainly in words of Foreign or Classical origin:

agend**a**	dat**a**	orchestr**a**	traum**a**
aren**a**	dilemm**a**	past**a**	ultr**a**
asthm**a**	eczem**a**	peninsul**a**	umbrell**a**
banan**a**	extr**a**	pizz**a**	vanill**a**
camer**a**	formul**a**	quot**a**	vill**a**
cinem**a**	oper**a**	sof**a**	...

/ə/ is spelled **ah** in these words of Foreign origin:

cheet**ah**	hook**ah**	loof**ah**	purd**ah**
halleluj**ah**	howd**ah**	pari**ah**	savann**ah**

Note: (1) **e** in 'gen**re**', 'raison d'et**re**', and 'til**de**'. (2) The weak forms of some grammatical words are pronounced /ə/: '**a**', 'int**o**', 'ont**o**', 'th**e**', and 't**o**'.

Inflection and word formation

Final silent **e** is dropped before a suffix beginning with a vowel:

e.g. press**ure** – press**uring** – press**ured** – press**urize**.

Pronunciation

/ə/ can be pronounced as a syllabic consonant before **l** and **n** and sometimes before **m**.

2.2 'Schwa' (/ə/) in word endings

2.2.1 -able or -ible?

The main problem for spelling is that these two adjective endings sound very similar.

Frequency

Five times more adjectives end in **-able**:

accept**able**	enjoy**able**	port**able**	unaccept**able**
avail**able**	fashion**able**	predict**able**	uncomfort**able**
cap**able**	formid**able**	profit**able**	understand**able**
comfort**able**	inevit**able**	reason**able**	valu**able**
compar**able**	li**able**	reli**able**	vari**able**
consider**able**	memor**able**	remark**able**	vi**able**
desir**able**	miser**able**	respect**able**	vulner**able**
dur**able**	not**able**	suit**able**	...

Fewer adjectives end in **-ible**, but some are fairly common:

ed**ible**	imposs**ible**	poss**ible**	terr**ible**
flex**ible**	incred**ible**	respons**ible**	vis**ible**
horr**ible**	invis**ible**	sens**ible**	...

History

Both **-able** and **-ible** come from a Latin suffix *-bilis*, which combined with verb stems to form adjectives:

e.g. *considerare* + *-bilis* = *considerabilis* : 'consider**able**'; *audire* + *-bilis* = *audibilis* : 'aud**ible**'.

In many cases, the original verb stem is not a current word in English, so the spelling of the word needs to be learned:

aff**able**	fe**asible**	leg**ible**	ten**able**
ar**able**	form**idable**	plaus**ible**	vulner**able**
ed**ible**	inev**itable**	prob**able**	...

However, the '**a**' or '**i**' was originally part of the Latin verb stem, so other words which are derived from the same verb are often spelled with the same vowel letter in the same position, and can be used as a clue to the spelling:

e.g. admir**a**tion – admir**a**ble; aud**i**tion – aud**i**ble; cap**a**city – cap**a**ble; cred**i**t – cred**i**ble; digest**i**ve – digest**i**ble; horr**i**d – horr**i**ble; imag**i**nation – imag**i**nable; prob**a**te – prob**a**ble; ten**a**city – ten**a**ble; toler**a**tion – toler**a**ble; vis**i**on – vis**i**ble.

-able or -ible?

Word formation

-able is a productive suffix in modern English, and is used to form adjectives from words of various origins (not just from words of Latin origin):

agree**able**	lov**able**	size**able**	understand**able**
enjoy**able**	manage**able**	suit**able**	unforget**table**
fashion**able**	pay**able**	tax**able**	unthink**able**
foresee**able**	reason**able**	unbear**able**	work**able**
knowledge**able**	remark**able**	unbeliev**able**	...

Note: Compare 'ed**ible**' (from Latin *edibilis*) with 'eat**able**' (from the English word 'eat').

-able is used to form adjectives from nouns as well as verbs:

comfort**able**	impression**able**	peace**able**	sale**able**
companion**able**	knowledge**able**	person**able**	size**able**
fashion**able**	marriage**able**	pleasur**able**	treason**able**
fission**able**	objection**able**	rate**able**	...

As **-able** can be a productive suffix, if the part of the word before the ending is a current word in English (especially if it is not a word of Latin origin) it is more likely to be **-able**. The most common words ending in **-able**, for example, have a current stem:

accept**able**	consider**able**	remark**able**	suit**able**
avail**able**	comfort**able**	reason**able**	...

Note: but '**cap**able', '**inevit**able', and '**vulner**able' (which were formed in Latin) cannot be analysed in this way ('**cap**able' is not related to the English word 'cap').

Most of the common adjectives ending in **-ible**, on the other hand, do not have a current stem:

compat**ible**	incred**ible**	poss**ible**	terr**ible**
elig**ible**	invis**ible**	suscept**ible**	vis**ible**
horr**ible**	plaus**ible**	tang**ible**	...

Note: but there are some exceptions: e.g. '**access**ible', '**convert**ible', and '**deduct**ible'.

'Schwa' /ə/ in word endings

2.2.2 -ant or -ent?

You cannot usually tell from the sound of an adjective or noun ending in /-ənt/ whether it is spelled -ent or -ant.

Note: Verbs ending in -ent and -ant usually have a strong vowel in the last syllable and can easily be distinguished: e.g. 'comm**ent**', 'dec**ant**', 'docum**ent**', 'pres**ent**', 'prev**ent**', and 'transpl**ant**'.

Frequency

Three times more words end in -ent:

accid**ent**	environ**ment**	pati**ent**	brilli**ant**
agree**ment**	equip**ment**	pres**ent**	const**ant**
announce**ment**	excell**ent**	presid**ent**	consult**ant**
argu**ment**	govern**ment**	rec**ent**	eleg**ant**
commit**ment**	incid**ent**	state**ment**	gi**ant**
correspond**ent**	independ**ent**	stud**ent**	import**ant**
curr**ent**	manage**ment**	treat**ment**	pregn**ant**
depart**ment**	mo**ment**	unemploy**ment**	reluct**ant**
develop**ment**	move**ment**	...	signific**ant**
differ**ent**	parlia**ment**	assist**ant**	...

Sound and spelling

Nearly all words pronounced /-mənt/ are abstract nouns ending in -ment:

agree**ment**	govern**ment**	mo**ment**	state**ment**
depart**ment**	invest**ment**	move**ment**	treat**ment**
develop**ment**	manage**ment**	parlia**ment**	...

Note: The only common words ending in -mant are the adjectives 'ada**mant**' and 'dor**mant**' and the nouns 'infor**mant**' and 'clai**mant**'.

The sounds /s/, /ʃ/, and /dʒ/ are nearly always followed by -ent:

abs**ent**	fluoresc**ent**	coeffici**ent**	conting**ent**
acc**ent**	indec**ent**	defici**ent**	deterg**ent**
adjac**ent**	innoc**ent**	effici**ent**	indulg**ent**
adolesc**ent**	magnific**ent**	pati**ent**	intellig**ent**
complac**ent**	rec**ent**	profici**ent**	pung**ent**
convalesc**ent**	reminisc**ent**	quoti**ent**	reg**ent**
cresc**ent**	retic**ent**	suffici**ent**	string**ent**
dec**ent**	...	...	urg**ent**
effervesc**ent**	anci**ent**	ag**ent**	...

Note: (1) /s/ is followed by -ant only in 'conver**sant**', 'convul**sant**', 'depre**ssant**', 'disper**sant**', 'inces**sant**', and 'suppre**ssant**'. (2) /ʃ/ is never followed by -ant. (3) /dʒ/ is followed by -ant only in 'ser**geant**' and 'pa**geant**'.

-ant or -ent?

The spelling **qu** is always followed by **-ent**:

| consequent | eloquent | grandiloquent | subsequent |
| delinquent | frequent | infrequent | |

Note: Except in 'piqu**ant**', which is of French origin.

The sounds /t/, /k/, /g/, and /f/ are nearly always followed by **-ant**:

accountant	instant	insignificant	elegant
assistant	irritant	lubricant	extravagant
blatant	militant	piquant	inelegant
constant	Protestant	significant	litigant
consultant	reluctant	supplicant	...
distant	resistant	vacant	elephant
expectant	resultant	...	infant
hesitant	...	arrogant	triumphant
important	applicant	congregant	...

Note: (1) But there are a few words spelled -tent: e.g. 'competent', 'consistent', 'existent', 'impotent', 'inadvertent', 'insistent', intermittent', 'latent', 'omnipotent', 'patent', 'penitent', 'persistent', and 'potent'. (2) /k/, /g/, and /f/ are never followed by -ent.

The sound /n/ can be followed by **-ant** or **-ent**:

consonant	pregnant	continent	opponent
dominant	remnant	eminent	permanent
indignant	stagnant	exponent	pertinent
malignant	tenant	immanent	prominent
pennant	...	imminent	proponent
poignant	component	impertinent	...

Grammar and spelling

Words with weak **-ment** are nearly all abstract nouns (see 'Sounds and spelling' section above).

Many other words ending in **-ent** are nouns:

| accident | client | parent | talent |
| agent | correspondent | student | ... |

Many other words ending in **-ent** are adjectives:

apparent	efficient	prominent	urgent
confident	excellent	recent	violent
different	frequent	silent	...

'Schwa' /ə/ in word endings

A large number of other words ending in **-ent** are both nouns and adjectives, but often with different meanings:

adolesc**ent**	conting**ent**	expedi**ent**	pati**ent**
astring**ent**	curr**ent**	incumb**ent**	pres**ent**
compon**ent**	deterg**ent**	independ**ent**	sali**ent**
constitu**ent**	dissid**ent**	innoc**ent**	solv**ent**
contin**ent**	equival**ent**	pat**ent**	...

Some words ending in **-ant** are nouns, mostly referring to people or living things:

account**ant**	defend**ant**	inf**ant**	serv**ant**
attend**ant**	eleph**ant**	merch**ant**	ten**ant**
consult**ant**	immigr**ant**	peas**ant**	...

Some words ending in **-ant** are adjectives:

arrog**ant**	eleg**ant**	redund**ant**	signific**ant**
brilli**ant**	ignor**ant**	relev**ant**	triumph**ant**
defi**ant**	pleas**ant**	reluct**ant**	vac**ant**
dist**ant**	pregn**ant**	resist**ant**	...

A few words ending in **-ant** are both nouns and adjectives:

clairvoy**ant**	const**ant**	gi**ant**	milit**ant**
concomit**ant**	devi**ant**	inst**ant**	...

A few words are spelled **-ant** when they are nouns, and **-ent** when they are adjectives:

e.g. depend**ant** – depend**ent**; descend**ant** – descend**ent**; pend**ant** – pend**ent**; propell**ant** – propell**ent**.

Word formation

Words spelled **-ant** often have related words with an **a** in the same position, which can help you to spell them:

e.g. account**ant** – account**a**ble; consult**ant** – consult**a**tion; domin**ant** – domin**a**tion; ignor**ant** – ignor**a**mus; immigr**ant** – immigr**a**tion; milit**ant** – milit**a**te; Protest**ant** – protest**a**tion; toler**ant** – toler**a**tion; triumph**ant** – triumph**a**l; vac**ant** – vac**a**te.

Words ending in **-ent** and **-ant** often have related nouns ending in **-ence** or **-ency**, or **-ance** or **-ancy**:

e.g. assist**ant** – assist**ance**; brilli**ant** – brilli**ance**; const**ant** – const**ancy**; correspond**ent** – correspond**ence**; differ**ent** – differ**ence**; dist**ant** – dist**ance**; import**ant** – import**ance**; independ**ent** – independ**ence**; pregn**ant** – pregn**ancy**; pres**ent** – pres**ence**; presid**ent** – presid**ency**; signific**ant** – signific**ance**.

2.2.3 -er, -or, or ar?

-er, -or, and -ar are the three main ways of spelling /ər/ at the end of a word.

Frequency

-er is one of the commonest word endings in English. Nearly three quarters of the words ending in /ər/ are spelled -er, including some very common words:

after	leader	other	together
better	mother	over	under
either	never	power	water
further	number	rather	whether
later	order	September	...

-er is the only one of these endings that can be used to form new nouns:

amplifier	eyeliner	humidifier	skateboarder
bleeper	go-getter	kidnapper	skier
cinematographer	hijacker	lifer	squatter
conditioner	hitchhiker	rapper	...

-er is also used to form the comparative of adjectives:

| earlier | higher | longer | older |
| greater | later | lower | ... |

Note: When -er is used to form nouns or the comparative of adjectives: (1) a final consonant will double after a short vowel: e.g. 'big – bigger' and 'squat – squatter'. (2) a final silent e will be dropped: e.g. 'late – later' and 'life – lifer'. (3) final -y after a consonant will be replaced by i: e.g. 'amplify – amplifier' and 'murky – murkier'.

There are a large number of words which are **not** spelled -er. These are listed in alphabetical order at the end of this entry.

Grammar and spelling

The most likely spelling of /ər/ often depends on the grammatical class of the word. -er, as indicated already, can occur at the end of words of many different classes: prepositions ('over' and 'under'), adverbs ('never' and 'together'), adjectives ('former' and 'further'), nouns ('leader' and 'power'), verbs ('consider' and 'remember'), and conjunctions ('either' and 'whether'). However, words ending in -or are mostly nouns, and words ending in -ar are mostly adjectives.

'Schwa' /ə/ in word endings

Nouns:

Most nouns which mean 'a person or thing that does a particular action or job, or that has a particular role or function' are spelled **-er**:

adviser	fighter	newscaster	singer
baker	hunter	officer	soldier
carrier	killer	owner	speaker
commander	lawyer	player	teacher
consumer	leader	prisoner	walker
dealer	lover	producer	winner
designer	maker	publisher	worker
driver	manager	reader	writer
farmer	minister	reporter	...

A large number of nouns with this meaning are spelled **-or**:

actor	doctor	monitor	solicitor
ambassador	editor	narrator	successor
author	governor	operator	translator
commentator	inspector	professor	victor
dictator	investor	prosecutor	visitor
director	mayor	senator	...

Note: (1) A few nouns with this meaning are spelled -ar: 'beggar', 'burglar', 'bursar', 'liar', 'pedlar', 'scholar', and 'vicar'. (2) Most of the nouns ending in -or are of Latin origin. Many of them end in -tor, or even more specifically in -ator, -ctor, -itor, and -utor. Nearly all of them are related to nouns ending in -tion: e.g. 'director – direction', 'editor – edition', 'narrator – narration', and 'prosecutor – prosecution'. (3) But note 'promoter – promotion' is unusual, whereas 'motor – motion' follows the normal pattern. (4) Most of these nouns ending in -er, -or, or -ar, are connected to English verbs: e.g. 'a **leader** leads', 'a **director** directs' and 'a **beggar** begs'. (5) Some are connected to other nouns: 'a **newscaster** reads a newscast' and 'a **senator** works in the Senate'. (6) Others have a less obvious relationship to other English words: an **officer** does not 'office', and is more likely to be in the armed forces or the police than to work in an office.

Most nouns with other meanings are spelled **-er**:

answer	December	November	quarter
border	dinner	number	river
cancer	letter	October	September
chapter	matter	offer	summer
corner	member	order	water
cover	murder	paper	wonder
danger	neither	power	...

-er, -or, or ar?

These words are spelled **-or**:

alligator	error	minor	squalor
ancestor	exterior	mirror	stupor
anchor	factor	Monsignor	successor
bachelor	horror	motor	tenor
castor	interior	pallor	terror
condor	languor	pastor	tractor
cursor	liquor	predecessor	traitor
denominator	mentor	razor	tremor
donor	metaphor	rotor	vector
Equator	meteor	sector	visor

These words are spelled **-our** in British spelling, but are usually spelled **-or** in American spelling:

arbour	demeanour	humour	saviour
ardour	endeavour	labour	savour
armour	favour	neighbour	splendour
behaviour	fervour	odour	succour
candour	flavour	parlour	tumour
clamour	glamour	rancour	valour
clangour	harbour	rigour	vapour
colour	honour	rumour	vigour

Note: 'glam**our**' is often spelled **-our** in American spelling as well as British.

These words are spelled **-ar**:

altar	cellar	grammar	pillar
briar	collar	hangar	poplar
calendar	cougar	molar	sugar
caterpillar	dollar	mortar	tartar
cedar	friar	nectar	vinegar

Comparative adjectives:

Comparative adjectives are usually formed with **-er**:

better	faster	higher	older
bigger	fewer	larger	stronger
closer	further	latter	upper
earlier	greater	longer	younger
easier	harder	lower	...

Note: A few words ending in **-ior** were originally comparative adjectives in Latin and can still be used with a comparative meaning: 'inferior', 'junior', 'prior', 'senior', and 'superior'. Compare 'He was **senior** to me' and 'He was **more important** than me'.

'Schwa' /ə/ in word endings

Other adjectives:

Most other adjectives end in **-ar**:

angular	jocular	perpendicular	stellar
avuncular	linear	polar	tabular
cellular	lumbar	popular	titular
circular	lunar	rectangular	tubercular
extracurricular	molecular	regular	tubular
familiar	muscular	secular	vascular
glandular	nuclear	similar	vehicular
globular	oracular	singular	vernacular
granular	particular	solar	vulgar
insular	peculiar	spectacular	...

A few other adjectives end in **-er**, and some are very common:

amber	eager	neuter	sinister
bitter	elder	other	sober
clever	former	premier	super
dapper	kosher	proper	utter

Note: A few other adjectives end in **-ior** or **-or**: 'exterior', 'interior', 'major', 'minor', 'posterior', and 'ulterior'. These were also originally comparative adjectives in Latin, but are no longer used with a comparative meaning.

Words that are not spelled -er:

acre	brassiere	clamour	demeanour
adaptor	brochure	clangour	dishonour
aggressor	burglar	closure	distributor
altar	bursar	colour	dollar
amateur	cadre	compositor	donor
ambassador	calibre	composure	editor
ancestor	candour	compressor	elixir
anchor	captor	confessor	embrasure
angular	carburettor	conqueror	endeavour
antimacassar	castor	conspirator	emperor
arbour	cedar	contributor	error
ardour	cellar	convenor	executor
armour	cellular	cougar	exhibitor
auditor	censor	councillor	exposure
augur	censure	counsellor	exterior
author	centre	creditor	failure
bachelor	chancellor	culture	favour
beggar	cheddar	cursor	femur
behaviour	circular	debtor	fervour

-er, -or, or -ar?

fibre	lumbar	poplar	sponsor
figure	lunar	popular	squalor
fissure	lustre	possessor	stupor
flavour	major	posterior	successor
funicular	manor	precursor	succour
future	martyr	predator	sugar
glamour	massacre	predecessor	suitor
glandular	meagre	pressure	sulphur
globular	measure	procedure	superior
goitre	mediocre	professor	supervisor
governor	metaphor	progenitor	survivor
grammar	meteor	proprietor	tailor
grandeur	metre	prosecutor	tenor
granular	minor	purveyor	tenure
hangar	mirror	rancour	terror
honour	mitre	razor	theatre
horror	molar	realtor	timbre
humour	molecular	receptor	titular
impostor	monitor	regular	tonsure
incisor	mortar	resistor	tormentor
inferior	motor	rigor	torpor
inheritor	murmur	rigour	transistor
injure	muscular	rumour	treasure
inquisitor	nature	sabre	tremor
insular	nectar	sailor	tubular
interceptor	neighbour	saltpetre	tumour
interior	non sequitur	satyr	tutor
interlocutor	nuclear	saviour	ulterior
inventor	ochre	savour	valour
investor	odour	sceptre	vapour
janitor	ogre	scholar	vehicular
jocular	oracular	sculptor	vendor
jugular	orator	secular	vernacular
junior	pallor	seizure	vicar
juror	parlour	senator	vigour
kilometre	particular	senior	vinegar
labour	peculiar	sensor	visitor
languor	pedlar	sepulchre	visor
leisure	perjure	singular	vulgar
lemur	perpendicular	solar	warrior
linear	persecutor	solicitor	zephyr
liquor	picture	sombre	
litre	pleasure	spectacular	
lucre	polar	splendour	

Note: Many words end in **-ator**, **-ctor**, and **-ture**: e.g. 'cul**ture**', 'dire**ctor**', 'do**ctor**', 'narr**ator**', 'na**ture**', and 'oper**ator**'.

'Schwa' /ə/ in word endings

2.2.4 -al, -el, -il, -le, -ol, or -ul?

The three main spellings are -le, -al, and -el.

The endings -il and -ol are fairly rare, so it is worth learning the few words that are spelled this way:

basil	daredevil	utensil	mongol
bedevil	devil	...	petrol
cavil	evil	carol	pistol
civil	pencil	gambol	symbol
council	stencil	idol	viol

-ul is common, but only in the adjective ending -ful. The only other words ending in -ul are 'consul' and 'mogul'.

Of the three main spellings, -al is the most common. Most of the words ending in -al are adjectives, but some are nouns:

central	natural	...	metal
final	official	animal	proposal
financial	personal	approval	rival
general	political	arrival	scandal
international	royal	capital	signal
local	several	festival	trial
medical	social	hospital	withdrawal
national	special	journal	...

The ending -le is more common than -el, and most of the words ending in -le or -el are nouns:

able	middle	title	model
article	people	trouble	novel
battle	principle	...	panel
couple	simple	angel	rebel
double	single	channel	travel
example	struggle	label	tunnel
little	table	level	...

Note: (1) But many adjectives end in -able or -ible: e.g. 'available', 'impossible', 'possible', and 'responsible'. See section 2.2.1 for '-able or -ible?'. (2) -le does not occur after /s/ spelled c, /dʒ/ spelled g, or m, n, r, s, v, or w. (3) -el does not occur after f, g, or k, except in words of Foreign origin: 'bagel', 'duffel', 'nickel'. (4) b, d, p, and t are much more commonly followed by -le than by -el.

2.3 The 24 main consonant sounds

/b/	but

This sound is nearly always spelled **b**. It is spelled **bb** after a short vowel, and before some Native endings. It is spelled **be** at the end of a word, after a long vowel.

Initial

/**b**/ is usually spelled **b**:

back	been	bid	but
be	before	both	by
because	between	build	...

Note: **bu** in '**bu**oy'.

Middle

/**b**/ is usually spelled **b**:

about	debate	number	problem
above	double	October	sober
cabinet	label	probably	...

/**b**/ is spelled **bb** after a short vowel, before the endings **-ed**, **-er**, **-ing**, **-ish**, **-le**, and **-y**:

bubble	hobby	rubber	snobbery
grabbed	lobby	rubbish	stabbed
grabbing	robber	rubble	...

/**b**/ is also spelled **bb** in these words:

abbey	dumbbell	rabbit	stubborn
abbot	gibbon	ribbon	yobbo
abbreviate	hubbub	Sabbath	
cabbage	kibbutz	sabbatical	
cabbie	rabbi	shibboleth	

Final

/**b**/ is usually spelled **b**:

absorb	crib	herb	rob
cab	curb	nib	squib
club	grab	pub	...

The 24 main consonant sounds

/**b**/ is spelled **be** after a long vowel:

ba**be**	descri**be**	pro**be**	wardro**be**
cu**be**	glo**be**	tu**be**	...

Note: **bb** in 'e**bb**'.

Inflection and word formation

Final silent **e** is dropped before suffixes that begin with a vowel:

e.g. describe – describ**ing** – describ**able**.

Final **b** is doubled after a short vowel, before suffixes that begin with a vowel:

e.g. club – clu**bb**able; snob – sno**bb**ish.

/k/   can

In most words, this sound is spelled **c**. Before **e** or **i** and at the end of a word, the most common spelling is **k**. After a short vowel, the spelling pattern **ck** occurs before some Native endings or at the end of a word. After a long vowel the pattern **ke** occurs at the end of a word. In most words, /ks/ is spelled **x**, and /kw/ is spelled **qu**. The other patterns are fairly rare.

Initial

/k/ is usually spelled **c**, especially before **a**, **o**, or **u**, and before **l** or **r**:

call	...	clock	cricket
can	cup	close	crime
...	cut	clothes	crisis
come	...	club	critical
company	claim	...	crowd
control	class	cream	crucial
could	clean	create	crunch
country	clear	credit	...

/k/ is spelled **k** before **a**, **o**, **u**, or **l** in these words of Foreign origin:

kaftan	kaput	...	...
kale	karaoke	koala	kudos
kaleidoscope	karate	kohl	kung fu
kamikaze	karma	koran	...
kangaroo	kayak	kosher	klaxon
kapok	kazoo	kowtow	kleptomania

Note: **kh** in 'khaki'.

/k/ is spelled **k** before **e** or **i**:

keel	kettle	kidney	kiss
keen	key	kill	kit
keep	...	kilometre	kitchen
kennel	kick	kind	kite
kerosene	kid	king	...

Note: **c** before **e** in '**C**elt' and '**c**eilidh'.

/k/ is spelled **ch** in some words of Greek origin:

chamomile	chemotherapy	chord	chromosome
chaos	chiropractic	choreography	chronic
character	chlorine	chorus	chronicle
charismatic	cholera	Christmas	chronology
chemical	cholesterol	chromium	...

The 24 main consonant sounds

Note: **qu** in '**qu**ay', '**qu**eue', '**qu**iche', and '**qu**oit'.

/**k**/ often occurs in the combination /**kw**/, which is usually spelled **qu**:

quack	**qu**antity	**qu**ell	**qu**ilt
quad	**qu**arrel	**qu**ench	**qu**intet
quaff	**qu**arry	**qu**ery	**qu**ip
quagmire	**qu**art	**qu**est	**qu**irk
quail	**qu**arter	**qu**estion	**qu**it
quaint	**qu**artz	**qu**ibble	**qu**ite
quake	**qu**ash	**qu**ick	**qu**iver
qualify	**qu**asi-	**qu**id	**qu**iz
quality	**qu**aver	**qu**iescent	**qu**o
qualm	**qu**easy	**qu**iet	**qu**ota
quandary	**qu**een	**qu**iff	**qu**ote
quango	**qu**eer	**qu**ill	...

Note: /**kw**/ is spelled **cho** in '**cho**ir', **co** in '**co**iffure', **cro** in '**cro**issant', and **cu** in '**cu**isine'.

Middle

/**k**/ is usually spelled **c**, especially before **a**, **o**, **u**, or a consonant:

across	become	fact	second
act	difficult	include	secretary
American	economy	local	security
article	education	political	vehicle
because	expect	record	...

Note: (1) **k** in the pattern **nkle** in 'ankle', 'crinkle', 'sprinkle', 'tinkle', 'twinkle', 'winkle', and 'wrinkle' (but **not** in 'uncle'). (2) **k** in these words, which are mostly of Foreign origin: 'alkali', 'eureka', 'kamikaze', 'leukaemia', 'paprika', 'polka', 'skate', 'skulk', 'skull', 'skunk', 'vodka'. (3) **k** in derived forms and compounds of words that end in **k**: e.g. 'bankrupt', 'breakfast', 'darkness', 'frankly', 'remarkable', 'risky', 'talks', 'workplace', and 'works'.

/**k**/ is usually spelled **k** before **e**, **i**, or **y**:

asked	likely	naked	snooker
baker	looking	skiing	taken
basket	maker	skipper	turkey
broken	market	sky	whisky
broker	monkey	smoked	...

Note: **c** before **e** in 'sceptic', 'sceptical', and 'scepticism', which are spelled with a **k** in American English: 'skeptic'.

/k/ is spelled **cc** in the patterns **acc-**, **occ-**, and **succ-** at the beginning of words:

a**cc**laim	a**cc**redit	o**cc**ult	...
a**cc**ommodation	a**cc**urate	o**cc**upation	**succ**our
a**cc**ompany	a**cc**use	o**cc**upy	**succ**ulent
a**cc**ording	...	o**cc**ur	**succ**umb
a**cc**ount	o**cc**asion	o**cc**urrence	...

/k/ is also spelled **cc** in these words:

bro**cc**oli	e**cc**lesiastical	me**cc**a	so**cc**er
bu**cc**aneer	hi**cc**up	ra**cc**oon	toba**cc**o
desi**cc**ated	impe**cc**able	re**cc**e	

Note: **cch** in 'sa**cch**arine' and 'zu**cch**ini'.

/k/ is spelled **ck** after a short vowel, before the endings **-ed**, **-en**, **-er**, **-est**, **-et**, **-ing**, **-ish**, **-le**, or **-y**:

bra**ck**en	fli**ck**er	qui**ck**est	ta**ck**y
chi**ck**en	ja**ck**et	sti**ck**y	wi**ck**ed
chu**ck**le	pe**ck**ish	sto**ck**ing	wi**ck**er
cri**ck**et	po**ck**et	ta**ck**le	...

/k/ is spelled **ck** before a vowel in these words:

be**ck**on	cu**ck**oo	jo**ck**ey	pa**ck**age
blo**ck**ade	ho**ck**ey	ma**ck**erel	re**ck**on
co**ck**erel	ja**ck**al	ni**ck**el	sto**ck**ade

/k/ is spelled **ck** in derived forms and compounds of words that end in **ck**:

atta**ck**s	ba**ck**wards	cra**ck**down	sto**ck**broker
ba**ck**ground	co**ck**tail	si**ck**ness	...

Note: **ck** in 'a**ck**nowledge'.

/k/ is spelled **ch**, usually in words of Greek origin:

a**ch**ing	ar**ch**ive	paro**ch**ial	s**ch**ool
anar**ch**y	e**ch**o	psy**ch**ic	te**ch**nical
an**ch**or	me**ch**anism	psy**ch**ological	te**ch**nology
ar**ch**etype	melan**ch**oly	s**ch**eme	...
ar**ch**itecture	or**ch**estra	s**ch**olarship	

/k/ is spelled **qu**, usually in words of French origin:

becquerel	croquet	mannequin	piquancy
bouquet	croquette	manqué	racquet
cliquey	etiquette	marquee	risqué
communiqué	lacquer	masquerade	soubriquet
conquer	liquor	mosquito	tourniquet
coquetry	liquorice	parquet	...

The 24 main consonant sounds

Note: **qu** spells /k/ in 'con**qu**er', but /kw/ in 'con**qu**est'.

/k/ often occurs in the combination /ks/, which is usually spelled **x**:

appro**x**imate	e**x**perience	fi**x**ed	se**x**ual
a**x**is	e**x**pert	fle**x**ible	si**x**ty
bo**x**ing	e**x**plain	ma**x**imum	ta**x**es
conte**x**t	e**x**port	mi**x**ed	ta**x**i
e**x**change	e**x**press	mi**x**ture	te**x**tile
e**x**cuse	e**x**tent	ne**x**t	te**x**ture
e**x**pect	e**x**tra	o**x**ygen	to**x**ic
e**x**pensive	e**x**treme	rela**x**ed	...

Note: (1) **xh** in 'e**xh**ibition'. (2) **xc** in 'e**xc**eed', 'e**xc**el', 'e**xc**ellence', 'e**xc**ept', 'e**xc**erpt', 'e**xc**ess', 'e**xc**ise', and 'e**xc**ite'.

/ks/ is spelled **cc** before **e** or **i** in these words:

a**cc**ede	a**cc**ess	su**cc**ess	o**cc**idental
a**cc**elerate	e**cc**entric	...	su**cc**inct
a**cc**ent	ina**cc**essible	a**cc**ident	va**cc**ine
a**cc**ept	su**cc**eed	fla**cc**id	

Note: (1) **cc** before **y** in 'co**cc**yx'. (2) **cs** in 'e**cs**tasy' and 'fa**cs**imile'. (3) **cz** in 'e**cz**ema'. (4) **ks** in compounds of words that end in **k**: e.g. 'bac**ks**tage', 'blac**ks**mith', 'boo**ks**tore', 'mar**ks**man', and 'ruc**ks**ack'.

/k/ often occurs in the combination /kʃ/, which is spelled **x** in these words:

an**x**ious	crucifi**x**ion	lu**x**ury	obno**x**ious
comple**x**ion	infle**x**ion	no**x**ious	se**x**ual

/kʃ/ is spelled **cti** in the ending -**cti**on:

a**cti**on	dire**cti**on	produ**cti**on	se**cti**on
colle**cti**on	ele**cti**on	rea**cti**on	...

Note: the rarer spellings 'conne**xion**' and 'infle**xion**'.

/k/ often occurs in the combination /kw/, which is usually spelled **qu**:

ade**qu**ate	be**qu**eath	e**qu**ity	re**qu**est
anti**qu**arian	be**qu**est	e**qu**ivalent	re**qu**ire
a**qu**alung	collo**qu**ial	fre**qu**ent	se**qu**ence
a**qu**amarine	conse**qu**ence	head**qu**arters	s**qu**are
a**qu**educt	earth**qu**ake	in**qu**iry	s**qu**eak
a**qu**iline	e**qu**al	li**qu**efy	subse**qu**ent
ban**qu**et	e**qu**ipment	li**qu**id	...

Note: (1) **cqu** in 'a**cqu**aint', 'a**cqu**iesce', 'a**cqu**ire', 'a**cqu**isition', and 'a**cqu**it'. (2) **kw** in 'aw**kw**ard', and in compounds of words that end in **k**: e.g. 'bac**kw**ard', 'bric**kw**ork', 'cloc**kw**ise', 'shoc**kw**ave', 'wal**kw**ay'.

Final

/k/ is spelled **k** after a vowel digraph or a consonant:

break	week	desk	thank
look	...	fork	think
meek	ask	mark	work
speak	bank	talk	...

/k/ is spelled **ke** after a long vowel:

cake	hike	like	spike
duke	joke	make	stroke
earthquake	lake	sake	...

/k/ is spelled **ck** after a short vowel:

attack	block	quick	track
back	check	rock	wick
black	lack	stock	...

Note: **k** in 'trek'.

/k/ is spelled **c** in the unstressed ending **-ic**:

basic	domestic	music	traffic
democratic	economic	public	...

/k/ is spelled **c** in some words of Classical or Foreign origin, and some shortened forms:

almanac	chic	hypochondriac	sync
arc	cognac	insomniac	talc
armagnac	cul-de-sac	lilac	tarmac
Aztec	disc	maniac	tic
bivouac	doc	mollusc	vac
bloc	elegiac	sec	zinc
bric-a-brac	franc	sic	zodiac
cardiac	havoc	spec	

/k/ is spelled **ch** in some words of Classical or Foreign origin, and some shortened forms:

Czech	loch	monarch	stomach
epoch	Mach	patriarch	synch
eunuch	matriarch	psych	tech

Note: **che** in 'ache' and its compounds such as 'headache'.

/**k**/ is spelled **que** in many words of French origin:

antique	discotheque	mystique	statuesque
baroque	cheque	oblique	technique
boutique	clique	physique	torque
brusque	critique	pique	unique
burlesque	grotesque	plaque	...

/**k**/ often occurs in the combination /**ks**/, which is usually spelled **x**:

apex	equinox	larynx	sex
appendix	fax	lynx	six
box	fix	matrix	sphinx
climax	flex	mix	syntax
coax	flux	orthodox	tax
complex	fox	paradox	telex
cox	hoax	phoenix	vortex
crucifix	index	reflex	wax
crux	influx	relax	...

Note: (1) **xe** in 'annexe', 'axe', and 'deluxe'. (2) 'annex' is an alternative spelling for 'annexe'. (3) 'ax' is an alternative spelling for 'axe' in American English.

/**ks**/ is spelled **cs** in the ending **-ics** in uncount nouns of Greek origin:

aerobics	electronics	linguistics	physics
athletics	ethics	mathematics	politics
economics	genetics	mechanics	...

Note: (1) Many of these nouns are related to adjectives that end in **-ic** or **-ical**, such as 'athletic' and 'ethical'. (2) /**ks**/ is spelled **chs**, **cks**, **cs**, **kes**, **ks**, or **ques** in inflected forms of words that end in /**k**/: e.g. 'stomachs', 'checks', 'clinics', 'cakes', 'breaks', and 'antiques'.

Inflection and word formation

Final silent **e** is dropped before a suffix beginning with a vowel:

e.g. stroke – stroking – stroked; mistake – unmistakable.

Note: but not in 'likeable'.

k is added to words ending in unstressed **-ic** before the suffixes **-ed**, **-er**, **-ing**, and **-y**:

colicky	mimicked	picnicker	trafficker
frolicking	panicky	politicking	...

Note: (1) 'finicky' does not have a related word ending in **-ic**. (2) Before suffixes other than **-ing** that begin with **i**, such as **-ism** or **-ity**, **k** is not added: e.g. 'critic –

criticism', 'electric -electricity', but the pronunciation of **ic** changes from /ɪk/ to /ɪs/. If the suffix has **i** followed by another vowel, the pronunciation of **ic** changes to /ʃ/: e.g. 'ma**g**ic – ma**g**ician', 'musi**c** -musi**c**ian'.

Nouns ending in -**ch** form their plurals regularly with **s**:

e.g. monar**ch** – monar**ch**s; stoma**ch** – stoma**ch**s.

Note: 'ache' drops its final **e** before suffixes that begin with a vowel: 'a**ch**ed – a**ch**ing – a**ch**y'.

Words ending in -**x** add **es** to form the plural of nouns or the third person singular present tense of verbs:

bo**xes**	fo**xes**	refle**xes**	wa**xes**
comple**xes**	mi**xes**	ta**xes**	...

Note: (1) Irregular plurals: 'appendi**x** – appendi**ces**', 'inde**x** – indi**ces** (or inde**xes**)', and 'matri**x** – matri**ces**'. (2) 'annexe' and 'axe' drop their final **e** before suffixes that begin with a vowel: 'anne**xe** (or annex) – anne**xing** – anne**xation**' and 'a**xe** – a**xing** – a**xed**'.

The 24 main consonant sounds

/tʃ/	child

In most words, this sound is spelled **ch**. After a short vowel, it is generally spelled **tch**. In the middle of words, however, **t** and **ti** are common, especially in a number of Classical endings.

Initial

/tʃ/ is usually spelled **ch**:

chair	chapter	child	choice
chance	check	children	church
change	chief	china	...

Note: **c** in these words of Italian origin: 'cellist', 'cello', 'ciabatta', and 'ciao'.

Middle

/tʃ/ is usually spelled **ch**:

achieve	exchange	merchant	treachery
archery	franchise	orchard	voucher
bachelor	macho	purchase	...

/tʃ/ is spelled **tch**, usually after a short vowel:

butcher	itchy	patchy	satchel
catchment	ketchup	pitcher	wretched
hatchet	kitchen	ratchet	...

/tʃ/ is spelled **ti** after **s**, in the Classical ending **-tion** in these words:

combustion	digestion	indigestion	suggestion
congestion	exhaustion	question	

/tʃ/ is spelled **t** before **u**, in the Classical endings **-tual, -tuary, -tuate, -tue, -tuous, -tural,** and **-ture**:

actual	accentuate	presumptuous	feature
habitual	fluctuate	virtuous	future
intellectual	perpetuate	voluptuous	literature
mutual	punctuate	...	mixture
spiritual	situate	architectural	nature
...	...	cultural	picture
actuary	statue	natural	temperature
estuary	virtue	structural	texture
mortuary	...	...	torture
obituary	contemptuous	capture	venture
sanctuary	fatuous	creature	...
...	impetuous	culture	

Note: (1) **t** before **u** in other words: e.g. 'bi**t**umen', 'congra**t**ulate', 'for**t**unate'. (2) **te** in 'pas**te**urized' and 'righ**te**ous'.

Final

/tʃ/ is commonly spelled **ch**, usually after two vowel letters or a consonant letter:

approa**ch**	pea**ch**	ben**ch**	mar**ch**
bea**ch**	prea**ch**	bir**ch**	per**ch**
bee**ch**	rea**ch**	bran**ch**	pin**ch**
brea**ch**	scree**ch**	bun**ch**	por**ch**
broo**ch**	slou**ch**	chur**ch**	pun**ch**
coa**ch**	spee**ch**	crun**ch**	quen**ch**
cou**ch**	tea**ch**	Fren**ch**	ran**ch**
crou**ch**	tou**ch**	in**ch**	resear**ch**
debau**ch**	vou**ch**	laun**ch**	sear**ch**
ea**ch**	...	lun**ch**	tor**ch**
moo**ch**	ar**ch**	lyn**ch**	...

/tʃ/ is usually spelled **tch** after a short vowel:

ba**tch**	e**tch**	no**tch**	swi**tch**
bi**tch**	fe**tch**	pa**tch**	tha**tch**
ca**tch**	ha**tch**	pi**tch**	twi**tch**
clu**tch**	hi**tch**	scra**tch**	ve**tch**
cru**tch**	hu**tch**	ske**tch**	wa**tch**
despa**tch**	i**tch**	sna**tch**	wi**tch**
dispa**tch**	ke**tch**	sti**tch**	wre**tch**
di**tch**	ma**tch**	stre**tch**	...

Note: (1) **ch** after a short vowel in 'atta**ch**', 'deta**ch**', and 'ri**ch**'; in the grammatical words 'mu**ch**', 'su**ch**', and 'whi**ch**'; and in the unstressed syllable in 'ostri**ch**', 'sandwi**ch**', and 'spina**ch**'. (2) In GenAm, **che** in 'avalan**che**' and 'ni**che**'.

Inflection and word formation

For words ending in /tʃ/, the plural form of nouns and third person singular present tense of verbs is formed with **es**:

e.g. bran**ch** – bran**ches**; ma**tch** – ma**tches**; rea**ch** – rea**ches**.

Pronunciation

Many speakers of English pronounce **tu** as /tʃuː/ in these words:

tuba	**tu**ition	**tu**mult	**tu**telage
tube	**tu**lip	**tu**na	**tu**tor
tubercular	**tu**lle	**tu**ne	**tu**torial
Tuesday	**tu**mour	**tu**nic	

/d/   do

In most words, this sound is spelled **d**. After a short vowel and before some Native endings it is spelled **dd**. After a long vowel at the end of a word it is spelled **de**. At the end of words, **ed** is common as a verb ending.

Initial

/**d**/ is usually spelled **d**:

day	**d**ecision	**d**ifferent	**d**own
deal	**d**evelopment	**d**o	**d**uring
death	**d**id	**d**oor	...

Middle

/**d**/ is usually spelled **d**:

a**d**equate	hun**d**red	mo**d**est	sche**d**ule
a**d**ult	inclu**d**ing	or**d**er	stu**d**ent
chil**d**ren	lea**d**er	pe**d**estal	to**d**ay
cre**d**it	me**d**icine	presi**d**ent	un**d**er
e**d**it	mo**d**erate	pro**d**uce	vi**d**eo
fe**d**eral	mo**d**ern	ra**d**io	...

/**d**/ is spelled **dd** in the pattern **add-** at the beginning of these words:

a**dd**	a**dd**er	a**dd**ition	a**dd**ress
a**dd**endum	a**dd**ict	a**dd**le	a**dd**uce

/**d**/ is spelled **dd** after a short vowel and before the endings **-ed, -en, -er, -est, -ie, -ing, -ish, -le,** and **-y**:

bu**dd**y	la**dd**er	pu**dd**ing	shu**dd**er
ca**dd**ie	mi**dd**le	re**dd**ish	su**dd**en
Da**dd**y	mu**dd**y	sa**dd**est	we**dd**ing
hi**dd**en	no**dd**ed	sa**dd**le	...

Note: (1) **dd** also in these words: 'Armage**dd**on', 'Bu**dd**ha', 'che**dd**ar', 'go**dd**ess', 'ha**dd**ock', 'o**dd**ity', 'pa**dd**ock', and 'ri**dd**ance'. (2) **dd** in compounds of words ending in **-d** and words beginning with **d-**: e.g. 'go**dd**amn', 'gran**dd**aughter', 'hea**dd**ress', 'mi**dd**ay'. (3) **d** (not **dd**) in 'body', 'consider', 'radish', and 'study'.

Final

/d/ is usually spelled **d**:

ai**d**	goo**d**	kin**d**	roa**d**
an**d**	groun**d**	lan**d**	roun**d**
aroun**d**	ha**d**	lea**d**	sai**d**
behin**d**	han**d**	le**d**	secon**d**
bloo**d**	har**d**	min**d**	thir**d**
chil**d**	hea**d**	nee**d**	thousan**d**
en**d**	hear**d**	ol**d**	tol**d**
fin**d**	hel**d**	perio**d**	worl**d**
foo**d**	hol**d**	rea**d**	woul**d**
Go**d**	hundre**d**	re**d**	...

/d/ is spelled **de** after a long vowel:

co**de**	inclu**de**	provi**de**	tra**de**
conce**de**	ma**de**	si**de**	...

Note: (1) **de** also in these words of French origin: 'ai**de**', 'avant-gar**de**', 'blon**de**', 'chara**de**', 'faca**de**', and 'promena**de**'. (2) **de** also in the English word 'ba**de**'.

/d/ is spelled **ed** in the past tense and past participle forms of regular verbs:

call**ed**	hurl**ed**	mann**ed**	turn**ed**
happen**ed**	kill**ed**	pull**ed**	...

Note: (1) **ed** also in adjectives formed from a regular verb or a noun: e.g. 'panell**ed**', 'schedul**ed**', 'skill**ed**', 'troubl**ed**', 'unparallel**ed**', and 'wall**ed**'. (2) **dd** in 'a**dd**' and 'o**dd**' because of the 'Three letter rule'. (3) silent l before **d** in the modal auxiliary verbs 'coul**d**', 'shoul**d**', and 'woul**d**'.

Inflection and word formation

Silent final **e** is dropped before suffixes that begin with a vowel:

e.g. provi**de** – provi**d**ing – provi**d**ed; ti**de** – ti**d**al.

Final **d** is doubled after a short vowel and before suffixes that begin with a vowel:

e.g. bi**d** – bi**dd**able; no**d** – no**dd**ed.

Note: Before some Classical endings which function as suffixes, such as **-ic**, **-ify** and **-ity**, final **d** does not double: e.g. 'aci**d** – aci**d**ic', 'liqui**d** – liqui**d**ity', and 'soli**d** – soli**d**ify'.

The 24 main consonant sounds

/f/	for

In most words, this sound is spelled **f**. It is spelled **ff** after a short vowel before some Native endings or at the end of a word, and also in some Classical patterns. After a long vowel at the end of a word, it is spelled **fe**. It is spelled **ph** in some words of Greek origin.

Initial

/f/ is usually spelled **f**:

face	few	foreign	free
family	five	former	from
far	food	found	full
feel	for	four	...

/f/ is spelled **ph** in most words of Greek origin:

phantom	phenomenon	phone	physical
pharmaceutical	philosophy	photograph	physiological
phase	phobia	phrase	...

Note: also in '**ph**ew' and '**ph**oney', which are not of Greek origin.

Middle

/f/ is usually spelled **f**:

afraid	defeat	professor	scientific
after	defence	profit	significance
before	deficiently	refer	surface
benefit	deficit	reference	terrific
café	definite	reform	theft
careful	often	refugee	uniform
conference	prefer	refuse	...

/f/ is spelled **ff** in the patterns **aff-**, **diff-**, **eff-**, **off-**, and **suff-** at the beginning of words:

affair	differ	efficient	office
affect	different	effigy	official
affiliated	difficult	effluent	...
affirmative	diffident	effort	suffer
afflict	diffuse	effusive	sufficient
affluent	...	...	suffocate
afford	effect	offensive	suffused
...	efficacy	offer	...

/f/ is spelled **ff** after a short vowel and before the endings **-ed**, **-er**, **-est**, **-ing**, **-ish**, **-le**, and **-y**:

baffle	jiffy	raffle	stiffen
buffer	muffle	reshuffle	stuffed
chuffed	offer	ruffle	stuffy
coffer	offing	scruffy	suffer
differ	proffer	scuffle	truffle
duffle	puffed	sniffed	...

/f/ is also spelled **ff** in these words:

boffin	chiffon	graffiti	ruffian
buffalo	coffee	kaffir	saffron
buffet	coiffeur	muffin	scaffold
buffoon	daffodil	offal	soufflé
caffeine	duffel	paraffin	toffee
chauffeur	giraffe	puffin	traffic

/f/ is spelled **ph** in these words of Greek origin:

alpha	catastrophic	geography	saxophone
alphabet	cellophane	graphic	schizophrenia
amorphous	cipher	graphite	siphon
amphetamines	claustrophobic	haemophiliac	sophisticated
amphibious	decipher	lymphocytes	sophomore
amphitheatre	diaphragm	metamorphosis	sphere
aphrodisiac	dolphin	metaphor	sphinx
apocryphal	elephant	morphine	sulphur
asphalt	emphasis	orphan	symphony
atmosphere	emphatic	pamphlet	syphilis
atrophy	emphysema	paraphernalia	telephone
biography	endorphins	periphery	triumphant
blasphemy	ephemeral	phosphate	trophy
cacophony	epiphany	phosphorus	typhoid
camphor	euphemism	photographer	typhoon
catastrophe	euphoria	prophet	unsophisticated

Note: (1) Other typical Greek features occur in many of these words: e.g. initial **eu**, non-final **y**, and silent **g**. (2) **pph** in 'sapphire'.

/f/ is spelled **gh** in words formed from 'cough', 'laugh', 'rough', and 'tough':

coughing	laughter	roughness	toughness
laughing	roughly	toughen	...

Final

/f/ is spelled **f** after a vowel digraph, or after **l** or **r**:

aloof	loaf	barf	scarf
beef	mischief	behalf	self
brief	proof	bookshelf	serf
chief	reef	calf	shelf
deaf	relief	dwarf	surf
grief	roof	elf	turf
handkerchief	sheaf	golf	wharf
hoof	spoof	gulf	wolf
leaf	...	half	...

Note: (1) It does not matter whether the **l** or **r** is pronounced or silent. (2) **f** after **m** in 'bumf'.

/f/ is spelled **ff** after a short vowel:

bailiff	duff	pontiff	snuff
bluff	fluff	puff	stiff
buff	gaff	ruff	stuff
chaff	gruff	scoff	tariff
cliff	midriff	sheriff	tiff
cuff	off	skiff	whiff
dandruff	plaintiff	sniff	...

Note: (1) **f**, **fe**, or **ffe** in 'carafe', 'chef', 'clef', and 'gaffe', which are of French origin. (2) **f** in the grammatical word 'if' and the abbreviation 'ref'.

/f/ is spelled **fe** after a long vowel:

chafe	life	safe	wife
knife	rife	strafe	...

Note: (1) **ffe** in 'giraffe', which is of Foreign origin. (2) **f** in 'aperitif', 'calif' (usually 'cali**ph**'), 'massif', and 'motif', which are of French origin.

/f/ is spelled **ph** in these words of Greek origin:

cenota**ph**	gra**ph**	lym**ph**	trium**ph**
epita**ph**	hierogly**ph**	nym**ph**	

Note: There are many compounds ending in '-gra**ph**': e.g. 'paragra**ph**', 'photogra**ph**', and 'telegra**ph**'.

/f/ is spelled **gh** in these words:

cou**gh**	lau**gh**	tou**gh**
enou**gh**	rou**gh**	

Inflection and word formation

When these words ending in **-f** or **-fe** are nouns, they have irregular plural forms ending in **-ves**:

calf – cal**ves**; elf – el**ves**; half – hal**ves**; hoof – hoo**ves**; knife – kni**ves**; leaf – lea**ves**; life – li**ves**; loaf – loa**ves**; scarf – scar**ves**; self – sel**ves**; sheaf – shea**ves**; shelf – shel**ves**; thief – thie**ves**; wife – wi**ves**; wolf – wol**ves**.

When these words are verbs, they have regular third person singular present tense forms ending in **-s**:

hoofs	leafs	wolfs
knifes	loafs	

In all other cases, final silent **e** is dropped before a suffix that begins with a vowel:

chaf**ed**   chaf**er**   knif**ing**   ...

Final **f** is doubled after a short vowel before a suffix that begins with a vowel:

iffy   reffed   ...

The 24 main consonant sounds

/g/	go

In most words, this sound is spelled **g**. It is spelled **gg** after a short vowel and before some Native endings. The other patterns are fairly rare. The common combination /**gz**/ is usually spelled **x** in the middle of a word.

Initial

/g/ is usually spelled **g**:

game	give	good	group
garden	glass	government	gulf
get	go	great	...

/g/ is sometimes spelled **gu**:

guarantee	**gu**ess	**gu**ile	**gu**ise
guard	**gu**est	**gu**illotine	**gu**itar
guardian	**gu**ide	**gu**ilty	**gu**y
guerrilla	**gu**ild	**gu**inea	...

/g/ is spelled **gh** in these words:

ghastly	ghetto	ghostly	ghoulish
gherkin	ghost	ghoul	

Middle

/g/ is usually spelled **g**:

again	figure	magazine	sugar
ago	language	programme	together
began	legal	single	...

Note: (1) **gh** in 'burgher' and 'spaghetti'. (2) **gu** in 'languor'.

/g/ is spelled **gg** in the pattern **agg-** at the beginning of these words:

agglomeration	aggravate	aggression	aggrieved
aggrandizement	aggregate	aggressive	aggro

/g/ is spelled **gg** after a short vowel and before the endings **-ed**, **-er**, **-est**, **-et**, **-ing**, **-ish**, **-le**, or **-y**:

baggy	digging	nugget	struggle
bigger	dragged	sluggish	...

/g/ is spelled **gg** after a short vowel and before another vowel in these words:

ba**gg**age	fa**gg**ot	lu**gg**age	tobo**gg**an
be**gg**ar	ha**gg**ard	ma**gg**ot	wa**gg**on
bra**gg**art	ha**gg**is	no**gg**in	
do**gg**erel	la**gg**ard	re**gg**ae	

/g/ often occurs in the combination /**gz**/, which is usually spelled **x**:

auxiliary	example	exhilarate	exotic
coexist	exasperate	exhort	exuberance
exacerbate	executive	exile	exude
exact	exempt	exist	exult
exaggerate	exert	exit	inexact
exalt	exhaust	exonerate	luxurious
exam	exhibit	exorbitant	...

Final

/g/ is usually spelled **g**:

ago**g**	do**g**	icebe**g**	sa**g**
ba**g**	dra**g**	ju**g**	shru**g**
be**g**	du**g**	le**g**	slo**g**
bi**g**	fi**g**	nutme**g**	snu**g**
bla**g**	flo**g**	pi**g**	thu**g**
bu**g**	fo**g**	plu**g**	wi**g**
cra**g**	fro**g**	ra**g**	zigza**g**
di**g**	hu**g**	ru**g**	...

Note: **gg** in 'e**gg**'.

/g/ is spelled **gue** after a long vowel in these words:

bro**gue**	fu**gue**	mor**gue**	va**gue**
collea**gue**	intri**gue**	pla**gue**	vo**gue**
fati**gue**	lea**gue**	ro**gue**	

Note: **ge** in 'rene**ge**'.

/g/ is spelled **gue** after short **o** in these words:

analo**gue**	dialo**gue**	pedago**gue**	travelo**gue**
catalo**gue**	epilo**gue**	prolo**gue**	
demago**gue**	monolo**gue**	synago**gue**	

Note: In American English, **g** is the usual spelling in 'analog' and 'catalog'.

/g/ in the combination /gz/ is usually spelled **gs**:

ba**gs**	dru**gs**	le**gs**	ru**gs**
do**gs**	e**ggs**	lo**gs**	...

Note: /gz/ is spelled **gues** in forms derived from words ending in **-gue**, e.g. 'catalo**gues**', 'collea**gues**', and 'pla**gues**'.

Inflection and word formation

Final silent **e** is dropped before suffixes and inflections that begin with a vowel:

e.g. demagogue – demagog**ery**; fatigu**e** – fatigu**ed**; plagu**e** – plagu**ing**.

Note: **u** is also dropped in 'demago**gic**' and 'pedago**gic**'.

Final **g** is doubled after a short vowel, before suffixes and inflections that begin with a vowel:

e.g. bi**g** – bi**gg**er – bi**gg**ish – bi**gg**est; dru**g** – dru**gg**ing – dru**gg**ed – dru**gg**ies.

Note: Final **g** in an unstressed syllable is not doubled: e.g. 'cataloging', 'cataloged' in American English.

/h/ have

This sound is nearly always spelled **h**, except for a few words in which it is spelled **wh**.

Initial

/h/ is usually spelled **h**:

had	head	here	house
half	health	high	how
hand	held	him	however
hard	help	himself	humble
have	her	his	hundred
he	herb	home	...

Note: **j** in these words of Foreign origin: 'jojoba' and 'junta'.

/h/ is spelled **wh** in these words:

who	wholesale	whooping cough
whoever	wholesome	whore
whole	whom	whose

Note: Most other words beginning **wh**-, such as 'what', 'when', 'whisper', and 'why', are pronounced /w/ in RP, but /hw/ by some people, including many GenAm speakers. See the entry for /w/ in this section.

Middle

/h/ is usually spelled **h**:

ahead	apprehend	behind	perhaps
alcohol	behaviour	comprehensive	...

Note: **j** in 'jojoba'.

Final

/h/ does not occur at the end of English words.

Pronunciation

Many American speakers do not pronounce the **h** in 'humble' and 'herb'.

The 24 main consonant sounds

/dʒ/	just

This sound is commonly spelled **j** at the beginning of a word, but in the middle of a word it is more frequently spelled **g**, or **dg** after a short vowel. **g** is usually followed by **e**, **i**, or **y**.

Initial

/dʒ/ is usually spelled **j** before **a**, **o**, and **u**:

jacket	jockey	judge	junk
jail	join	juice	jury
jazz	joke	July	just
job	journal	jump	...

Note: **g** before **a** in '**gaol**'.

/dʒ/ is usually spelled **g** before **e**, **i**, and **y**:

gender	gentle	giant	gypsum
gene	genuine	gin	gypsy
general	geography	ginger	gyrate
genetic	gesture	gym	...

/dʒ/ is spelled **j** before **e** or **i** in these words:

jealous	jerk	jettison	jihad
jeans	jerkin	jewel	jilt
jeep	jerry-built	Jewish	jingle
jeer	jersey	jib	jingoism
jejune	jest	jibe	jinx
jelly	Jesus	jig	jittery
jemmy	jet	jiggle	jive
jeopardy	jetsam	jigsaw	

Note: '**jibe**' can also be spelled '**gibe**'.

Middle

/dʒ/ is usually spelled **g**:

a**g**ency	fra**g**ile	ori**g**inal	strate**g**ic
a**g**enda	**g**inger	passen**g**er	strate**g**y
an**g**el	ima**g**ine	refri**g**erator	sur**g**eon
dan**g**er	intelli**g**ence	refu**g**ee	sur**g**ery
dan**g**erous	le**g**end	re**g**ime	tra**g**edy
di**g**estion	le**g**islation	re**g**ion	tra**g**ic
di**g**ital	lo**g**ical	re**g**ister	ur**g**ent
eli**g**ible	ma**g**ic	reli**g**ion	ve**g**etables
emer**g**ency	ma**g**istrates	ri**g**id	vir**g**in
en**g**ine	mar**g**in	ser**g**eant	...

Note: **gg** in 'exa**gg**erate', 'lo**gg**ia', 'su**gg**est', and 've**gg**ie'.

/dʒ/ is spelled **dg** after a short vowel in these words:

ba**dg**er	co**dg**er	fi**dg**et	mi**dg**et
blu**dg**eon	cu**dg**el	ga**dg**et	pi**dg**in
bri**dg**es	do**dg**em	ju**dg**ement	pu**dg**y
bu**dg**erigar	do**dg**er	ke**dg**eree	squi**dg**y
bu**dg**et	dru**dg**ery	lo**dg**er	sto**dg**y
bu**dg**ie	du**dg**eon	lo**dg**ings	

/dʒ/ is spelled **j** in the Classical patterns **abj-, adj-, conj-, ej-, inj-, obj-, perj-, proj-, rej-,** and **subj-** at the beginning of words:

ab**j**ect	con**j**unction	ob**j**ect	re**j**oin
ab**j**ure	e**j**aculation	per**j**ury	re**j**uvenate
ad**j**acent	e**j**ect	pro**j**ect	sub**j**ect
ad**j**ust	in**j**ect	re**j**ect	sub**j**ugate
con**j**ecture	in**j**ure	re**j**oice	...

Note: but **ing** in '**ing**enious', '**ing**enuity', '**ing**enuous', and '**ing**est'.

/dʒ/ is spelled **j** in these words:

a**j**ar	en**j**oy	ma**j**or	pe**j**orative
ban**j**o	hi**j**ack	ma**j**ority	py**j**amas
ca**j**ole	inter**j**ection	mar**j**oram	so**j**ourn
en**j**oin	ma**j**estic	pa**j**amas	tra**j**ectory

Note: **j** in compounds in which the second word begins with **j**-: e.g. 'kill**j**oy', 'log**j**am', 'lumber**j**ack', 'over**j**oyed', and 'un**j**ust'.

/dʒ/ is spelled **d** before **u** in some words of Classical origin:

a**d**ulation	e**d**ucate	indivi**d**ual	proce**d**ure
ar**d**uous	frau**d**ulent	mo**d**ulate	resi**d**ual
cre**d**ulous	glan**d**ular	no**d**ule	un**d**ulate
deci**d**uous	gra**d**uate	pen**d**ulum	...

Final

/dʒ/ is usually spelled **ge**:

age	emerge	page	siege
arrange	huge	plunge	stage
challenge	indulge	range	urge
change	large	refuge	wage
charge	orange	revenge	...

/dʒ/ is spelled **dge** after a short vowel:

badge	edge	ledge	ridge
budge	fridge	lodge	wedge
dodge	judge	midge	...

Note: but not in 'allege' and 'veg'.

When /dʒ/ occurs in unstressed /ɪdʒ/, it is usually spelled **age**:

advantage	image	manage	village
damage	language	package	...

Note: There are several rarer patterns for unstressed /ɪdʒ/: **edge** in 'knowledge'; **ege** in 'college', 'privilege', and 'sacrilege'; **iage** in 'marriage' and 'carriage'; **idge** in 'cartridge', 'partridge', and 'porridge'; and **ige** in 'vestige'.

/dʒ/ is not spelled **j** at the end of words, except in words of Foreign origin such as 'raj'.

Inflection and word formation

Final silent **e** is only dropped before suffixes which begin with **e** or **i**:

e.g. change – changed – changing – changeable; knowledge – knowledgeable.

Note: (1) 'aging' can also be spelled 'ageing'. (2) **e** is not dropped in 'singeing' and 'swingeing' (to avoid confusion with 'singing' and 'swinging'). (3) **e** can be dropped before **ment** in 'abridgment', 'acknowledgment', and 'judgment'.

Pronunciation

Many speakers of English pronounce **d** as /dʒ/ in these words:

deuce	due	dune	duration
dew	duel	duo	duress
dual	duet	duplicate	during
dubious	duly	durable	duty

/l/   like

In most words, this sound is spelled **l**, but **ll** is much more common than other double letters, because it occurs not only after short vowels, but also after long vowels and 'schwa' (/ə/).

Initial

/l/ is usually spelled **l**:

last	like	long	luck
left	little	look	...

Note: **ll** only in 'llama'.

Middle

/l/ is usually spelled **l**:

already	early	old	problem
believe	family	only	public
black	help	place	told
child	include	police	world
clear	military	political	...

/l/ is spelled **ll** in the Classical patterns **all-**, **coll-**, and **ill-** at the beginning of words:

a**ll**ege	a**ll**y	co**ll**ide	i**ll**egitimate
a**ll**ergy	...	co**ll**iery	i**ll**icit
a**ll**iance	co**ll**aborate	co**ll**oquial	i**ll**ness
a**ll**ocate	co**ll**ar	co**ll**usion	i**ll**uminate
a**ll**ow	co**ll**ect	...	i**ll**usion
a**ll**ure	co**ll**ege	i**ll**egal	...

/l/ is spelled **ll** after a short vowel before the endings **-ar**, **-ed**, **-en**, **-er**, **-et**, **-ing**, **-ow**, and **-y**:

be**ll**y	fo**ll**ow	po**ll**en	unwi**ll**ing
bu**ll**et	jo**ll**y	ski**ll**ed	ye**ll**ow
ce**ll**ar	mi**ll**er	te**ll**ing	...

Note: but single **l** after a short vowel before **ar** in the pattern **-ular** at the end of many adjectives: e.g. 'circ**ular**', 'irreg**ular**', 'partic**ular**', 'pop**ular**', 'reg**ular**', and 'sing**ular**'.

/l/ is spelled **ll** after 'schwa' (/ə/) before the endings **-ed**, **-er**, **-ing**, **-or**, and **-y**:

chance**ll**or	jewe**ll**er	specifica**ll**y
counse**ll**ing	signa**ll**ed	...

Note: single **l** in the American spelling of 'counseling', 'jeweler', and 'signaled'.

/l/ is also spelled **ll** in these words:

artillery	challenge	medallist	tonsillitis
ballad	excellent	million	tranquillity
ballistic	fallacy	pallid	umbrella
balloon	gallery	panellist	valley
billion	gallon	parallel	vanilla
brilliant	gallop	pollution	villa
bulletin	guerrilla	rebellious	village
callous	hallucination	satellite	volley
cancellation	intellectual	scallop	wholly
caterpillar	intelligent	surveillance	woollen
cellular	marvellous	syllable	woolly

Final

/l/ is usually spelled **l**:

control	hospital	oil	school
feel	level	powerful	...

/l/ is spelled **ll** after a short vowel in words of one syllable:

bill	pull	shall	well
dull	sell	still	...

/l/ is spelled **ll** after the long vowel sounds /ɔ:/ spelled **a**, and /oʊ/ spelled **o**, in these words of one syllable:

all	hall	tall	poll
ball	pall	thrall	roll
call	small	wall	scroll
fall	squall	...	stroll
gall	stall	droll	toll

Note: (1) /l/ is usually spelled l in words of more than one syllable. But some words are spelled l in British English and ll in American English: e.g. 'appal – appall', 'distil – distill', 'enrol – enroll', and 'fulfil – fulfill'. (2) ll in compounds ending in a common -ll word: e.g. 'football', 'goodwill', 'recall', and 'waterfall'. (3) But compounds of 'full' end in '-ful': e.g. 'armful', 'careful', 'doubtful', 'grateful', 'spoonful', and 'useful'.

/l/ is usually spelled **le** after a long vowel:

file	rule	smile	while
hole	scale	style	...

/l/ is spelled **al**, **el**, **il**, **le**, **ol**, or **ul** when it is pronounced as a separate syllable:

loc**al**	...	midd**le**	cons**ul**
nation**al**	civ**il**	...	mog**ul**
...	penc**il**	id**ol**	powerf**ul**
chann**el**	...	petr**ol**	successf**ul**
lab**el**	ab**le**	...	...

For more details, see the entry at 2.2.4: **-al**, **-el**, **-il**, **-le**, **-ol**, or **-ul**?

/l/ in GenAm is also spelled **ile** when it is pronounced as a separate syllable:

frag**ile**	host**ile**	ster**ile**	versat**ile**
fut**ile**	miss**ile**	text**ile**	...

Inflection and word formation

Final silent **e** is dropped before suffixes that begin with a vowel:

e.g. styl**e** – styl**ing** – styl**ish** – styl**istic**.

Final **l** is doubled after a short vowel, after /ɔː/ spelled **a**, or after /oʊ/, before suffixes that begin with a vowel:

e.g. contr**ol** – contr**olling** – contr**olled** – contr**ollable**.

Final **l** becomes **ll** when **ly** is added:

e.g. cool + ly = coo**lly**.

Final **l** is doubled after 'schwa' (/ə/) before the suffixes **-ed**, **-er**, **-ing**, and **-or** in British spelling, but not in American spelling:

e.g. British: counsel – counse**lled** – counse**lling** – counse**llor**; travel – trave**lled** – trave**lling** – trave**ller**; American: counsel – counse**led** – counse**ling** – counse**lor**; travel – trave**led** – trave**ling** – trave**ler**.

Note: 'parall**el**ed' is correct in both British and American spelling.

Final **ll** becomes **l** in many compounds of words that end in **ll**:

e.g. a**ll** – a**l**most, a**l**ready, a**l**though, a**l**ways; be**ll** – be**l**fry; chi**ll** – chi**l**blain; fu**ll** – fu**l**some, successfu**l**; insta**ll** – insta**l**ment; we**ll** – we**l**come, we**l**fare.

Note: (1) This sometimes happens to both parts of a compound: 'skill' and 'full' in 'skilful'; and 'will' and 'full' in 'wilful'. (2) In British spelling, also 'full' and 'fill' in 'fulfil', but only 'full' in the American spelling: 'fulfill'. (3) Final **ll** becomes **l** when **-ly** is added: e.g. 'chill – chilly' and 'smell – smelly'.

The 24 main consonant sounds

| /m/ | more |

In most words, this sound is spelled **m**. After a short vowel before some Native endings, it is spelled **mm**. It is spelled **me** after a long vowel at the end of a word, and in the very common words 'come' and 'some'. The other spelling patterns are fairly rare.

Initial

/m/ is usually spelled **m**:

major	market	million	much
man	may	more	must
many	might	most	...

Middle

/m/ is usually spelled **m**:

almost	demand	important	small
among	economic	limit	women
company	family	number	...

/m/ is spelled **mm** in the Classical patterns **amm-**, **comm-**, **imm-**, and **summ-**, at the beginning of words:

ammo	common	immense	summary
ammonia	communist	immigration	summer
ammunition	community	immortal	summit
...	...	immune	summon
committee	immediate	...	...

Note: not in all words of Classical origin: e.g. 'comet', 'comic', 'image', and 'imitate'.

/m/ is spelled **mm** after a short vowel before the endings **-ed**, **-er**, **-ing**, and **-y**:

| dummy | mummy | summer | trimmed |
| hammer | slammed | swimming | ... |

/m/ is spelled **mm** before a vowel in these words:

cummerbund	inflammable	plummet	scrimmage
flummox	mammal	pommel	symmetry
gimmick	mammary	pummel	trammel
grammar	mammoth	rummage	

/m/ is spelled **lm**, **mb**, or **mn** in these words:

144

almond	...	numbness	condemning
alms	bombshell	plumber	
salmon	combed	...	

Note: **thm** in 'as**thm**a', with silent **th**.

Final

/m/ is usually spelled **m**:

arm	freedom	problem	team
film	from	room	term
form	him	seem	...

/m/ is spelled **me** after a long vowel:

assume	home	same	time
extreme	prime	syndrome	volume
game	rhyme	theme	...

/m/ is spelled **me** in 'co**me**', 'so**me**', and compound words that end in **-come** and **-some**:

become	welcome	cumbersome	troublesome
income	...	gruesome	wholesome
overcome	awesome	handsome	...

Note: **mme** in 'gra**mme**' and 'progra**mme**' ('progr**am**' in American English).

/m/ is spelled **gm**, **lm**, **mb**, or **mn** in these words:

diaphragm	...	lamb	column
paradigm	aplomb	limb	condemn
phlegm	bomb	plumb	damn
...	climb	succumb	hymn
balm	comb	thumb	solemn
palm	dumb	tomb	
psalm	honeycomb	womb	
qualm	jamb	...	

Inflection and word formation

Final silent **e** is dropped before a suffix beginning with a vowel:

e.g. extreme – extre**m**ist; programme – program**m**able; time – ti**m**ing.

Final **-m** is doubled after a short vowel before a suffix beginning with a vowel:

e.g. hum – hu**mm**able; swim – swi**mm**ing.

Note: but not before suffixes which change the pronunciation of the base word: e.g. 'atom – ato**m**ic', and 'synonym – synony**m**ous'.

The 24 main consonant sounds

/n/	**n**ot

In most words this sound is spelled **n**. After a short vowel before some Native endings it is spelled **nn**. It is spelled **ne** at the end of a word after a long vowel, and in the very common words 'do**ne**', 'go**ne**', 'no**ne**', and 'o**ne**'. The other spelling patterns are fairly rare, and usually involve silent letters, as in **gn** and **kn**.

Initial

/n/ is usually spelled **n**:

nation	new	no	now
need	next	north	number
never	night	nothing	...

/n/ is spelled **gn** or **kn** in these words:

gnarled	knacker	knew	knobbly
gnash	knapsack	knick-knacks	knock
gnat	knave	knickers	knoll
gnaw	knavery	knife	knot
gnome	knead	knight	knotty
gnomic	knee	knighthood	know
gnu	kneel	knit	knowledge
...	knell	knives	known
knack	knelt	knob	knuckle

Note: (1) **mn** in '**mn**emonic'. (2) **pn** in '**pn**eumatic' and '**pn**eumonia'.

Middle

/n/ is usually spelled **n**:

any	minister	pound	united
country	money	think	want
general	only	under	...

Note: (1) **dne** in 'We**dne**sday'. (2) **nd** in some compound words: e.g. 'gra**nd**child' and 'ha**nd**kerchief'.

/n/ is spelled **nn** in the Classical patterns **ann-**, **conn-**, and **inn-** at the beginning of words:

annexe	...	connotation	innocent
announce	connect	...	innovation
annoy	connoisseur	innate	...

Note: (1) These words have the pattern **ann** or **enn** because they are derived from the Latin word *annus* meaning 'year': '**ann**al', '**ann**iversary', '**ann**ual', 'annuity', 'biennial', 'centennial', 'millennium', and 'perennial'. (2) Not all words of Classical origin have these patterns: e.g. 'analysis', 'anatomy', 'another', 'coniferous', 'conundrum', 'conurbation', 'inevitable', and 'initial'.

/n/ is spelled **nn** after a short vowel and before the endings **-ed**, **-el**, **-er**, **-ing**, and **-y**:

banned	channel	funny	planned
beginning	cunning	manner	tunnel
canny	dinner	penny	...

Note: but not in 'any', 'many', and 'panel'.

/n/ is also spelled **nn** in these words:

antenna	ennoble	minnow	savannah
bandanna	ennui	nunnery	sonnet
bannister	gonna	openness	spinney
belladonna	henna	pannier	tannin
bonnet	legionnaire	pennant	tennis
cannabis	madonna	pinnacle	tinnitus
cannibal	manna	punnet	tonnage
cannon	mannequin	reconnaissance	unnecessary
cinnamon	mayonnaise	rennet	winnow

Final

/n/ is usually spelled **n**:

been	man	often	when
down	mean	seen	won
in	million	taken	...

Note: **nn** in 'inn'.

/n/ is spelled **ne** after a long vowel:

airline	fortune	phone	tone
alone	line	plane	whine
decline	mine	scene	wine
fine	nine	stone	...

Note: (1) also **ne** in these words ending in **-one**: 'done', 'gone', 'none', and 'one' (and their compounds: e.g. 'bygone', 'nonetheless', 'someone', and 'undone'). (2) also **ne** in the common ending **-ine**: e.g. 'determine', 'engine', 'genuine', 'imagine', 'machine', 'magazine', 'medicine', and 'routine'. (3) **gne** in 'champagne', **ne** in 'nocturne', and **nne** in 'comedienne' and 'doyenne', which are all of French origin.

/n/ is spelled **gn** in these words:

ali**gn**	consi**gn**	forei**gn**	resi**gn**
assi**gn**	desi**gn**	impu**gn**	si**gn**
beni**gn**	ensi**gn**	mali**gn**	soverei**gn**
campai**gn**	fei**gn**	rei**gn**	

Inflection and word formation

Final silent **e** is dropped before suffixes beginning with a vowel:

e.g. line – lin**ing**; phone – phon**ed**; sane – san**ity**; tone – ton**ic**.

Final **n** is doubled before common Native suffixes after a short vowel:

e.g. don – do**nn**ish; thin – thi**nn**est; win – wi**nn**er.

Note: Final **n** is not doubled before Classical endings which can function as suffixes, such as **-ic**, **-ify** and **-ity**: e.g. 'hum**an** – huma**nity**', 'org**an** – orga**nic**', and 'pers**on** – perso**nify**'. Note also that the original words have 'schwa' (/ə/), and not a short vowel, before final **n**.

/ŋ/ sing

This sound is usually spelled **n** in the middle of words and **ng** at the end of words.

Initial

/ŋ/ does not occur at the beginning of English words.

Middle

/ŋ/ occurs before /k/ or /g/ in stressed syllables, and is spelled **n** before **c**, **g**, or **k**:

concrete	...	single	bunker
function	congress	...	monkey
include	England	ankle	zonked
uncle	longer	blanket	...

Final

/ŋ/ is spelled **ng**:

along	during	sing	throng
among	king	strong	young
bring	long	thing	...

Note: **ng** is very common as part of the -**ing** form of verbs: e.g. 'be**ing**', 'go**ing**', 'hav**ing**', and 'tak**ing**'.

Inflection and word formation

When suffixes are added to words ending in -**ng**, the **g** usually remains silent:

e.g. bri**ng**ing (/ˈbrɪŋɪŋ/), lo**ng**ing, si**ng**er.

Note: but with adjectives ending in -**ng**, the **g** usually becomes pronounced when suffixes are added: e.g. 'lo**ng**er' (/ˈlɒŋɡəʳ/), 'lo**ng**est', 'stro**ng**er', 'stro**ng**est', 'you**ng**er', and 'you**ng**est'.

The 24 main consonant sounds

/p/	put

In most words, this sound is spelled **p**. It is spelled **pp** after a short vowel before some Native endings, and **pe** after a long vowel at the end of a word.

Initial

/**p**/ is usually spelled **p**:

party	**p**oint	**p**ower	**p**ublic
past	**p**olice	**p**resent	**p**ump
people	**p**olitical	**p**resident	**p**ut
place	**p**ound	**p**roblem	...

Middle

/**p**/ is usually spelled **p**:

ca**p**ital	Euro**p**ean	reci**p**e	Se**p**tember
de**p**artment	inde**p**endent	re**p**ort	...

/**p**/ is spelled **pp** in the Classical patterns **app-**, **opp-**, and **supp-** at the beginning of words:

a**pp**ear	...	o**pp**osition	su**pp**ort
a**pp**ly	o**pp**onent	...	su**pp**ose
a**pp**roach	o**pp**ortunity	su**pp**ly	...

/**p**/ is spelled **pp** after a short vowel before the endings **-ed**, **-er**, **-ing**, **-le**, and **-y**:

a**pp**le	kidna**pp**ed	slo**pp**y	tra**pp**ing
cri**pp**le	pe**pp**er	to**pp**ed	u**pp**er
ha**pp**y	sho**pp**ing	tra**pp**ed	...

/**p**/ is also spelled **pp** in these words:

ca**pp**uccino	hi**pp**o	sni**pp**et	u**pp**ity
co**pp**ice	pu**pp**et	sto**pp**age	worshi**pp**ing
fli**pp**ant	ra**pp**ort	tu**pp**ence	ze**pp**elin
ha**pp**en	sli**pp**age	unsto**pp**able	

Final

/**p**/ is usually spelled **p**:

cam**p**	grou**p**	shar**p**	to**p**
championshi**p**	hel**p**	sho**p**	tri**p**
dee**p**	kee**p**	slee**p**	u**p**
develo**p**	relationshi**p**	ste**p**	...

/p/ is spelled **pe** after a long vowel:

archety**pe**	esca**pe**	ra**pe**	telesco**pe**
co**pe**	gra**pe**	ri**pe**	ty**pe**
do**pe**	ho**pe**	sha**pe**	wi**pe**
envelo**pe**	pi**pe**	ta**pe**	...

Note: (1) also **pe** in 'cre**pe**', 'escalo**pe**', 'Euro**pe**', 'hy**pe**', and 'trou**pe**'. (2) **ppe** in 'ste**ppe**'.

Inflection and word formation

Final silent **e** is dropped before suffixes beginning with a vowel:

e.g. hope – hop**ing**; telescope – telescop**ic**; troupe – troup**er**; type – typ**ist**.

Final **p** is doubled after a short vowel before suffixes beginning with a vowel:

dro**pp**ed	handica**pp**ed	worshi**pp**ed
sto**pp**age	u**pp**ity	...

Note: (1) But **p** in 'gossi**p**ing' and 'gossi**p**ed'. (2) In American English, **p** in 'worshi**p**ing' and 'worshi**p**ed'. (3) After 'schwa' (/ə/), as in 'develo**p**ing', **p** is not doubled. (4) Before Classical endings such as **-ic** and **-ify**, which can function as suffixes, **p** is not doubled: e.g. 'microscope – microscop**ic**' and 'type – typ**ify**'. Note also that the original words do not have short vowels.

The 24 main consonant sounds

/r/	run

In most words, this sound is spelled **r**. It is spelled **rr** in a large number of Classical spelling patterns, but otherwise **rr** after a short vowel is very restricted in use.

Initial

/r/ is usually spelled **r**:

radio	reason	rest	round
rather	recent	result	royal
read	record	right	rumour
real	reports	role	run
really	research	room	...

/r/ is spelled **rh** in these words, which are mostly of Greek origin:

rhapsody	rheumatic	rhino	rhubarb
rhesus	rheumatism	rhinoceros	rhyme
rhetoric	rhinestone	rhododendron	rhythm

Note: There are other typical Greek features in these words: e.g. **y** in 'rhythm' and 'rhyme', and **eu** in 'rheumatic'.

/r/ is spelled **wr** in these words:

wraith	wreck	wretched	writhe
wrangle	wreckage	wriggle	written
wrap	wren	wring	wrong
wrath	wrench	wrinkly	wrote
wreak	wrest	wrist	wrought
wreath	wrestle	writ	wrung
wreathe	wretch	write	wry

Note: Many of these words have **homophones** which start with r: e.g. 'wrap – rap', 'wrest – rest', 'wring – ring', and 'write – right – rite'. But they usually have very different meanings and often belong to different word classes: compare **write** (verb – 'use a pen'), **right** (adjective and verb – 'correct', and noun – 'entitlement'), and **rite** (noun – 'sacred ceremony').

Middle

This section deals only with **r** before a vowel. See Section One: 'Silent consonants' for information about **silent r**.

/r/ run

/r/ is usually spelled r, after consonant sounds or vowel sounds:

already	three	different	period
control	through	during	security
country	...	European	series
free	American	experience	serious
from	area	foreign	several
prime	around	general	story
problem	average	interest	very
street	conference	military	...

/r/ is spelled rr after a short vowel or 'schwa' (/ə/) in these patterns:

arrange	raspberry	erratic	surrogate
array	strawberry	error	surrounded
arrears	...	...	...
arrest	correct	horrible	deterrent
arrive	correlate	horrific	terrace
arrogant	correspondent	horror	terrestrial
...	corridor	...	terrible
barracks	corrugate	interrogate	terrier
barrage	corrupt	interrupt	terrific
barrel	...	...	terrine
barren	currant	irrelevant	territory
barricade	currency	irresistible	terrorist
barrier	current	irresponsible	...
barrister	curriculum	irritate	warrant
embarrass	curry	...	warren
...	...	resurrection	warrior
blackberry	errand	surreal	...
cranberry	errata	surrender	

Note: (1) There are words that do not belong to these patterns and are spelled r: e.g. 'Arab', 'arena', 'arise', 'baron', 'bury', 'coral', 'coroner', 'erase', 'erect', 'erode', 'erotic', 'erudite', 'erupt', 'horizontal', 'horoscope', 'interact', and 'interest'. (2) rrh in 'cirrhosis', 'diarrhoea', 'gonorrhoea', 'haemorrhage', and 'haemorrhoids'.

/r/ is also spelled rr after a short vowel before the endings -ow or -y:

arrow	sparrow	ferry	parry
borrow	tomorrow	harry	sherry
farrow	...	lorry	sorry
marrow	carry	marry	worry
sorrow	curry	merry	...

Note: but r in 'very'.

/r/ is also spelled **rr** in these words:

carriage	harrier	parrot	torrent
carrot	herring	porridge	torrid
garrison	marriage	quarrel	
guerrilla	mirror	squirrel	

/r/ after /ɑː/ or /ɜː/ is also spelled **rr** before the endings **-ing** and **-y**:

recurring	stirring	...	starry
referring	warring	furry	...

Final

Final **r** is usually silent in RP but pronounced in GenAm and other **r accents**.

/s/ say

In most words, this sound is spelled **s**. It is often spelled **ss** after a short vowel. In words of Classical origin, it is often spelled **c** before **e**, **i**, or **y**.

Initial

/s/ is usually spelled **s**:

say	**s**et	**s**ome	**s**till
school	**s**kin	**s**outh	**s**uch
second	**s**mall	**s**pecial	**s**ystem
see	**s**o	**s**tate	...

/s/ is spelled **c** before **e**, **i**, or **y**, usually in words of Classical origin, and especially in the patterns **cel-**, **cell-**, **cent-**, **cert-**, **circ-**, **cit-**, **civ-**, **cy-**, and **cycl-** at the beginning of words:

celebrate	**cent**ral	**cit**adel	**cy**linder
celery	**cent**ury	**cit**e	**cy**mbals
celestial	...	**cit**izen	**cy**nical
celibate	**cert**ain	**cit**y	**cy**press
...	**cert**ificate	...	**cy**stic
cell	**cert**itude	**civ**ic	...
cellar	...	**civ**ilian	**cycl**e
cellular	**circ**le	**civ**ilization	**cycl**ical
cellulose	**circ**uit	...	**cycl**ist
...	**circ**ulate	**cy**anide	**cycl**one
cent	**circ**us	**cy**bernetics	...
centimetre	...	**cy**gnet	

/s/ is also spelled **c** in these words:

cease	**c**ensus	**c**ervical	**c**inder
ceiling	**c**eramic	**c**ider	**c**inema
cement	**c**eremony	**c**igarette	**c**issy

Note: **Cae** in '**Cae**sarian'.

/s/ is spelled **sc** in these words:

scenario	**sc**eptre	**sc**imitar	**sc**ion
scene	**sc**iatica	**sc**intilla	**sc**issors
scent	**sc**ience	**sc**intillating	**sc**ythe

/s/ is spelled **ps** in these words of Greek origin:

psalm	**ps**eud	**ps**ychiatrist	**ps**ychology
psephologist	**ps**yche	**ps**ychic	**ps**ychotic

Middle

Before a consonant:

/s/ is usually spelled **s**:

again**s**t	de**s**cribe	ho**s**pital	**s**ystem
an**s**wer	de**s**pite	indu**s**try	ye**s**terday
a**s**k	ea**s**t	la**s**t	...
corre**s**pondent	fir**s**t	new**s**paper	

Note: /s/ followed by the inflectional ending **-ed** is pronounced /st/ and can be spelled **-ced**: e.g. 'announ**ced**' and 'for**ced**'; **-sed**: e.g. 'ba**sed**' and 'increa**sed**'; and **-ssed**: e.g. 'expre**ssed**' and 'pa**ssed**'.

Before a vowel and after a short vowel:

/s/ is usually spelled **ss**:

amba**ss**ador	e**ss**ay	ma**ss**ive	po**ss**ible
a**ss**et	expre**ss**ed	me**ss**age	profe**ss**or
cla**ss**ic	fo**ss**il	pa**ss**age	...

/s/ is spelled **c** in the endings **-acity**, **-icit**, and **-icity**:

aud**acity**	...	sol**icit**	electr**icity**
cap**acity**	def**icit**	...	publ**icity**
ten**acity**	ill**icit**	domest**icity**	...

/s/ is also spelled **c** in these words:

a**c**etate	exa**c**erbate	ne**c**essary	re**c**itation
a**c**etone	fa**c**et	pa**c**ifist	spe**c**ify
a**c**id	fa**c**ile	pla**c**id	spe**c**imen
anti**c**ipate	gla**c**ier	pre**c**edent	ta**c**it
de**c**ibel	la**c**erate	pre**c**ipice	thora**c**ic
de**c**imate	medi**c**inal	re**c**ipe	va**c**illate

Note: **cc** in 'fla**cc**id'.

/s/ is spelled **s** in the prefixes **dis-** and **mis-**, and the ending **-osity**:

disappear	**mis**inform	curi**osity**
disorder	**mis**understand	gener**osity**
...	...	...

/s/ is also spelled **s** in these words:

a**s**inine	de**s**ecrate	ga**s**oline	pro**s**ecute
ba**s**alt	de**s**olate	ma**s**ochist	
chry**s**alis	dy**s**entery	philo**s**ophy	

/s/ is spelled **sc** in the endings **-esce**, **-escence**, **-escent**, and **-escension**:

acquie**sc**e	coale**sc**e	convale**sc**ence	obsole**sc**ence
adole**sc**ent	conde**sc**ension	efferve**sc**ence	...

/s/ is also spelled **sc** in these words:

a**sc**ertain	fa**sc**inate	omni**sc**ience	probo**sc**is
corpu**sc**le	iso**sc**eles	o**sc**illate	resu**sc**itate
di**sc**ipline	mi**sc**ellaneous	pre**sc**ient	

Before a vowel and after other vowels:

/s/ is usually spelled **c**:

criticism	facing	policy	recession
December	licence	precise	society
decision	magnificent	process	specific
deficit	medicine	received	suicide
facility	officer	recent	...

/s/ is spelled **c** in the ending **-acy**:

accur**acy**	democr**acy**	leg**acy**	suprem**acy**
conspir**acy**	diplom**acy**	priv**acy**	...

/s/ is spelled **s** in the endings **-sis** and **-sive**:

analy**sis**	deci**sive**	exclu**sive**	offen**sive**
cri**sis**	empha**sis**	hypno**sis**	...

/s/ is also spelled **s** in these words:

aside	ecstasy	idiosyncrasy	premises
asylum	episode	isolate	sausage
basic	heresy	mason	supersede
crusade	hypocrisy	nuisance	

/s/ is spelled **ss** in the beginning **ass-**:

assail	**ass**ent	**ass**iduous	**ass**ociate
assassin	**ass**ert	**ass**ign	**ass**orted
assault	**ass**ess	**ass**imilate	**ass**ume
assemble	**ass**et	**ass**ist	...

/s/ is also spelled **ss** in these words:

emba**ss**y	e**ss**ential	nece**ss**ary

/s/ is spelled **sc** in these words:

a**sc**ent	de**sc**ent	di**sc**iple	su**sc**eptible
conde**sc**end	di**sc**ern	plebi**sc**ite	

The 24 main consonant sounds

After a consonant:

/s/ is usually spelled **s**:

absolute	circumstance	itself	subsidy
also	compulsive	offset	university
amidst	conservative	outside	upset
backstage	insult	person	...

Note: **sc** in 'abscess', 'obscene', and 'transcend'.

/s/ is sometimes spelled **c** after **l**, **n**, or silent **r**:

calcium	cancel	council	exercise
halcyon	chancellor	incident	merciful
ulcer	coincidence	principle	parcel
...	conception	...	perception
agency	concern	enforcement	...

/s/ often occurs in the combination /ks/, which is usually spelled **x**, often **cc**, and more rarely **xc**:

boxing	sixty	succeed	excellent
excuse	taxi	vaccine	except
mixed	...	...	exciting
next	accept	exceed	...

Note: For full details about /ks/, see the entry for /k/ in this section.

Final

After a short vowel:

/s/ is usually spelled **ss**:

across	discuss	mass	process
boss	guess	miss	puss
congress	less	press	...

Note: In most non-RP accents, the vowel in 'class', 'glass', 'grass', and 'pass' is also short.

/s/ is spelled **s** in these words, which are of Classical origin:

aegis	catharsis	gravitas	plus
alas	chaos	hubris	portcullis
apotheosis	clematis	iris	proboscis
appendicitis	clitoris	kudos	psychosis
aurora borealis	cosmos	marquis	pus
bathos	epidermis	paterfamilias	symbiosis
bronchitis	extremis	pathos	syphilis
bus	gas	pelvis	trellis
cannabis	glottis	penis	tuberculosis

Note: (1) The ending -**sis** occurs in many of the words, but -**scis** in 'proboscis'. (2) The technical names of many illnesses end in -**itis**. (3) -**s** also in 'alas', 'Bros.', 'haggis', 'tennis', 'this', and 'us'.

/s/ is spelled **ce** after **i** in these words:

accomplice	cornice	interstice	practice
armistice	cowardice	jaundice	precipice
avarice	crevice	lattice	pumice
bodice	edifice	malice	service
chalice	hospice	notice	solstice
coppice	injustice	novice	

Note: (1) **ce** after **a** in 'volte-face'. (2) **se** in 'diocese', 'practise', 'premise', and 'promise'. (3) **sce** in 'acquiesce', 'coalesce', 'convalesce', and 'reminisce'. (4) **sse** in 'crevasse', 'en masse', 'finesse', 'impasse', and 'lacrosse', which are of French origin. (5) In British English, 'practice' is a noun, and 'practise' is a verb. In American English 'practise' is used in both cases.

After 'schwa' (/ə/):

/s/ is usually spelled **s**:

alias	garrulous	miraculous	scandalous
anomalous	genius	nebulous	scurrilous
atlas	jealous	pendulous	stylus
bias	Judas	perilous	surplus
credulous	libellous	populous	tremulous
fabulous	marvellous	querulous	zealous
frivolous	meticulous	ridiculous	...

Note: **se** in 'porpoise', 'purchase', 'purpose', and 'tortoise'.

/s/ is spelled **ss** in these words:

business	carcass	embarrass	mattress
buttress	compass	fortress	windlass
canvass	cypress	harass	

Note: **ss** in the common endings -**ess**, -**less**, and -**ness**: e.g. 'darkness', 'endless', and 'waitress'.

/s/ is spelled **ce** in these words:

furnace	menace	populace	surface
grimace	necklace	preface	surplice
lettuce	palace	solace	terrace

After a long vowel or vowel digraph:

/s/ is usually spelled **se** or **ce**:

abuse	increase	choice	police
base	lease	dice	price
case	moose	face	produce
cease	mouse	ice	reduce
chase	mousse	introduce	rice
close	obese	juice	sacrifice
concise	paradise	lace	sauce
crease	precise	nice	spice
dose	use	niece	trace
excuse	verbose	pace	twice
geese	...	peace	vice
grandiose	ace	piece	voice
grease	advice	place	...

Note: the American spelling 'vise' for 'vice' (meaning 'a tool').

/s/ is spelled **ss** in these words:

bass	glass	gross
class	grass	pass

Note: In most non-RP accents, 'class', 'glass', 'grass', and 'pass' have a short vowel.

After a consonant:

/s/ is spelled **s** in the plural form of nouns and the third person singular present tense of verbs:

minutes	reports	students	weeks
months	states	talks	...

/s/ is usually spelled **se** at the end of adjectives:

false	immense	intense	...

/s/ is more commonly spelled **ce** than **se** in other words:

chance	prince	collapse	else
conference	science	copse	glimpse
defence	since	corpse	lapse
experience	violence	course	relapse
once	...	eclipse	sense
performance	apocalypse	elapse	...

Note: **ce** in British spelling of 'defence', 'licence', 'offence', and 'pretence', but **se** in American spelling: 'defense', 'license', 'offense', and 'pretense'.

/s/ is spelled **z** in these words of Foreign origin:

blitz	glitz	quartz
ersatz	hertz	waltz

/s/ often occurs in the combination /**ks**/, which is usually spelled **x**, and often **cs**:

box	matrix	telex	genetics
coax	mix	wax	graphics
fax	paradox	...	linguistics
fix	relax	athletics	mathematics
flex	sex	dynamics	physics
index	six	economics	politics
larynx	tax	ethics	...

Note: For full details about /**ks**/, see the entry for /**k**/ in this section.

Inflection and word formation

Before a suffix which begins with a vowel:

Final silent **e** is dropped:

e.g. place – placing – placed; promise – promising.

If a short vowel is followed by a single **s**, the **s** is doubled when forming verb inflections but not when forming the plural of nouns:

e.g. bus – busses – bussing – bussed; gas – gasses – gassing – gassed; bus – buses; gas – gases; plus – pluses; yes – yeses.

Note: The verbs 'bias' and 'focus' can have **ss** in inflected forms, even though their second syllable is unstressed: 'bias – biasses – biassing – biassed'; 'focus – focusses – focussing – focussed'.

Plurals:

Many words which end in **s** have irregular plurals:

e.g. alum**nus** – alum**ni**; analy**sis** – analy**ses**; a**xis** – a**xes**; ba**sis** – ba**ses**; cor**pus** – cor**pora**; cri**sis** – cri**ses**; diagno**sis** – diagno**ses**; empha**sis** – empha**ses**; fun**gus** – fun**gi** (or fungu**ses**); ge**nus** – ge**nera**; hypothe**sis** – hypothe**ses**; lo**cus** – lo**ci**; neuro**sis** – neuro**ses**; nucle**us** – nucle**i**; o**pus** – o**pera**; stimu**lus** – stimu**li**; the**sis** – the**ses**.

For plurals of words ending in /**ks**/, see the entry for /**k**/ in this section.

/ʒ/ measure

This sound usually occurs between vowels in the middle of words and is most commonly spelled **s**. The other spellings, **g**, **j**, and **ge**, are of French origin.

Initial

/ʒ/ is spelled **g** or **j** in these words of French origin:

gendarme   genre   joie de vivre

Middle

/ʒ/ is most commonly spelled **s**, usually after a vowel and before **i** or **u**:

casual	illusion	occasion	treasure
decision	invasion	pleasure	usual
division	measure	television	...

/ʒ/ is spelled **g** or **j** in these words of French origin:

aubergine	ingenue	protégé	bijou
bourgeois	lingerie	regime	déjà vu
courgette	negligee	...	objet d'art

Final

/ʒ/ is spelled **ge** in these words of French origin:

badinage	corsage	garage	prestige
barrage	cortege	massage	rouge
beige	dressage	melange	sabotage
camouflage	entourage	menage	
collage	espionage	mirage	
concierge	fuselage	montage	

Inflection and word formation

Final silent **e** is dropped before a suffix which begins with a vowel:

e.g. camouflage – camouflage**s** – camouflag**ing** – camouflag**ed**; massage – massage**s** – massag**ing** – massag**ed**.

/ʃ/ show

In most words which begin or end with this sound, it is spelled **sh**. In the middle of a word there are several spelling patterns, but **ti** is the most common. In words of French origin, **ch**, or **che** at the end of a word, are common.

Initial

/ʃ/ is usually spelled **sh**:

shall	she	shot	show
share	shop	should	shut
sharp	short	shoulder	...

/ʃ/ is spelled **ch** in these words of French origin:

chagrin	chaperone	chateau	chicane
chaise longue	charabanc	chauvinist	chicanery
chalet	charade	chef	chiffon
chamois	chargé d'affaires	cheroot	chivalry
champagne	charlatan	chevron	chute
chandelier	chassis	chic	

/ʃ/ is spelled **sch** in these words:

schedule	schlock	schmaltzy	schnapps
schlep	schmaltz	schmooze	schwa

/ʃ/ is spelled **s** in these words:

spiel	sugary	surely
sugar	sure	surety

Middle

Before '-al':

/ʃ/ is most frequently spelled **ti**:

confidential	initial	potential	spatial
essential	martial	preferential	substantial
impartial	partial	residential	...

Note: Some of these words are related to nouns which end in **ce**: e.g. 'essence – essential', 'space – spatial'.

The 24 main consonant sounds

/ʃ/ is often spelled **ci**:

artificial	facial	official	social
beneficial	financial	provincial	special
commercial	glacial	racial	superficial
crucial	judicial	sacrificial	...

Note: (1) /ʃ/ is spelled si in 'controversial'. (2) /kʃ/ is spelled x in 'sexual'.

Before '-an':

/ʃ/ is most frequently spelled **ci**, usually in words describing people's occupations:

beautician	magician	obstetrician	politician
dietician	mathematician	optician	technician
electrician	musician	physician	...

Note: (1) also 'patrician', which is not an occupation. (2) ce in 'ocean'. (3) ss in 'Russian'. (4) ti in 'alsatian', 'dalmatian', 'martian', and 'Venetian blind'.

Before '-on':

/ʃ/ is most frequently spelled **ti**, after a consonant, a long a, e, o, or u, or a short i:

action	competition	nation	situation
administration	education	operation	station
association	election	position	...
attention	information	production	

/ʃ/ is often spelled **ssi**, always after a short vowel:

admission	depression	passion	session
aggression	discussion	permission	submission
commission	expression	possession	succession
compassion	impression	profession	suppression
concession	mission	recession	transmission
confession	obsession	repression	...

Note: (1) Many of these words are related to words which end in -ss: e.g. 'confess – confession', 'depress – depression', 'discuss – discussion', and 'express – expression'. (2) But words which end in -**mission** are often related to words that end in -**mit**: e.g. 'admit – admission', 'commit – commission', and 'permit – permission'.

/ʃ/ is often spelled **si**, usually after l, n, or silent r:

apprehension	dimension	extension	subversion
compulsion	diversion	incursion	suspension
conversion	expansion	mansion	tension
convulsion	expulsion	pension	...

Note: (1) **ci** in 'coer**ci**on' and 'suspi**ci**on'. (2) **shi** in 'cu**shi**on' and 'fa**shi**on'.

/ʃ/ in the combination /kʃ/ is spelled **cti**:

a**cti**on	dire**cti**on	produ**cti**on	se**cti**on
colle**cti**on	ele**cti**on	prote**cti**on	...
conne**cti**on	infle**cti**on	rea**cti**on	

Note: (1) **x** in 'comple**x**ion', 'crucifi**x**ion', and the rare alternative spellings 'conne**x**ion' and 'infle**x**ion'. (2) For full details, see the entry for /k/ in this section.

Before '-ous':

/ʃ/ is most frequently spelled **ci**:

atro**ci**ous	fero**ci**ous	perni**ci**ous	tena**ci**ous
auda**ci**ous	gra**ci**ous	pre**ci**ous	vi**ci**ous
capri**ci**ous	judi**ci**ous	spa**ci**ous	vora**ci**ous
deli**ci**ous	mali**ci**ous	suspi**ci**ous	...

/ʃ/ is often spelled **ti**:

ambi**ti**ous	ficti**ti**ous	nutri**ti**ous	sedi**ti**ous
cau**ti**ous	flirta**ti**ous	ostenta**ti**ous	supersti**ti**ous
conscien**ti**ous	frac**ti**ous	preten**ti**ous	surrepti**ti**ous
face**ti**ous	infec**ti**ous	propi**ti**ous	...

Note: (1) **sci** in 'con**sci**ous' and 'lu**sci**ous'. (2) **ce** in 'curva**ce**ous' and 'herba**ce**ous'. (3) In some accents, **se** in 'ga**se**ous'. (4) /ʃ/ in the combination /kʃ/ is spelled **xi** in 'an**xi**ous', 'no**xi**ous', and 'obno**xi**ous'.

Otherwise:

/ʃ/ is usually spelled **sh**:

aba**sh**ed	bu**sh**el	gei**sh**a	sea**sh**ore
a**sh**amed	ca**sh**ew	in**sh**ore	sling**sh**ot
a**sh**en	ca**sh**ier	ko**sh**er	wor**sh**ip
a**sh**ore	en**sh**rine	mu**sh**room	ya**sh**mak
bi**sh**op	galo**sh**es	ricks**h**aw	...

Note: **sh** in the common ending -**ship**: e.g. 'champion**ship**', 'leader**ship**', and 'owner**ship**'.

/ʃ/ is spelled **ch** in words of French origin:

atta**ch**é	cou**ch**ette	ma**ch**ine	re**ch**er**ch**é
bro**ch**ure	cro**ch**et	non**ch**alant	ri**co**ch**et
cach**et	e**ch**elon	para**ch**ute	sa**ch**et
cli**ch**é	ma**ch**ete	rappro**ch**ement	...

The 24 main consonant sounds

In words of Classical origin, /ʃ/ is spelled **t** before **i**, or **c** before **i**, or **ss**, **s**, or **sc**:

dementia	potential	depreciate	reassure
differentiate	quotient	efficient	tissue
ex gratia	ratio	excruciating	...
expatiate	satiate	ex officio	censure
inertia	tertiary	judiciary	ensure
ingratiate	vitiate	sociable	insure
initiate	...	species	tonsure
insatiable	acacia	sufficient	...
militia	ancient	...	conscience
minutiae	appreciate	assure	crescendo
nasturtium	associate	fissure	fascia
negotiate	beneficiary	issue	fascism
patience	deficient	pressure	...

Note: (1) **chs** in 'fuchsia' (/fjuːʃə/). (2) /kʃ/ is spelled **x** in 'luxury'.

Final

/ʃ/ is usually spelled **sh**:

abolish	dish	harsh	rubbish
accomplish	distinguish	lavish	rush
anguish	establish	marsh	selfish
ash	finish	parish	sluggish
brush	fish	polish	smash
bush	flash	publish	squash
cash	flourish	punish	stylish
crash	flush	push	wash
crush	foolish	rash	wish
dash	fresh	relish	...

/ʃ/ is spelled **che** in words of French origin:

cache	gauche	niche	quiche
crèche	microfiche	panache	tranche
douche	moustache	pastiche	...

Note: All other words with final /ʃ/ are spelled **sh**, whatever their origin: e.g. 'abolition' but 'abolish'.

/t/	time

In most words, this sound is spelled **t**. After a short vowel and before some Native endings, it is spelled **tt**. After a long vowel at the end of a word, it is spelled **te**. As a verb ending, **ed** is very common.

Initial

/t/ is usually spelled **t**:

take	tell	together	trade
taking	time	too	try
talk	to	took	turn
team	today	town	...

Note: (1) **pt** in 'pterodactyl'. (2) **th** in 'thyme'. (3) **tw** in 'two'.

Middle

/t/ is usually spelled **t**:

after	into	still	until
between	party	system	yesterday
city	political	united	...

/t/ is spelled **tt** in the pattern **att-** at the beginning of words:

attach	**att**empt	**att**itude	**att**ract
attack	**att**ention	**att**orney	...

/t/ is also spelled **tt** after a short vowel and before the endings **-ed**, **-en**, **-er**, **-est**, **-ing**, **-le**, **-on**, and **-y**:

battle	fittest	little	sitting
better	flatten	pretty	spotted
cotton	hottest	rotten	witty
fitted	letter	setting	...

Note: but not in 'baton', 'city', and 'pity'.

/t/ is also spelled **tt** in words containing /mɪt/ followed by a vowel:

admitted	committee	permitting	...
committal	intermittent	remittance	

/t/ is also spelled **tt** in many words of Italian origin:

Beretta	ghetto	regatta	terracotta
confetti	grotto	risotto	vendetta
dilettante	libretto	spaghetti	...
falsetto	motto	stiletto	

The 24 main consonant sounds

/t/ is also spelled **tt** in these words:

acquittal	buttress	lettuce	rebuttal
attic	cottage	mattress	regrettable
battalion	forgettable	ottoman	settee
battery	gotta	pattern	skittish
bottom	guttural	petticoat	tattoo
boycotted	jettison	pitta	
buttock	lattice	pottery	

Final

After a consonant sound:

/t/ is usually spelled **t**:

correct	first	left	support
difficult	government	next	want
fact	just	part	...

Note: **t** often follows silent consonant letters: e.g. 'de**b**t', 'dou**b**t', 'indi**c**t', 'ni**gh**t', 'recei**p**t', and 'thou**gh**t'.

/t/ is spelled **ed** in the past tense and past participle forms of regular verbs:

asked	fixed	introduced	sniffed
briefed	glanced	looked	stopped
discussed	helped	passed	...

Note: These irregular past tense forms end in '-**t**': 'burst', 'cast', 'cost', 'crept', 'kept', 'left', 'lost', 'slept', 'swept', 'thrust', and 'wept'.

/t/ is also spelled **ed** in adjectives formed from a regular verb or from a noun:

biased	handicapped	scuffed	...
convinced	marked	sexed	
depressed	perplexed	shaped	

/t/ is spelled **te** when **s** is preceded by long **a**:

baste	haste	taste	...
chaste	paste	waste	

/t/ is also spelled **te** in these words of French origin:

à la carte	debutante	poste restante
artiste	detente	riposte
caste	entente	svelte

After a short vowel:

/t/ is usually spelled **t**:

bat	fit	hot	sat
cut	get	not	...

Note: **te** in 'dovecote'.

/t/ is spelled **tte** in these words of French origin:

brunette	diskette	launderette	statuette
cassette	etiquette	palette	suffragette
cigarette	garrotte	roulette	vignette
courgette	gazette	silhouette	vinaigrette

/t/ is spelled **tt** in these words:

boycott	matt	watt
butt	putt	

After a long vowel:

/t/ is usually spelled **te**:

absolute	dispute	rate	white
complete	erudite	state	wrote
despite	obsolete	vote	...

After 'schwa' (/ə/):

/t/ is usually spelled **te**:

appropriate	delicate	immediate	separate
climate	favourite	moderate	ultimate
corporate	graduate	private	...

Note: (1) In this case, 'moderate' and 'separate' are adjectives, not verbs. (2) **tte** in 'omelette' and 'palette'.

/t/ is spelled **t** in these words:

abbot	diet	mascot	riot
ballot	faggot	pallet	scarlet
bigot	gamut	pamphlet	secret
cabinet	garret	parrot	sherbet
carat	idiot	patriot	tablet
carrot	ingot	pilot	toilet
chariot	maggot	pivot	violet
claret	magnet	quiet	zealot

/t/ is also spelled **t** after /ər/ in these words:

braggart	covert	effort	yoghurt
comfort	culvert	sievert	yogurt
concert	desert	stalwart	

Note: In many non-RP accents, including GenAm, the **r** in these words is pronounced.

The 24 main consonant sounds

After unstressed /ɪ/:

/t/ is usually spelled **t**:

benefit	limit	spirit	visit
budget	market	summit	...
credit	profit	target	

/t/ is spelled **te** in these words:

composite	incarnate	perquisite
exquisite	minute	requisite
granite	opposite	respite

Note: In this case, 'minute' is a noun, not an adjective.

After vowel digraphs:

/t/ is usually spelled **t**:

about	feet	meet	wait
eat	great	suit	...

/t/ is spelled **te** in these words:

route   suite

Note: /t/ is also spelled **te** in 'ate', 'fete', and 'petite'.

Inflection and word formation

Final silent **e** is dropped before a suffix that begins with a vowel:

e.g. rate – rating – rated; taste – tasting – tasted – tasty – tastier.

Final **t** is doubled after a short vowel before a suffix that begins with a vowel:

e.g. fit – fitting – fitted – fitter – fittest.

Note: (1) but not after 'schwa' (/ə/) or unstressed /ɪ/: e.g. 'target – targeting – targeted'. (2) and not before the Classical ending **-ic** that can function as a suffix: e.g. 'automate – automatic' and 'democrat – democratic'.

/θ/ thank

This sound is always spelled **th**.

Initial

thank	**th**ink	**th**ousand	**th**rough
theory	**th**ought	**th**ree	...

Middle

au**th**or	au**th**ority	no**th**ing	...

Final

bo**th**	heal**th**	pa**th**	wrea**th**
dea**th**	mon**th**	wor**th**	...

/ð/   than

This sound is nearly always spelled **th**, except at the end of words, where it is usually spelled **the**.

Initial

/ð/ is always spelled **th**, and usually occurs in grammatical words:

than	**th**eir	**th**ese	**th**ose
that	**th**en	**th**ey	**th**us
the	**th**ere	**th**is	...

Middle

/ð/ is always spelled **th**:

clo**th**es	fur**th**er	o**th**er	wea**th**er
ei**th**er	mo**th**er	ra**th**er	whe**th**er
fa**th**er	nor**th**ern	toge**th**er	...

Final

/ð/ is usually spelled **the**:

ba**the**	la**the**	see**the**	tee**the**
bli**the**	li**the**	shea**the**	wrea**the**
brea**the**	loa**the**	soo**the**	wri**the**
clo**the**	scy**the**	swa**the**	...

/ð/ is spelled **th** in these words:

bequea**th**	boo**th**	smoo**th**	wi**th**

Inflection and word formation

Final silent **e** is dropped before suffixes that begin with a vowel:

e.g. brea**the** – brea**thes** – brea**thing** – brea**thed**.

Note: 'bath' has the form 'baths', and 'bathe' has the form 'bathes', but both have the forms 'bathing – bathed'.

/v/			very

In most words, this sound is spelled **v**. At the end of words it is usually spelled **ve**. It is spelled **f** only in the word 'of', which is the second commonest word in English, **vv** in the middle of a few informal words, and **v** at the end of a few abbreviations and informal words.

Initial

/v/ is always spelled **v**:

value	victory	visit	vote
various	view	voice	vulgar
very	violence	volume	...

Middle

/v/ is nearly always spelled **v**:

development	level	private	several
even	never	service	university
government	over	seven	...

/v/ is spelled **vv** in these informal words:

bovver	civvy	navvy	skivvy
chivvy	luvvies	savvy	

Final

/v/ is nearly always spelled **ve**:

above	effective	leave	receive
active	executive	live	save
alternative	five	love	serve
believe	gave	move	twelve
conservative	give	positive	...
drive	have	prove	

/v/ is spelled **v** in these abbreviations and informal words:

adv.	guv	Nov.	Rev.
gov.	luv	rev	spiv

Note: (1) also **v** in 'Molotov cocktail', 'Slav', and 'Yugoslav'. (2) **f** only in the word 'of'.

Inflection and word formation

Final silent **e** is dropped before a suffix that begins with a vowel:

e.g. love – lov**ed** – lov**ing** – lov**able**.

Final **v** in 'rev' is doubled before a suffix that begins with a vowel: 'revving – revved'.

The 24 main consonant sounds

/w/	was

In most words, this sound is spelled **w**, but it is spelled **wh** at the beginning of many words.

Initial

/w/ is usually spelled **w**:

wall	way	wife	women
want	we	will	won
wanted	week	win	work
war	well	with	world
was	went	within	would
wash	were	without	wound
water	west	woman	...

/w/ is spelled **wh** in these words:

whack	when	while	whirl
whale	whenever	whilst	whisk
wharf	where	whim	whisky
what	whereas	whimper	whisper
whatever	whether	whine	whistle
wheat	which	whinge	white
wheel	whiff	whip	why

Note: (1) Some speakers, including many GenAm speakers, pronounce these words /hw/. (2) Some common words beginning with **wh** are pronounced /h/: e.g. 'who', 'whole', 'whom', and 'whose'. (3) Initial /wʌ/ is spelled **o** in 'once' and 'one'.

Middle

/w/ is usually spelled **w**:

always	forward	software	twenty
anyway	framework	sweep	twice
aware	hardware	switch	twin
away	railway	toward	twist
awkward	reward	towards	unwilling
between	sandwich	tweed	...

Note: (1) Many of these are compounds of words beginning with **w**: e.g. 'way – always, anyway, away, railway'. (2) Similarly, **wh** occurs in compounds of words beginning with **wh**: e.g. 'elsewhere' and 'meanwhile'. (3) /w/ is spelled **ju** in 'marijuana'.

/w/ often occurs in the combination /kw/, which is usually spelled **qu**:

quality	...	frequent	square
question	equal	inquiry	squash
quite	equipment	require	...

Note: For full details about /kw/, see the entry for /k/ in this section.

/w/ also occurs in the combinations /gw/ and /sw/, which are spelled **gu** and **su** in these words:

an**gu**ish	**gu**ava	san**gu**ine	per**su**ade
distin**gu**ish	lan**gu**age	...	**su**ave
extin**gu**ish	lan**gu**id	as**su**age	**su**ede
guano	lan**gu**ish	dis**su**ade	**su**ite

Note: (1) /w/ is spelled **hu** in 'chi**hu**ahua'. (2) /nw/ is spelled **nu** in 'en**nu**i'. (3) /w/ occurs in various other combinations in words of French origin: /wɑːʳ/ is spelled **oir** in 'abatt**oir**', 'boud**oir**', 'reserv**oir**' and 'sav**oir**-faire', and **oire** in 'bete n**oire**' and 'repert**oire**'; /wɑː/ is spelled **oi** in 'c**oi**ffure' and 's**oi**ree', **oid** in 'sang-fr**oid**', **oie** in 'j**oie** de vivre', and **ois** in 'cham**ois**', 'menage a tr**ois**', and 'pat**ois**'; /wæ/ is spelled **oi** in 'cr**oi**ssant'; /waɪ/ is spelled **oy** in 'v**oy**eur'.

Final

/w/ does not occur at the end of words in English.

The 24 main consonant sounds

| /j/ | yes |

In most words, this sound is not represented by a separate letter in the spelling. It occurs most frequently in the combinations /**ju:**/ and /**jə**/, both of which are usually spelled **u**. The letter **y** can represent the sound /**j**/ at the beginning of words and before a vowel.

Initial

/j/ is usually spelled **y**:

yacht	yellow	yoga	young
yard	yesterday	yoghurt	yuppie
year	yield	yolk	...

/j/ often occurs in the combination /**ju:**/, which is usually spelled **u**, or **eu** in some words of Greek origin:

uniform	use	eulogy	eureka
union	...	euphemism	...

Note: For more details, see the entry for /**ju:**/ in this section.

Middle

/j/ is most commonly spelled **i**:

behaviour	companion	onion	saviour
billion	junior	opinion	...

/j/ is spelled **y** in these words:

| banyan | beyond | canyon | lawyer |

/j/ often occurs in the combination /**ju:**/, which is usually spelled **u**, **eu** in some words of Greek origin, or more rarely **ew**:

human	...	pneumonia	steward
popular	neutral	...	...

Note: For more details, see the entry for /**ju:**/ in this section.

/j/ often occurs in the combination /**jə**/, which is spelled **u** in many words:

document	invaluable	nebula	tenure
failure	January	ocular	...

Note: (1) In GenAm, also **u** in 'er**u**dite' and 'fig**u**re' and their compounds. (2) /nj/ in some words of Foreign origin is spelled **gn**: e.g. 'co**gn**oscenti', 'lasa**gn**e', and 'poi**gn**ant'. (3) /j/ is spelled **ll** in these words of Foreign origin: 'bouillabaisse' and 'tortilla'.

Final

/j/ does not occur at the end of words in English.

/z/	zone

This sound is usually spelled **z** at the beginning of words, and **s** in the middle. At the end of grammatical words and inflected forms it is spelled **s**, at the end of other words it is usually **se** or **ze**. The less common patterns **z** and **zz** occur more often in the middle of words than at the end.

Initial

/z/ is usually spelled z:

zeal	zest	zodiac	zoom
zenith	zinc	zone	zucchini
zero	zip	zoo	...

Note: (1) **cz** in 'czar', 'czarina', and 'czarist'. (2) **ts** in 'tsar', 'tsarina', and 'tsarist'. (3) **x** in 'xenophobia', 'xenophobic', 'Xerox', and 'xylophone'.

Middle

/z/ is usually spelled s:

advertising	easy	position	result
business	housing	present	season
desert	husband	president	thousand
design	museum	prison	Thursday
desire	music	reason	using
disaster	opposition	resolution	visit
disease	physical	resource	...

Note: also **s** in the common ending **-ism**: e.g. 'capital**ism**', 'critic**ism**', and 'mechan**ism**'.

The 24 main consonant sounds

/z/ is spelled **z** in these words:

Amazon	eczema	influenza	seize
bamboozle	emblazon	kamikaze	size
bazaar	enzyme	lapis lazuli	sleazy
bazooka	freeze	lazy	stanza
bizarre	frieze	lizard	teazel
blazer	frenzy	lozenge	teazle
bonanza	frozen	magazine	tweezers
brazier	gazelle	marzipan	wheezy
cadenza	gazette	muzak	wizard
chimpanzee	geezer	ouzo	wizened
citizen	hazard	ozone	woozy
crazy	hazel	plaza	yakuza
denizens	hazy	prize	zigzag
dozen	horizon	razor	

/z/ is spelled **zz** in these words:

blizzard	fizzle	jacuzzi	puzzle
buzzard	fizzy	mezzanine	quizzical
buzzer	frazzle	muezzin	razzle
dazzle	frizzy	muzzle	sizzle
dizzy	fuzzy	nozzle	snazzy
drizzle	grizzly	nuzzle	sozzled
embezzle	guzzle	pizzazz	tizzy

Note: **x** in 'anxiety'.

Final

/z/ is spelled **s** at the end of plural forms of nouns and third person singular present tense forms of regular verbs:

counties	hours	says	wars
days	pounds	things	years
forces	problems	times	...

/z/ is also spelled **s** at the end of some grammatical words, some adverbs, adjectives and prepositions, and some non-plural nouns:

as	was	inwards	gallows
does	yours	overseas	innings
has	...	sideways	lens
his	always	towards	measles
is	besides	unawares	news
ours	downstairs	...	series
theirs	indoors	diabetes	...

Otherwise, /z/ is usually spelled **se**:

because	exercise	raise	these
cause	lose	rise	use
close	pause	suppose	whose
disease	please	surprise	...

Note: also **se** in 'pekinese', and in all nationality adjectives ending in /iːz/: e.g. 'Burmese', 'Chinese', 'Maltese', 'Siamese', and 'Sudanese'.

/z/ is spelled **ze** in these words:

amaze	daze	glaze	seize
assize	doze	graze	size
blaze	faze	haze	sleaze
booze	freeze	maize	sneeze
breeze	frieze	maze	snooze
bronze	froze	ooze	squeeze
capsize	gauze	prize	trapeze
craze	gaze	raze	wheeze

Note: (1) Most verbs ending in /aɪz/ can be spelled **-ize** or **-ise**, e.g. 'apolog**ize** – apolog**ise**', 'emphas**ize** – emphas**ise**', 'organ**ize** – organ**ise**', 'real**ize** – real**ise**', 'recogn**ize** – recogn**ise**', and 'stabil**ize** – stabil**ise**'. In the past, British writers preferred **-ise**, and American writers preferred **-ize**, but **-ize** is now becoming standard. (2) These verbs can only be spelled **-ise**:

advertise	compromise	exercise	supervise
advise	despise	franchise	surmise
arise	devise	improvise	surprise
chastise	disguise	revise	televise
circumcise	excise	rise	

/z/ is spelled **z** or **zz** in these words:

quiz	whiz	fizz
topaz	...	jazz
waltz	buzz	whizz

Inflection and word formation

Final silent **e** is dropped before a suffix that begins with a vowel:

e.g. advertise – advertis**ing** – advertis**ement**; organize – organiz**ing** – organiz**ation**.

Note: (1) Final **-z** is doubled in 'quiz' before a suffix that begins with a vowel: 'quiz – quiz**zes** – quiz**zing** – quiz**zed**'. (2) Both 'whiz' and 'whizz' have the forms 'whiz**zes** – whiz**zing** – whiz**zed**'.

3 Word Lists

/æ/
/æb/

ab:
abacus
abattoir
abdicate
abdomen
abdominal
abdominals
abduct
aberrant
aberration
abhor
abhorrence
abhorrent
abject
abjure
abnormal
abnormality
abolition
abolitionist
aboriginal
Aborigine
abracadabra
abrogate
abscess
abscond
abseil
absence
absent
absentee
absenteeism
absentia
absinthe
absolute
absolutely
absolution
absolutism
absolve
abstain
abstemious
abstention
abstinence
abstract
abstracted
abstraction
abstruse
absurd
absurdist
abyss

abb:
abbess
abbey
abbot

/æk/

ac:
academe
academia
academic
acme
acne
acolyte
acrid
acrimonious
acrimony
acrobat
acrobatic
acrobatics
acronym
acrylic
act
acting
action
actionable
activate
active
activism
activist
activity
actor
actress
actual
actuality
actually
actuarial
actuary
actuate
acuity
acumen
acupressure
acupuncture
acupuncturist

acc:
acclamation
accolade
accompli
accuracy
accurate
accusation

ack:
acknowledge
acknowledgement

/æks/

acc:
accede
accelerate
acceleration
accelerator
accent
accented
accentuate
accept
acceptable
acceptance
accepted
access
accessible
accession
accessorize
accessory
accident
accidental

ax:
axe
axeman
axiom
axiomatic
axis
axle

/ækw/

acqu:
acquiesce
acquiescence
acquiescent
acquisition

aqu:
aqua
aquamarine
aqueduct
aquifer
aquiline

/æd/

ad:
ad
adage
adamant
Adam's apple
adaptation
adenoidal
adenoids
adept
adequacy
adequate
adhere
adherence
adherent
adhesion
adhesive
ad hoc
ad infinitum
adman
admin
administer
administration
administrative
administrator
admirable
admiral
Admiralty
admiration
admissible
admission
admit
admittance
admittedly
admixture
admonish
admonition
adolescence
adolescent
adoration
adult
adulthood
advance
advanced
advancement
advantage
advantaged
advantageous
advent
adventure
adventurer
adventurism
adventurist
adventurous
adverb
adverbial
adversarial
adversary
adverse
adversity
advert
advertise
advertisement
advertiser
advertising
advertorial
advice
advisable
advise
advisedly
advisement
adviser
advisory
advocacy
advocate

add:
add

/æf/ /æn/

added
adder
addict
additive
addle
addled
addressee
adduce

/æf/

af:
Afghan
African
Afrikaans
Afrikaner
Afro
Afro-
after

aff:
affable
affectation
affidavit
affix
affluence
affluent
afforestation

aph:
aphorism
aphrodisiac

/æg/

ag:
agate
agnostic
agnosticism
agonize
agonized
agonizing
agony
agoraphobia
agoraphobic
agribusiness
agricultural
agriculturalist
agriculture
agro-

agg:
aggravate
aggravated
aggregate
aggro

/ædʒ/

adj:
adjectival
adjective

adjunct
adjutant

adu:
adulation
adulatory

ag:
agile
agitate
agitated
agitation
agitator
agitprop

/æl/

al:
alabaster
Albanian
albatross
albino
album
albumen
albumin
alchemical
alchemist
alchemy
alcohol
alcoholic
alcoholism
alcove
al dente
alec
aleck
alfalfa
alfresco
algae
algal
algebra
algebraic
Algerian
algorithm
alibi
alimentary canal
alimony
alkali
alkaline
alma mater
aloe vera
alpaca
alphabet
alphabetical
alpine
alpines
Alsatian
altimeter
altitude
alto
altruism
altruistic
aluminium

Alzheimer's Disease

all:
Allah
allegation
allegorical
allegory
alleluia
allergen
allergist
allergy
alley
alleyway
allied
alligator
allocate
allocation
alloy
ally

/æm/

am:
am
amateur
amateurish
amateurism
Amazon
Amazonian
ambassador
ambassadorial
amber
ambergris
ambiance
ambidextrous
ambience
ambient
ambiguity
ambiguous
ambit
ambition
ambitious
ambivalent
amble
ambrosia
ambulance
ambulanceman
ambush
Amerindian
amethyst
amicable
amity
amnesia
amnesiac
amnesty
amniocentesis
amorous
amour
amp
ampère
amphetamine

amphibian
amphibious
amphitheatre
ample
amplifier
amplify
amplitude
ampoule
amputate
amputee
amulet

amm:
ammo
ammunition

im:
impasse

/æn/

an:
an
anabolic steroid
anaesthesia
anaesthetic
anagram
analgesic
analogue
analyse
analyser
analyst
analytic
analytical
analyze
anarchic
anarchism
anarchist
anarchistic
anarcho-
anarchy
anatomical
ancestor
ancestral
ancestry
anchovy
ancillary
and
andante
androgynous
androgyny
android
anecdotal
anecdote
anesthesia
anesthesiologist
anesthetic
angelic
angelica
angina
animal
animate

181

/æŋ/

animated
animation
animator
animosity
animus
anise
aniseed
anode
anodyne
anorak
anorexia
anorexic
ant
antacid
antagonise
antagonism
antagonist
antagonistic
antagonistic
antagonize
Antarctic
ante
anteater
antecedent
antechamber
antediluvian
antelope
antenatal
antenna
anterior
anteroom
anthem
anthill
anthology
anthracite
anthrax
anthropology
anthropomorphic
anthropomorphism
anti
anti-
antibiotic
antibody
anticipate
anticipated
anticipation
anticipatory
anticlimax
anticlockwise
antics
anticyclone
antidote
antifreeze
antihistamine
antimatter
antipathy
Antipodean
Antipodes
antiquarian
antiquary

antiquated
antique
antiqued
antiquity
anti-Semite
anti-Semitism
antiseptic
antithesis
antithetical
antitrust
antler
antonym
antsy
anvil

ann:
annals
annex
annexe
anniversary
annotate
annotation
annual
annum

aun:
aunt
auntie

in:
ingenue

/æŋ/

anch:
anchor
anchorage
anchorman
anchorwoman

ang:
anger
angle
angler
Anglican
Anglicanism
anglicize
angling
Anglo-
Anglophile
Anglophone
Angolan
angora
angry
angst
anguish
anguished
angular

ank:
ankle

anx:
anxiety
anxious

/æp/

ap:
apathetic
apathy
aperitif
aperture
apogee
apologia
apoplectic
apoplexy
Apostolic
apres-ski
apropos
apt
aptitude

app:
apparatchik
apparatus
apparition
appellation
appetite
appetizer
appetizing
apple
applecart
applicable
applicant
application
applicator
apposite
apposition
apprehend
apprehension
apprehensive
approbation

/ær/

ar:
Arab
arabesque
Arabic
Arabist
arable
arid
aristocracy
aristocrat
arithmetic
arithmetical
aromatic

arr:
arrant
arriviste
arrogant
arrogate
arrow
arrowhead
arrowroot

/æs/

ac:
acetate
acetone
acid

as:
asbestos
ascertain
ascorbic acid
asinine
aspect
aspen
asperity
asphalt
asphyxia
asphyxiate
aspic
aspiration
aspirational
aspirin
asterisk
asteroid
asthma
asthmatic
astrakhan
astral
astro-
astronaut
astronomical
astrophysicist
astrophysics

ass:
ass
assay
asset
asshole
assignation

/æʒ/

ag:
agent provocateur

az:
azure

/æʃ/

ash:
ash
ashen
ashtray

/æt/

at:
at
atavistic
atlas
atmosphere
atmospheric

/æθ/

atmospherics
atoll
atom
atrophy

att:
attaché
attic
attitude
attitudinal
attribute

/æθ/

ath:
athlete
athletic
athleticism
athletics

/æv/

av:
avalanche
avant-garde
avarice
avaricious
avenue
average
avid
avocado
avocation

/æz/

as:
as

/eɪ/

a:
A,a
a-
ABC
A-bomb
AC
AD
AGM
AI
A level
a.m.
a priori
asap
ATM
A to Z

eh:
eh

/eɪɔ:/

aor:
aorta

/eɪb/

ab:
able
able-bodied
ably

/eɪk/

ac:
acorn
acre
acreage

ach:
ache
achingly
achy

aqu:
aqueous

ec:
ecru
ecu

/eɪtʃ/

h:
H,h
HIV
HM
HMS
HNC
HP
HQ
HRH
HRT

/eɪd/

aid:
aid
aide
aide-de-camp
aide-memoire
AIDS

/eɪf/

aph:
aphid

/eɪdʒ/

ag:
aging

age:
age
aged
ageing
ageism
ageist
ageless
agency

agent

/eɪl/

ail:
ail
aileron
ailing
ailment

al:
ale
alehouse
alia
alias
alien
alienate

él:
élan

/eɪm/

aim:
aim
aimless

am:
amiability
amiable
Amir
amoral

/eɪn/

ain:
ain't

an:
anal
ancient
angel
anus

/eɪp/

ap:
ape
apex
apolitical
apricot
April
apron

ép:
épée

/eɪs/

ac:
ace

as:
asexual
asymmetric
asymmetrical

asymmetry
asymptomatic

/eɪʒ/

as:
Asian
Asiatic

/eɪt/

at:
atonal
atrium
atypical

eight:
eight
eighteen
eighteenth
eighth
eightieth
eighty

/eɪθ/

ath:
atheism
atheist
atheistic

/eɪv/

av:
aviary
aviation
aviator
avionics

/eɪw/

aw:
AWOL

/ɑ:/

aah:
aah

ah:
ah

are:
are

r:
R,r
RAF
R&B
R&D
RC
R.E.
REM
Rh factor
R.I.P.
RM

/ɑːb/

RN
RNA
RP
rpm
RSI
RSVP
RV

/ɑːb/

arb:
arbiter
arbitrage
arbitrager
arbitrary
arbitrate
arbitration
arboreal
arboretum
arbour

/ɑːk/

arc:
arc
arcade
arcane
arctic

arch:
archaeology
archaic
archangel
archeology
archetypal
archetype
archetypical
archipelago
architect
architectural
architecture
archival
archive
archivist

ark:
ark

/ɑːtʃ/

arch:
arch
arch-
archbishop
archdeacon
archdiocese
arched
archer
archery
archway

/ɑːd/

ard:
ardent
ardor

ardour

/ɑːf/

af:
aft
after
after-
afterglow
afterlife
aftermath
afternoon
aftershave
aftershock
aftertaste
afterthought
afterwards

/ɑːg/

arg:
argon
argot
arguable
arguably
argue
argument
argumentation
argumentative

/ɑːh/

ah:
aha

/ɑːdʒ/

ard:
arduous

arg:
Argentine
Argentinian

/ɑːl/

à l:
à la
à la carte

/ɑːm/

alm:
almond
almoner
alms
almshouse

am:
amen

arm:
arm
armada
armadillo
Armageddon

Armagnac
armament
armband
armchair
armed
armful
armhole
armistice
armload
armor
armored
armorer
armory
armour
armoured
armourer
armoury
armpit
armrest
army

/ɑːn/

an:
answer
answerable
answerphone

aren:
aren't

aun:
aunt
auntie

/ɑːr/

ar:
aria

/ɑːs/

ars:
arse
arsehole
arsenal
arsenic
arson
arsonist

as:
ask

/ɑːt/

art:
art
Art Deco
artefact
arterial
arteriosclerosis
artery
artful
artichoke

article
articled
articulate
articulated
articulation
artifact
artifice
artificial
artillery
artilleryman
artisan
artist
artiste
artistic
artistry
artless
Art Nouveau
artsy
artwork
arty

/ɑːθ/

arth:
arthritic
arthritis

/eə/

air:
air

ere:
ere

heir:
heir

/eəb/

airb:
airbag
airbed
airborne
airbrush
Airbus

/eək/

airc:
aircraft
aircrew

/eəf/

airf:
airfare
airfield
airframe

/eəg/

airg:
airgun

/eəh/

airh:
airhead

/eəl/

airl:
airless
airlift
airline
airliner
airlock

heirl:
heirloom

/eəm/

airm:
airmail
airman

/eəp/

airp:
airplane
airplay
airport

/eər/

aer:
aerate
aerial
aero-
aerobatics
aerobic
aerobics
aerodrome
aerodynamic
aerodynamics
aeronautical
aeronautics
aeroplane
aerosol
aerospace

air:
airy

ar:
area
Aries

heir:
heiress

/eəs/

airs:
airspace
airspeed
airstrip

/eəʃ/

airsh:
airship
airshow

/eət/

aert:
Aertex

airt:
airtight

/eəw/

airw:
airwaves
airway
airwoman
airworthy

/eəz/

ers:
ersatz

/e/

/eb/

eb:
ebony

ebb:
ebb

/ek/

ech:
echo

/eks/

ecc:
eccentricity

ecs:
ecstasy
ecstatic
eczema

ex:
ex
ex-
excavate
excavator
excellence
Excellency
excellent
excerpt
excess
excise
exclamation
excommunicate
excrement
execrable
execute
executioner
exegesis
exercise
ex gratia
exhale
exhibition
exhibitionism
exhibitionist
exhume
exigency
exile
exodus
ex officio
exorcism
exorcist
exorcize
expat
expatriate
expectation
expedite
expedition
expeditionary force
expeditious
expert
expertise
expiate
expiration
explanation
explicate
exploit
exponential
export
exporter
exposé
exposition
expropriate
expurgate
extant
extra
extra-
extract
extracurricular
extradite
extraordinaire
extraterrestrial
extricate
extrovert
extroverted

x:
X,x

/ekw/

equ:
equable
equanimity
equatorial
equine
equitable
equity

/etʃ/

etch:
etch
etching

/ed/

ed:
eddy
edible
edification
edifice
edifying
edit
editor
editorial
editorialize
editorship
Edwardian

/ef/

eff:
effervescent
efficacious
efficacy
effigy
effing
effluent
effort
effortless

f:
F,f
FBI
FM

/eg/

egg:
egg
egghead
eggnog
eggplant
eggshell

/egz/

ex:
exaltation
existential
existentialism
existentialist
exit

/edʒ/

edg:
edge
edged
edgeways
edging
edgy

edu:
educate
educated
education
educational

/el/

educationalist
educationist
educative
educator
edutainment

/el/

el:
elbow
elder
elderberry
elderly
eldest
elegant
elegiac
elegy
element
elemental
elementary
elephant
elephantine
elevate
elevated
elevation
elevator
elf
elfin
eligible
elk
elm
elocution
eloquent
else
elsewhere
elves

l:
L,l
LCD
LP
LSD

/em/

em:
emanate
emanation
embassy
ember
emblem
emblematic
embryo
embryonic
emcee
emerald
emigrant
emigrate
émigré
eminence
eminent
eminently
emir
emirate
emissary
empathetic
empathize
empathy
emperor
emphasis
emphasize
empire
emporium
empress
emptiness
empty
emulate

m:
M,m
MA
MBA
MBE
MC
MD
MEP
MOT
MP
mpg
MS
MSc
MSG

/en/

an:
any
anybody
anyhow
anymore
anyone
anyplace
anything
anytime
anyway
anyways
anywhere

en:
end
endemic
ending
endive
endless
endocrine
enema
enemy
energetic
energize
energy
enervated
enervating
engine
engineer
engineering
enigmatic
enmity
ensign
enter
enterprise
enterprising
entertain
entertainer
entertainment
entity
entomology
entrails
entrance
entrant
entropy
entry
envelope
enviable
envious
envoy
envy
enzyme

n:
N,n
NB
NCO
NHS
nth

/eŋ/

en:
enclave

/ep/

ep:
epaulette
epic
epicentre
epicure
epicurean
epidemic
epidermis
epidural
epigram
epilepsy
epileptic
epilogue
episode
episodic
epitaph
epithet
Epsom salts

/er/

er:
erudite
erudition

/eθ/

err:
errand
errant
error

/es/

es:
escalate
escalator
escalope
escapade
escapologist
escort
Eskimo
Esperanto
espionage
esplanade
espresso
esprit de corps
estimable
estimate
estimation
estuary

ess:
essay
essayist
essence

s:
S,s
s.a.e.
SAS
SF
SOS
STD

/eʃ/

ech:
echelon

/et/

at:
ate

et:
et al
etc
etcetera
etiquette
etymological
etymology

/eθ/

eth:
ethic
ethical
ethnic
ethnicity
ethnocentric

/ev/

ethnographic
ethnography

/ev/

ev:
evanescent
ever
ever-
evergreen
everlasting
every
everybody
everyday
everyman
everyone
everything
everywhere
evidence
evident
evidently

/iː/

e:
E,e
ECG
EFL
e.g.
ELT
EP
E number
ESL
ESP
EU

/iːɒ/

aeo:
aeon

eo:
eon

/iːk/

ec:
eco-
ecological
economic
economical
economics
ecosystem
ecumenical

ek:
eke

equ:
equal
equalize
equalizer
equally
equidistant
equilateral
equilibrium
equinox

/iːtʃ/

each:
each

/iːd/

ed:
edict

oed:
Oedipus complex

/iːg/

eag:
eager
eagle

eg:
ego
egocentric
egoism
egoist
egoistic
egomania
egomaniac
egotism
egotist
egotistic

/iːdʒ/

aeg:
aegis

/iːl/

eel:
eel

el:
elasticity
elongate
elongated

/iːm/

em:
email
emu

/iːp/

ep:
epoch

/iːs/

aes:
aesthete
aesthetic
aesthetics

eas:
east
eastbound
Easter
easterly
eastern
easterner
easternmost
eastward

es:
esoteric
esthete
esthetic
estrogen

oes:
oesophagus
oestrogen

/iːt/

aet:
aetiology

eat:
eat
eaten
eater
eatery

et:
etiology

/iːθ/

eth:
ether
Ethiopian
ethos

/iːv/

eav:
eaves
eavesdrop

ev:
evangelical
eve
even
evening
evens
evensong
evil
evildoer
evocation
evolution
evolutionary

/iːz/

eas:
ease
easel
easily
easy

/ɜː/

er:
er

err:
err

/ɜːb/

urb:
urban
urbane
urbanization
urbanized

/ɜːk/

irk:
irk
irksome

/ɜːtʃ/

urch:
urchin

/ɜːg/

erg:
ergo
ergonomics

/ɜːdʒ/

urge:
urge
urgent

/ɜːl/

earl:
earl
earldom
earlier
earliest
early

/ɜːm/

erm:
ermine

/ɜːn/

earn:
earn
earner
earnest
earnestly
earnings

urn:
urn

/ɜːs/

ers:
erstwhile

/ɜːθ/

earth:
earth
earthbound
earthling
earthly
earthquake
earthwork
earthworm
earthy

/ɜːð/

earthe:
earthen
earthenware

/ɪə/

ear:
ear

/ɪəd/

eard:
eardrum

/ɪəf/

earf:
earful

earph:
earphone

/ɪəl/

earl:
earlobe

/ɪəm/

earm:
earmark
earmuffs

/ɪəp/

earp:
earpiece
earplug

/ɪər/

ear:
earache
earring

eer:
eerie

er:
era

eyr:
eyrie

/ɪəʃ/

earsh:
earshot

/ɪəw/

earw:
earwig

/ɪ/

/ɪb/

eb:
ebullient

/ɪk/

ec:
eclectic
eclecticism
eclipse
ecologist
ecology
economist
economize
economy
ecumenism

éc:
éclair

ecc:
ecclesiastic
ecclesiastical

/ɪks/

ecc:
eccentric

ex:
exceed
exceedingly
excel
except
excepted
excepting
exception
exceptional
excess
excessive
exchange
Exchequer
excise
excitable
excite
excited
excitement
exciting
exclaim
exclude
excluding
exclusion
exclusionary
exclusive
exclusively
excoriate
excrescence
excreta
excrete
excruciating
excursion
excusable
excuse
expand
expanse
expansion
expansionary
expansionism
expansionist
expansive
expect
expectancy
expectant
expectorant
expediency
expedient
expel
expend
expendable
expenditure
expense
expensive
experience
experienced
experiential
experiment
experimental
expire
expiry
explain
explanatory
expletive
explicable
explicit
explode
exploit
exploitable
exploitative
exploiter
exploratory
explore
explorer
explosion
explosive
exponent
export
exportable
expose
exposed
expostulate
exposure
expound
express
expression
expressionism
expressionist
expressionless
expressive
expressway
expulsion
expunge
exquisite
extemporize
extend
extendable
extended
extension
extensive
extent
extenuating
exterior
exterminate
exterminator
external
externalize
externals
extinct
extinction
extinguish
extinguisher
extol
extort
extortion
extortionate
extortionist
extract
extraction
extractor
extraneous
extraordinary
extrapolate
extravagance
extravagant
extravaganza
extreme
extremely
extremis
extremism
extremist
extremity
extrinsic
extrude
extrusion

/ɪkw/

equ:
equality
equate
equation

/ɪtʃ/

equator
equerry
equestrian
equestrianism
equip
equipment
equivalence
equivalent
equivocal
equivocate

/ɪtʃ/

itch:
itch
itchy

/ɪd/

ed:
edition

id:
ideogram
idiocy
idiom
idiomatic
idiosyncrasy
idiosyncratic
idiot
idiotic
idyll
idyllic

/ɪf/

eff:
efface
effect
effective
effectively
effectual
effeminate
effete
efficiency
efficient
effrontery
effusion
effusive

eph:
ephemera
ephemeral

if:
if
iffy

/ɪg/

eg:
egalitarian
egalitarianism
egregious

ig:
igloo
igneous
ignite
ignition
ignoble
ignominious
ignominy
ignoramus
ignorance
ignorant
ignore
iguana

/ɪgz/

ex:
exacerbate
exact
exacting
exactitude
exactly
exactness
exaggerate
exaggerated
exalt
exalted
exam
examination
examine
examinee
examiner
example
exasperate
exasperated
exasperating
executive
executor
exemplar
exemplary
exemplify
exempt
exert
exhaust
exhaustion
exhaustive
exhibit
exhibitor
exhilarated
exhilarating
exhilaration
exhort
exist
existence
existent
existing
exonerate
exorbitant
exotic
exotica
exoticism

exuberance
exuberant
exude
exult
exultant

/ɪdʒ/

eg:
Egyptian

ej:
ejaculate
eject

/ɪl/

el:
elaborate
elapse
elastic
elasticated
elated
elation
elect
election
electioneering
elective
elector
electoral
electorate
electric
electrical
electrician
electricity
electrics
electrification
electrified
electrify
electro-
electrocardiogram
electrocute
electrode
electrolysis
electrolyte
electromagnetic
electron
electronic
electronics
electroplate
eleven
elevenses
eleventh
elicit
elide
eliminate
eliminator
elite
elitism
elitist
elixir
Elizabethan

elope
elucidate
elude
elusive

ell:
ellipse
ellipsis
elliptical

il:
il-
ilk

ill:
ill
ill-
illegal
illegible
illegitimacy
illegitimate
illiberal
illicit
illiteracy
illiterate
illness
illogical
illuminate
illuminated
illumination
illumine
illusion
illusionist
illusory
illustrate
illustration
illustrative
illustrator
illustrious

/ɪm/

em:
em-
emaciated
emancipate
emancipated
emasculate
embalm
embankment
embargo
embark
embarrass
embarrassed
embarrassing
embarrassment
embattled
embed
embellish
embellishment
embezzle
embezzlement

/ɪm/ /m/

embittered
emblazoned
embodiment
embody
embolden
embossed
embrace
embroider
embroidery
embroil
embroiled
emerge
emergence
emergency
emergent
emeritus
emetic
emission
emit
emollient
emolument
emotion
emotional
emotionless
emotive
emphatic
emphatically
empirical
empiricism
emplacement
employ
employable
employee
employer
employment
empower
empowerment
emulsifier
emulsify
emulsion

im:
im-
image
imagery
imaginable
imaginary
imagination
imaginative
imagine
imaging
imaginings
imam
imbalance
imbalanced
imbecile
imbibe
imbroglio
imbue
imitate

imitation
imitative
imitator
imp
impact
impair
impairment
impale
impart
impartial
impassable
impassioned
impassive
impatient
impeach
impeachment
impeccable
impecunious
impede
impediment
impel
impending
impenetrable
imperative
imperceptible
imperfect
imperfection
imperial
imperialism
imperialist
imperialistic
imperil
imperious
imperishable
impermanent
impermeable
impersonal
impersonate
impersonator
impertinence
impertinent
imperturbable
impervious
impetuosity
impetuous
impetus
impinge
impious
impish
implacable
implant
implausible
implement
implicate
implicated
implication
implicit
implode
implore
imploring

imply
impolite
imponderable
import
importance
important
importer
importunate
importune
impose
imposing
impossible
impostor
impotence
impotent
impound
impoverish
impoverishment
impracticable
impractical
imprecation
imprecise
imprecision
impregnable
impregnate
impresario
impress
impression
impressionable
Impressionism
impressionist
impressionistic
impressive
imprint
imprison
imprisonment
improbable
impromptu
improper
impropriety
improve
improvement
improvident
improvise
imprudent
impudent
impugn
impulse
impulsive
impunity
impure
impurity
impute

imm:
immaculate
immanent
immaterial
immature
immeasurable

immeasurably
immediacy
immediate
immediately
immemorial
immense
immensely
immerse
immersion
immigrant
immigrate
immigration
imminent
immobile
immobilize
immoderate
immodest
immoral
immortal
immortalize
immovable
immune
immunize
immutable

/m/

en:
en-
enable
enact
enactment
enamel
enamelled
enamelling
enamoured
encamped
encampment
encapsulate
encase
enchant
enchanting
enchantment
enchantress
encircle
enclose
enclosed
enclosure
encode
encompass
encounter
encourage
encouragement
encouraging
encroach
encroachment
encrustation
encrusted
encumber
encumbrance
encyclical

encyclopedia
encyclopedic
endanger
endear
endearing
endearment
endeavour
endorse
endorsement
endow
endowment
endurance
endure
enfeebled
enfold
enforce
enforceable
enforcement
enfranchise
enfranchisement
engage
engaged
engagement
engaging
engender
engorged
engrave
engraved
engraver
engraving
engrossed
engrossing
engulf
enhance
enhancement
enhancer
enigma
enjoin
enjoy
enjoyable
enjoyment
enlarge
enlargement
enlighten
enlightened
enlightenment
enlist
enlisted
enlistment
enliven
enmeshed
enormity
enormous
enough
enquire
enquirer
enquiry
enrage
enrapture
enrich

enrichment
enrol
enrolment
ensconced
enshrine
enshroud
enslave
enslavement
ensnare
ensue
ensuing
ensure
entail
entangle
entanglement
enthral
enthrone
enthronement
enthuse
enthusiasm
enthusiast
enthusiastic
entice
enticement
enticing
entire
entirely
entirety
entitle
entitlement
entomb
entrance
entrap
entrapment
entreat
entreaty
entrench
entrenchment
entrust
entwine
enumerate
enunciate
envelop
environment
environmental
environmentalism
environmentalist
environs
envisage
envision

enn:
ennoble

in:
in
in-
inability
inaccessible
inaccuracy
inaccurate

inaction
inactive
inadequacy
inadequate
inadmissible
inadvertent
inadvisable
inalienable
inane
inanimate
inapplicable
inappropriate
inarticulate
inasmuch as
inattention
inattentive
inaudible
inaugural
inaugurate
inauspicious
inboard
inborn
inbound
inbred
inbreeding
inbuilt
incalculable
incandescent
incantation
incapable
incapacitate
incapacity
incarcerate
incarnate
incarnation
incautious
incendiary
incense
incentive
inception
incessant
incest
incestuous
inch
inchoate
incidence
incident
incidental
incidentally
incinerate
incinerator
incipient
incise
incision
incisive
incisor
incite
incitement
inclement
inclination

incline
inclined
include
included
including
inclusion
inclusive
incognito
incoherent
income
incomer
incoming
incommunicado
incomparable
incomparably
incompatible
incompetence
incompetent
incomplete
incomprehensible
incomprehension
inconceivable
inconclusive
incongruity
incongruous
inconsequential
inconsiderable
inconsiderate
inconsistency
inconsistent
inconsolable
inconspicuous
incontinence
incontinent
incontrovertible
inconvenience
inconvenient
incorporate
incorrect
incorrigible
incorruptible
increase
increasingly
incredible
incredulity
incredulous
increment
incremental
incriminate
incubate
incubator
inculcate
incumbent
incur
incurable
incursion
indebted
indecency
indecent
indecipherable

indecision
indecisive
indeed
indefatigable
indefensible
indefinable
indefinite
indefinitely
indelible
indelicate
indemnify
indemnity
indent
indentation
indented
indentured
independence
independent
indescribable
indestructible
indeterminacy
indeterminate
index
Indian
indicate
indication
indicative
indicator
indices
indict
indictment
indie
indifference
indifferent
indigenous
indigent
indigestible
indigestion
indignant
indignation
indignity
indigo
indirect
indiscipline
indiscreet
indiscretion
indiscriminate
indispensable
indisposed
indisputable
indissoluble
indistinct
indistinguishable
individual
individualism
individualist
individualistic
individuality
individualize

indivisible
Indo-
indoctrinate
indolence
indolent
indomitable
Indonesian
indoor
indoors
indubitable
induce
inducement
induct
induction
inductive
indulge
indulgence
indulgent
industrial
industrialise
industrialism
industrialist
industrialize
industrialized
industrious
industry
inebriated
inedible
ineffable
ineffective
ineffectual
inefficient
inelegant
ineligible
ineluctable
inept
ineptitude
inequality
inequitable
inequity
ineradicable
inert
inertia
inescapable
inessential
inestimable
inevitability
inevitable
inevitably
inexact
inexcusable
inexhaustible
inexorable
inexpensive
inexperience
inexperienced
inexpert
inexplicable
inexpressible

in extremis
inextricable
inextricably
infallible
infamous
infamy
infancy
infant
infanticide
infantile
infantry
infantryman
infatuated
infatuation
infect
infected
infection
infectious
infective
infer
inference
inferior
infernal
inferno
infertile
infest
infidel
infidelity
infill
infiltrate
infiltrator
infinite
infinitesimal
infinitive
infinitum
infinity
infirm
infirmary
inflame
inflamed
inflammable
inflammation
inflammatory
inflatable
inflate
inflation
inflationary
inflect
inflection
inflexible
inflexion
inflict
inflow
influence
influential
influenza
influx
info
infobahn

infomercial
inform
informal
informant
information
informational
informative
informed
informer
infotainment
infra-red
infrastructure
infrequent
infringe
infringement
infuriate
infuriating
infuse
infusion
ingenious
ingenuity
ingenuous
ingest
inglorious
ingrained
ingratiate
ingratiating
ingratitude
ingredient
ingrown
inhabit
inhabitant
inhalation
inhale
inhaler
inherent
inherit
inheritance
inheritor
inhibit
inhibited
inhibition
inhospitable
inhuman
inhumane
inhumanity
inimical
inimitable
iniquitous
iniquity
initial
initially
initiate
initiation
initiative
initiator
inject
injection
injudicious

injunction
injure
injured
injurious
injury
injustice
inlaid
inland
inlay
inlet
inmate
inmost
inoculate
inoffensive
inoperable
inoperative
inopportune
inordinate
inorganic
input
inquest
inquire
inquirer
inquiring
inquiry
inquisition
inquisitive
inquisitor
inquisitorial
inroads
insane
insanitary
insanity
insatiable
inscribe
inscription
inscrutable
insect
insecticide
insecure
inseminate
insensitive
inseparable
insert
inset
inshore
inside
insider
insidious
insight
insightful
insignia
insignificance
insignificant
insincere
insinuate
insinuating
insipid
insist

insistence
insistent
in situ
insofar as
insole
insolent
insoluble
insolvency
insolvent
insomnia
insomniac
insouciance
insouciant
inspect
inspector
inspectorate
inspiration
inspirational
inspire
inspiring
instability
install
installation
instalment
instance
instant
instantaneous
instead
instep
instigate
instigator
instil
instinct
instinctive
instinctual
institute
institution
institutional
institutionalize
instruct
instruction
instructional
instructive
instructor
instrument
instrumental
instrumentalist
instrumentation
insubordinate
insubordination
insubstantial
insufferable
insufficient
insular
insulate
insulation
insulator
insulin
insult

insulting
insuperable
insupportable
insurance
insure
insured
insurer
insurgency
insurgent
insurmountable
insurrection
intact
intake
intangible
integer
integral
integrate
integrated
integrity
intellect
intellectual
intelligence
intelligent
intelligentsia
intelligible
intemperate
intend
intended
intense
intensifier
intensify
intensive
intent
intention
intentional
inter
inter-
interact
interactive
inter alia
intercede
intercept
interceptor
intercession
interchange
interchangeable
intercollegiate
intercom
interconnect
interconnection
intercontinental
intercourse
intercut
interdependence
interdependent
interdict
interdiction
interdisciplinary
interest

interested
interesting
interestingly
interface
interfere
interference
interfering
interim
interior
interject
interjection
interlaced
interlink
interlock
interlocutor
interloper
interlude
intermarriage
intermarry
intermediary
intermediate
interment
interminable
intermingle
intermission
intermittent
intern
internal
internalize
international
internationalism
internationalist
internationalize
internecine
internee
Internet
internment
interpersonal
interplay
interpolate
interpolation
interpose
interpret
interpretation
interpretative
interpreter
interpretive
interregnum
interrelate
interrelationship
interrogate
interrogation
interrogative
interrupt
intersect
intersection
intersperse
interspersed
interstate

/ɪŋ/

interstellar
intertwine
interval
intervene
intervening
intervention
interventionist
interview
interviewee
interviewer
interweave
intestinal
intestine
intimacy
intimate
intimation
intimidate
intimidated
intimidating
into
intolerable
intolerance
intolerant
intonation
intone
intoxicated
intoxicating
intoxication
intractable
intransigence
intransigent
intransitive
intravenous
intrepid
intricacies
intricacy
intricate
intrigue
intrigued
intriguing
intrinsic
introduce
introduction
introductory
introspection
introspective
introvert
introverted
intrude
intruder
intrusion
intrusive
intuit
intuition
intuitive
Inuit
inundate
inure
invade

invader
invalid
invalidate
invalidity
invaluable
invariable
invariably
invasion
invasive
invective
inveigh
inveigle
invent
invention
inventive
inventor
inventory
inverse
inversion
invert
invertebrate
invest
investigate
investigative
investigator
investigatory
investiture
investment
investor
inveterate
invidious
invigilate
invigorate
invigorating
invincible
inviolable
inviolate
invisible
invitation
invite
inviting
in vitro
invocation
invoice
invoke
involuntary
involve
involved
involvement
invulnerable
inward
inwards

inn:
inn
innards
innate
inner
innermost
inning

innings
innkeeper
innocence
innocent
innocently
innocuous
innovate
innovation
innovative
innovator
innovatory
innuendo
innumerable

/ɪŋ/

en:
English
Englishman
Englishwoman

in:
ingot
ink
inkling
inkwell
inky

/ɪp/

ep:
Epiphany
episcopal
Episcopalian
epistle
epistolary
epitome
epitomize
eponymous

/ɪr/

er:
eradicate
erase
eraser
erasure
erect
erection
erode
erogenous
erosion
erotic
erotica
eroticism
erupt

err:
erratic
erroneous

ir:
ir-
Iranian

/ɪs/

Iraqi
irascible
iridescent

irr:
irradiate
irrational
irreconcilable
irredeemable
irreducible
irrefutable
irregular
irrelevance
irrelevancy
irrelevant
irreligious
irremediable
irreparable
irreplaceable
irrepressible
irreproachable
irresistible
irresolute
irrespective
irresponsible
irretrievable
irreverent
irreversible
irrevocable
irrigate
irritable
irritant
irritate
irritating
irritation

/ɪs/

es:
escape
escapee
escapism
escapist
escarpment
eschew
escort
esophagus
especial
especially
espousal
espouse
espy
esquire
establish
established
establishment
estate
esteem
esteemed
estranged
estrangement

/ɪt/

ess:
essential
essentially

is:
issue
isthmus

/ɪt/

et:
eternal
eternity

it:
it
Italian
italic
it'd
it'll
its
it's
itself

/ɪθ/

eth:
ethereal

/ɪv/

ev:
evacuate
evacuee
evade
evaluate
evaluative
evangelism
evangelist
evangelize
evaporate
evasion
evasive
event
eventful
eventual
eventuality
eventually
evict
eviction
evince
eviscerate
evocative
evoke
evolve

/ɪz/

is:
is
Islam
Islamic
isn't
Israeli

/aɪ/

aye:
aye

eye:
eye

i:
I, i
ID
i.e.
IMF
IOU
IQ
ITV
IUD

/aɪoʊ/

io:
iota

/aɪb/

eyeb:
eyeball
eyebrow

/aɪk/

ic:
icon
iconic
iconoclast
iconoclastic
iconography

ik:
ikon

/aɪd/

eid:
eiderdown

I'd:
I'd

id:
idea
ideal
idealise
idealism
idealistic
idealize
ideally
identical
identifiable
identification
identify
identikit
identity
ideological
ideologist
ideologue
ideology
idle
idler
idol
idolatry
idolize

/aɪf/

eyef:
eyeful

/aɪl/

aisl:
aisle

eyel:
eyelash
eyelet
eyelid
eyeliner

I'll:
I'll

isl:
island
islander
isle
islet

/aɪm/

I'm:
I'm

/aɪp/

eyep:
eyepiece

/aɪr/

ir:
irate
ironic
ironically
ironist
irony

/aɪs/

eis:
eisteddfod

eyes:
eyesight
eyesore

ic:
ice
iceberg
icebox
iced

Icelander
Icelandic
icicle
icing
icy

is:
isolate
isolated
isolation
isolationism
isometrics
isotope

/aɪt/

it:
item
itemize
itinerant
itinerary

/aɪð/

eith:
either

/aɪv/

iv:
ivory
ivy

I've:
I've

/aɪw/

eyew:
eyewitness

/aɪə/

aya:
ayatollah

i:
iris
Irish
Irishman
Irishwoman

io:
iodine
ion
ionizer

ire:
ire

iro:
iron
ironclad
ironmonger
ironmongery
ironwork

/ɒ/
/ɒb/

ob:
obduracy
obdurate
obelisk
obfuscate
object
objet d'art
obligate
obligated
obligation
oblong
obnoxious
obscene
obscenity
obscurantism
obscurantist
obscure
obscurity
obsequious
observation
observational
obsolescence
obsolescent
obsolete
obstacle
obstetrician
obstetrics
obstinate
obstreperous
obstruct
obstruction
obstructionism
obstructive
obtain
obtainable
obtrude
obtrusive
obverse
obviate
obvious
obviously

/ɒk/

oc:
octagon
octagonal
octane
octave
octet
October
octogenarian
octopus
ocular

occ:
occult
occultist
occupancy
occupant
occupation
occupational
occupier
occupy

/ɒks/

occ:
occidental

ox:
ox
Oxbridge
oxcart
oxidation
oxide
oxidize
oxtail
oxygen
oxygenate
oxymoron

/ɒd/

od:
odyssey

odd:
odd
oddball
oddity
oddly
oddment
odds

/ɒf/

off:
off
offal
offbeat
off-Broadway
offer
offering
offertory
office
officer
offing
offload
offset
offshoot
offshore
offside
offspring
offstage

oft:
oft-
often
oftentimes

oph:
ophthalmic
ophthalmologist
ophthalmology

/ɒl/

ol:
olfactory
oligarchy
olive

/ɒm/

om:
ombudsman
omelette
ominous
omnibus
omnipotence
omnipotent
omnipresent
omniscient
omnivorous

/ɒn/

en:
en bloc
enfant terrible
en masse
ennui
en route
ensemble
en suite
entente
entourage
entrée
entrepreneur
entrepreneurial
envelope

hon:
Hon.
honest
honestly
honesty
honor
honorable
honorarium
honorary
honorific
honour
honourable
Hons

on:
on
oncoming
ongoing
online
onlooker
onomatopoeia
onomatopoeic
onrush
onrushing
onset
onshore
onslaught
onstage
onto
ontology
onward
onyx

/ɒŋ/

en:
encore

/ɒp/

op:
op
op. cit.
opera
operandi
operate
operatic
operation
operational
operative
operator
operetta
opt
optic
optical
optician
optics
optimal
optimism
optimist
optimistic
optimize
optimum
option
optional
opulent

opp:
opportune
opportunism
opportunist
opportunistic
opportunity
opposite
opposition

/ɒr/

or:
oracle
orange
orangery
orangey
orator
oratorical
oratorio
oratory

/ɒs/

oregano
orifice
origami
origin

/ɒs/

aus:
Australasian
Australian
Austrian
Austro-

os:
oscillate
osmosis
ostensible
ostentation
ostentatious
osteopath
osteoporosis
ostracism
ostracize
ostrich

oss:
ossify

/ɒt/

ott:
otter

/ɒv/

of:
of

ov:
ovulate

/ɒz/

auss:
Aussie

/ɒx/

och:
och

/oʊ/

au:
au fait
au pair

eau:
eau de cologne

o:
O,o
OAP
OD
OHMS
OHP

OK
OTT

oh:
oh

owe:
owe

/oʊeɪ/

oa:
oasis

/oʊb/

aub:
aubergine

ob:
obedient
obeisance
obese
obey
obituary
oblique
oboe
oboist

/oʊk/

oak:
oak
oaken

och:
ochre

ok:
okay
okra

/oʊd/

od:
ode
odious
odium
odor
odour
odourless

/oʊf/

oaf:
oaf
oafish

/oʊg/

og:
ogle
ogre

/oʊl/

aul:
Auld Lang Syne

ol:
old
olde
olden
oldie
ole
oleander

/oʊm/

ohm:
ohm

om:
omen
omission
omit

/oʊn/

on:
onerous
only
onus

own:
own
owner
ownership

/oʊp/

op:
opacity
opal
opalescent
opaque
open
opencast
opener
opening
openly
opiate
opine
opium
opus

/oʊʃ/

oce:
ocean
oceanic
oceanography

/oʊt/

haut:
haute couture
hauteur

oat:
oatmeal
oats

/oʊθ/

oath:
oath

/oʊv/

ov:
ova
oval
ovarian
ovary
ovation
over
over-
overact
overall
overarching
overarm
overawe
overbalance
overbearing
overblown
overboard
overbook
overbooked
overburdened
overcame
overcast
overcharge
overcoat
overcome
overcrowded
overcrowding
overdo
overdone
overdose
overdraft
overdrawn
overdressed
overdrive
overdue
overeat
overemphasis
overemphasize
overestimate
overexposed
overextended
overflight
overflow
overfly
overground
overgrown
overhang
overhaul
overhead
overheads
overhear
overheat
overheated
overhung

/oʊz/

overindulge
overjoyed
overkill
overland
overlap
overlay
overleaf
overload
overlook
overlord
overly
overmanned
overmanning
overmuch
overnight
overpaid
overpass
overpay
overplay
overpopulated
overpopulation
overpower
overpowering
overpriced
overran
overrate
overreach
overreact
override
overriding
overrule
overrun
overseas
oversee
overseer
oversell
oversexed
overshadow
overshoot
oversight
oversimplify
oversize
oversleep
overspend
overspill
overstaffed
overstate
overstatement
overstay
overstep
overstretch
overstretched
oversubscribed
overt
overtake
overtax
overthrow
overtime
overtired
overtone

overtook
overture
overturn
overuse
overvalue
overview
overweening
overweight
overwhelm
overwhelming
overwork
overworked
overwrought
ovum

/oʊz/

oz:
ozone

/ɔː/

awe:
awe

oar:
oar

o'er:
o'er

or:
or

ore:
ore

/ɔːb/

aub:
auburn

orb:
orb
orbit
orbital

/ɔːk/

auc:
auction
auctioneer

auk:
auk

awk:
awkward

orch:
orchestra
orchestral
orchestrate
orchestration
orchid

/ɔːtʃ/

orch:
orchard

/ɔːd/

aud:
audacious
audacity
audible
audience
audio
audit
audition
auditor
auditorium
auditory

hors d':
hors d'oeuvre

ord:
ordain
ordeal
order
ordered
orderly
ordinal number
ordinance
ordinand
ordinarily
ordinary
ordination
ordnance

/ɔːf/

awf:
awful

orph:
orphan
orphanage

/ɔːg/

aug:
augment
augur
augury
august
August

org:
organ
organdie
organic
organisation
organisational
organise
organiser
organism
organist

organization
organizational
organize
organized
organizer
organza
orgasm
orgasmic

/ɔːgz/

aux:
auxiliary

/ɔːdʒ/

org:
orgiastic
orgy

/ɔːl/

al:
albeit
alder
alderman
all
all-
allspice
almanac
almanack
almighty
almost
already
alright
also
altar
alter
alteration
altercation
alternate
alternative
alternatively
alternator
although
altogether
always

/ɔːn/

awn:
awning

orn:
ornament
ornamental
ornamentation
ornamented
ornate
ornery
ornithology

/ɔːr/

aur:
aura
aural

or:
oral
orang-outan
orient
Orient
oriental
orientalist
orientate
orientated
orientation
oriented
orienteering

/ɔːs/

aus:
auspices
auspicious
austere
austerity

awes:
awesome
awestruck

/ɔːt/

aut:
autism
autistic
auto
autobahn
autobiographical
autobiography
autocracy
autocrat
autocratic
autocue
autograph
automate
automated
automatic
automaton
automobile
automotive
autonomous
autonomy
autopilot
autopsy
autumn
autumnal

ought:
ought
oughtn't

/ɔːθ/

auth:
authentic
authenticate
author
authoress
authorial
authorise
authoritarian
authoritarianism
authoritative
authority
authorize
authorship

orth:
orthodontist
orthodox
orthodoxy
orthopaedic

/ɔɪ/

/ɔɪk/

oik:
oik

/ɔɪl/

oil:
oil
oilcloth
oiled
oilfield
oilman
oilseed rape
oilskins
oily

/ɔɪn/

oin:
ointment

/ɔɪs/

oys:
oyster
oystercatcher

/ʊ/

/ʊm/

oom:
oomph

um:
umlaut

/ʊp/

oop:
oops

/uː/

oo:
oo
ooh

/uːd/

ood:
oodles

/uːt/

out:
outré

/uːz/

ooz:
ooze

ouz:
ouzo

/ʊə/

/ʊəd/

urd:
Urdu

/aʊ/

ow:
ow

/aʊtʃ/

ouch:
ouch

outsh:
outshine

/aʊl/

owl:
owl
owlish

/aʊn/

oun:
ounce

/aʊs/

ous:
oust

/aʊt/

out:
out
out-
outage
outback
outbid
outboard
outbound
outbreak
outbuilding
outburst
outcast
outclass
outcome
outcrop
outcry
outdated
outdid
outdistance
outdo
outdoor
outdoors
outer
outermost
outerwear
outfall
outfield
outfielder
outfit
outfitter
outflank
outflow
outfox
outgoing
outgoings
outgrow
outgrowth
outguess
outgun
outhouse
outing
outlandish
outlast
outlaw
outlay
outlet
outline
outlive
outlook
outlying
outmanoeuvre
outmoded
outnumber
outpace
outpatient
outperform
outplacement
outplay
outpoint
outpost
outpouring
output
outrage
outrageous
outran
outrank
outreach

/aʊəg/

outrider
outright
outrun
outsell
outset
outshine
outside
outsider
outsize
outskirts
outsmart
outsold
outspoken
outstanding
outstandingly
outstay
outstretched
outstrip
outvote
outward
outwardly
outwards
outweigh
outwit
outworn

/aʊə/

hour:
hour

our:
our

/aʊəg/

hourg:
hourglass

/aʊəl/

hourl:
hourly

/aʊəs/

ours:
ourself
ourselves

/aʊəz/

ours:
ours

/ʌ/

/ʌd/

udd:
udder

/ʌg/

ug:
ugly

/ʌl/

ul:
ulcer
ulcerated
ulterior
ultimate
ultimately
ultimatum
ultra-
ultramarine
ultrasonic
ultrasound
ultraviolet

/ʌm/

um:
umber
umbilical cord
umbrage
umbrella
umpire
umpteen
umpteenth

/ʌn/

on:
onion

un:
un-
unabashed
unabated
unable
unabridged
unacceptable
unaccompanied
unaccountable
unaccounted for
unaccustomed
unacknowledged
unacquainted
unadorned
unadulterated
unaffected
unafraid
unaided
unalloyed
unalterable
unaltered
unambiguous
unambitious
unannounced
unanswerable
unanswered
unappealing
unappetizing
unapproachable
unarguable
unarmed
unashamed

unasked
unassailable
unassisted
unassuming
unattached
unattainable
unattended
unattractive
unauthorized
unavailable
unavailing
unavoidable
unaware
unawares
unbalance
unbalanced
unbearable
unbeatable
unbeaten
unbecoming
unbeknown
unbelievable
unbeliever
unbelieving
unbend
unbending
unbiased
unbidden
unbind
unblemished
unblinking
unborn
unbound
unbounded
unbreakable
unbridgeable
unbridled
unbroken
unbuckle
unburden
unbutton
uncalled for
uncanny
uncared for
uncaring
unceasing
unceremoniously
uncertain
uncertainty
unchallenged
unchangeable
unchanged
unchanging
uncharacteristic
uncharitable
uncharted
unchecked
uncivilized
unclaimed
unclassified

/ʌn/

unclean
unclear
unclothed
uncluttered
uncoil
uncombed
uncomfortable
uncommitted
uncommon
uncommunicative
uncomplaining
uncomplicated
uncomprehending
uncompromising
unconcealed
unconcern
unconcerned
unconditional
unconfirmed
uncongenial
unconnected
unconscionable
unconscious
unconstitutional
uncontrollable
uncontrolled
unconventional
unconvinced
unconvincing
uncooked
uncooperative
uncoordinated
uncork
uncorroborated
uncountable noun
uncount noun
uncouth
uncover
uncovered
uncritical
uncultivated
uncultured
uncut
undamaged
undated
undaunted
undecided
undefeated
undemanding
undemocratic
undemonstrative
undeniable
under
under-
underachieve
underarm
underbelly
underbrush
undercarriage
underclass

underclothes
underclothing
undercoat
undercover
undercurrent
undercut
underdeveloped
underdog
underdone
underemployed
underestimate
underexposed
underfed
underfinanced
underfoot
underfunded
undergarment
undergo
undergraduate
underground
undergrowth
underhand
underlay
underlie
underline
underling
underlying
undermanned
undermine
underneath
undernourished
undernourishment
underpaid
underpants
underpass
underpin
underplay
underpopulated
underprivileged
underrate
underscore
undersea
undershirt
underside
undersigned
undersized
understaffed
understand
understandable
understanding
understate
understated
understatement
understood
understudy
undertake
undertaker
undertaking
undertone
undertook

undertow
underused
underutilized
undervalue
underwater
underway
underwear
underweight
underwent
underwhelmed
underwhelming
underworld
underwrite
underwriter
undeserved
undesirable
undetected
undeveloped
undid
undies
undignified
undiluted
undisciplined
undisclosed
undiscovered
undisguised
undismayed
undisputed
undistinguished
undisturbed
undivided
undo
undoing
undone
undoubted
undreamed of
undress
undressed
undue
undulate
unduly
undying
unearned income
unearth
unearthly
unease
uneasy
uneconomic
uneconomical
uneducated
unemotional
unemployable
unemployed
unemployment
unending
unendurable
unenviable
unequal
unequalled
unequivocal

unerring
unescorted
unethical
uneven
uneventful
unexceptionable
unexceptional
unexciting
unexpected
unexplained
unfailing
unfair
unfaithful
unfamiliar
unfashionable
unfasten
unfathomable
unfavourable
unfeasible
unfeeling
unfettered
unfinished
unfit
unflagging
unflappable
unflattering
unflinching
unfocused
unfold
unforeseeable
unforeseen
unforgettable
unforgivable
unforgiving
unformed
unfortunate
unfortunately
unfounded
unfriendly
unfruitful
unfulfilled
unfunny
unfurl
unfurnished
ungainly
ungenerous
ungodly
ungovernable
ungracious
ungraded
ungrateful
unguarded
unhampered
unhappily
unhappy
unharmed
unhealthy
unheard
unheeded
unhelpful

unheralded
unhesitatingly
unhinge
unhinged
unholy
unhook
unhurried
unhurt
unhygienic
unidentifiable
unidentified
unimaginable
unimaginative
unimpaired
unimpressed
unimpeachable
unimpeded
unimportant
unimpressed
unimpressive
uninformed
uninhabitable
uninhabited
uninhibited
uninitiated
uninspired
uninspiring
unintelligent
unintelligible
unintended
unintentional
uninterested
uninteresting
uninterrupted
uninvited
unjust
unjustifiable
unjustified
unkempt
unkind
unknowable
unknowing
unknowingly
unknown
unlawful
unleaded
unlearn
unleash
unleavened
unless
unlike
unlikely
unlimited
unlisted
unlit
unload
unlock
unlovable
unloved
unlovely
unloving

/ʌn/

unluckily
unlucky
unmade
unmanageable
unmanly
unmanned
unmarked
unmarried
unmask
unmatched
unmentionable
unmercifully
unmet
unmissable
unmistakable
unmitigated
unmolested
unmoved
unmusical
unnamed
unnatural
unnaturally
unnecessary
unnerve
unnerving
unnoticed
unobserved
unobtainable
unobtrusive
unoccupied
unofficial
unopened
unopposed
unorthodox
unpack
unpaid
unpalatable
unparalleled
unpardonable
unpick
unplayable
unpleasant
unplug
unplugged
unpolluted
unpopular
unprecedented
unpredictable
unprepared
unprepossessing
unpretentious
unprincipled
unprintable
unproductive
unprofessional
unprofitable
unpromising
unpronounceable
unprotected
unprovoked
unpublished
unpunished
unqualified
unquestionable
unquestioned
unquestioning
unquote
unravel
unread
unreadable
unreal
unrealistic
unreasonable
unreasoning
unrecognizable
unrecognized
unreconstructed
unrecorded
unrefined
unrehearsed
unrelated
unrelenting
unreliable
unrelieved
unremarkable
unremarked
unremitting
unrepentant
unrepresentative
unrepresented
unrequited
unreserved
unresolved
unresponsive
unrest
unrestrained
unrestricted
unrewarded
unrewarding
unripe
unrivalled
unroll
unruffled
unruly
unsafe
unsaid
unsaleable
unsanitary
unsatisfactory
unsatisfied
unsatisfying
unsavoury
unscathed
unscheduled
unschooled
unscientific
unscramble
unscrew
unscripted
unscrupulous
unseasonably
unseat
unsecured
unseeded
unseeing
unseemly
unseen
unselfish
unsentimental
unsettle
unsettled
unsettling
unshaded
unshakeable
unshaken
unshaven
unsightly
unsigned
unskilled
unsmiling
unsociable
unsocial
unsold
unsolicited
unsolved
unsophisticated
unsound
unspeakable
unspecified
unspectacular
unspoiled
unspoken
unsporting
unstable
unstated
unsteady
unstick
unstinting
unstoppable
unstressed
unstructured
unstuck
unsubstantiated
unsuccessful
unsuitable
unsuited
unsullied
unsung
unsupported
unsure
unsurpassed
unsurprising
unsuspected
unsuspecting
unsweetened
unswerving
unsympathetic
untamed
untangle
untapped
untenable
untested
unthinkable
unthinking
untidy
untie
until
untimely
untiring
unto
untold
untouchable
untouched
untoward
untrained
untrammelled
untreated
untried
untroubled
untrue
untrustworthy
untruth
untruthful
untutored
untypical
unusable
unused
unusual
unusually
unutterable
unvarying
unveil
unwaged
unwanted
unwarranted
unwary
unwashed
unwavering
unwelcome
unwelcoming
unwell
unwholesome
unwieldy
unwilling
unwind
unwise
unwitting
unworkable
unworldly
unworthy
unwound
unwrap
unwritten
unyielding
unzip

/ʌŋ/

un:
uncle
Uncle Sam

/ʌp/

unctuous

/ʌp/

up:
up
upbeat
upbraid
upbringing
upcoming
upcountry
update
upend
upgrade
upheaval
upheld
uphill
uphold
upholder
upholstered
upholsterer
upholstery
upkeep
upland
uplift
uplifted
uplifting
upmarket
upraised
upright
uprising
uproar
uproarious
uproot
upscale
upset
upshot
upside down
upstage
upstairs
upstanding
upstart
upstate
upstream
upsurge
upswing
uptake
uptight
uptown
uptrend
upturn
upturned
upward
upwards
upwind

upp:
upper
uppercut
uppermost
uppity

/ʌs/

us:
us

/ʌʃ/

ush:
usher
usherette

/ʌt/

ut:
utmost

utt:
utter
utterance
utterly
uttermost

/ʌð/

oth:
other
otherness
otherwise

/ʌv/

of:
of

ov:
oven
ovenproof

/ju:/

ewe:
ewe

u:
U,u
UFO
UHF
UHT
UK
UN
US
USA
USAF

yew:
yew

you:
you

/ju:æ/

yua:
yuan

/ju:b/

ub:
ubiquitous
ubiquity

/ju:k/

euc:
eucalyptus

euch:
Eucharist

uk:
ukulele

/ju:d/

you'd:
you'd

/ju:f/

euph:
euphemism
euphemistic
euphoria
euphoric

/ju:g/

ug:
Ugandan

yug:
Yugoslav
Yugoslavian

/ju:dʒ/

eug:
eugenics

/ju:l/

eul:
eulogize
eulogy

ul:
ululate

you'll:
you'll

yul:
Yule
Yuletide

/ju:n/

eun:
eunuch

un:
unanimity
unanimous
unicorn
unification
uniform
uniformed
uniformity
unify
unilateral
unilateralism
union
unionism
unionization
unionized
unique
unisex
unison
unit
unitary
unite
united
unity
universal
universally
universe
university

/ju:s/

us:
usage
use
used
useful
useless

/ju:ʒ/

us:
usual
usually
usury

/ju:t/

ut:
utensil
uterine
uterus
utilise
utilitarian
utilitarianism
utility
utilize
utopia
utopian

/ju:θ/

euth:
euthanasia

youth:
youth
youthful

/ju:v/

you've:
you've

/juːz/

us:
usable
use
used
user
usurp
usurper

/jʊə/

eur:
Eurasian
Euro-
Eurocentric
Eurocrat
Europe
European

ur:
urinary
urinate
urine

/ə/

a:
a

are:
are

or:
or

/əb/

ab:
aback
abandon
abandoned
abandonment
abashed
abate
abatement
abbreviate
abbreviation
abdominal
abduct
aberrant
abet
abeyance
abhor
abhorrence
abide
abiding
ability
abjure
ablaze
ablutions
aboard
abode
abolish
abominable
abomination
abort
abortion
abortionist
abortive
abound
about
above
abrade
abrasion
abrasive
abreast
abridge
abridged
abroad
abrupt
abscond
absent
absolve
absorb
absorbed
absorbent
absorber
absorbing
absorption
abstain
abstemious
abstention
abstract
abstraction
absurd
abundance
abundant
abundantly
abuse
abusive
abut
abuzz
abysmal
abyss

ob:
obedient
obese
obey
obituary
object
objection
objectionable
objective
objector
obligatory
oblige
obliging
oblique
obliterate
oblivion
oblivious
obnoxious
obscene
obscure
obsequious
observable
observance
observant
observatory
observe
observer
obsess
obsessed
obsession
obsessional
obsessive
obstetrics
obstreperous
obstruct
obtain
obtrude
obtuse

/ək/

ac:
acacia
academician
academy
acoustic
acoustical
across
acrylic
acuity
acute
acutely

acc:
acclaim
acclimatize
accommodate
accommodating
accommodation
accompaniment
accompanist
accompany
accomplice
accomplish
accomplished
accomplishment
accord
accordance
accordingly
accordion
accost
account
accountable
accountancy
accountant
accounting
accoutrement
accredit
accretion
accrual
accrue
accumulate
accumulation
accumulative
accumulator
accursed
accusative
accusatory
accuse
accused
accuser
accusing
accustom
accustomed

ach:
Achilles heel
Achilles tendon

ack:
acknowledge
acknowledgement

ak:
akimbo
akin

o'c:
o'clock

occ:
occasion
occasional
occult
occur
occurrence

/əks/

acc:
accede
accelerate
acceleration
accelerator
accentuate
accept
acceptable
acceptance
accepted
accessible
accession
accessory

/əkw/

acqu:
acquaint
acquaintance
acquaintanceship
acquainted
acquire
acquirer

/ətʃ/

acquisitive
acquit
acquittal

aqu:
aquarium
Aquarius
aquatic

/ətʃ/

ach:
achievable
achieve
achievement
achiever

/əd/

ad:
adagio
adapt
adaptable
adapted
adaption
adaptive
adaptor
adept
adhere
adherence
adherent
adhesion
adieu
administer
administration
administrative
administrator
admire
admirer
admiring
admissible
admission
admit
admittance
admittedly
admonish
ado
adobe
adopt
adorable
adore
adoring
adorn
adornment
adrenalin
adrift
adroit
adulterate
adulterer
adulteress
adulterous
adultery

advance
advanced
advancement
advantage
advantaged
adventure
adventurer
adventurism
adventurist
adventurous
adverbial
adversity
advertisement
advice
advisable
advise
advisedly
advisement
adviser
advisory

add:
addendum
addicted
addiction
addictive
addition
additional
additionally
address
adduce

/əf/

af:
afar
aficionado
afield
afire
aflame
afloat
afoot
aforementioned
aforesaid
afoul
afraid
afresh

aff:
affair
affect
affected
affecting
affection
affectionate
affiliate
affiliated
affiliation
affinity
affirm
affirmative
affix

afflict
affliction
afford
affordable
afforestation
affray
affront

aph:
aphasia

off:
offence
offend
offender
offending
offense
offensive
official
officialdom
officiate
officious

/əg/

ag:
again
against
agape
aglow
agnostic
ago
agog
agrarian
agree
agreeable
agreed
agreement
agronomist
aground

agg:
agglomeration
aggrandize
aggrandizement
aggression
aggressive
aggressor
aggrieved

agh:
aghast

/əh/

ah:
ahead
ahold
ahoy

/ədʒ/

adj:
adjacent
adjoin

adjourn
adjournment
adjudge
adjudicate
adjust
adjustable
adjuster
adjustment

ag:
agenda

aj:
ajar

/əl/

al:
alacrity
alarm
alarmed
alarming
alarmist
alas
alert
alight
align
alignment
alike
alive
aloft
alone
along
alongside
aloof
aloud
aluminum
alumnus

all:
allay
allege
alleged
allegiance
allegro
allergic
alleviate
alliance
alliteration
alliterative
allot
allotment
allow
allowable
allowance
allude
allure
alluring
allusion
allusive
alluvial
ally

205

/əm/ /əs/

ol:
Olympian
Olympic

/əm/

am:
am
amalgam
amalgamate
amass
amaze
amazement
amazing
ameliorate
amenable
amend
amendment
amenity
America
American
Americana
Americanism
Americanize
amid
amidships
amidst
amino acid
amiss
amoeba
amok
among
amongst
amorphous
amortize
amount
amour
amuse
amused
amusement
amusing

amm:
ammonia

om:
omission
omit
omnipotence
omnipotent

/ən/

an:
an
anachronism
anachronistic
anaemia
anaemic
anaesthetist
anaesthetize
analogous

analogy
analysis
anathema
anatomist
anatomize
anatomy
and
anemia
anemic
anemone
anesthetist
anesthetize
anew
anoint
anomalous
anomaly
anon
anonymous
another

ann:
annex
annihilate
announce
announcement
announcer
annoy
annoyance
annoyed
annoying
annuity
annul
annulment
Annunciation

un:
unless
until

/əp/

ap:
apace
apart
apartheid
apartment
aperitif
apiece
aplenty
aplomb
apocalypse
apocalyptic
apocryphal
apologetic
apologise
apologist
apologize
apology
apostasy
apostate
apostle
apostrophe

apothecary
apotheosis

app:
appal
appalled
appalling
apparel
apparent
apparently
appeal
appealing
appear
appearance
appease
appeasement
appellant
appellate court
append
appendage
appendices
appendicitis
appendix
applaud
applause
appliance
applicable
applied
applique
appliqued
apply
appoint
appointed
appointee
appointment
apportion
appraisal
appraise
appraiser
appreciable
appreciate
appreciation
appreciative
apprentice
apprenticeship
apprise
approach
approachable
appropriate
appropriation
approval
approve
approved
approving
approximate
approximation

op:
opine
opinion
opinionated

opossum

opp:
opponent
oppose
opposed
opposing
oppress
oppressed
oppression
oppressive
oppressor
opprobrium

up:
upon

/ər/

ar:
Arabian
arena
arise
aristocratic
arithmetic
aroma
aromatherapist
aromatherapy
arose
around
arousal
arouse

arr:
arraign
arraignment
arrange
arranged
arrangement
arranger
array
arrayed
arrears
arrest
arrival
arrive

awr:
awry

or:
orang-outan
oration
original
originally
originate
originator

/əs/

ac:
acerbic
acerbity

/əʃ/

acetic acid
acetylene
acidic

as:
aside
askance
askew
asleep
asparagus
aspersions
asphyxia
aspirant
aspire
aspiring
astern
astigmatism
astonish
astonished
astonishing
astonishment
astound
astounded
astounding
astray
astride
astringent
astrologer
astrology
astronomer
astronomy
astute
asunder
asylum

asc:
ascend
ascendancy
ascendant
ascendency
ascending
ascension
ascent
ascetic
asceticism
ascribe

ass:
assail
assailant
assassin
assassinate
assault
assemblage
assemble
assembler
assembly
assemblyman
assemblywoman
assent
assert

assertive
assess
assessment
assessor
assiduous
assign
assignment
assimilate
assist
assistance
assistant
associate
associated
association
associative
assorted
assortment
assuage
assume
assuming
assumption

us:
us

/əʃ/

ash:
ashamed
ashore

ass:
assurance
assure
assured
assuredly

/ət/

at:
at
atelier
atishoo
atomic
atone
atonement
atop
atrocious
atrocity

att:
attach
attaché
attached
attachment
attack
attacker
attain
attainable
attainment
attempt
attempted
attend

attendance
attendant
attendee
attender
attention
attentive
attenuate
attenuated
attest
attire
attired
attorney
attract
attraction
attractive
attributable
attribute
attrition
attuned

/əv/

av:
avail
available
avenge
aver
averse
aversion
avert
avoid
avoidable
avoidance
avow
avowed
avuncular

of:
of

ov:
ovation

/əw/

aw:
await
awake
awaken
awakening
award
aware
awash
away
awhile
awoke
awoken

/əz/

as:
as

/b/
/bæ/

ba:
babble
baboon
baccalaureate
bachelor
back
backache
backbencher
backbenches
backbiting
backbone
backcloth
backcomb
backdate
backdoor
backdrop
backer
backfire
backgammon
background
backhand
backhanded
backhander
backing
backlash
backless
backlog
backpack
backpacker
backpacking
backrest
backside
backsliding
backstage
backstroke
backtrack
backup
backward
backwards
backwash
backwater
backwoods
backwoodsman
backyard
bacteria
bacterial
bacteriology
bacterium
bad
baddy
bade
badge
badger
badinage
badly
badminton
bad-mouth

/beɪ/   /beə/

baffle
bafflement
bag
baggage
baggy
bagpipes
baguette
balaclava
balance
balanced
balcony
ballad
ballast
ballerina
ballet
balletic
ballot
ballyhoo
balustrade
bamboo
bamboozle
ban
band
bandage
bandanna
banded
bandit
banditry
bandleader
bandsman
bandstand
bandwagon
bandy
bang
banger
Bangladeshi
bangle
banish
banishment
banister
banjo
bank
bankable
banked
banker
banking
banknote
bankroll
bankrupt
bankruptcy
banner
bannister
banns
banquet
banqueting
banquette
banshee
bantam
bantamweight

banter
Bantu
bap
baptise
baptism
baptismal
Baptist
baptize
baritone
barometric pressure
baron
baroness
baronet
barony
barrack
barracuda
barrage
barrel
barren
barricade
barrier
barrister
barrow
basalt
bash
bashful
basil
bass
basset hound
bastion
bat
batch
bath
batman
baton
batsman
batten
batter
battered
batterer
battering
battery
battle
battlefield
battleground
battlements
battleship
batty

/beɪ/

ba:
babe
babel
baby
baby boomer
babyhood
babyish
babysit
bacon

bagel
bake
Bakelite
baker
bakery
bakeware
baking
bale
baleful
bane
basal
base
baseball
based
baseless
baseline
basement
bases
basic
basically
basics
basin
basis
bass
bassist
baste
bated
bathe
bathed
bather
bathing cap
bathing costume
bathing suit
bathing trunks
bathos

bai:
bail
bailiff
bait
baize

bay:
bay
bayonet

bei:
beige

/bɑː/

ba:
bask
basket
basketball
bastard
bastardized
bath
bathmat
bathrobe
bathroom
bathtub

bah:
bah

bal:
balm
balmy

bar:
bar
barb
Barbadian
barbarian
barbaric
barbarism
barbarity
barbarous
barbecue
barbed
barber
barbie
barbiturate
bard
barf
barfly
bargain
barge
bark
barker
barley
barmaid
barman
bar mitzvah
barmy
barn
barnacle
barnstorm
barnstorming
barnyard
bartender
barter

barr:
barring
barrio
barroom

bas:
bas-relief

/beə/

bair:
bairn

bar:
barium

bare:
bare
bareback
barefoot
bareheaded
barely

/be/

bear:
bear
bearable
bearer
bearing
bearish
bearskin

/be/

be:
beck
beckon
bed
bedbug
bedchamber
bedclothes
bedding
bedfellow
bedhead
bedlam
Bedouin
bedpan
bedpost
bedridden
bedrock
bedroll
bedroom
bedside
bedsit
bedsitter
bedsores
bedspread
bedstead
bedtime
bedwetting
beg
beggar
belch
belfry
Belgian
belt
belted
belter
bell
bellboy
belle
bellicose
bellow
bellwether
belly
bellyache
bench
benchmark
bend
bended
bender
bendy
Benedictine
benediction
benefactor

beneficial
beneficiary
benefit
Bengali
bent
benzene
beret
berry
best
bestial
bestiality
bet
bete noire
better
betterment
betting
bevelled
beverage
bevvy
bevy

bu:
burial
bury

/biː/

b:
B, b
BA
B&B
BBC
BC
BEd
B.O.
BS
BSc
BSE

be:
be
bebop
being
beta blocker

bea:
beach
beachcomber
beachfront
beachhead
beacon
bead
beaded
beading
beady
beagle
beak
beaker
beam
bean
beanfeast
beanpole

beast
beastly
beat
beatable
beaten
beater
beatific
beating
beatnik
beaver

bee:
bee
Beeb
beech
beef
beefburger
beefcake
Beefeater
beefsteak
beefy
beehive
beekeeper
beekeeping
beeline
beep
beeper
beeswax
beet
beetle
beetroot

bi:
bidet
bijou
bistro

/bɜː/

ber:
Berber
berk
berth

bir:
birch
bird
birdcage
birdie
birdlife
birdlike
birdsong
birth
birthdate
birthday
birthing
birthmark
birthplace
birthright

bour:
bourbon

/bɪ/

bur:
burble
burden
burdened
burdensome
burgeon
burger
burgher
burglar
burglarize
burglary
burgle
burgundy
burlap
burlesque
burly
Burmese
burn
burner
burning
burnish
burnished
burnt
burp
burr
bursar
bursary
burst
bursting

/bɪə/

bear:
beard
bearded

beer:
beer
beermat
beery

/bɪ/

be:
be
be-
beatify
becalmed
became
because
become
becoming
bedazzled
bedeck
bedecked
bedevil
bedraggled
befall
befit
before
beforehand
befriend

/baɪ/

befuddle
began
beget
begetter
begin
beginner
beginning
begonia
begot
begotten
begrudge
begrudgingly
beguile
beguiling
begun
behalf
behave
behaviour
behavioural
behaviourism
behead
beheld
behemoth
behest
behind
behindhand
behold
beholden
beholder
behove
bejewelled
belabour
belated
beleaguered
belie
belief
believable
believe
believer
belittle
belligerent
belong
belongings
beloved
below
bemoan
bemuse
bemused
beneath
beneficent
benevolent
benighted
benign
bequeath
bequest
berate
bereaved
bereavement
bereft
beseech

beseeching
beset
beside
besides
besiege
besmirch
besotted
bespeak
bespectacled
bespoke
bestow
bestride
betide
betoken
betray
betrayal
betrothal
betrothed
between
bewail
beware
bewilder
bewildered
bewildering
bewilderment
bewitch
beyond

bee:
been

bi:
bib
biblical
bibliography
bicker
bid
bidden
bidder
bidding
biddy
biff
big
bigamist
bigamous
bigamy
biggie
biggish
bigot
bigoted
bigotry
bigwig
bikini
bilge
bilious
bilk
bill
billboard
billet
billfold
billiards

billion
billionaire
billionth
billow
billy goat
bimbo
bin
binge
bingo
binoculars
Biro
biscuit
bishop
bishopric
bit
bitch
bitchy
bitten
bitter
bitterly
bitty
bitumen
bivouac
biz
bizarre

bu:
busily
business
businesslike
businessman
businesswoman
busy
busybody

bui:
build
builder
building
built

by:
byzantine

/baɪ/

bay:
bayou

bi:
bi-
biannual
bias
biased
Bible
bicarb
bicarbonate of soda
bicentenary
bicentennial
biceps
bicycle
bicyclist

bide
biennial
bifocals
bike
biker
bilateral
bile
bilingual
bilingualism
bimonthly
binary
bind
binder
binding
bio-
biochemical
biochemist
biochemistry
biodegradable
biodiversity
biographer
biographical
biography
biological
biology
bionic
biopic
biopsy
biosphere
biotech
biotechnology
bipartisan
biped
biplane
bipolar
bisect
bisexual
bison
bite
biting
biweekly

buy:
buy
buyout

by:
by
bye
bygone
bylaw
bypass
bystander
byte
byway
byword

/baɪə/

bir:
Biro

/bɒ/

buyer:
buyer

byre:
byre

/bɒ/

bo:
bob
bobbed
bobbin
bobble
bobby
bobcat
bobsled
bobsleigh
bod
bodge
bodice
bodily
body
bodybuilder
bodybuilding
bodyguard
bodysuit
bodywork
boffin
bog
boggle
boggy
bolero
bollard
bollocks
Bolshevik
Bolshevism
bolshy
bomb
bombard
bombardment
bombast
bombastic
bomber
bombshell
bonce
bond
bondage
bonded
bondholder
bonfire
bong
bongo
bonhomie
bonk
bonkers
bon mot
bonnet
bonny
bonsai
bon voyage
bop

bopper
borrow
borrower
borrowing
boss
bossy
botanist
botany
botch
bother
bothersome
bottle
bottled
bottleneck
bottler
bottom
bottomless
botulism
box
boxed
boxer
boxing
boxwood
boxy

/boʊ/

beau:
beau

bo:
bode
Boer
bogey
bogeyman
bogus
bohemian
Bohemian
bold
bolster
bolt
bona fide
bona fides
bone
bonus
bony
bosun
both
bovine
bozo

boa:
boa
boast
boastful
boat
boatbuilder
boatbuilding
boater
boathouse
boating
boatload

boatman
boatyard

bou:
boulder
bouquet
bouquet garni

bow:
bow
bowed
bowl
bowler
bowlful
bowling
bow tie

/bɔː/

ba:
bald
balderdash
balding
balk
Balkanization
ball
ballgown
ballpark
ballplayer
ballpoint
ballroom
balls
balsa
balsam
balsamic vinegar
balti

bau:
bauble
baulk
bauxite

baw:
bawdy
bawl

boar:
boar
board
boarder
boarding
boardroom
boardwalk

bor:
borax
bordello
border
borderland
borderline
bore
bored
boredom

borehole
boring
born
borne
borstal

bough:
bought

/bɔɪ/

boi:
boil
boiler
boiling
boisterous

boy:
boy
boycott
boyfriend
boyhood
boyish

buoy:
buoy
buoyancy
buoyant

/bʊ/

bo:
bosom

boo:
book
bookable
bookbinder
bookbinding
bookcase
bookend
bookie
booking
bookish
bookkeeper
bookkeeping
booklet
bookmaker
bookmaking
bookmark
bookseller
bookshelf
bookshop
bookstall
bookstore
bookworm

bu:
Buddha
Buddhism
Buddhist
buffet
bull

/bu:/

bulldog
bulldoze
bulldozer
bullet
bulletin
bullfight
bullfighter
bullfighting
bullfinch
bullfrog
bullhorn
bullion
bullish
bullock
bullring
bullshit
bullwhip
bully
bulwark
bush
bushed
bushel
Bushman
bushy
butch
butcher
butchery

/bu:/

boo:
boo
boob
booby prize
booby-trap
boogie
boom
boomerang
boon
boost
booster
boot
bootee
booth
bootlace
bootleg
bootstraps
booty
booze
boozed
boozer
boozy

bou:
boudoir
bouffant
bougainvillaea
bouillabaisse
bouillon
boules
boulevard

boutique

bu:
bulimia
bulimic

/bʊə/

boor:
boor
boorish

bour:
bourgeois
bourgeoisie

/baʊ/

bou:
bounce
bouncer
bouncing
bouncy
bound
boundary
bounder
boundless
bountiful
bounty
bout

bough:
bough

bow:
bow
bowdlerize
bowed
bowel

/baʊə/

bower:
bower

/bʌ/

bo:
borough

bu:
bubble
bubbly
buccaneer
buccaneering
buck
bucket
bucketful
buckle
buckled
buckshot
buckskin
buckwheat
bud
budding

buddy
budge
budgerigar
budget
budgetary
budgie
buff
buffalo
buffer
buffet
buffoon
buffoonery
bug
bugbear
bugger
buggered
buggery
buggy
bulb
bulbous
Bulgarian
bulge
bulk
bulkhead
bulky
bum
bumble
bumblebee
bumbling
bumf
bummer
bump
bumper
bumph
bumpkin
bumptious
bumpy
bun
bunch
bundle
bung
bungalow
bungee jumping
bungle
bungler
bunion
bunk
bunker
bunkum
bunny
bunting
burrow
bus
busk
busker
busload
busman's holiday
bust
bustier
bustle

busty
but
butler
butt
butter
buttercup
butterfly
buttermilk
butterscotch
buttery
buttock
button
buttonhole
buttress
butty
buxom
buzz
buzzard
buzzer
buzzword

/bju:/

beau:
beaut
beauteous
beautician
beautiful
beautify
beauty

bu:
bubonic plague
bucolic
bugle
bugler
butane

/bjʊə/

bur:
bureau
bureaucracy
bureaucrat
bureaucratic
bureaux

/bə/

ba:
Bahamian
ballistic
ballistics
balloon
balloonist
baloney
banal
banana
barometer
baronial
baroque
basilica
bassoon

212

/bl/

bassoonist
batik
battalion
bazaar
bazooka

ber:
berserk

bo:
bolero
Bolivian
bonanza
botanic
botanical

bu:
buffet
but

/bl/

bl:
blab
black
blackball
blackberry
blackbird
blackboard
blackcurrant
blacken
blackguard
blackhead
blackish
blacklist
blackmail
blackness
blackout
blacksmith
blacktop
bladder
blade
blag
blah
blame
blameless
blanch
blancmange
bland
blandishments
blandly
blank
blanket
blare
blarney
blasé
blaspheme
blasphemous
blasphemy
blast
blasted
blatant

blatantly
blather
blaze
blazer
blazing
bleach
bleachers
bleak
bleary
bleat
bled
bleed
bleeding
bleep
bleeper
blemish
blemished
blend
blender
bless
blessed
blessing
blew
blight
blighter
Blighty
blimey
blimp
blind
blinder
blindfold
blinding
blindly
blink
blinkered
blinkers
blip
bliss
blissful
blister
blistering
blithe
blitz
blitzkrieg
blizzard
bloated
bloating
blob
bloc
block
blockade
blockage
blockbuster
blockbusting
bloke
blonde
blood
bloodbath
bloodhound
bloodless

bloodline
bloodshed
bloodshot
bloodstain
bloodstained
bloodstock
bloodstream
bloodsucker
bloodthirsty
bloody
Bloody Mary
bloom
bloomers
blooming
blooper
blossom
blot
blotch
blotched
blotchy
blotter
blouse
blow
blower
blowlamp
blown
blowtorch
blub
blubber
bludgeon
blue
bluebell
blueberry
bluebottle
bluegrass
blueish
blueprint
blue riband
bluestocking
bluesy
bluff
bluish
blunder
blunt
blur
blurb
blurry
blurt
blush
blusher
bluster
blustery

/br/

br:
bra
brace
bracelet
bracing
bracken

bracket
brackish
brag
Brahman
Brahmin
braid
braided
Braille
brain
brainchild
brainless
brainpower
brainstorm
brainwash
brainwave
brainy
braise
brake
bramble
bran
branch
brand
branded
brandish
brandy
brash
brass
brasserie
brassica
brassiere
brassy
brat
bravado
brave
bravery
bravo
bravura
brawl
brawn
brawny
bray
brazen
brazier
Brazilian
breach
bread
breadboard
breadbox
breadcrumb
breadfruit
breadline
breadth
breadwinner
break
breakable
breakage
breakaway
breakdown
breaker
breakfast

/kæ/   /kæ/

breakneck
breakout
breakthrough
breakwater
breast
breastbone
breastplate
breaststroke
breath
breathable
breathalyze
breathalyzer
breathe
breather
breathless
breathtaking
breathy
bred
breech
breeches
breed
breeder
breeding
breeze
breezy
brethren
brevity
brew
brewer
brewery
briar
bribe
bribery
bric-a-brac
brick
brickbat
brickie
bricklayer
brickwork
bridal
bride
bridegroom
bridesmaid
bridge
bridgehead
bridle
bridleway
Brie
brief
briefcase
briefer
briefing
briefly
brig
Brig.
brigade
brigadier
brigand
bright
brighten

brill
brilliant
brim
brimful
brimstone
brine
bring
bringer
brink
brinkmanship
brioche
brisk
brisket
bristle
bristling
bristly
Brit
British
Britisher
Briton
brittle
broach
broad
broadcast
broadcaster
broadcasting
broaden
broadly
broadminded
broadsheet
broadside
brocade
broccoli
brochure
brogue
broil
broiler
broiling
broke
broken
broker
brokerage
brolly
bromide
bronchial
bronchitis
bronco
brontosaurus
bronze
bronzed
bronzing
brooch
brood
brooding
broody
brook
broom
broomstick
broth
brothel

brother
brotherhood
brotherly
brought
brouhaha
brow
browbeat
brown
brownie
brownish
brownstone
browse
bruise
bruiser
bruising
Brummie
brunch
brunette
brunt
brush
brushed
brushstroke
brushwood
brushwork
brusque
brussels sprout
brutal
brutalise
brutality
brutalize
brute
brutish

/k/
/kæ/

ca:
cab
cabaret
cabbage
cabbie
cabin
cabinet
cache
cachet
cack-handed
cackle
cactus
cad
caddie
cadge
cadmium
café
cafeteria
caff
caffeine
caftan
cal
calcium
calculable

calculate
calculated
calculating
calculation
calculator
calculus
calendar
caliber
calibrate
calibre
calico
caliper
calisthenics
calliper
callisthenics
callous
calloused
callow
callus
calorie
calorific
calumny
Calvinist
camaraderie
camber
camcorder
camel
Camembert
cameo
camera
cameraman
camerawork
camisole
camomile
camouflage
camp
campaign
campaigner
camped
camper
campground
camphor
campsite
campus
campy
camshaft
can
canapé
canard
cancel
cancer
cancerous
candelabra
candelabrum
candid
candidacy
candidate
candidature
candied
candle

/keɪ/

candlelight
candlelit
candlestick
candour
candy
candyfloss
canister
canker
cannabis
canned
cannelloni
cannery
cannibal
cannibalism
cannibalistic
cannibalize
cannon
cannonade
cannot
canny
canon
canonize
canopied
canopy
cant
cantaloupe
cantankerous
cantata
canteen
canter
cantilever
cantilevered
canton
Cantonese
cantonment
canvas
canvass
canyon
cap
capital
capitalise
capitalism
capitalist
capitalistic
capitalize
cappuccino
caprice
capricious
Capricorn
capsicum
capsize
capstan
capsule
captain
captaincy
caption
captivate
captivating
captive
captivity

captor
capture
caramel
caramelize
carapace
carat
caravan
caravanning
caraway
Caribbean
caribou
caricature
caricaturist
carob
carol
carousel
carriage
carriageway
carrier
carrion
carrot
carry
carrycot
cascade
cash
cashew
cashier
cashmere
cashpoint
casserole
cassock
castanets
castellated
castigate
castrate
casual
casualty
casuistry
cat
cataclysm
cataclysmic
catacomb
Catalan
catalogue
catalyse
catalyst
catalytic
catamaran
catapult
cataract
catastrophic
catatonic
catbird seat
catcall
catch
Catch 22
catcher
catching
catchment
catchy

catechism
categoric
categorical
categorize
category
caterpillar
caterwaul
catfish
catherine wheel
catheter
Catholic
catkin
catnap
catsuit
catsup
cattery
cattle
cattleman
catty
catwalk
cavalcade
cavalier
cavalry
cavalryman
caveat
caveat emptor
cavern
cavernous
caviar
cavil
cavity

cha:
chamomile
character
characterful
characteristic
characterization
characterize
characterless
charismatic
chasm

ka:
kaftan
kamikaze
kangaroo
karaoke

/keɪ/

ca:
caber
cable
cabling
cadence
cage
caged
cagey
Cajun
cake
caked

caliph
came
cane
canine
capability
capable
cape
caper
capon
case
casebook
caseload
casement
casework
caseworker
casing
cater
caterer
catering
cave
caveman
caver

cei:
ceilidh

cha:
chaos
chaotic

k:
K,k
KO
kph

ka:
kale

/kɑː/

ca:
cadre
can't
cask
casket
cast
castaway
caste
caster
casting
castle
castor

cal:
calf
calfskin
calm
calmly
calve

car:
car
carbine

/keə/

carbohydrate
carbolic acid
carbon
carbonate
carbonated
carbuncle
carburettor
carcass
carcinogen
carcinogenic
carcinoma
card
cardamom
cardboard
cardholder
cardiac
cardie
cardigan
cardinal
cardiologist
cardiology
cardiovascular
cargo
carjacking
carload
carmine
carnage
carnal
carnation
carnival
carnivore
carnivorous
carp
carpenter
carpentry
carpet
carpetbagger
carpeting
cart
carte blanche
cartel
carthorse
cartilage
cartographer
cartography
carton
cartoon
cartoonist
cartridge
cartwheel
carve
carver
carving

kar:
karma
kart

kha:
khaki

/keə/

cair:
cairn

car:
caries
caring

care:
care
carefree
careful
careless
carelessly
carer
caretaker
careworn

/ke/

ce:
Celt
Celtic

che:
chemical
chemist
chemistry

ke:
kedgeree
keg
kelp
ken
kennel
Kenyan
kept
kerosene
kestrel
ketch
ketchup
kettle
kettledrum

/kiː/

che:
chemotherapy

chi:
chiaroscuro

kee:
keel
keen
keep
keeper
keepsake

key:
key
keyboard
keyboarder

keyboarding
keyboardist
keyhole
keynote
keystone

ki:
kilo
kiosk
kiwi

quay:
quay
quayside

qui:
quiche

/kɜː/

colo:
colonel

cour:
courteous
courtesy

cur:
cur
curb
curd
curdle
curfew
curl
curler
curlew
curlicue
curly
curse
cursed
cursor
cursory
curt
curtail
curtailment
curtain
curtained
curtsy
curvaceous
curvature
curve
curved
curvy

ker:
kerb
kerchief
kernel

kir:
kirk

/kɪə/

kir:
kirsch

/kɪ/

chi:
chiropodist
chiropody

ki:
kibbutz
kick
kickback
kid
kiddie
kidnap
kidney
kill
killer
killing
killjoy
kiln
kilo-
kilobyte
kilogram
kilohertz
kilometre
kilowatt
kilt
kimono
kin
kindergarten
kindle
kindling
kindred
kinetic
king
kingdom
kingfisher
kingly
kingpin
kingship
kink
kinky
kinship
kinsman
kinswoman
kip
kipper
kiss
kit
kitbag
kitchen
kitchenette
kith and kin
kitsch
kitten
kitty

/kaɪ/

cay:
cayenne pepper

chi:
chimera

/kaɪə/

coy:
coyote

kay:
kayak

ki:
kind
kindly
kindness
kite
Kitemark

/kaɪə/

chir:
chiropractic
chiropractor

/kɒ/

cau:
cauliflower

cho:
cholera
choleric
choreograph
choreographed
choreographer
choreographic
choreography
chorister

co:
cob
cobble
cobbled
cobbler
cobblestone
cobweb
cobwebbed
coccyx
cochineal
cochlea
cock
cockatoo
cockerel
cocker spaniel
cockeyed
cockle
cockney
cockpit
cockroach
cocksure
cocktail
cocky
cod
coddle
codger
codpiece
codswallop
coffee
coffer
coffin
cog
cogitate
cognac
cognate
cognisance
cognisant
cognition
cognitive
cognizance
cognizant
cognoscenti
colada
colander
colic
colicky
collage
collagen
collar
collarless
colleague
college
collie
colliery
collocate
collocation
colloquy
colonist
colonize
colonnade
colonnaded
colony
coloratura
column
columnist
combat
combatant
combative
combine
combination
combo
comedy
comet
comic
comical
comma
commandant
commandeer
comment
commentary
commentate
commentator
commerce
commie
commissariat
commissary
commodore
common
commonality
commoner
commonplace
commonwealth
communal
commune
communism
communist
compact
comparable
compartmentalize
compensate
compensation
compensatory
compere
competence
competency
competent
competition
compilation
complement
complementary
complementation
complex
complicate
complicated
complication
compliment
complimentary
composite
composition
compositional
compost
compote
compound
compounded
comprehend
comprehensible
comprehension
comprehensive
comprehensively
compress
compromise
compromising
computation
computational
comrade
comradely
comradeship
con
concatenation
concave
concentrate
concentrated
concentration
concept
concert
concertgoer
concertina
conch
concierge
conclave
concord
concourse
concrete
concubine
condemnation
condemnatory
condensation
condescend
condescending
condescension
condiment
condo
condom
condominium
condor
conduct
conduit
conference
confidant
confidante
confidence
confident
confidential
confidentially
confines
confiscate
conflagration
conflict
confluence
confrontation
confrontational
conga
conger
congregant
congregate
congregation
congress
congressman
congressperson
congresswoman
congruence
congruent
conical
conifer
conjugal
conjugate
conk
conker
connoisseur
connotation
conquer
conqueror
conquest
conquistador
conscience
conscientious
conscious
consciousness
conscript

/koʊ/

consecrate
consequence
consequent
consequential
consequently
conservation
conservationist
conserve
console
consommé
consonant
consort
constancy
constant
constellation
consternation
constipated
constipation
constitute
constitution
constitutional
constitutionality
construct
consul
consular
consulate
consultation
consummate
contact
contemplate
content
contest
context
continent
continental
continuity
contour
contoured
contraband
contraception
contraceptive
contract
contractor
contradict
contradiction
contradictory
contraflow
contraindication
contrary
contrast
contravene
contretemps
contribution
controversial
controversy
conurbation
convalesce
convalescence
convalescent
convent

conversation
conversational
conversationalist
converse
conversely
convert
convex
convict
convocation
convoluted
convolution
convoy
cop
copier
copper
coppery
coppice
copse
copter
Coptic
copula
copulate
copy
copybook
copycat
copyist
copyright
copyrighted
copywriter
coquette
coquettish
coracle
coral
coriander
coronary
coronation
coroner
coronet
correlate
correlation
correlative
correspond
correspondence
correspondent
correspondingly
corridor
corrugated
coruscating
cosh
cosmetic
cosmic
cosmology
cosmonaut
cosmopolitan
cosmos
cosset
cost
costing
costly
costume

costumier
cot
cottage
cottager
cottaging
cotton
cottonwood
cough
Coventry
cox
coxswain

/koʊ/

caʊ:
cause célèbre

co:
co-
coagulate
cobalt
cobra
cocaine
cocoa
coconut
coda
code
coded
codeine
codex
codices
codicil
codify
coding
coefficient
coerce
coercion
coercive
coexist
coexistence
cogent
cohabit
cohere
coherence
coherent
cohesion
cohesive
cohort
coincide
coincidence
coincident
coincidental
coincidentally
coital
coitus
coke
cola
cold
coleslaw
colon
colt

coltish
coma
comatose
comb
cone
co-ordinate
cope
copious
cosy
coterie
cove
cozy

coa:
coach
coachload
coachman
coal
coalesce
coalface
coalfield
coalition
coast
coastal
coaster
coastguard
coastline
coat
coating
coax

ko:
koala
kosher

koh:
kohl
kohlrabi

/kɔː/

ca:
caldron
call
caller
calling

cau:
Caucasian
caucus
caught
cauldron
causal
causality
causation
causative
cause
causeway
caustic
cauterize
caution
cautionary

/kɔɪ/

cautious

caw:
caw

chor:
choral
chorale
chord
chorus

coar:
coarse
coarsen

cor:
cor
cord
cordial
cordite
cordless
cordon
cordon bleu
corduroy
core
corgi
cork
corker
corkscrew
cormorant
corn
cornbread
cornea
corneal
corned beef
corner
cornerstone
cornet
cornfield
cornflake
cornflour
cornflower
cornice
Cornish
cornmeal
cornstarch
cornucopia
corny
corpora
corporal
corporate
corporation
corporatism
corporatist
corporeal
corps
corps de ballet
corpse
corpulent
corpus
corpuscle
corsage
corset
corseted
cortege
cortex
cortisone
corvette

cour:
course
coursing
court
courtesan
courthouse
courtier
courtly
courtroom
courtship
courtyard

kor:
Koran
Koranic
Korean

qur:
Quran
Quranic

/kɔɪ/

coi:
coil
coiled
coin
coinage
coir

coy:
coy
coypu

quoi:
quoit

/kʊ/

coo:
cook
cookbook
cooker
cookery
cookie
cooking
cookout
cookware

cou:
could
couldn't
could've
courier

cu:
cuckoo
cushion

cushioning
cushy

ku:
Kuwaiti

/ku:/

coo:
coo
cool
coolant
cooler
coolie
coon
coop
cooped up
cooper
coot

cou:
couchette
cougar
coup
coup de grace
coup d'état
coupé
coupon
couscous
couture
couturier

koo:
kooky

/kʊə/

cour:
courgette

/kaʊ/

cou:
couch
council
councillor
councilman
councilwoman
counsel
counselling
counsellor
count
Count
countable noun
countdown
countenance
counter
counter-
counteract
counterbalance
counterblast
counterclockwise
counterfeit
counterfoil
countermand
counterpane
counterpart
counterpoint
countersign
countertenor
countervailing
counterweight
countess
counting
countless
county

cow:
cow
cowbell
cowboy
cowhide
cowl
cowling
cowpat
cowshed
cowslip

kow:
kowtow

/kaʊə/

cowar:
coward
cowardice
cowardly

cower:
cower

/kʌ/

co:
color
coloration
colorization
colorized
colour
colourant
coloured
colourful
colouring
colourist
colourless
come
comeback
comely
comer
comeuppance
comfort
comfortable
comfortably
comforter
comforting
comfrey

/kju:/

comfy
coming
company
compass
conjure
conjurer
conjuror
constable
coven
covenant
cover
coverage
covered
covering
coverlet
covert
covet
coveted
covetous
covey

cou:
countrified
country
countryman
countryside
countrywide
countrywoman
couple
couplet
coupling
courage
cousin

cu:
cub
cubby-hole
cuckold
cud
cuddle
cuddly
cudgel
cuff
cufflink
cul-de-sac
culinary
cull
culminate
culmination
culpable
culprit
cult
cultivate
cultivated
cultivator
cultural
culture
cultured
culvert
cumbersome
cumin

cummerbund
cunnilingus
cunning
cunt
cup
cupboard
cupcake
cupful
cuppa
currant
currency
current
curried
curry
cusp
cuss
cussed
custard
custodial
custodian
custody
custom
customary
customer
customize
customs
cut
cutaway
cutback
cutlass
cutlery
cutlet
cutter
cutting
cuttlefish

ku:
kung fu

/kju:/

cu:
Cuban
cube
cubic
cubicle
cubism
Cubist
cucumber
cue
culottes
cumulative
cumulus
cupid
cupidity
cupola
cute
cutesy
cuticle

ku:
kudos

q:
Q,q
QC

queue:
queue

/kjʊə/

cur:
curable
curate
curative
cure
curio
curiosity
curious

/kə/

ca:
cabal
cacophonous
cacophony
cadaver
cadaverous
cadenza
cadet
cahoots
cajole
calamitous
calamity
calligrapher
calligraphy
caloric
calypso
camellia
can
Canadian
canal
canary
canoe
canoeing
canoeist
canonical
canoodle
capacious
capacitor
capacity
capillary
capitulate
carafe
careen
career
careerist
caress
carotid artery
carouse
casino
cassava
cassette
catalysis

/kə/

catarrh
catastrophe
catharsis
cathartic
cathedral
Catholicism
cavort

cha:
chameleon
charisma

cho:
cholesterol

co:
cocoon
cocooned
colitis
collaborate
collaboration
collaborationist
collaborative
collaborator
collapse
collapsible
collate
collateral
collect
collectable
collected
collectible
collecting
collection
collective
collectivise
collectivism
collectivist
collectivize
collector
collegiate
collide
collision
colloquial
colloquialism
colloquium
collude
collusion
collusive
cologne
Colombian
colonial
colonialism
colonialist
colossal
colossus
colostomy
combat
combine
combined
combustible

/kə/   /kə/

- combustion
- comedian
- comedic
- comedienne
- command
- commander
- commanding
- commandment
- commando
- commemorate
- commemorative
- commence
- commencement
- commend
- commendable
- commensurate
- commercial
- commercialism
- commercialize
- commiserate
- commission
- commissioner
- commit
- commitment
- committal
- committee
- commode
- commodious
- commodity
- commotion
- commune
- communicable
- communicant
- communicate
- communication
- communicative
- communion
- communiqé
- community
- commute
- compact
- companion
- companionable
- companionship
- companionway
- comparative
- compare
- compared
- comparison
- compartment
- compassion
- compassionate
- compatible
- compatriot
- compel
- compelling
- compendium
- compete
- competing
- competitive
- competitor
- compile
- compiler
- complacency
- complacent
- complain
- complainant
- complainer
- complaint
- complaisant
- complete
- complex
- complexion
- complexities
- complexity
- compliance
- compliant
- complicity
- comply
- component
- comport
- compose
- composed
- composer
- compositor
- composure
- compound
- compress
- compressed
- compressor
- comprise
- comptroller
- compulsion
- compulsive
- compulsory
- compunction
- compute
- computer
- computerate
- computerize
- computerized
- computing
- conceal
- concealment
- concede
- conceit
- conceited
- conceivable
- conceive
- concentric
- conception
- conceptual
- conceptualize
- concern
- concerned
- concerning
- concerted
- concerto
- concession
- concessionaire
- concessionary
- concessive clause
- conciliate
- conciliation
- conciliatory
- concise
- conclude
- conclusion
- conclusive
- concoct
- concoction
- concomitant
- concordance
- concur
- concurrence
- concurrent
- concussed
- concussion
- condemn
- condemned
- condense
- condensed
- condenser
- condition
- conditional
- conditioner
- condolence
- condone
- conducive
- conduct
- conduction
- conductive
- conductor
- confection
- confectioner
- confectionery
- confederacy
- confederate
- confederation
- confer
- confess
- confessed
- confession
- confessional
- confessor
- confetti
- confide
- configuration
- confine
- confined
- confinement
- confirm
- confirmed
- conflate
- conflict
- conform
- conformist
- conformity
- confound
- confront
- confuse
- confused
- confusing
- confusion
- congeal
- congenial
- congenital
- congested
- congestion
- congestive
- conglomerate
- conglomeration
- congratulate
- congratulations
- congratulatory
- congressional
- coniferous
- conjectural
- conjecture
- conjoin
- conjunction
- conjunctivitis
- connect
- connected
- connection
- connective
- connector
- connexion
- connivance
- connive
- conniving
- connote
- conscript
- conscription
- consecutive
- consensual
- consensus
- consent
- consenting
- conservancy
- conservatism
- conservative
- conservatoire
- conservator
- conservatory
- conserve
- consider
- considerable
- considerate
- consideration
- considered
- considering
- consign
- consignment
- consist
- consistency
- consistent
- console
- consolidate
- consort

/kl/

consortium
conspicuous
conspiracy
conspirator
conspiratorial
conspire
constabulary
constituency
constituent
constrain
constraint
constrict
constriction
construct
construction
constructive
constructor
construe
consult
consultancy
consultant
consultative
consumable
consume
consumed
consumer
consumerism
consumerist
consuming
consummate
consumption
consumptive
contagion
contagious
contain
container
containment
contaminant
contaminate
contemplative
contemporaneous
contemporary
contempt
contemptible
contemptuous
contend
contender
content
contented
contention
contentious
contentment
contest
contestant
contextual
contiguous
contingency
contingent
continual
continuance

continuation
continue
continuous
continuum
contort
contortion
contortionist
contract
contraction
contractual
contralto
contraption
contrarian
contrast
contribute
contributor
contributory
contrite
contrivance
contrive
contrived
control
controllable
controller
contusion
conundrum
convection
convene
convener
convenience
convenient
convenor
convention
conventional
conventioneer
converge
convergence
conversant
converse
conversion
convert
converter
convertible
convey
conveyance
conveyancing
conveyor belt
convict
conviction
convince
convinced
convincing
convivial
convulse
convulsion
convulsive
corollary
corona
corral
correct

correction
correctional
corrective
corroborate
corroborative
corrode
corrosion
corrosive
corrupt
corruption

cou:
could
courageous

cur:
curmudgeon
curmudgeonly

curr:
curriculum
curriculum vitae

ka:
kaleidoscope
kaleidoscopic
kaput
karate
kazoo

ke:
kebab

ker:
kerfuffle

/kl/

chl:
chloride
chlorinated
chlorine
chlorofluorocarbon
chloroform
chlorophyll

cl:
clack
clad
cladding
claim
claimant
clairvoyant
clam
clamber
clammy
clamorous
clamour
clamp
clampdown
clan
clandestine
clang

clanger
clank
clannish
clansman
clap
clapboard
clapperboard
claptrap
claret
clarify
clarinet
clarinettist
clarity
clash
clasp
class
classic
classical
classically
classicism
classicist
classification
classified
classifieds
classify
classless
classmate
classroom
classy
clatter
clause
claustrophobia
claustrophobic
clavichord
clavicle
claw
clawback
clay
clean
cleaner
cleanliness
cleanse
cleanser
clear
clearance
clearing
cleat
cleavage
cleave
cleaver
clef
cleft
clematis
clemency
clement
clementine
clench
clergy
clergyman
cleric

/kr/

clerical
clerk
clever
cliché
clichéd
click
client
clientele
cliff
clifftop
climactic
climate
climatic
climatologist
climax
climb
climber
climbing
clime
clinch
clincher
cling
clingfilm
clingy
clinic
clinical
clinician
clink
clip
clipboard
clipped
clipper
clipping
clique
cliquey
clitoral
clitoris
cloak
cloakroom
clobber
cloche
clock
clockwise
clockwork
clod
clog
cloister
cloistered
clone
close
Close
close-cropped
closed
close-fitting
close-knit
close-run
close season
closet
closeted
close-up

closing
closure
clot
cloth
clothe
clothed
clothes
clothesline
clothespin
clothing
cloud
cloudburst
cloudless
cloudy
clout
clove
cloven hoof
clover
clown
clownish
cloying
cloze
club
clubbable
clubber
clubbing
clubby
clubhouse
clubland
cluck
clue
clueless
clump
clumpy
clumsy
clung
clunk
clunker
clunky
cluster
clustered
clutch
clutter

kl:
Kleenex
kleptomaniac

/kr/

chr:
Christ
christen
Christendom
christening
Christian
Christianity
Christmas
Christmassy
chrome
chromium

chromosomal
chromosome
chronic
chronicle
chronological
chronology
chronometer
chrysalis
chrysanthemum

cr:
crab
crabbed
crabby
crabmeat
crack
crackdown
cracked
cracker
cracking
crackle
crackly
crackpot
cradle
craft
craftily
craftsman
craftsmanship
craftspeople
craftswoman
crafty
crag
craggy
cram
crammed
crammer
cramp
cramped
crampon
cranberry
crane
cranefly
cranial
cranium
crank
crankshaft
cranky
cranny
crap
crappy
crash
crass
crate
crater
cratered
cravat
crave
craven
crawl
crayfish

crayon
craze
crazed
crazily
crazy
creak
creaky
cream
creamer
creamery
creamy
crease
create
creation
creative
creator
creature
crèche
cred
credence
credentials
credibility
credible
credit
creditable
creditor
creditworthy
credo
credulity
credulous
creed
creek
creep
creeper
creepy
creepy-crawly
cremate
crematorium
crème de la crème
crenellated
creole
creosote
crepe
crept
crepuscular
crescendo
crescent
cress
crest
crested
crestfallen
cretin
cretinous
crevasse
crevice
crew
crewman
crib
crick
cricket

/kw/

cricketer
cricketing
crier
crikey
crime
criminal
criminalize
criminology
crimp
crimplene
crimson
cringe
crinkle
crinkly
crinoline
cripple
crippling
crisis
crisp
crispbread
crispy
criss-cross
criterion
critic
critical
criticise
criticism
criticize
critique
critter
croak
croaky
crochet
crock
crockery
crocodile
crocus
croft
crofter
crofting
crone
crony
cronyism
crook
crooked
croon
crooner
crop
cropped
cropper
croquet
croquette
cross
crossbar
crossbones
crossbow
crossfire
crossing
crossover
crossroads
crosswalk
crosswind
crosswise
crossword
crotch
crotchet
crotchety
crouch
croup
croupier
crouton
crow
crowbar
crowd
crowded
crown
crucial
crucible
crucifix
crucifixion
cruciform
crucify
crude
crudites
cruel
cruelty
cruet
cruise
cruiser
cruiserweight
crumb
crumble
crumbly
crummy
crumpet
crumple
crunch
crunchy
crusade
crusader
crush
crusher
crushing
crushingly
crust
crustacean
crusted
crusty
crutch
crux
cry
crying
cryogenics
crypt
cryptic
crypto-
crystal
crystalline
crystallize
crystallized

kr:
Kremlin

/kw/

cho:
choir
choirboy
choirmaster

co:
coiffed
coiffure
coiffured

cro:
croissant

cu:
cuisine

qu:
quack
quackery
quad
quadrangle
quadrant
quadraphonic
quadriceps
quadrille
quadriplegic
quadrophonic
quadruped
quadruple
quadruplet
quaff
quagmire
quail
quaint
quake
Quaker
qualification
qualified
qualifier
qualify
qualitative
quality
qualm
quandary
quango
quantifiable
quantifier
quantify
quantitative
quantity
quantum
quarantine
quark
quarrel
quarrelsome
quarry
quart
quarter
quarterly
quartet
quartz
quasar
quash
quasi-
quaver
queasy
queen
queenly
queer
quell
quench
querulous
query
quest
questing
question
questionable
questioner
questioning
questionnaire
quibble
quick
quick-
quicken
quickfire
quickie
quicksand
quicksilver
quid
quids
quiescent
quiet
quieten
quietude
quiff
quill
quilt
quilted
quince
quinine
quintessence
quintessential
quintet
quip
quirk
quirky
quisling
quit
quite
quitter
quiver
quixotic
quiz
quizmaster
quizzical
quo
Quonset hut

/tʃæ/

quorate
quorum
quota
quotable
quotation
quote
quoth
quotidian
quotient

qw:
Qwerty

/tʃ/
/tʃæ/

cha:
chaffinch
chalice
challenge
challenged
challenger
challenging
champ
champion
championship
channel
chap
chapel
chaplain
chaplaincy
chapped
chappy
chapter
chariot
charioteer
charitable
charity
chastise
chastisement
chastity
chat
chatline
chattel
chatter
chatterbox
chatterer
chatty

/tʃeɪ/

cha:
chafe
chamber
chamberlain
chambermaid
change
changeable
changeling
changeover
chase
chaser

chaste
chasten
chastening

chai:
chain
chained

/tʃɑː/

cha:
cha-cha
chaff
chance
chancel
chancellery
Chancellor
chancellorship
Chancery
chancy
chant

char:
char
charcoal
chard
charge
chargeable
charged
charger
charleston
charm
charmed
charmer
charming
charmless
charnel house
charred
chart
charter
chartered
charwoman

/tʃeə/

chair:
chair
chairman
chairmanship
chairperson
chairwoman

char:
chary

/tʃe/

ce:
cellist
cello

che:
check
checkbook

checked
checker
checkerboard
checkered
checklist
checkmate
checkout
checkpoint
cheddar
cheque
chequerboard
chequered
cherish
cherry
cherub
Cheshire cat
chess
chessboard
chest
chestnut
chesty

cze:
Czech
Czechoslovak
Czechoslovakian

/tʃiː/

chea:
cheap
cheapen
cheapo
cheapskate
cheat
cheater

chee:
cheek
cheekbone
cheeky
cheese
cheeseboard
cheeseburger
cheesecake
cheesecloth
cheesed off
cheesy
cheetah

chie:
chief
chiefly
chieftain

chi:
chinos

/tʃɜː/

cher:
chervil

chir:
chirp
chirpy

chur:
church
churchgoer
churchman
churchwarden
churchyard
churlish
churn
churning

/tʃɪə/

cheer:
cheer
cheerful
cheerio
cheerleader
cheerless
cheery

/tʃɪ/

chi:
chicano
chick
chicken
chickenpox
chickweed
chicory
chihuahua
chilblain
children
chili
chill
chiller
chilli
chilli con carne
chilling
chilly
chimney
chimneypiece
chimp
chimpanzee
chin
chink
chintz
chintzy
chip
chipboard
chipmunk
Chippendale
chipper
chippings
chippy
chirrup
chisel
chiselled
chit

225

/tʃaɪ/

chivvy

/tʃaɪ/

chi:
chide
child
childbearing
childbirth
childcare
childhood
childish
childless
childlike
childminder
childminding
childproof
chime
china
Chinatown
Chinese
chives

/tʃɒ/

cho:
choc-ice
chock-a-block
chock-full
chocoholic
chocolate
chomp
chop
chopper
choppy
chopstick
chop suey

/tʃoʊ/

cho:
choke
choked
choker
chose
chosen

/tʃɔː/

chal:
chalk
chalkboard
chalky

chor:
chore
chortle

/tʃɔɪ/

choi:
choice

/tʃuː/

chew:
chew
chewy

choo:
choose
choosy

/tʃaʊ/

chow:
chow
chowder
chow mein

ciao:
ciao

/tʃʌ/

chu:
chubby
chuck
chuckle
chuffed
chug
chum
chummy
chump
chunk
chunky
chutney

/tʃə/

cher:
cherubic

cia:
ciabatta

/d/

/dæ/

da:
dab
dabble
dacha
dachshund
Dacron
dad
daddy
daddy longlegs
daffodil
daffy
dagger
dalliance
dally
Dalmatian
dam
damage
damask
dammit
damn
damnable
damnation
damned
damnedest
damning
Damocles
damp
dampen
dampener
damper
dampness
damsel
damson
dandelion
dandruff
dandy
dangle
dank
dapper
dappled
dash
dashboard
dashing
dastardly
DAT
dazzle
dazzling

/deɪ/

da:
dace
dado
dale
dame
Dane
danger
dangerous
Danish
data
database
date
dated
dative
datum
daze
dazed

dah:
dahlia

dai:
daily
dainty
dais
daisy

day:
day
daybreak
daydream
Day-glo
daylight
daylights
daytime

de:
debacle
debris
debut
decor
de facto
déjà vu
de jure
denouement
detente

dei:
deification
deify
deign
deity

/dɑː/

da:
daft
dance
dancer
dancing

dar:
dark
darken
darkened
darkroom
darling
darn
dart
dartboard

der:
derby

/deə/

dair:
dairy

dar:
dare
daredevil
daren't
daresay
daring

/de/

dea:
dead
deadbeat
deaden
deadening
deadline

/diː/

deadlock
deadlocked
deadly
deadpan
deaf
deafen
deafening
dealt
death
deathbed
deathly
death row

de:
deb
debit
debonair
debt
debtor
debutante
decade
decadent
decibel
decimal
decimate
deck
deckchair
deckhand
declaration
decorate
decoration
decorative
decorator
decorous
dedicate
dedicated
dedication
defamation
defecate
deference
deferential
deficit
definite
definitely
definition
deft
degradation
delegate
delegation
deleterious
delicacy
delicate
delicatessen
dell
delphinium
delta
deluge
delve
demagogic
demagogue

demagogy
demerara sugar
demigod
demo
democrat
democratic
demographic
demolition
demonstrate
demonstration
demonstrator
den
denier
denigrate
denim
denims
denizen
dense
density
dent
dental
dentist
dentistry
dentures
deposition
depot
deprecate
deprecating
depredation
deprivation
depth
deputation
deputize
deputy
derelict
dereliction
derivation
derrick
derring-do
descant
desecrate
desert
desert island
desiccated
desiccation
designate
designation
desk
desktop
desolate
desolation
desperado
desperate
desperation
despot
despotism
destination
destined
destiny
destitute

destitution
desultory
detente
detonate
detonation
detonator
detriment
detrimental
devastate
devastated
devastating
devastation
devil
devilish
devotee
dexterity
dexterous
dextrose

/diː/

d:
D,d
D.A.
DC
DDT
DIY
DJ
DNA
DT's

de:
de-
debrief
debriefing
debug
debunk
decaf
decaffeinated
decelerate
decency
decent
decentralize
declassify
decode
decoder
decolonization
decommission
decompose
decomposition
decompression
decongestant
deconstruct
decontaminate
decontrol
decouple
decoy
decrease
decriminalize
deed
deem

deep
deepen
defect
deflation
deflationary
deflower
defoliant
defoliate
deforest
defrost
defuse
dehumanize
dehydrate
delectation
demarcate
demarcation
demerge
demerger
demerit
demilitarize
demob
demobbed
demobilize
demon
demonize
demonology
demystify
denationalize
departmental
depersonalize
depopulate
deportee
derail
derailment
deregulate
deregulation
desalination
deseed
desegregate
desensitize
destabilize
detail
detailed
detainee
dethrone
detour
detox
detoxification
detoxify
devalue
deviant
deviate
deviation
devious
devolution

dea:
deacon
deal
dealer

/dɪ/

dealership
dealings
dean

di:
diva

die:
diesel

/dɪ/

de:
deactivate
deodorant
deodorize

/dɜː/

dear:
dearth

der:
dermatitis
dermatologist
dervish

dir:
dirge
dirt
dirty

/dɪə/

dear:
dear
dearest
dearie
dearly

deer:
deer

/dɪ/

de:
debacle
debar
debase
debasement
debatable
debate
debater
debauched
debauchery
debenture
debilitate
debility
decamp
decant
decanter
decapitate
decathlon
decay
deceased

deceit
deceitful
deceive
December
deception
deceptive
decide
decided
decidedly
decider
deciduous
decipher
decision
decisive
declaim
declamatory
declare
decline
decorum
decrease
decree
decree nisi
decrepit
decrepitude
decry
deduce
deduct
deduction
deductive
deface
defamatory
defame
default
defaulter
defeat
defeatism
defeatist
defect
defective
defector
defence
defenceless
defend
defendant
defender
defense
defensible
defensive
defer
deferment
deferral
defiance
defiant
deficiency
deficient
defile
definable
define
defined
definitive

deflate
deflect
deflection
deform
deformity
defraud
defray
defunct
defy
degeneracy
degenerate
degenerative
degrade
degree
dejected
dejection
delay
delectable
delete
deliberate
deliberation
delicious
delight
delighted
delightful
delimit
delineate
delinquency
delinquent
delirious
delirium
deliver
deliverance
delivery
delude
deluded
delusion
deluxe
demand
demanding
demean
demeaning
demeanour
demented
dementia
demise
democracy
democratize
demography
demolish
demonic
demonstrable
demonstrative
demoralize
demoralizing
demote
demotic
demur
demure
denial

denomination
denominational
denominator
denote
denounce
denude
denunciation
deny
depart
departed
department
departure
depend
dependable
dependant
dependence
dependency
dependent
depict
depiction
depilatory
deplete
deplorable
deplore
deploy
deployment
deport
deportment
depose
deposit
depositor
depository
deprave
depraved
depravity
depreciate
depress
depressed
depressing
depression
depressive
deprive
deprived
depute
deranged
derangement
deride
derision
derisive
derisory
derivative
derive
derogatory
descend
descendant
descended
descending
descent
describe
description

descriptive
desert
deserter
desertification
deserve
deservedly
deserving
design
designer
desirable
desire
desirous
desist
despair
despatch
despicable
despise
despite
despoil
despondency
despondent
despotic
dessert
dessertspoon
dessertspoonful
destroy
destroyer
destruction
destructive
detach
detachable
detached
detachment
detain
detect
detectable
detection
detective
detector
detention
deter
detergent
deteriorate
determinant
determinate
determination
determine
determined
determiner
determinism
determinist
deterministic
deterrence
deterrent
detest
detestable
detract
detractor
detritus
develop

developed
developer
developing
development
developmental
device
devise
devoid
devolve
devote
devoted
devotion
devotional
devotions
devour
devout
devoutly

di:
dibber
dick
dicker
dictate
dictation
dictator
dictatorial
dictatorship
diction
dictionary
dictum
did
diddle
didn't
differ
difference
different
differential
differentiate
difficult
difficulty
diffident
diffuse
dig
digger
digit
digital
digitize
dignified
dignify
dignitary
dignity
diktat
dilapidated
dilatory
dildo
dilettante
diligent
dill
dim
diminish

diminution
diminutive
dimmer
dimple
dimpled
dimwit
din
ding-dong
dinghy
dingo
dingy
dinky
dinner
dinnertime
dint
dip
diphtheria
diphthong
diploma
diplomacy
diplomat
diplomatic
dippy
dipstick
dis-
disability
disable
disabled
disablement
disabuse
disadvantage
disadvantaged
disadvantageous
disaffected
disaffection
disagree
disagreeable
disagreement
disallow
disappear
disappearance
disappoint
disappointed
disappointing
disappointment
disapproval
disapprove
disapproving
disarm
disarmament
disarming
disarray
disassemble
disassociate
disaster
disastrous
disavow
disavowal
disband
disbelief

disbelieve
disburse
disbursement
disc
discard
discern
discernible
discerning
discernment
discharge
disciple
disciplinarian
disciplinary
discipline
disciplined
disclaim
disclaimer
disclose
disclosure
disco
discography
discolour
discomfit
discomfiture
discomfort
disconcert
disconcerting
disconnect
disconnected
disconnection
disconsolate
discontent
discontented
discontinue
discontinuity
discontinuous
discord
discordant
discotheque
discount
discounter
discourage
discouragement
discourse
discourteous
discourtesy
discover
discovery
discredit
discreditable
discreet
discrepancy
discrete
discretion
discretionary
discriminate
discriminating
discrimination
discriminatory
discursive

/daɪ/

discus
discuss
discussion
disdain
disdainful
disease
diseased
disembark
disembodied
disembowel
disenchanted
disenchantment
disenfranchise
disengage
disengaged
disengagement
disentangle
disequilibrium
disestablish
disfavour
disfigure
disfigurement
disgorge
disgrace
disgraced
disgraceful
disgruntled
disguise
disgust
disgusted
disgusting
dish
disharmony
dishcloth
disheartened
disheartening
dishevelled
dishonest
dishonesty
dishonour
dishonourable
dishwasher
dishwater
dishy
disillusion
disillusioned
disillusionment
disincentive
disinclination
disinclined
disinfect
disinfectant
disinflation
disinformation
disingenuous
disinherit
disinherited
disintegrate
disinter
disinterest
disinterested
disjointed
disk
diskette
dislike
dislocate
dislocation
dislodge
disloyal
disloyalty
dismal
dismantle
dismay
dismember
dismemberment
dismiss
dismissal
dismissive
dismount
disobedience
disobedient
disobey
disorder
disordered
disorderly
disorganization
disorganized
disorient
disorientate
disown
disparage
disparagement
disparaging
disparate
disparity
dispassionate
dispatch
dispel
dispensable
dispensary
dispensation
dispense
dispenser
dispersal
disperse
dispersed
dispersion
dispirited
dispiriting
displace
displacement
display
displease
displeased
displeasure
disport
disposable
disposal
dispose
disposed
disposition
dispossess
disproportion
disproportionate
disprove
disputation
dispute
disqualify
disquiet
disquisition
disregard
disrepair
disreputable
disrepute
disrespect
disrespectful
disrobe
disrupt
disruption
disruptive
dissatisfaction
dissatisfied
dissemble
disseminate
dissension
dissent
dissenter
dissertation
disservice
dissident
dissimilar
dissimulate
dissipate
dissipated
dissipation
dissociate
dissolute
dissolution
dissolve
dissonance
dissuade
distance
distant
distantly
distaste
distasteful
distemper
distend
distension
distil
distiller
distillery
distinct
distinction
distinctive
distinguish
distinguishable
distinguished
distort
distortion
distract
distracted
distracting
distraction
distraught
distress
distribute
distributed
distribution
distributional
distributive
distributor
distributorship
district
distrust
distrustful
disturb
disturbance
disturbed
disturbing
disunited
disunity
disuse
disused
ditch
dither
ditto
ditty
divan
divide
dividend
divider
divination
divine
divinity
divisible
division
divisional
divisive
divorce
divorced
divorcee
divot
divvy
Diwali
dizzy

dy:
dynasty
dysentery
dysfunction
dysfunctional
dyslexia
dyslexic
dyspepsia
dystrophy

/daɪ/

dai:
daiquiri

/daɪə/

di:
diabetes
diabetic
diabolic
diabolical
diadem
diagnose
diagnosis
diagnostic
diagonal
diagram
diagrammatic
dial
dialect
dialectic
dialectical
dialogue
dialysis
diamante
diameter
diametrically
diamond
diaper
diaphanous
diaphragm
diaspora
diatribe
dice
dicey
dichotomy
didactic
die
diehard
diet
dietary
dieter
dietetic
dietician
digest
digestible
digestion
digestive
digress
dike
dilate
dilemma
dilute
dilution
dime
dimension
dimensional
dine
diner
dinosaur
diocesan
diocese
dioxide
dioxin
direct
direction

directional
directionless
directive
directly
director
directorate
directorial
directorship
directory
dissect
diurnal
dive
diver
diverge
divergence
divergent
diverse
diversify
diversion
diversionary
diversity
divert
diverting
divest
diving
divulge

dy:
dye
dying
dyke
dynamic
dynamism
dynamite
dynamo
dynastic

/daɪə/

dia:
diarist
diarrhoea
diary

dire:
dire

diu:
diuretic

/dɒ/

do:
doc
dock
docker
docket
dockland
dockyard
doctor
doctoral
doctorate
doctrinaire

doctrinal
doctrine
docudrama
document
documentary
documentation
doddering
doddery
doddle
dodge
dodgem
dodger
dodgy
doff
dog
dogfight
dogfish
dogged
doggerel
doggie
doggy
doghouse
dogleg
dogma
dogmatic
dogmatism
dogsbody
Dolby
doldrums
doll
dollar
dollop
dolly
dolphin
domicile
domiciled
dominance
dominant
dominate
dominating
domineering
domino
don
Don Juan
donkey
donnish
doss
dosser
dossier
dot
dotted
dotty

/doʊ/

do:
doberman
docile
dodo
dole
doleful

dolt
domain
dome
domed
domesticity
donate
donation
donor
don't
donut
dope
dopey
dosage
dose
dotage
dote
doting
dove
doze
dozy

doe:
doe

dou:
dough
doughnut
doughy

/dɔː/

dau:
daub
daunt
daunting
dauntless
dauphin

daugh:
daughter

daw:
dawdle
dawn

door:
door
doorbell
doorkeeper
doorknob
doorman
doormat
doorstep
doorstop
doorway

dor:
dork
dorm
dormant
dormer
dormitory
dormouse

dorsal

/dɔɪ/

doi:
doily

doy:
doyen
doyenne

/du:/

do:
do
doer
doings

doo:
doodad
doodah
doodle
doom
doomed
doomsday

dou:
double entendre
douche

du:
duvet

/dʊə/

dour:
dour

/daʊ/

dou:
douse

doub:
doubt
doubter
doubtful
Doubting Thomas
doubtless

dough:
doughty

dow:
dowager
dowdy
dowel
down
downbeat
downcast
downer
downfall
downgrade
downhearted
downhill
Downing Street
download
downmarket
downplay
downpour
downright
downs
downside
downsize
downspout
downstage
downstairs
downstream
downswing
downtime
downtown
downtrend
downtrodden
downturn
downward
downwards
downwind
downy
dowry
dowse

/daʊə/

dowr:
dowry

/dʌ/

do:
does
doesn't
done
dost
doth
double
double bass
doublespeak
doublet
doubly
dove
dovecote
dovetail
dovish
dozen

du:
dub
duchess
duchy
duck
duckling
duct
dud
dudgeon
duff
duffel
duffel bag
duffel coat
duffer
duffle
dug
dugout
dulcet
dull
dullard
dumb
dumb-bell
dumbfound
dumbfounded
dumbstruck
dum-dum
dummy
dump
dumpling
Dumpster
dumpy
dun
dunce
dung
dungarees
dungeon
dunk
dusk
dusky
dust
dustbin
dustcart
duster
dustman
dustpan
dusty
Dutch
Dutchman

w:
W,w
WC
WPC

/dju:/

deu:
deuce

dew:
dew
dewy

du:
dual
dualism
duality
dubious
ducal
dude
due
duel
duet
duke
dukedom
duly
dune
duo
duodenal
duodenum
duopoly
dupe
duplex
duplicate
duplication
duplicity
dutiful
duty

d'you:
d'you

/djʊə/

dur:
durable
duration
duress
Durex
during

/də/

de:
de rigueur

do:
do
does
domestic
domesticate
domesticated
dominion

du:
dunno

/dr/

dr:
drab
drachma
draconian
draft
draftee
draftsman
drafty
drag
dragnet
dragon
dragonfly
dragoon
drain
drainage
drainpipe
drake

/dw/   /feɪ/

dram
drama
dramatic
dramatics
dramatis personae
dramatist
dramatize
drank
drape
draper
drapery
drastic
draught
draughtsman
draughtsmanship
draughty
draw
drawback
drawbridge
drawer
drawing
drawl
drawn
drawstring
dray
dread
dreaded
dreadful
dreadfully
dreadlocks
dream
dreamer
dreamily
dreamland
dreamless
dreamlike
dreamt
dreamy
dreary
dredge
dredger
dregs
drench
dress
dressage
dressed
dresser
dressing
dressmaker
dressmaking
dressy
drew
dribble
dribs and drabs
dried
drier
drift
drifter
driftwood
drill

drily
drink
drinkable
drinker
drinking
drip
dripping
drippy
drive
drivel
driven
driver
driveway
driving
drizzle
drizzly
droll
drone
drool
droop
droopy
drop
droplet
dropper
droppings
dross
drought
drove
drover
droves
drown
drowse
drowsy
drudge
drudgery
drug
druggie
druggist
drugstore
Druid
drum
drumbeat
drummer
drumming
drumstick
drunk
drunkard
drunken
dry
dryer

/dw/
dw:
dwarf
dweeb
dwell
dweller
dwelling
dwelt

dwindle

/f/
/fæ/
fa:
fab
fabric
fabricate
fabulous
facet
facile
facsimile
fact
faction
factional
factionalism
factor
factory
factotum
factual
faculty
fad
faddish
faddy
faff
fag
faggot
Fahrenheit
fallacy
fallible
fallow
family
famine
famished
fan
fancier
fanciful
fancy
fandango
fanfare
fang
fanlight
fanny
fantasia
fantasist
fantasize
fantastic
fantasy
fanzine
farrier
fascinate
fascinated
fascinating
fascination
fascism
fascist
fashion
fashionable
fastidious

fat
fathom
fathomless
fatten
fattening
fatty
fatuous
fatwa
fax

fe:
femme fatale

fi:
fin de siècle

pha:
phalanx
phallic
phallus
phantasmagorical
phantasy
phantom
Pharisee

/feɪ/
fa:
fable
fabled
face
facecloth
faceless
facelift
facial
facie
facing
fade
fake
fame
famed
famous
famously
fascia
fatal
fatalism
fatalistic
fate
fated
fateful
favour
favourable
favourite
favouritism
faze

fai:
fail
failing
failure
faint
faintest

/fɑː/

fait accompli
faith
faithful
faithfully
faithless

fe:
fete

fei:
feign
feint

fey:
fey

pha:
phase

/fɑː/

fa:
fast
fasten
fastener
fastening
fastness
father
fatherhood
fatherland
fatherless
fatherly

far:
far
faraway
farce
farcical
farm
farmer
farmhand
farmhouse
farming
farmland
farmyard
fart
farther
farthest
farthing

phar:
pharmaceutical
pharmacist
pharmacology
pharmacopoeia
pharmacy

/feə/

fair:
fair
fairground
fairly
fairness

fairway
fairy
fairyland

fare:
fare
farewell

phar:
pharaoh

/fe/

fea:
feather
feathered
featherweight
feathery

fe:
February
feckless
fed
federal
federalism
federalist
federated
federation
fell
fella
fellow
fellowship
felon
felony
felt
feminine
femininity
feminism
feminist
feminize
fen
fence
fencing
fend
fender
fennel
feral
ferret
ferrous
ferrule
ferry
ferryboat
fester
festival
festive
festivity
festoon
fetch
fetching
fetid
fetish
fetishism

fetishist
fetlock
fetter
fettle
fez

pf:
pfennig

ph:
pheasant
pheromone

/fiː/

fae:
faecal
faeces

fe:
febrile
fecal
feces
fecund
feline
female
femur
fetal
fetus
fever
fevered
feverish

fea:
fealty
feasible
feast
feat
feature
featureless

fee:
fee
feeble
feed
feedback
feeder
feel
feeler
feelgood
feeling
feelingly
feet

fi:
fiat

fie:
fief
field
fielder
fieldwork
fiend

fiendish

foe:
foetal
foetid
foetus

phoe:
phoenix

/fi/

fi:
fiancé
fiancée
fiasco
fiesta

/fɜː/

fer:
ferment
fern
fertile
fertilize
fertilizer
fervent
fervour

fir:
fir
firm
firmament
first
firstly

fur:
fur
furl
furlong
furlough
furnace
furnish
furnished
furnishings
furniture
furry
further
furtherance
furthermore
furthermost
furthest
furtive

/fɪə/

fear:
fear
fearful
fearless
fearsome

fier:
fierce

/fɪ/

fe:
fedora
felicitous
felicity

fi:
fib
fibula
fickle
fiction
fictional
fictionalize
fictitious
fiddle
fiddler
fiddlesticks
fiddling
fiddly
fidelity
fidget
fidgety
fifteen
fifteenth
fifth
fiftieth
fifty
fig
figment
figurative
figure
figurehead
figurine
filament
filch
filial
filibuster
filigree
Filipino
fill
filler
fillet
filling
fillip
filly
film
filmic
filming
filmy
filter
filth
filthy
filtration
fin
finale
finch
finesse
finger
fingering
fingermark
fingernail
fingerprint
fingertip
finicky
finish
finished
Finn
Finnish
fiscal
fish
fisherman
fishery
fishing
fishmonger
fishnet
fishwife
fishy
fission
fissure
fist
fistful
fisticuffs
fit
fitful
fitted
fitter
fitting
fix
fixated
fixation
fixative
fixed
fixedly
fixer
fixings
fixity
fixture
fizz
fizzle
fizzy

phe:
phenomena
phenomenal
phenomenology
phenomenon

phi:
philanderer
philandering
philanthropic
philanthropist
philanthropy
philatelist
philately
philharmonic
Philippine
philistine
philistinism
philology
philosopher
philosophic
philosophical
philosophize
philosophy

phy:
physical
physician
physicist
physics
physio
physiognomy
physiology
physiotherapist
physiotherapy
physique

/faɪ/

fei:
feisty

fi:
fibre
fibreglass
fibroid
fibrous
fife
fight
fightback
fighter
file
Filofax
final
finalise
finalist
finality
finalize
finally
finance
financial
financier
find
finder
finding
fine
finery
finite
five
fiver

phi:
phial

/faɪə/

fier:
fiery

fire:
fire
firearm
fireball
firebomb
firebrand
firebreak
firecracker
firefight
firefly
fireguard
firelight
fireman
fireplace
firepower
fireproof
fireside
firestorm
firewood
firework

/fɒ/

fo:
fob
fodder
fog
fogbound
foggy
foghorn
follicle
follow
follower
following
folly
fond
fondant
fondle
fondue
font
foppish
forage
foray
forehead
foreign
foreigner
forest
forested
forester
forestry
fossil
fossilize
foster
fox
foxglove
foxhole
foxhound
foxy

pho:
phonic
phosphate
phosphorescence
phosphorescent
phosphoric acid

/foʊ/

phosphorus

/foʊ/

faux:
faux pas

fo:
focal
focus
focused
foe
fogey
fogy
fold
folder
foliage
folio
folk
folklore
folksy
foment

foa:
foal
foam
foamy

pho:
phobia
phobic
phone
phoneme
phoney
phonograph
phony
photo
photo-
photocopier
photocopy
Photofit
photogenic
photograph
photographic
photojournalism
photon
photostat
photosynthesis

/fɔ:/

fa:
falcon
falconer
falconry
fall
fallback
fallen
fallout
false
falsehood
falsetto
falsify

falter
faltering

fau:
faucet
fault
faultless
faulty
faun
fauna

faw:
fawn

for:
for
forbear
forbearance
forbearing
force
forced
forceful
forceps
forcible
ford
forfeit
forfeiture
forge
forgery
forgo
fork
forked
forkful
forlorn
form
formal
formaldehyde
formalise
formalism
formality
formalize
format
formation
formative
former
formerly
Formica
formidable
formless
formula
formulaic
formulate
formulation
fornicate
forswear
forsythia
fort
forte
forth
forthcoming
forthright

forthwith
fortieth
fortification
fortify
fortissimo
fortitude
fortnight
fortnightly
fortress
fortuitous
fortunate
fortunately
fortune
forty
forum
forward
forwards
forwent

fore:
fore
forearm
forearmed
forebear
foreboding
forecast
forecaster
foreclose
forecourt
forefather
forefinger
forefoot
forefront
forego
foregoing
foregone
foreground
forehand
foreknowledge
foreleg
forelock
foreman
foremost
forename
forenoon
foreplay
forerunner
foresee
foreseeable
foreshadow
foreshore
foreshorten
foresight
foreskin
forestall
foretaste
foretell
forethought
foretold
forewarn

forewent
foreword

fough:
fought

four:
four
foursome
fourteen
fourteenth
fourth
fourthly

/fɔɪ/

foi:
foible
foil
foist

foy:
foyer

/fʊ/

foo:
foot
footage
football
footballer
footballing
footbridge
footfall
foothills
foothold
footing
footlights
footloose
footman
footnote
footpath
footplate
footprint
footsie
footsore
footstep
footstool
footwear
footwork

fu:
fulcrum
fulfil
fulfilment
full
fullness
fully
fulminate
fulsome

/fu:/

foo:
food
foodie

/faʊ/

foodstuff
fool
foolhardy
foolish
foolproof
foolscap

fu:
futon

/faʊ/

fou:
foul
found
foundation
founded
founder
founding
foundling
foundry
fount
fountain

fow:
fowl

/fʌ/

fu:
fuck
fucker
fucking
fuddy-duddy
fudge
fug
fumble
fun
function
functional
functionalism
functionary
fund
fundamental
fundamentalism
fundamentally
fundamentals
funding
fundraiser
funfair
fungal
fungi
fungicide
fungus
funk
funky
funnel
funnily
funny
furrier
furrow
fuss

fussed
fussy
fusty
fuzz
fuzzy

/fju:/

feu:
feud
feudal
feudalism

few:
few

fu:
fuchsia
fuel
fuelled
fugitive
fugue
fume
fumigate
funeral
funerary
funereal
funicular
fuse
fused
fuselage
fusillade
fusion
futile
futility
future
futurism
futurist
futuristic
futurology

phew:
phew

/fjʊə/

fur:
furious
fury

/fjɔ:/

fjor:
fjord

/fə/

fa:
facade
facetious
facilitate
facilitator
facility
fallacious

fallopian tube
familial
familiar
familiarity
familiarize
familiarly
fanatic
fanatical
fanaticism
farrago
fatality
fatigue
fatigued
fatiguing

fe:
fellatio
ferocious
ferocity

fer:
ferment

for:
for
forbade
forbid
forbidden
forbidding
forensic
forever
forgave
forget
forgetful
forgettable
forgivable
forgive
forgiveness
forgiving
forgot
forgotten
forsake
forsaken

pha:
phalanges

pho:
phonetics
phonology
photographer
photography

/fl/

fl:
flab
flabbergasted
flabby
flaccid
flag
flagellation
flagged

flagon
flagpole
flagrant
flagship
flagstaff
flagstone
flail
flair
flak
flake
flaky
flambée
flamboyant
flame
flamenco
flameproof
flaming
flamingo
flammable
flan
flange
flank
flannel
flap
flapjack
flare
flared
flash
flashback
flashbulb
flasher
flashgun
flashlight
flashpoint
flashy
flask
flat
flatfish
flatmate
flatten
flatter
flattered
flattering
flattery
flatulence
flatware
flaunt
flautist
flavour
flavoured
flavouring
flavourless
flaw
flawed
flawless
flax
flaxen
flay
flea
fleapit

/fr/

fleck
flecked
fled
fledgling
flee
fleece
fleecy
fleet
fleeting
Flemish
flesh
fleshy
flew
flex
flexible
flexitime
flick
flicker
flier
flight
flightless
flighty
flimsy
flinch
fling
flint
flintlock
flinty
flip
flippant
flipper
flipping
flirt
flirtatious
flirty
flit
float
flock
floe
flog
flood
floodgates
flooding
floodlight
floor
floorboard
floored
flooring
floozy
flop
floppy
flora
floral
florid
florin
florist
floss
flotation
flotilla
flotsam

flounce
flounder
flour
flourish
floury
flout
flow
flower
flowerbed
flowered
flowering
flowerpot
flowery
flown
flu
fluctuate
flue
fluent
fluff
fluffy
fluid
fluke
flummox
flung
flunk
flunkey
fluorescent
fluoridation
fluoride
flurry
flush
flushed
fluster
flute
fluted
fluting
flutist
flutter
flux
fly
flyaway
flyby
flyer
flying
flyleaf
flyover
flypast
flywheel

phl:
phlegm
phlegmatic

/fr/

fr:
fracas
fractal
fraction
fractional

fractious
fracture
fragile
fragment
fragmentary
fragrance
fragrant
frail
frailty
frame
framework
franc
franchise
franchisee
franchiser
frank
frankfurter
frankincense
frankly
frantic
fraternal
fraternity
fraternize
fratricidal
fratricide
fraud
fraudster
fraudulent
fraught
fray
freak
freakish
freaky
freckle
freckled
free
freebie
freedom
freefone
freehand
freehold
freeholder
freelance
freelancer
freeloader
freely
freeman
Freemason
freemasonry
Freepost
freer
freesia
freest
freestyle
freeway
freewheel
freewheeling
freeze
freezer
freezing

freight
freighter
French
Frenchman
Frenchwoman
frenetic
frenzied
frenzy
frequency
frequent
fresco
fresh
fresh-
freshen
fresher
freshly
freshman
freshwater
fret
fretful
fretwork
Freudian
friar
friction
Friday
fridge
friend
friendless
friendly
friendship
frieze
frigate
frigging
fright
frighten
frightened
frightening
frightful
frigid
frill
frilled
frilly
fringe
fringed
frippery
Frisbee
frisk
frisky
frisson
fritter
frivolity
frivolous
frizz
frizzy
fro
frock
frogman
frogspawn
frolic

/gæ/

from
frond
front
frontage
frontal
frontbencher
frontier
frontispiece
frost
frostbite
frostbitten
frosted
frosting
frosty
froth
frothy
frown
froze
frozen
frugal
fruit
fruitcake
fruitful
fruition
fruitless
fruity
frumpy
frustrate
fry

phr:
phrasal verb
phrase
phraseology
phrasing
phrenology

/g/
/gæ/

ga:
gab
gabardine
gabble
gad
gadfly
gadget
gadgetry
gaff
gaffe
gaffer
gag
gaggle
gal
galaxy
gallant
gallantry
galleon
gallery
galley
Gallic
gallivant
gallon
gallop
gallows
galvanize
galvanized
gambit
gamble
gambler
gambling
gambol
gamine
gamma
gammon
gamut
gander
gang
gangland
gangling
gangly
gangplank
gangrene
gangrenous
gangster
gangway
gantry
gap
garage
garret
garrison
garrulous
gas
gaseous
gash
gasket
gaslight
gasman
gasoline
gasometer
gassy
gastric
gastroenteritis
gastronome
gastronomic
gastronomy
gasworks
gateau
gather
gatherer
gathering
gavel
gazetteer

gua:
guarantee
guaranteed
guarantor

/geɪ/

ga:
gable
gabled
gale
game
Gameboy
gamekeeper
gamely
gamesmanship
gaming
gape
gate
gatecrash
gatehouse
gatekeeper
gatepost
gateway
gator
gave
gaze

gae:
Gaelic

gai:
gaiety
gaily
gain
gainer
gainful
gainsay
gait
gaiter

gau:
gauge

gay:
gay

gei:
geisha

/gɑ:/

ga:
gaga
gala
gasp

gar:
garb
garbage
garbed
garbled
garden
gardener
gardenia
gargantuan
gargle
gargoyle
garland
garlic
garlicky
garment
garner
garnet
garnish
garter

gha:
Ghanaian
ghastly

guar:
guard
guarded
guardian
guardianship
guardrail
guardsman

/geə/

gar:
garish

/ge/

ge:
gelding
get
getaway
getting

ghe:
ghetto

gue:
guess
guesstimate
guesswork
guest

/gi:/

gee:
geek
geese
geezer

gey:
geyser

/gɜ:/

gher:
gherkin

gir:
gird
girder
girdle
girl
girlfriend
girlhood

/gɪə/

girlie
girlish
girth

gur:
gurgle

/gɪə/

gear:
gear
gearbox
gearshift

/gɪ/

gi:
gibbon
giddy
gift
gifted
gig
giggle
giggly
gild
gilding
gill
gilt
gimlet
gimmick
gimmickry
gimmicky
gingham
git
give
giveaway
given
giver
gizmo

gui:
guild
guilder
guildhall
guillotine
guilt
guilty
guinea
guitar
guitarist

/gaɪ/

gei:
Geiger counter

gui:
guidance
guide
guidebook
guideline
guile
guileless

guise

guy:
guy
Guy Fawkes Night

gy:
gynaecology

/gɒ/

go:
gob
gobbet
gobble
gobbledygook
goblet
goblin
gobsmacked
god
godchild
goddammit
goddamn
goddamned
goddaughter
goddess
godfather
Godhead
godless
godlike
godliness
godly
godmother
godparent
godsend
godson
Godspeed
goggle
golf
golfer
golfing
golly
gondola
gone
goner
gong
gonna
gonorrhoea
gosh
gosling
gospel
gossamer
gossip
gossipy
got
Gothic
gotta
gotten

/goʊ/

gau:
gauche

gho:
ghost
ghostly

go:
go
gofer
going
gold
golden
goldfish
goldmine
goldsmith
gopher

goa:
goad
goal
goalie
goalkeeper
goalkeeping
goalless
goalmouth
goalpost
goat
goatee

/gɔː/

ga:
gall
gallstone

gau:
gaudy
gaunt
gauntlet
gauze
gauzy

gaw:
gawd
gawk
gawky
gawp

gor:
gore
gorge
gorgeous
gormless
gorse
gory

/gɔɪ/

goi:
goitre

/gʊ/

goo:
good
goodbye

goodie
goodly
goodness
goodnight
goods
goodwill
goody
gooseberry

/guː/

ghou:
ghoul
ghoulish

goo:
goo
gooey
goof
goofy
googly
goon
goose

gu:
gubernatorial
guru

/gʊə/

gour:
gourd
gourmand
gourmet

/gaʊ/

gou:
gouge
gout

gow:
gown

/gʌ/

go:
govern
governance
governess
governing
government
governmental
governor
governorship

gu:
guff
guffaw
gulch
gulf
gull
gullet
gulley

/gə/

gullible
gully
gulp
gum
gumboot
gummy
gumption
gun
gunboat
gunfire
gunge
gunman
gunner
gunnery
gunpoint
gunpowder
gunship
gunshot
gunsmith
guppy
gush
gusset
gust
gusto
gusty
gut
gutless
gutsy
gutted
gutter
guttering
guttural
guv
guvnor
guzzle

/gə/

ga:
galactic
galore
galoshes
garrotte
gazebo
gazelle
gazette
gazump

ge:
gestalt

go:
gorilla

gue:
guerrilla

/gl/

gl:
glacé
glacial
glacier
glad
gladden
glade
gladiator
glamor
glamorize
glamorous
glamour
glance
glancing
gland
glandular
glare
glaring
glasnost
glass
glasshouse
glassware
glassy
glaucoma
glaze
glazed
glazier
gleam
glean
glee
gleeful
glen
glib
glide
glider
gliding
glimmer
glimmering
glimpse
glint
glisten
glitch
glitter
glitterati
glittering
glittery
glitz
glitzy
gloat
glob
global
globalize
globe
globular
globule
glockenspiel
gloom
gloomy
glorified
glorify
glorious
glory
gloss
glossary
glossies
glossy
glove
gloved
glow
glower
glowering
glowing
glucose
glue
glum
glut
glutamate
gluten
glutinous
glutton
gluttonous
gluttony
glycerine

/gr/

gr:
grab
grace
graceful
graceless
gracious
gradation
grade
graded
gradient
gradual
graduate
graduated
graduation
graffiti
graft
Grail
grain
grainy
gram
grammar
grammarian
grammatical
gramme
gramophone
gran
granary
grand
grandad
grandaddy
grandchild
granddad
granddaughter
grandee
grandeur
grandfather
grandiloquent
grandiose
grandly
grandma
Grandmaster
grandmother
grandpa
grandparent
Grand Prix
grandson
grandstand
granite
granny
grant
granted
granular
granulated sugar
granule
grape
grapefruit
grapevine
graph
graphic
graphical
graphite
graphology
grapple
grasp
grasping
grass
grasshopper
grassland
grassy
grata
grate
grateful
grater
gratify
grating
gratis
gratitude
gratuitous
gratuity
grave
gravedigger
gravel
gravelled
gravelly
graveside
gravestone
graveyard
gravitas
gravitate
gravitation
gravitational
gravity
gravy
gray
graze
grazing
grease
greasepaint
greaseproof paper

/gw/

greasy
great
great-
Great Britain
greatcoat
greater
greatly
Grecian
greed
greedy
Greek
green
greenback
greenery
greenfly
greengage
greengrocer
greenhouse
greening
greenish
greenroom
Greenwich Mean Time
greeny
greet
greeting
gregarious
gremlin
grenade
grew
grey
greyhound
greyish
grid
griddle
gridiron
gridlock
grief
grievance
grieve
grievous
griffin
grill
grille
grim
grimace
grime
grimy
grin
grind
grinder
grinding
grindstone
gringo
grip
gripe
griping
grisly
grist
gristle

grit
gritty
grizzled
grizzly
groan
grocer
grocery
grog
groggy
groin
groom
groomed
grooming
groove
grooved
groovy
grope
gross
grotesque
grotto
grotty
grouch
grouchy
ground
groundbreaking
groundcloth
groundhog
grounding
groundless
groundnut
groundsheet
groundsman
groundswell
groundwater
groundwork
group
groupie
grouping
grouse
grove
grovel
grow
grower
growl
grown
growth
grub
grubby
grudge
grudging
gruel
gruelling
gruesome
gruff
grumble
grumpy
grunge
grunt

/gw/

gu:
guano
guava

/h/

/hæ/

ha:
haberdasher
haberdashery
habit
habitable
habitat
habitation
hack
hacker
hacking
hackles
hackneyed
hacksaw
had
haddock
hadn't
hag
haggard
haggis
haggle
halcyon
halibut
halitosis
hallelujah
hallo
hallowed
Halloween
ham
hamburger
hamlet
hammer
hammock
hamper
hamster
hamstring
hand
hand-
handbag
handball
handbill
handbook
handbrake
handcart
handcuff
handful
handgun
handhold
handicap
handicapped
handicraft
handiwork
handkerchief

handle
handlebar
handler
handmade
handmaiden
handout
handover
handrail
handset
handshake
handsome
handstand
handwriting
handwritten
handy
handyman
hang
hangar
hangdog
hanger
hanging
hangman
hangout
hangover
hank
hanker
hankering
hanky
hanky-panky
hansom
haphazard
hapless
happen
happening
happenstance
happily
happy
hara-kiri
harass
harassed
harassment
haricot bean
harridan
harrow
harrowing
harry
has
hash
hashish
hasn't
hassle
hassock
hast
hat
hatband
hatbox
hatch
hatchback
hatchery
hatchet

/heɪ/

hatchway
hath
hatpin
hatstand
have
haven't
haversack
haves
havoc
hazard
hazardous

/heɪ/

ha:
habeas corpus
Hades
hail
hailstone
hailstorm
hake
hale
halfpenny
halo
haste
hasten
hasty
hate
hateful
hater
hatred
haven
haze
hazel
hazelnut
hazy

hay:
hay
haystack
haywire

hei:
heinous

hey:
hey
heyday

/hɑː/

cha:
Chanukah

ha:
ha
hah
half
halfway
halve
Hanukkah
hasp

har:
harbinger
harbour
harbourmaster
hard
hardback
hardboard
harden
hardened
hardline
hardliner
hardly
hardship
hardware
hardwood
hardworking
hardy
harem
hark
harlequin
harlot
harm
harmful
harmless
harmonic
harmonica
harmonious
harmonize
harmony
harness
harp
harpist
harpoon
harpsichord
harpy
harsh
harvest
harvester

hear:
heart
heartache
heartbeat
heartbreak
heartbreaking
heartbroken
heartburn
hearten
heartfelt
hearth
heartland
heartless
heartstrings
hearty

/heə/

hair:
hair
hairbrush
haircut

hairdo
hairdresser
hairdressing
hairdryer
hairgrip
hairless
hairline
hairnet
hairpiece
hairpin
hairspray
hairstyle
hairstylist
hairy

hare:
hare

/he/

hae:
haemorrhage
haemorrhoid

hea:
head
headache
headband
headboard
headdress
header
headgear
headhunt
headhunter
heading
headlamp
headland
headless
headlight
headline
headlined
headlong
headman
headmaster
headmistress
headphones
headquartered
headquarters
headrest
headroom
headscarf
headset
headship
headstone
headstrong
headway
headwind
headword
heady
health
healthful
healthy

heather
heaven
heavenly
heavenward
heavily
heavy
heavyweight

he:
heck
heckle
hectare
hectic
hector
hedge
hedgehog
hedgerow
hefty
held
helicopter
helipad
heliport
hell
Hellenic
hellhole
hellish
hello
helluva
helm
helmet
helmsman
help
helper
helpful
helping
helpless
helpline
helpmate
helter-skelter
hem
hemisphere
hemline
hemlock
hemorrhage
hemorrhoid
hemp
hen
hence
henceforth
henceforward
henchman
henhouse
henna
hepatitis
heptathlon
herald
heraldry
heresy
heretic
heritage

/hiː/

heroin
heroine
heroism
heron
herring
herringbone
hesitant
hesitate
hesitation
hessian
heterodox
heterogeneous
heterosexual
het up
hexagon
hexagonal

heɪ:
heifer

/hiː/

hae:
haemoglobin
haemophilia
haemophiliac

he:
he
Hebrew
hedonism
hedonist
hedonistic
heed
heedless
heel
helium
helix
hemoglobin
hemophilia
hemophiliac

hea:
heal
healer
heap
heaped
heat
heated
heater
heath
heathen
heating
heatwave
heave

/hi/

he:
he

/hɜː/

hear:
hearse

her:
her
herb
herbaceous
herbal
herbalism
herbalist
herbicide
herbivore
herculean
herd
herdsman
hermaphrodite
hermetic
hermit
hernia
herpes
hers

hir:
hirsute

hur:
hurdle
hurdler
hurl
hurly-burly
hurt
hurtful
hurtle

/hɪə/

hear:
hear
hearer
hearing
hearsay

her:
hero

here:
here
hereabouts
hereafter
hereby
herein
heretofore
herewith

/hɪ/

he:
he'd
hegemony
he'll
hereditary
heredity
heretical
heroic
he's

/hɪ/

hi:
hibiscus
hiccup
hick
hid
hidden
hideous
hideously
higgledy-piggledy
hilarious
hilarity
hill
hillbilly
hillock
hillside
hilltop
hilly
hilt
him
himself
hinder
Hindi
hindrance
Hindu
Hinduism
hinge
hinged
hint
hinterland
hip
hippie
hippo
Hippocratic oath
hippopotamus
hippy
hipster
his
Hispanic
hiss
historian
historic
historical
history
histrionic
histrionics
hit
hitch
hitchhike
hither
hitherto
hitman
hitter

hy:
hymn
hymnal
hypnosis
hypnotherapist
hypnotherapy
hypnotic

/haɪ/

hypnotise
hypnotism
hypnotize
hypocrisy
hypocrite
hypocritical
hysterectomy
hysteria
hysterical
hysterics

/haɪ/

hei:
height
heighten
heist

hi:
hi
hiatus
hibernate
hide
hideaway
hidebound
hideout
hiding
hi-fi
high
highborn
highbrow
highfalutin
highlands
highlight
highlighter
highly
Highness
highway
highwayman
hijack
hijacker
hike
hiker
hind
hindquarters
hindsight
hive
hiya

hy:
hyacinth
hybrid
hybridize
hydrant
hydrate
hydraulic
hydraulics
hydrocarbon
hydrochloric acid
hydroelectric
hydro-electricity
hydrofoil

/haɪə/

hydrogen
hydroplane
hydrotherapy
hyena
hygiene
hygienic
hygienist
hymen
hype
hyper
hyper-
hyperactive
hyperbole
hyperbolic
hyperinflation
hypermarket
hypersensitive
hypertension
hypertext
hyperventilate
hyphen
hyphenated
hypochondria
hypochondriac
hypodermic
hypotenuse
hypothermia
hypothesis
hypothesize
hypothetical

/haɪə/

hier:
hierarchical
hierarchy
hieroglyph
hieroglyphics

higher:
higher

hire:
hire
hireling

/hɒ/

ho:
hob
hobble
hobby
hobbyist
hobnob
hock
hockey
hod
hodgepodge
hog
Hogmanay
hogwash
holiday

holidaymaker
holler
hollow
holly
Hollywood
holocaust
hologram
hols
homage
homicidal
homicide
homily
homogeneity
homogeneous
homophobia
homophobic
homophone
homosexual
honk
honky-tonk
hop
hopper
hopscotch
horizontal
horoscope
horrible
horrid
horrify
horrifying
horror
horror-stricken
hospice
hospitable
hospital
hospitality
hospitalize
hostage
hostel
hostelry
hostile
hostilities
hostility
hot
hotbed
hotch-potch
hothead
hothouse
hotline
hotly
hotplate
hotpot
hotshot
hovel
hover
hovercraft

/hoʊ/

ho:
hobo
hocus-pocus

ho hum
hokum
hold
holdall
holder
holding
holdout
hole
holiness
holism
holistic
holster
holy
holy of holies
home
homecoming
homeland
homeless
homely
homemaker
homeopath
homeopathic
homeopathy
homesick
homespun
homestead
hometown
homeward
homework
homey
homing
homoeopath
homo sapiens
hone
hope
hopeful
hopefully
hopeless
hose
hosepipe
hosiery
host
hostess
hotel
hotelier
hove

hoa:
hoax
hoaxer

hoe:
hoe

jo:
jojoba

who:
whole
wholefood
wholegrains
wholehearted

wholemeal
wholeness
wholesale
wholesaler
wholesaling
wholesome
wholewheat
wholly

/hɔ:/

ha:
hall
hallmark
hallway
halt
halter
halting

hau:
haughty
haul
haulage
hauler
haulier
haunch
haunt
haunted
haunting

haw:
haw
hawk
hawker
hawkish
hawser
hawthorn

hoar:
hoard
hoarding
hoarse
hoary

hor:
horde
hormonal
hormone
horn
horned
hornet
hornpipe
horny
horse
horseback
horsehair
horseman
horsemanship
horseplay
horsepower
horseradish
horseshoe

/hɔː/

horsewhip
horsewoman
horsey
horticultural
horticulturalist
horticulture

whor:
whore
whorehouse

/hɔɪ/

hoi:
hoi polloi
hoist

/hʊ/

chu:
chutzpah

hoo:
hood
hooded
hoodwink
hook
hooked
hooker
hooky
hooray

hu:
hurray

/huː/

hoo:
hooch
hoodlum
hoof
hoofer
hooligan
hooliganism
hoop
hooped
hoot
hooter
hoover
hooves

hou:
houmous

hu:
hummus
humus

who:
who
who'd
whodunnit
whoever
who'll

whom
whomever
whooping cough
who're
who's
whose
whosoever
who've

/haʊ/

hou:
hound
house
houseboat
housebound
houseboy
housebreaker
housebreaking
housecoat
household
householder
househusband
housekeeper
housekeeping
housemaid
houseman
housemaster
housemate
houseproud
houseroom
housewares
housewarming
housewife
housework
housing

how:
how
howdy
however
howitzer
howl
howler

/hʌ/

ho:
honey
honeybee
honeycomb
honeyed
honeymoon
honeypot
honeysuckle

hu:
hub
hubbub
hubby
hubcap
huckster

huddle
huff
huffy
hug
huh
hulk
hulking
hull
hullabaloo
hullo
hum
humble
humbug
humdinger
humdrum
hummingbird
hummock
hump
humpback
humped
hunch
hunchback
hunched
hundred
hundredth
hundredweight
hung
Hungarian
hunger
hungover
hungry
hunk
hunker
hunt
hunter
hunting
huntsman
hurricane
hurried
hurry
husband
husbandry
hush
hushed
husk
husky
hussy
hustings
hustle
hustler
hut
hutch

/hjuː/

hew:
hew

hu:
hubris
huge

human
humane
humanise
humanism
humanistic
humanitarian
humanitarianism
humanity
humanize
humankind
humanly
humid
humidifier
humidity
humiliate
humiliating
humiliation
humility
humor
humorist
humorous
humour
humourless
humungous

hue:
hue

/hjʊə/

heur:
heuristic

/hə/

ha:
habitual
habituated
habitué
had
hallucinate
hallucination
hallucinatory
hallucinogen
hallucinogenic
harangue
has
have

he:
heraldic

her:
her
herself

ho:
homogenize
homogenized
homogenous
horizon
horrendous
horrific

/dʒ/

/dʒæ/

ja:
jab
jabber
jack
jackal
jackboot
jackdaw
jacket
jackpot
Jacobean
jagged
jaguar
jam
jamb
jamboree
jammy
jangle
janitor
January
Japanese
jasmine
javelin
jazz
jazzy

/dʒeɪ/

ga:
gaol
gaoler

j:
J,j
JP

ja:
jade
jaded
jape

jai:
jail
jailbird
jailbreak
jailer
jailhouse

jay:
jay
jaywalking

/dʒɑː/

jar:
jar
jargon

/dʒe/

ge:
gel
gelatine

gelignite
gem
Gemini
gemstone
gen
gender
genera
general
generalise
generalissimo
generality
generalization
generalize
generalized
generally
generate
generation
generational
generative
generator
generosity
generous
genesis
genital
genitalia
genitive
genocidal
genocide
genome
gent
genteel
gentian
Gentile
gentility
gentle
gentleman
gentlemanly
gentlewoman
gentry
genuflect
genuine
genus
geriatric
gerontology
gerrymandering
gerund
gestation
gesticulate
gestural
gesture

jea:
jealous
jealousy

je:
jell
jellied
jelly
jellyfish
jerry-built

jest
jester
Jesuit
jet
jetliner
jetsam
jettison
jetty

jeo:
jeopardize
jeopardy

/dʒiː/

g:
G,g
GB
GBH
GCE
GCSE
GDP
GHQ
GI
GMT
GNP
GP
GRE
G-string

ge:
gene
genealogy
genial
genie
genius
geographical
geological
geometric
geophysical
geophysicist
geophysics
geopolitical
geopolitics

gee:
gee
gee whiz

je:
Jesus

jea:
jeans

jee:
Jeep

/dʒi/

ge:
geographer
geography
geology

geometry

ji:
jihad

/dʒɜː/

ger:
gerbil
germ
German
germane
Germanic
germinate

jer:
jerk
jerkin
jerky
jersey

jour:
journal
journalism
journalist
journalistic
journey
journeyman

/dʒɪə/

jeer:
jeer

/dʒɪ/

ge:
gelatinous
generic
geneticist
genetics
geranium

gi:
gibber
gibberish
gibbet
giblets
gigolo
gin
ginger
gingerbread
gingerly
gingery
ginseng
gipsy
giraffe
gist

gy:
gym
gymkhana
gymnasium
gymnast

/dʒaɪ/

gymnastics
gypsum
gypsy

je:
Jehovah
jejune

ji:
jib
jiffy
jig
jiggery-pokery
jiggle
jigsaw
jilt
jingle
jingoism
jingoistic
jink
jinx
jinxed
jitters
jittery

/dʒaɪ/

gi:
giant
giantess
gibe
gigantic

gy:
gyrate
gyroscope

ji:
jibe
jive

/dʒaɪə/

gir:
giro

/dʒɒ/

jo:
job
jobbing
jobless
jobsworth
jock
jockey
jockstrap
jocular
jodhpurs
jog
jogger
jollity
jolly
joss stick
jostle

jot
jotting

/dʒəʊ/

jo:
joke
joker
jokey
jokingly
jolt
jovial

/dʒɔ:/

geor:
Georgian

jau:
jaundice
jaundiced
jaunt
jaunty

jaw:
jaw
jawbone
jawline

jor:
Jordanian

/dʒɔɪ/

joi:
join
joiner
joinery
joint
jointed
joist

joy:
joy
joyful
joyless
joyous
joyride
joyrider
joyriding
joystick

/dʒʊ/

ju:
July

/dʒu:/

jew:
Jew
jewel
jewelled
jeweller
jewellery

Jewish
Jewishness

jou:
joule

ju:
jubilant
jubilation
jubilee
Judaic
Judaism
Judas
judicial
judiciary
judicious
judo
jukebox
June
junior
juniper
jute
juvenile

jui:
juice
juicy

/dʒʊə/

jew:
Jewry

jur:
jurisdiction
jurisprudence
jurist
juror
jury

/dʒaʊ/

jou:
joust

jow:
jowl
jowly

/dʒʌ/

ju:
judder
judge
judgment
judgmental
jug
juggernaut
juggle
juggler
jugular
jumble
jumbled
jumbo

jump
jumper
jump leads
jumpsuit
jumpy
junction
juncture
jungle
junk
junket
junkie
junkyard
junta
just
justice
justifiable
justification
justified
justify
justly
jut
juxtapose
juxtaposition

/dʒə/

ja:
Jacuzzi
Jamaican

/l/

/læ/

la:
lab
labrador
labyrinth
labyrinthine
lacerate
laceration
lachrymose
lack
lackadaisical
lackey
lacking
lacklustre
lacquer
lacquered
lactation
lactic acid
lactose
lad
ladder
laddie
lag
laggard
lagging
lam
lamb
lambast
lambing

/leɪ/ /le/

lamentable
lamentation
laminate
laminated
lamp
lamplight
lampoon
lampshade
land
landed
landfall
landfill
landing
landlady
landless
landlocked
landlord
landlubber
landmark
landmine
landowner
landowning
landscape
landslide
landslip
landward
language
languid
languish
languor
languorous
lank
lanky
lantern
lap
lapis lazuli
lapse
laptop
lapwing
laryngitis
larynx
lash
lashing
lass
lassie
lassitude
lasso
latch
latchkey
lateral
Latin
Latino
latitude
latter
latterly
lattice
latticed
latticework
lavatorial
lavatory

lavender
lavish
lax
laxative

li:
lingerie

/leɪ/

la:
label
labor
laborer
labour
laboured
labourer
lace
lacy
laden
ladle
lady
ladybird
ladybug
ladylike
Ladyship
lake
lakeside
lame
lane
Laotian
laser
late
latecomer
lately
latent
later
latest
latex
lathe
laze
lazy

lai:
laid
lain
laissez-faire
laity

lay:
lay
layabout
layer
layered
layman
layoff
layout
layperson

/lɑ:/

la:
la-di-da
lager

lama
lamé
lance
last
lasting
lastly
lather
lava

lar:
larceny
larch
lard
larder
large
largely
largesse
largish
largo
lark
larva
larval

lau:
laugh
laughable
laughingly
laughter

lla:
llama

/leə/

lair:
lair
laird

/le/

lea:
lead
leaded
leaden
lead-free
leant
leapt
leather
leathery
leaven
leavened

le:
Lebanese
lecher
lecherous
lechery
lectern
lecture
lecturer
lectureship
led
ledge

ledger
left
leftism
leftist
leftover
leftward
lefty
leg
legacy
legate
legend
legendary
leggings
leggy
legible
legislate
legislation
legislative
legislator
legislature
legless
legume
lemming
lemon
lemonade
lemongrass
lemony
lend
lender
length
lengthen
lengthways
lengthwise
lengthy
lens
lent
lentil
leper
leprosy
lesbian
lesbianism
less
lessee
lessen
lesser
lesson
lest
let
lethargy
let's
letter
letterbox
lettered
letterhead
lettering
lettuce
level
leveller
levitate
levity

/liː/

levy
lexical
lexicography
lexicon
lexis

leɪ:
leisure
leisured
leisurely
leisurewear

leo:
leopard

lie:
lieutenant

/liː/

lea:
lead
leader
leadership
lead-in
leading
lead singer
lead-up
leaf
leafless
leaflet
leafy
league
leak
leakage
leaker
leaky
lean
leaning
leap
leapfrog
lease
leasehold
leaseholder
leash
least
leave
leaves

lee:
lee
leech
leek
leeway

le:
legal
legalise
legalistic
legalize
legion
lemur
leniency

lenient
Leo
leonine
leotard
lesion
lethal
lever
leverage
Levi's

li:
Libra
lido
lima bean
liter
litre

/li/

le:
legality

li:
liaise
liaison

/lɜː/

lear:
learn
learned
learner
learning
learnt

lur:
lurch
lurk

/lɪə/

leer:
leer
leery

lir:
lira

/lɪ/

le:
legation
legitimate
legitimize
lethargic
leviathan

li:
lib
Lib Dem
liberal
liberalism
liberalize
liberate
liberated

liberator
libertarian
libertine
liberty
libidinous
libido
librettist
libretto
Libyan
lick
licking
licorice
lid
lidded
lift
ligament
lilt
lilting
lily
limb
limber
limbo
limerick
limit
limitation
limited
limitless
limousine
limp
limpet
limpid
linchpin
linden
lineage
lineal
linear
linen
linger
lingo
lingua franca
linguist
linguistics
liniment
link
linkage
linoleum
linseed oil
lint
lintel
lip
liposuction
lip-read
lipstick
liquefy
liqueur
liquid
liquidate
liquidator
liquidity
liquidize

/laɪ/

liquidizer
liquor
liquorice
lisp
list
listed
listen
listener
listing
listless
lit
litany
literacy
literal
literally
literary
literate
literati
literature
lithograph
lithography
Lithuanian
litigant
litigate
litigation
litigator
litigious
litmus test
litter
little
littoral
liturgical
liturgy
live
live-in
liver
liveried
livery
livid
living
lizard

ly:
lymph gland
lynch
lynchpin
lynx
lyric
lyrical
lyricism
lyricist

/laɪ/

lei:
leitmotif

li:
liability
liable

/laɪə/

libation
libel
libellous
Liberian
librarian
library
lice
licence
license
licensed
licensee
licentious
lichen
life
lifebelt
lifeblood
lifeboat
lifeguard
lifeless
lifelike
lifeline
lifelong
lifer
lifesaver
lifespan
lifestyle
lifetime
likable
like
likeable
likelihood
likely
liken
likeness
likewise
liking
lilac
lime
limelight
limestone
limey
line
lined
liner
linesman
lining
lino
lion
lioness
lionize
lithe
live
livelihood
lively
liven
livestock
live wire

lie:
lie

ligh:
light
lighten
lighter
lighthouse
lighting
lightning
lightship
lightweight

ly:
lychee
Lycra
lying

/laɪə/

liar:
liar

lyre:
lyre

/lɒ/

lau:
laurel

lo:
lob
lobby
lobbyist
lobster
loch
lock
locked
locker
locket
lodge
lodger
lodging
loft
lofty
log
logarithm
logger
loggerheads
loggia
logging
logic
logical
logjam
loll
lollipop
lollop
lolly
long
longevity
longhand
longing
longingly
longish
longitude
longitudinal
longshoreman
lop
lopsided
lorry
loss
lost
lot
lottery
lozenge

/loʊ/

lo:
lo
lobe
local
locale
locality
localize
localized
locate
located
location
loci
locomotion
locomotive
locum
locus
locust
loganberry
logo
lone
loneliness
lonely
loner
lonesome
lope
loth
lotion
lotus

loa:
load
loaded
loaf
loafer
loam
loan
loath
loathe
loathing
loathsome
loaves

low:
low
lowbrow
lower
lowlands
lowly

/lɔ:/

lau:
laud
laudable
laudatory
launch
launder
launderette
laundromat
laundry

law:
law
lawful
lawless
lawmaker
lawman
lawn
lawnmower
lawsuit

lor:
lord
lordly
Lordship
lore

/lɔɪ/

lawy:
lawyer

loi:
loin
loincloth
loiter

loy:
loyal
loyalist
loyalty

/lʊ/

loo:
look
looker
lookout

/lu:/

lo:
lose
loser

loo:
loo
loofah
loom
loony
loop
loophole
loose
loosen

/lu/

loot
looter

lou:
louche
louvre

lu:
lubricant
lubricate
lucerne
lucid
lucrative
lucre
ludicrous
lugubrious
lukewarm
luminary
luminescence
luminosity
luminous
lunacy
lunar
lunatic
lute

/lu/

leu:
leukaemia

/laʊ/

lou:
loud
loudhailer
loudmouth
loudspeaker
lounge
louse
lousy
lout
loutish

/lʌ/

lo:
lovable
love
lovebirds
loveless
lovelorn
lovely
lover
lovesick
lovey-dovey
loving

lu:
luck
luckily
luckless
lucky

Luddite
lug
luggage
lull
lullaby
lumbago
lumbar
lumber
lumberjack
lumberyard
lump
lumpectomy
lumpen
lumpy
lunch
luncheon
lunchroom
lunchtime
lung
lunge
lungful
luscious
lush
lust
lustful
lustre
lustrous
lusty
luv
luvvie
luxuriance
luxuriant
luxuriate
luxurious
luxury

/lju:/

lew:
lewd

lieu:
lieu

/ljʊə/

lur:
lure
lurid

/lə/

la:
laboratory
laborious
laburnum
laconic
lacrosse
lacuna
lagoon
lament
lapel
lasagne

lascivious
latrine
legit

lo:
lobotomy
logician
logistic
logistics
loquacious

/m/

/mæ/

ma:
ma'am
mac
macaroni
macaroon
macerate
Mach
Machiavellian
machinations
machismo
macho
macintosh
mackerel
mackintosh
macro
macro-
macrobiotic
macrobiotics
macrocosm
macroeconomic
mad
madam
madcap
madden
maddening
madhouse
madly
madman
madrigal
madwoman
mafia
mag
magazine
maggot
magic
magical
magisterial
magistrate
magnanimity
magnanimous
magnate
magnesium
magnet
magnetic
magnetism
magnetize
magnification

magnificent
magnify
magnitude
magnolia
magnum
magpie
majesty
mal-
maladjusted
maladministration
maladroit
malady
malaise
malcontent
malefactor
malevolent
malformation
malformed
malfunction
malice
mallard
malleable
mallet
malnourished
malnutrition
malodorous
malpractice
maltreat
maltreatment
mam
mammal
mammalian
mammary
mammogram
Mammon
mammoth
mammy
man
manacle
manage
manageable
management
manager
manageress
managerial
mandarin
mandate
mandatory
mandible
mandolin
manfully
manganese
mangle
mango
mangrove
manhandle
manhole
manhood
manhunt
manic

/meɪ/

manicure
manicured
manicurist
manifest
manifestation
manifesto
manifold
mankind
manly
manna
manned
mannequin
manner
mannered
mannerism
mannish
manor
manpower
manse
manservant
mansion
manslaughter
mantel
mantelpiece
mantelshelf
mantle
mantlepiece
mantra
manual
manufacture
manufacturer
manuscript
Manx
map
marathon
marigold
marijuana
marinade
marinate
mariner
marionette
marital
maritime
marriage
marriageable
married
marrow
marry
mascara
mascot
masculine
masculinity
masculinize
mash
masochism
masochistic
masquerade
mass
massacre
massage

massed
masseur
masseuse
massif
massive
mastectomy
masticate
mastiff
masturbate
mat
matador
match
matchbox
matched
matching
matchless
matchmaker
matchmaking
matchstick
math
mathematical
mathematician
mathematics
maths
matinee
matrimonial
matrimony
matt
matted
matter
matting
mattress
maturation
maverick
max
maxim
maximize
maximum

/meɪ/

meɪ:
mace
made
major
majorette
make
makeover
maker
makeshift
makeweight
making
male
mane
manger
mangy
mania
maniac
maple
mason
masonry

mate
matey
matriarch
matriarchal
matriarchy
matrices
matrix
matron
maze

maeː
maelstrom

maɪ:
maid
maiden
mail
mailbag
mailbox
mailing
mailman
mailshot
maim
main
mainframe
mainland
mainline
mainly
mainspring
mainstay
mainstream
maintain
maintenance
maisonette
maize

maɪ:
may
May
maybe
Mayday
mayfly
mayhem
mayn't
mayo
mayonnaise
may've

meː
melange
menage
menage a trois
mesa

/mɑː/

mɑː:
ma
maharaja
mamma
mask
masked

/mɑː/

mast
master
masterclass
masterful
masterly
mastermind
masterpiece
masterstroke
masterwork
mastery
masthead

mɑr:
mar
marble
marbled
march
marchioness
margarine
marge
margin
marginal
marginalize
marginally
marjoram
mark
marked
marker
market
marketable
marketeer
marketer
marketing
marketplace
marking
marksman
marksmanship
marmalade
marmoset
marque
marquee
marquis
marsh
marshal
marshland
marshmallow
marshy
marsupial
mart
martial
Martian
martin
martinet
martyr
martyrdom
martyred
marvel
marvellous
Marxism
Marxist

/meə/

marzipan

/meə/

mare:
mare

mayor:
mayor
mayoress

/me/

ma:
many

me:
mecca
mechanise
mechanism
mechanistic
mechanize
medal
medallist
meddle
meddlesome
mediaeval
medic
medical
medicated
medication
medicinal
medicine
medieval
meditate
meditation
meditative
Mediterranean
medley
mega
mega-
megabyte
megahertz
megalomania
megalomaniac
megaphone
megaton
megawatt
melancholia
melancholic
melancholy
melanin
melanoma
melee
mellow
melodrama
melodramatic
melody
melon
melt
meltdown
member
membership
membrane
memo
memoir
memorabilia
memorable
memorandum
memorize
memory
memsahib
men
menace
menacing
mend
mendacious
mendacity
mending
menfolk
meningitis
menopause
menstrual
menstruate
menswear
mental
mentality
menthol
mention
mentor
menu
meretricious
merit
meritocracy
meritocratic
meritorious
merrily
merriment
merry
mesa
mesh
mesmerize
mess
message
messenger
messianic
Messrs
messy
met
metabolic
metal
metalanguage
metalled
metallurgist
metallurgy
metalwork
metamorphose
metamorphosis
metaphor
metaphorical
metaphysical
metaphysics
method
Methodism
Methodist
methodology
meths
methylated spirits
metier
metric
metro
metronome
metronomic
metropolitan
mettle
Mexican
mezzanine
mezzo

mea:
meadow
meant
measurable
measure
measured
measurement
measuring

/mi:/

me:
me
media
median
mediate
mediocre
mediocrity
medium
meek
meet
meeting
menial
mete
meteor
meteoric
meteorite
meteorological
meteorology
meter
methane
metre

mea:
mead
meagre
meal
mealtime
mealy
mealy-mouthed
mean
meaning
meaningful
meaningfully
meaningless

/mɪə/

means
meantime
meanwhile
measles
measly
meat
meatball
meaty

mi:
mien
migraine
milieu

/mi/

me:
me
meander

mi:
miaow
miasma

/mɜ:/

mer:
mercantile
mercenary
merchandise
merchandiser
merchandising
merchant
merciful
mercifully
merciless
mercurial
mercury
mercy
merge
merger
mermaid

mir:
mirth
mirthless

mur:
murder
murderer
murderess
murderous
murderously
murk
murky
murmur
murmurings

/mɪə/

mere:
mere
merely

/mɪ/

me:
mechanic
mechanical
medallion
mellifluous
melodic
melodious
memento
memorial
memorialize
messiah
metabolism
metabolize

mi:
mickey
mid-
midday
middle
middlebrow
middleman
middling
midge
midget
Midlands
midnight
midpoint
midriff
midsized
midst
midstream
midsummer
midway
midweek
Midwest
Midwestern
midwife
midwifery
midwinter
miffed
mildew
mildewed
militant
militarism
militarist
militaristic
militarized
military
militate
militia
militiaman
milk
milkmaid
milkman
milkshake
milky
mill
millennium
miller

millet
milli-
milligram
millilitre
millimetre
milliner
millinery
milling
million
millionaire
millionairess
millionth
millipede
millisecond
millstone
mimetic
mimic
mimicry
minaret
mince
mincemeat
mincer
mineral
minestrone
mingle
mini
mini-
miniature
miniaturize
minibar
minibus
minicab
minim
minimal
minimalism
minimalist
minimize
minimum
minion
minister
ministerial
ministrations
ministry
mink
minnow
minority
minstrel
mint
minted
minuet
minuscule
minute
miracle
miraculous
mirage
mirror
mis-
misadventure
misanthrope
misanthropic

misanthropy
misapplication
misapply
misapprehension
misappropriate
misbehave
misbehaviour
miscalculate
miscarriage
miscarry
miscast
miscellaneous
miscellany
mischief
mischievous
misconceived
misconception
misconduct
misconstrue
miscreant
misdeed
misdemeanour
misdirect
miserable
misery
misfire
misfit
misfortune
misgiving
misguided
mishandle
mishap
mishear
mishmash
misinform
misinformation
misinterpret
misjudge
misjudgement
mislay
mislead
misleading
misled
mismanage
mismanagement
mismatch
misnamed
misnomer
misogynist
misogyny
misplace
misplaced
misprint
mispronounce
misquote
misread
misrepresent
misrule
miss
Miss

misshapen
missile
missing
mission
missionary
missive
misspell
misspend
missus
mist
mistake
mistaken
mister
mistime
mistletoe
mistook
mistreat
mistreatment
mistress
mistrial
mistrust
mistrustful
misty
misunderstand
misunderstanding
misunderstood
misuse
mitigate
mitigating
mitigation
mitt
mitten
mix
mixed
mixer
mixture

mr:
Mr
Mrs

my:
myriad
mysterious
mystery
mystic
mystical
mysticism
mystify
mystique
myth
mythic
mythical
mythology

/maɪ/

mae:
maestro

mi:
mica
mice

/maɪə/

micro-
microbe
microbiological
microbiology
microchip
microcosm
microelectronics
microfiche
microfilm
microphone
microprocessor
microscope
microscopic
microsecond
microsurgery
microwave
migrant
migrate
migratory
mike
mild
mildly
mile
mileage
milestone
mime
mind
minded
minder
mindful
mindless
mindset
mine
minefield
miner
minesweeper
mining
minor
minus
minute
minutely
minutiae
miser
miserly
mite

migh:
might
mightily
mightn't
might've
mighty

my:
my
myopia
myopic
myself

/maɪə/

mire:
mire

/mɒ/

ma:
Maltese
manqué

mo:
mob
mobster
moccasin
mock
mockery
mocking
mod
model
modeller
moderate
moderation
moderator
modern
modernise
modernism
modernist
modernistic
modernize
modest
modesty
modicum
modifier
modify
modular
modulate
module
moggy
molecule
mollify
mollusc
mollycoddle
Molotov cocktail
mom
momma
mommy
monarch
monarchical
monarchist
monarchy
monastery
Mongol
Mongolian
monitor
mono
mono-
monochrome
monocle
monogram
monogrammed
monograph

monolingual
monolith
monolithic
monologue
monorail
monosodium
 glutamate
monosyllabic
monosyllable
monotone
Monsignor
monsoon
monster
monstrosity
monstrous
montage
monument
monumental
mop
moral
moralise
moralist
moralistic
moralize
moratorium
moribund
morris dancer
morris dancing
morrow
Moslem
mosque
mosquito
moss
mossy
moth
mothball
motley
mottled
motto

/moʊ/

mau:
mauve

mo:
mo
mobile
mobilize
modal
mode
modem
modish
modus operandi
modus vivendi
mogul
mohair
molar
mold
molding
moldy

mole
molehill
molten
moment
momentarily
momentary
momentous
momentum
mope
moped
mosaic
mosey
most
mostly
motel
motif
motion
motionless
motivate
motivation
motive
motor
motorbike
motorboat
motorcade
motorcycle
motorcyclist
motoring
motorised
motorist
motorized
motorway

moa:
moan
moaner
moat

mou:
mould
moulder
moulding
mouldy
moult

mow:
mow
mower

/mɔː/

ma:
mall
malt
malted

mau:
maudlin
maul
Maundy Thursday
mausoleum

/mɔɪ/

maw:
maw
mawkish

mor:
morbid
mordant
more
moreover
mores
morgue
Mormon
morn
morning
moron
moronic
morpheme
morphine
morphology
morse code
morsel
mortal
mortality
mortar
mortgage
mortice lock
mortician
mortification
mortified
mortify
mortifying
mortuary

mou:
mourn
mourner
mournful
mourning

/mɔɪ/

moi:
moist
moisten
moisture
moisturize
moisturizer

/mʊ/

mou:
moussaka

mu:
mullah
Muslim

/mu/

mu:
muezzin

/mu:/

mo:
movable
move
moveable
movement
mover
movie
moviegoer
moving

moo:
moo
mooch
mood
moody
moon
moonbeam
moonless
moonlight
moonlit
moonshine
moose
moot

mou:
mousse

/mʊə/

moor:
moor
mooring
Moorish
moorland

/maʊ/

mao:
Maori

mou:
mound
mount
mountain
mountaineer
mountaineering
mountainous
mountainside
mounted
mouse
mousetrap
mousey
mousy
mouth
mouthful
mouthpiece
mouthwash

/mʌ/

mo:
Monday
monetarism
monetarist
monetary
money
moneyed
moneylender
mongrel
monied
monk
monkey
month
monthly
mother
motherfucker
motherhood
motherland
motherless
motherly

mu:
much
much-
muck
mucky
mud
muddle
muddled
muddy
mudflats
mudguard
mudslide
muff
muffin
muffle
muffled
muffler
mug
mugger
muggy
mulberry
mulch
mull
mulled
mullet
multi-
multicoloured
multicultural
multiculturalism
multifarious
multilateral
multilingual
multimedia
multinational
multiple
multiple sclerosis
multiplex
multiplication
multiplicity
multiply
multiracial
multitude
mum
mumble
mumbo jumbo
mummify
mummy
mumps
munch
mundane
muscle
muscular
muscular dystrophy
musculature
mush
mushroom
mushy
musk
musket
musky
muslin
mussel
must
must-
mustard
muster
mustn't
must've
musty
mutt
mutter
mutton
muzzle
muzzy

/mju:/

mew:
mew
mews

mu:
mucous membrane
mucus
mule
municipal
municipality
munificent
munitions
muse
museum
music
musical
musician
musicianship
mutant
mutate
mute
muted
mutilate
mutineer
mutinous
mutiny

/mjʊə/

mutual
muzak

mue:
muesli

/mjʊə/

mur:
mural

/mə/

m:
McCoy
Ms

ma:
macabre
machete
machine
machinery
machinist
Madonna
madras
magenta
magician
mahogany
majestic
majority
malaria
malarial
Malay
Malaysian
malicious
malign
malignancy
malignant
malinger
mama
maneuver
maniacal
manila
manipulate
manipulative
manipulator
manoeuvrable
manoeuvre
manure
marauder
marauding
marina
marine
maroon
marooned
Masonic
material
materialise
materialism
materialist
materialistic
materialize

maternal
maternity
matriculate
mature
maturity

mau:
Mauritian

me:
menagerie
meridian
meringue
metallic
methodical
meticulous
metropolis

mo:
molasses
molecular
molest
monastic
monogamous
monogamy
monopolistic
monopolize
monopoly
monotonous
monotony
monoxide
morale
morality
morass
Moroccan
morose

mou:
moustache
moustachioed

mu:
must
mustache

/n/

/næ/

gna:
gnash
gnat

kna:
knack
knacker
knackered
knapsack

na:
nab
naff
nag
nagging

nan
nanny
nannying
nap
napkin
nappy
narrative
narrow
narrowly
NASA
nascent
nasturtium
natch
national
nationalise
nationalism
nationalist
nationalistic
nationality
nationalize
natter
natty
natural
naturalism
naturalist
naturalistic
naturalize
naturalized
naturally
navigable
navigate
navigation
navigational
navigator
navvy

/neɪ/

kna:
knave

na:
nadir
naked
name
nameless
namely
nameplate
namesake
napalm
nape
nasal
nation
nationhood
nationwide
native
NATO
nature
naturism
naval
nave

/ne/

navel
navy

nai:
nail
nail polish

nay:
nay

née:
née

neigh:
neigh
neighbour
neighbourhood
neighbouring
neighbourly

/nɑː/

gnar:
gnarled

na:
nasty
Nazi
Nazism

naa:
naan

nar:
narcissi
narcissism
narcissistic
narcissus
narcolepsy
narcotic
narked

/ne/

kne:
knelt

ne:
nebula
nebulous
necessarily
necessary
neck
neckerchief
necklace
neckline
necktie
necromancy
necrophilia
necropolis
necrosis
nectar
nectarine
negative

/niː/

negligee
negligence
negligent
negligible
nemesis
nephew
nepotism
nest
nestle
nestling
net
netball
nether
netherworld
nett
netting
nettle
network
networking
never
nevertheless
next
nexus

/niː/

knea:
knead

knee:
knee
kneecap
kneel

ne:
Negress
Negro
negroid
neo-
neoclassical
neolithic
neologism
neon
neonatal
neophyte

nea:
neat

nee:
need
needful
needle
needless
needlework
needn't
needy

ni:
niche

nie:
niece

/nɪ/

ne:
neanderthal

/nɜː/

ner:
nerd
nerve
nervosa
nervous
nervy

nur:
nurse
nursemaid
nursery
nurseryman
nursing
nurture

/nɪə/

near:
near
nearby
nearly
nearside

nir:
nirvana

/nɪ/

kni:
knickers
knick-knacks
knit
knitting
knitwear

mne:
mnemonic

ne:
necessitate
necessity
nefarious
negate
negation
neglect
neglectful
negotiable
negotiate
negotiation
negotiator

ni:
nib
nibble
nick
nickel
nickname
nicotine
nifty
niggardly
nigger
niggle
niggling
Nikkei average
nil
nimble
nimbus
nimby
ninny
nip
nipper
nipple
nippy
Nissen hut
nit
nitpicking
nitty-gritty
nitwit

ny:
nymph
nymphomaniac

/naɪ/

kni:
knife
knifeman
knifepoint
knifing
knight
knighthood
knightly
knives

nai:
naive

nei:
neither

ni:
niacin
nice
nicely
nicety
Nigerian
nihilism
nihilistic
nine
ninepins
nineteen
nineteenth
ninetieth
ninety
ninth
nitrate
nitric
nitro-
nitrogen
nitroglycerin
nitrous

nigh:
nigh
night
nightcap
nightclothes
nightclub
nightclubbing
nightdress
nightfall
nightgown
nightie
nightingale
nightlife
nightly
nightmare
nightmarish
nightshirt
nightspot
nightstick
nightwatchman
nightwear

ny:
nylon

/nɒ/

kno:
knob
knobbly
knock
knockabout
knockdown
knocker
knockout
knot
knotty

know:
knowledge
knowledgeable

no:
nob
nobble
nocturnal
nocturne
nod
nodule
nom de guerre
nom de plume
nominal
nominate
nomination
nominative
nominee
non-
nonchalant
noncommittal

/noʊ/

nonconformist
nonconformity
nondescript
nonentity
nonplussed
nonsense
nonsensical
non sequitur
nosh
nostalgia
nostalgic
nostril
nostrum
not
notch
notwithstanding
novel
novelist
novelty
novice
noxious
nozzle

/noʊ/

gno:
gnome
gnomic

kno:
knoll

know:
know
knowing
knowingly
known

no:
no
nobility
noble
nobleman
noblesse oblige
noblewoman
nobody
node
Noel
nomad
nomadic
nomenclature
nomenklatura
nope
nose
nosebleed
nosedive
nosey
nosy
notable
notably
notary
notation

note
notebook
noted
notepad
notepaper
noteworthy
notice
noticeable
noticeboard
notifiable
notification
notify
notion
notional
notoriety
notorious
novella
November

now:
nowhere

/nɔ:/

gnaw:
gnaw

nau:
nausea
nauseam
nauseate
nauseating
nauseous
nautical

naugh:
naught
naughty

nor:
nor
Nordic
norm
normal
normalcy
normality
normalize
normally
Norman
normative
Norse
Norseman
north
northbound
northerly
northern
northerner
northernmost
northward
Norwegian

nough:
nought

/nɔɪ/

noi:
noise
noiseless
noisome
noisy

/nʊ/

noo:
nook
nookie

/nu:/

gnu:
gnu

noo:
noodle
noon
noonday
noose

nou:
nougat
nouveau-riche
nouvelle cuisine

/naʊ/

nou:
noun
nous

now:
now
nowadays
nowt

/nʌ/

knu:
knuckle

no:
none
nonetheless
nothing
nothingness

nou:
nourish
nourishment

nu:
nub
nudge
nugget
null
nullify
numb
number
numberless
numbskull

nun
nuncio
nunnery
nuptial
nut
nutcase
nutcracker
nutmeg
nutshell
nutter
nutty
nuzzle

/nju:/

knew:
knew

neu:
neuter
neutral
neutralize
neutron

new:
new
new-
newborn
newcomer
new-fangled
newly
newlywed
news
newsagent
newscast
newscaster
newsflash
newsletter
newsman
newspaper
newspaperman
newsprint
newsreader
newsreel
newsroom
newsstand
newsworthy
newt
New Zealander

nu:
nuance
nubile
nuclear
nucleic acid
nucleus
nude
nudism
nudity
nuke
numeracy
numeral

/njʊə/

numerate
numerical
numerology
numerous
numinous
nutrasweet
nutrient
nutrition
nutritional
nutritionist
nutritious
nutritive

nui:
nuisance

pneu:
pneumatic
pneumonia

/njʊə/

neur:
neural
neuralgia
neuro-
neurological
neurology
neuron
neurosis
neurotic

/nə/

na:
narrate
Nativity

no:
nomenclature

/p/
/pæ/

pa:
pachyderm
pacifier
pacifism
pacifist
pacify
pack
package
packaging
packed
packer
packet
packing
pact
pad
padding
paddle
paddock
paddy

padlock
pageant
pageantry
pah
pal
palace
palaeontology
palatable
palate
Palestinian
palette
palimony
palindrome
palisade
pallet
palliative
pallid
pallor
pally
palomino
palpable
palpitate
palpitation
pampas
pamper
pamphlet
pamphleteer
pan
pan-
panacea
panama hat
pancake
pancreas
pancreatic
panda
pandemic
pandemonium
pander
Pandora
panegyric
panel
panelled
panelling
panellist
pang
panhandle
panhandler
panic
panicky
pannier
panoply
panorama
panoramic
pansy
pant
pantaloons
pantechnicon
pantheism
pantheistic
pantheon

panther
panties
panto
pantomime
pantry
pants
pantyhose
pap
paparazzo
papier-mâché
para
para.
parable
parabolic
paracetamol
parachute
parachuting
parachutist
paradigm
paradigmatic
paradise
paradox
paradoxical
paraffin
paragon
paragraph
parakeet
paralegal
parallax
parallel
parallelism
parallelogram
paralyse
paralytic
paramedic
paramedical
paramilitary
paramount
paramour
paranoia
paranoiac
paranoid
paranormal
parapet
paraphernalia
paraphrase
paraplegia
paraplegic
parapsychology
paraquat
parasite
parasitic
parasol
paratrooper
paratroops
parenthetical
parish
Parisian
parity
parody

/peɪ/

paroxysm
parrot
parry
passage
passageway
passé
passenger
passim
passion
passionate
passionless
passive
passivize
pasta
pastel
pastiche
pastille
pastrami
pasty
pat
patch
patchwork
patchy
pâté
patent
pathogen
pathogenic
pathological
patina
patio
patois
patrimony
patriot
patriotic
patriotism
patronage
patronise
patronising
patronize
patronizing
patsy
patter
pattern
patterned
patterning
patty
pavlova

pi:
pince-nez

/peɪ/

pa:
pace
paced
pacemaker
pacesetter
pagan
paganism
page

/pɑː/

pageboy
pager
pale
pane
papacy
papal
paper
paperback
paperboy
papergirl
paperless
paperweight
paperwork
papery
papist
paste
pasting
pastry
pasty
pate
patent
pathos
patience
patient
patriarch
patriarchal
patriarchy
patron
patroness
pave
pavement
paving

paɪ:
paid
pail
pain
pained
painful
painfully
painkiller
painless
painstaking
paint
paintbox
paintbrush
painter
painterly
painting
paintwork
paisley

paɪ:
pay
payable
payback
paydirt
payee
payer
payload
paymaster

payment
payoff
payola
payout
payphone
payroll
payslip

pe:
peso

/pɑː/

pɑː:
pa
padre
Pakistani
palm
palmcorder
palmistry
palmtop
pas de deux
pass
passable
passbook
passing
Passover
passport
password
past
pasteurized
pastime
pastor
pastoral
pasture
path
pathfinder
pathway

pɑː:
par
parboil
parcel
parched
parchment
pardon
pardonable
par excellence
park
parka
parked
parking
parkland
parkway
parlance
parley
parliament
parliamentarian
parliamentary
parlour
parlourmaid
parlous

Parmesan
parquet
parse
parsimonious
parsimony
parsley
parsnip
parson
parsonage
part
part-
partake
partial
partially
participant
participate
participative
participatory
participial
participle
particle
parting
partisan
partisanship
partition
partly
partner
partnership
partook
partridge
party
partygoer
party pooper
parvenu

/peə/

peə:
pair
pairing

peə:
pare
parent
parentage
parenthood
parenting
paring

peə:
pear

/pe/

pe:
pebble
pebbly
pec
peccadillo
peck
pecker
peckish

pectin
pectoral
pedagogic
pedagogical
pedagogue
pedagogy
pedal
pedant
pedantry
peddle
peddler
pedestal
pedicure
pedigree
pediment
pedlar
peg
pelican
pellet
pell-mell
pellucid
pelmet
pelota
pelt
pelvic
pelvis
pen
penalty
penance
pence
pencil
pendant
pending
pendulous
pendulum
penetrate
penetrating
penetrative
penguin
penicillin
penitence
penitent
penitential
penitentiary
penknife
penmanship
pennant
pennies
penniless
penn'orth
penny
pension
pensionable
pensioner
pensive
pentagon
pentameter
pentathlon
Pentecost
Pentecostal

/piː/

penthouse
pent-up
penultimate
penumbra
penury
pep
pepper
peppercorn
peppermill
peppermint
pepperoni
pepperpot
peppery
peppy
peptic ulcer
peregrine falcon
perestroika
peril
perilous
perinatal
periodontal
peripatetic
periscope
perish
perishable
perished
peritonitis
periwinkle
peroration
pesky
pessary
pessimism
pessimist
pessimistic
pest
pester
pesticide
pestilence
pestilential
pestle
pesto
pet
petal
petard
pethidine
petit bourgeois
petit bourgeoisie
petit four
petrel
petrified
petrify
petrochemical
petrodollars
petrol
petticoat
pettifogging
petting
petty
petulance
petulant

pea:
peasant
peasantry

/piː/

p:
P,p
PA
PAYE
PC
PE
PG
PGCE
pH
PhD
plc
PM
p.m.
PMS
PMT
PO
PO Box
POW
PPS
PR
PS
PTA
PTO
PVC

pae:
paean
paediatrician
paediatrics
paedophile
paedophilia
paeony

pe:
pecan
pediatrician
pediatrics
pedophile
pedophilia
pee
peek
peekaboo
peel
peeler
peelings
peep
peepbo
peephole
peepshow
peeved
peevish
pekinese
penal
penalize
penile
penis

peony
people
peter

pea:
pea
peace
peaceable
peaceably
peaceful
peacefully
peacekeeper
peacekeeping
peacemaker
peacemaking
peacenik
peacetime
peach
peachy
peacock
peak
peaked
peal
peanut
peat
peaty

pi:
pianist
pianola
pilau
pina colada
piquant
pique
piqued
piste
pita
pizza
pizzeria

pie:
piece
piecemeal
piecework
pierrot

/pi/

pi:
pianissimo
piano
pianoforte
piazza
pièce de résistance
pied-à-terre

/pɜː/

pear:
pearl
pearly

per:
per
perch

percolate
percolator
perdition
perfect
perfectly
perfidy
perforate
perforation
perfume
perfumed
pergola
perjure
perjured
perjury
perk
perky
perm
permafrost
permanent
permeable
permeate
permit
permutation
perpendicular
perpetrate
perpetuity
perquisite
persecute
persecution
persecutor
perseverance
persevere
Persian
persimmon
person
personable
personage
personal
personality
personalize
personally
personnel
perspex
perspicacious
perspiration
pert
pertinacious
pertinent
perturbation
pervert

pur:
purchase
purdah
purgative
purgatory
purge
purloin
purple
purplish

/pɪə/

purpose
purposeful
purposeless
purposely
purr
purse
purser
purview

/pɪə/

peer:
peer
peerage
peeress
peerless

per:
period
periodic
periodical

pier:
pier
pierce
piercing

/pɪ/

pe:
peculiar
peculiarity
pecuniary
pedantic
pedestrian
pedestrianized
petunia

pi:
pic
picador
picaresque
piccolo
pick
pickaxe
picker
picket
pickings
pickle
pickled
pickpocket
picky
picnic
pictorial
picture
picturesque
piddle
piddling
pidgin
piffle
piffling
pig
pigeon

piggery
piggy
piggyback
piglet
pigment
pigmentation
pigmented
pigmy
pigpen
pigskin
pigsty
pigswill
pigtail
pilaf
pilaster
pilchard
pilfer
pilgrim
pilgrimage
pill
pillage
pillar
pillared
pillbox
pillion
pillock
pillory
pillow
pillowcase
pimento
pimp
pimpernel
pimple
pimply
pin
PIN
pinafore
pinball
pincer
pinch
pinched
pincushion
ping
pinhead
pinhole
pinion
pink
pinkie
pinko
pinky
pinnace
pinnacle
pinny
pinpoint
pinprick
pinstripe
pinstriped
pip
pipit
piranha

pirouette
piss
pissed
pistachio
pistol
piston
pit
pitch
pitched
pitcher
pitchfork
piteous
pitfall
pith
pithead
pithy
pitiable
pitiful
pitiless
pitman
pitta
pittance
pitted
pituitary gland
pity
pitying
pivot
pivotal
pixel
pixie
pizzazz
pizzicato

py:
pygmy
pyjamas
pyramid
pyramidal
pyrrhic victory

/paɪ/

pae:
paella

pi:
pi
pike
pile
piling
pilot
pine
pineapple
pinewood
pint
pioneer
pioneering
pious
pipe
pipeline
piper
pipework

piping
piracy
pirate
Pisces

pie:
pie
piebald
pieties
piety

py:
pylon
pyrotechnics
python

/paɪə/

pyr:
pyre
Pyrex
pyromaniac

/pɒ/

pe:
penchant

po:
pocked
pocket
pocketbook
pockmark
pockmarked
pod
podgy
pogrom
policy
policyholder
policymaker
polish
polished
Politburo
politic
politician
politicking
politics
polity
polka
pollen
pollinate
pollinator
poltergeist
poly
poly-
polyester
polyethylene
polyglot
polygraph
polymath
polymer
polyp
polypropylene

/poʊ/

polystyrene
polytechnic
polythene
polyunsaturate
polyunsaturated
polyurethane
pom
pomegranate
pommy
pomp
pomposity
pompous
ponce
poncho
pond
ponder
ponderous
pong
pontiff
pontificate
pontoon
pop
pop.
popcorn
poplar
poplin
poppadom
popper
poppy
populace
popular
popularize
popularly
populate
population
populism
populist
populous
porridge
posh
posit
positive
positively
positivism
poss
posse
possibility
possible
possibly
possum
posterior
posterity
posthumous
postulate
postural
posture
pot
potash
potboiler
pothole

potholing
potted
potter
pottery
potty
poverty
pox
poxy

/poʊ/

po:
podium
po-faced
poke
poker
poky
polar
polarise
polarity
polarize
Polaroid
pole
polecat
polio
poliomyelitis
Polish
polka dots
poll
polling
pollster
polo
pony
ponytail
pope
pose
poser
poseur
post
post-
postage
postal
postbag
postcard
postcode
poster
poste restante
postgrad
postgraduate
posting
postman
postmark
postmarked
postmaster
postmistress
post-mortem
postnatal
postoperative
postpone
postponement
post-prandial

postscript
posy
potable
potency
potent
potentate
potion

poa:
poach

poe:
poem
poet
poetess
poetic
poetical
poet laureate
poetry

pot:
potpourri

pou:
poultice
poultry

/pɔː/

pa:
pall
pallbearer
palsy
paltry

pau:
paucity
paunch
paunchy
pauper
pause

paw:
paw
pawn
pawnbroker
pawpaw

por:
porcelain
porch
porcine
porcupine
pore
pork
porn
porno
pornographer
pornographic
pornography
porosity
porous
porpoise

port
portable
portal
portcullis
portend
portent
portentous
porter
portfolio
porthole
portico
portion
portly
portrait
portraitist
portraiture
portray
portrayal
Portuguese

pour:
pour

/pɔɪ/

poi:
poignancy
poignant
poinsettia
point
pointed
pointer
pointing
pointless
pointy
poise
poised
poison
poisoner
poisonous

/pʊ/

poo:
poof
poofter

pou:
pouf

pu:
pud
pudding
pull
pulley
Pullman
pullover
pulpit
push
pushchair
pushed
pusher
pushing

/pu:/

pushover
pushy
puss
pussy
pussycat
pussyfoot
put
putsch

/pu:/
poo:
poo
pooch
poodle
pooh-pooh
pool
poop
pooped

/pʊə/
poor:
poor
poorhouse
poorly

/paʊ/
pou:
pouch
pounce
pound
pounding
pout

pow:
powder
powdered
powdery
pow-wow

/paʊə/
power:
power
powerboat
powerful
powerhouse
powerless

/pʌ/
po:
pommel

pu:
pub
public
publican
publication
publicise
publicist
publicity
publicize

publish
publisher
publishing
puck
pucker
puckish
puddle
pudgy
puff
puffball
puffed
puffin
puffy
pug
pugnacious
pugnacity
pukka
pulmonary
pulp
pulpy
pulsar
pulsate
pulse
pulverize
pumice
pummel
pump
pumpernickel
pumpkin
pun
punch
Punch and Judy
  show
punchbag
punchline
punchy
punctilious
punctual
punctuate
punctuation
puncture
pundit
pungent
punish
punishable
punishing
punishment
Punjabi
punk
punnet
punt
punter
pup
puppet
puppeteer
puppy
pus
pustule
putt
putter

putting green
putty
puzzle
puzzled
puzzlement

/pju:/
pew:
pew
pewter

pu:
puberty
pubescent
pubic
puce
pugilist
puke
puma
punitive
puny
pupa
pupil
pusillanimous
putative
putrefaction
putrefy
putrid

/pjʊə/
puer:
puerile

pur:
pure
puree
purely
purifier
purify
purism
purist
puritan
puritanical
puritanism

/pə/
pa:
pacific
pagoda
pajamas
palatial
palaver
panache
papa
papaya
paprika
papyrus
parabola
parade
paralysis

parameter
parental
parenthesis
pariah
parishioner
parochial
parochialism
parole
paternal
paternalism
paternalist
paternalistic
paternity
pathetic
pathologist
pathology
patisserie
patrician
patrol
patrolman
pavilion

par:
particular
particularity
particularize
particularly
particulars

pe:
pejorative
pellagra
peninsula
perambulate
per annum
peremptory
perennial
perimeter
peripheral
periphery
perusal
peruse
Peruvian
peseta
petite
petition
petitioner
petroleum

per:
per capita
perceive
per cent
percentage
perceptible
perception
perceptive
perceptual
perchance
percussion
percussionist

/pl/

percussive
perfect
perfection
perfectionism
perfectionist
perfidious
perforce
perform
performance
performer
perfumery
perfunctory
perhaps
permissible
permission
permissive
permit
pernicious
pernickety
peroxide
perpetual
perpetuate
perplex
perplexed
perplexing
perplexity
persist
persistence
persistent
persistently
persona
persona non grata
personification
personify
perspective
perspire
persuade
persuasion
persuasive
pertain
perturb
perturbed
pertussis
pervade
pervasive
perverse
perversion
pervert
perverted

po:
podiatry
polemic
polemical
polemicist
police
policeman
policewoman
polite
political

politicize
politico
politico-
pollutant
pollute
polluter
pollution
polygamous
polygamy
position
possess
possessed
possession
possessive
possessor
potassium
potato
potential
potentiality

pur:
purport
purportedly
pursuance
pursuant
pursue
pursuer
pursuit
purvey
purveyor

/pl/
pl:
placard
placate
placatory
place
placebo
placeman
placement
placenta
placid
placings
plagiarism
plagiarize
plague
plaice
plaid
plain
plainly
plaint
plaintiff
plaintive
plait
plan
plane
planeload
planet
planetarium
planetary

plangent
plank
planking
plankton
planner
planning
plant
plantain
plantation
planter
plaque
plasma
plaster
plasterboard
plastered
plasterer
plaster of Paris
plastic
Plasticine
plate
plateau
plated
plateful
platelet
platform
plating
platinum
platitude
platonic
platoon
platter
plaudits
plausible
play
playback
playboy
player
playful
playground
playgroup
playhouse
playmate
playpen
playroom
playschool
plaything
playtime
playwright
plaza
plea
plead
pleading
pleasant
pleasantry
please
pleased
pleasing
pleasurable
pleasure
pleat

pleated
pleb
plebeian
plebiscite
pledge
plenary
plenipotentiary
plenitude
plentiful
plenty
plenum
plethora
pleurisy
plexus
pliable
pliant
pliers
plight
plimsoll
plinth
plod
plodder
plonk
plonker
plop
plot
plotless
plotter
plough
ploughman
ploughshare
plover
plow
plowshare
ploy
pluck
plucky
plug
plughole
plum
plumage
plumb
plumber
plumbing
plume
plumed
plummet
plummy
plump
plunder
plunge
plunger
plunging
plunk
pluperfect
plural
pluralism
pluralist
pluralistic
plurality

/pr/

plus
plush
plutocracy
plutocrat
plutonium
ply
plywood

/pr/

pr:
practicable
practical
practicality
practically
practice
practise
practised
practitioner
praesidium
praetorian guard
pragmatic
pragmatics
pragmatism
prairie
praise
praiseworthy
praline
pram
prance
prank
prankster
prat
pratfall
prattle
prawn
pray
prayer
pre-
preach
preacher
preamble
prearrange
prearranged
precarious
precaution
precautionary
precede
precedence
precedent
precept
precinct
precious
precipice
precipitate
precipitation
precipitous
précis
precise
precisely
precision

preclude
precocious
precocity
preconceived
preconception
precondition
precursor
predate
predator
predatory
predecease
predecessor
predestination
predestined
predetermined
predeterminer
predicament
predicate
predict
predictable
prediction
predictive
predictor
predilection
predispose
predisposition
predominance
predominant
predominantly
predominate
predominately
pre-empt
pre-emptive
preen
prefab
prefabricated
preface
prefect
prefecture
prefer
preferable
preference
preferential
preferment
prefigure
prefix
prefixed
pregnancy
pregnant
preheat
prehistoric
prehistory
prejudge
prejudice
prejudiced
prejudicial
prelate
preliminary
prelude
premarital

premature
premeditated
premeditation
premenstrual
premier
premiere
premiership
premise
premised
premiss
premium
premonition
prenatal
preoccupation
preoccupied
preoccupy
preordained
prep
prepaid
preparation
preparatory
prepare
prepared
preparedness
preponderance
preposition
prepositional phrase
preposterous
preppy
pre-prandial
prepubescent
prequel
Pre-Raphaelite
prerequisite
prerogative
presage
Presbyterian
presbytery
pre-school
preschooler
prescient
prescribe
prescription
prescriptive
presence
present
presentable
presentation
presenter
presentiment
presently
preservationist
preservative
preserve
preset
preside
presidency
president
presidential
presidium

press
pressed
pressing
pressman
pressure
pressurize
pressurized
prestige
prestigious
presumably
presume
presumption
presumptuous
presuppose
presupposition
pretence
pretend
pretender
pretension
pretentious
preternatural
pretext
prettify
pretty
pretzel
prevail
prevailing
prevalent
prevaricate
prevent
preventable
preventative
preventive
preview
previous
previously
prey
price
priceless
pricey
prick
prickle
prickly
pride
priest
priestess
priesthood
priestly
prig
priggish
prim
primacy
prima donna
primaeval
prima facie
primal
primarily
primary
primate
prime

primer
primeval
primitive
primordial
primrose
primula
Primus
prince
princely
princess
principal
principality
principally
principle
principled
print
printable
printer
printing
printmaking
printout
prior
prioress
prioritize
priority
priory
prise
prism
prison
prisoner
prissy
pristine
privacy
private
privately
privation
privatize
privet
privilege
privileged
privy
prize
pro
pro-
proactive
probabilistic
probability
probable
probably
probate
probation
probationary
probationer
probe
probity
problem
problematic
problematical
procedural
procedure

proceed
proceeding
process
procession
processional
processor
proclaim
proclamation
proclivity
procrastinate
procreate
procurator
procure
procurement
prod
prodigal
prodigious
prodigy
produce
producer
product
production
productive
productivity
Prof.
profane
profanity
profess
profession
professional
professionalism
professionalize
professor
professorial
professorship
proffer
proficiency
proficient
profile
profit
profitable
profiteer
profiteering
profligacy
profligate
pro forma
profound
profundity
profuse
profusion
progenitor
progeny
progesterone
prognosis
prognostication
program
programmable
programmatic
programme
programmer

progress
progression
progressive
prohibit
prohibition
prohibitive
project
projectile
projection
projectionist
projector
prolapse
prole
proletarian
proletariat
proliferate
prolific
prologue
prolong
prolonged
prom
promenade
prominence
prominent
promiscuous
promise
promising
promisingly
promissory note
promo
promontory
promote
promoter
promotion
promotional
prompt
prompting
promptly
promulgate
prone
prong
pronominal
pronoun
pronounce
pronounced
pronouncement
pronto
pronunciation
proof
proofread
prop
propaganda
propagandist
propagandize
propagate
propane
propel
propellant
propeller
propensity

proper
properly
propertied
property
prophecy
prophesy
prophet
prophetic
prophylactic
propitiate
propitious
proponent
proportion
proportional
proportionality
proportionate
proposal
propose
proposition
propound
proprietary
proprieties
proprietor
proprietorial
proprietress
propriety
propulsion
pro rata
prosaic
proscenium
proscribe
proscription
prose
prosecute
prosecution
prosecutor
proselytize
prospect
prospective
prospectus
prosper
prosperity
prosperous
prostate
prosthesis
prosthetic
prostitute
prostitution
prostrate
protagonist
protean
protect
protected
protection
protectionism
protectionist
protective
protector
protectorate
protégé

/ps/

protein
pro tem
protest
Protestant
Protestantism
protestation
protester
proto-
protocol
proton
prototype
prototypical
protozoan
protracted
protractor
protrude
protrusion
protuberance
protuberant
proud
prove
proven
provenance
proverb
proverbial
provide
provided
providence
providential
providing
province
provincial
provincialism
provision
provisional
proviso
provocateur
provocation
provocative
provoke
provost
prow
prowess
prowl
prowler
proximity
proxy
prude
prudence
prudent
prudery
prudish
prune
prurience
prurient
pry

pte:
Pte

/ps/
pss:
psst

/r/

/ræ/
ra:
rabbi
rabbinical
rabbit
rabble
rabid
raccoon
rack
racket
racketeer
racketeering
racking
raconteur
racoon
racquet
radical
radicalism
radicalize
radicchio
radish
raffia
raffish
raffle
rag
ragamuffin
ragbag
ragged
raggedy
ragout
ragtag
ragtime
rally
ram
RAM
Ramadan
ramble
rambler
rambling
ramblings
rambunctious
ramekin
ramification
ramp
rampage
rampant
rampart
ramrod
ramshackle
ran
rancid
rancor
rancorous
rancour

rand
random
randomize
randy
rang
rank
ranking
rankle
ransack
ransom
rant
rap
rapid
rapids
rapper
rapport
rapporteur
rapprochement
rapt
raptor
rapture
raptures
rapturous
rash
rasher
Rasta
Rastafarian
rat
ratatouille
ratbag
ratchet
ratification
ratify
ration
rational
rationale
rationalism
rationalist
rationalize
rationing
rattan
rattle
rattler
rattlesnake
ratty
ravage
ravages
ravenous
ravioli
ravish
ravishing
razzamatazz
razzle-dazzle
razzmatazz

rha:
rhapsodic
rhapsodize
rhapsody

wra:
wrangle
wrap
wrapper
wrapping

/reɪ/
ra:
rabies
race
racecourse
racegoer
racehorse
racer
racetrack
racial
racialism
racing
racism
racist
racy
radar
radial
radiance
radiant
radiate
radiation
radiator
radii
radio
radioactive
radiocarbon
radiographer
radiography
radiological
radiologist
radiology
radiotherapist
radiotherapy
radium
radius
radon
rage
raging
rake
raked
rakish
range
rangefinder
ranger
rangy
rape
rapier
rapist
rate
rateable value
ratepayer
rating
ratio
rave

/rɑː/

raven
raver
raving
ravings
raze
razor

raɪ:
raid
raider
rail
railcard
railing
railroad
railway
railwayman
raiment
rain
rainbow
raincoat
raindrop
rainfall
rainforest
rainstorm
rainwater
rainy
raise
raisin
raison d'etre

reɪ:
ray
rayon

reɪ:
regime

reɪ:
reign
reigning
rein
reindeer

wraɪ:
wraith

/rɑː/

rɑ:
raft
rafter
rafting
raga
Raj
ranch
rancher
ranching
rascal
rascally
rasp
raspberry
raspy
rata

rather

/reə/

reə:
rare
rarefied
rarely
raring
rarity

/re/

reɑ:
read
readily
ready
realm

re:
rebel
recce
recipe
reciprocity
recitation
reckless
reckon
reckoning
reclamation
recognise
recognition
recognizable
recognize
recollect
recollection
recommend
recommendation
recompense
reconcile
reconciliation
reconnoitre
record
recreation
recreational
rectal
rectangle
rectangular
rectification
rectify
rectitude
rector
rectory
rectum
red
redbrick
redcurrant
redden
reddish
redhead
redheaded
redneck
redness

redolent
redwood
ref
referee
reference
referendum
reformation
refuge
refugee
refuse
refutation
reggae
regicide
regimen
regiment
regimental
regimentation
regimented
register
registered
registrar
registration
registry
regular
regularity
regularize
regulate
regulation
regulator
relative
relatively
relativism
relativist
relativity
relegate
relevance
relevant
relic
reliquary
relish
remedy
reminisce
reminiscence
reminiscent
remnant
remonstrate
rend
render
rendering
rendition
renegade
renovate
rent
rental
rep
reparation
repartee
repertoire
repertory
repetition

repetitious
replica
replicate
reprehensible
represent
representation
representational
representative
reprimand
reprobate
reptile
reptilian
reputable
reputation
requiem
requisite
requisition
rescue
reservation
reservoir
residence
residency
resident
residential
residue
resignation
resin
resinous
resolute
resolution
resonance
resonant
resonate
respiration
respirator
respiratory
respite
rest
restaurant
restaurateur
rested
restful
restitution
restive
restless
Restoration
résumé
resurrect
Resurrection
retch
reticent
retina
retinal
retinue
retribution
retro
retro-
retroactive
retrofit
retrograde

/ri:/

retrogression
retrogressive
retrospect
retrospective
rev
revel
revelation
revelatory
reveller
revelry
revenue
reverence
Reverend
reverent
reverential
reverie
revolution
revolutionary
revolutionize

rhe:
rhetoric
rhetorician

wre:
wreck
wreckage
wren
wrench
wrest
wrestle
wrestler
wrestling
wretch
wretched

/ri:/

re:
re
re-
readjust
readjustment
reaffirm
reafforestation
reappear
reappearance
reappraisal
reappraise
rearm
rearmament
rearrange
rearrangement
reassemble
reassert
reassess
reassessment
reassurance
reassure
reassured
reassuring
reawaken

rebate
rebirth
reborn
rebound
rebuild
recall
recap
recapitalize
recapitulate
recapture
recast
recent
recently
recessed
recharge
rechargeable
recoil
recommence
recondition
reconfirm
reconnect
reconquer
reconsider
reconstitute
reconstruct
reconstruction
reconstructive
reconvene
recount
recreate
recreation
recyclable
recycle
redecorate
redefine
redefinition
redeploy
redeployment
redesign
redevelop
redevelopment
redirect
rediscover
rediscovery
redistribute
redo
redouble
redraft
redraw
refill
refinance
refit
reflate
reflex
reflexology
reforest
reforestation
refuel
refund
refurbish

refurbishment
regal
regency
regent
region
regional
regionalism
regroup
rehab
rehabilitate
rehash
rehouse
reimburse
reimbursement
reincarnate
reincarnation
reinforce
reinforcement
reinstate
reinstatement
reissue
reiterate
reject
rejig
rejoin
rekindle
relapse
relaxation
relay
relive
reload
relocate
remake
remarriage
remarry
remaster
rematch
remit
remix
remodel
remould
remount
renal
rename
repatriate
repercussion
rephrase
replay
repossess
repossession
repot
reprint
reproduce
reproduction
reproductive
re-run
resat
reschedule
resell
reset

resettle
resettlement
reshape
reshuffle
resit
resold
restart
restate
restatement
restock
restructure
resurface
retail
retailer
retailing
retake
retard
retardation
retell
rethink
rethought
retold
retook
retool
retouch
retrain
retread
retrial
reunification
reunion
reunite
reusable
reuse
revalue
revamp
reverb
revisit
revitalize
revivify
rewind
rewire
reword
rework
rewound
rewrite

rea:
reach
reaches
read
readable
reader
readership
reading
readout
real
realign
realignment
realise
realism

/ri/

realist
realistic
realistically
realizable
realize
reallocate
really
realtor
ream
reap
reaper
reason
reasonable
reasoned
reasoning

ree:
reed
reedy
reef
reefer
reek
reel

rhe:
rhesus factor

wrea:
wreak
wreath
wreathe

/ri/

re:
re-
react
reaction
reactionary
reactivate
reactive
reactor
reagent
reality
reopen
reorganize

/rɪə/

rear:
rear
rearguard
rearward

/rɪ/

re:
rebel
rebellion
rebellious
rebound
rebuff
rebuke

rebut
rebuttal
recalcitrant
recall
recant
recede
receipt
receive
received
receiver
receivership
receptacle
reception
receptionist
receptive
receptor
recess
recession
recessional
recessionary
recessive
recidivist
recipient
reciprocal
reciprocate
recital
recite
reclaim
recline
recluse
reclusive
recognizance
recoil
recondite
reconnaissance
record
recorder
recording
recount
recoup
recourse
recover
recoverable
recovery
recrimination
recruit
recruitment
recumbent
recuperate
recuperative
recur
recurrence
recurrent
redeem
redeemable
Redeemer
redemption
redemptive
redoubt
redoubtable

redound
redress
reduce
reducible
reduction
reductionist
reductive
redundancy
redundant
refectory
refer
referral
refine
refined
refinement
refiner
refinery
reflect
reflection
reflective
reflector
reflexive
reform
reformer
reformism
reformist
refract
refractory
refrain
refresh
refreshing
refreshment
refrigerate
refrigerator
refund
refundable
refusal
refuse
refute
regain
regale
regalia
regard
regarding
regardless
regatta
regenerate
regenerative
regress
regressive
regret
regretful
regrettable
regurgitate
rehearsal
rehearse
reject
rejoice
rejoin
rejoinder

rejuvenate
relapse
relate
related
relation
relational
relationship
relax
relaxed
relaxing
relay
release
relent
relentless
reliable
reliance
reliant
relief
relieve
relieved
religion
religiosity
religious
religiously
relinquish
reluctant
rely
remain
remainder
remaining
remand
remark
remarkable
remedial
remember
remembrance
remind
reminder
remiss
remission
remit
remittance
remorse
remorseful
remorseless
remote
remotely
removable
removal
remove
removed
remover
remunerate
remuneration
remunerative
renaissance
renege
renew
renewable
renewal

/rɪ/ /rɪ/

renounce	requirement	retaliate	**rhy:**	
renown	rescind	retaliatory	rhythm	
renowned	research	retard	rhythmic	
renunciation	resemblance	retarded		
repaid	resemble	retention	**ri:**	
repair	resent	retentive	rib	
repairman	resentful	retire	ribald	
repast	resentment	retired	ribbed	
repay	reserve	retiree	ribbing	
repayable	reserved	retirement	ribbon	
repayment	reservist	retiring	rich	
repeal	reside	retort	richly	
repeat	residual	retrace	Richter scale	
repeated	resign	retract	rick	
repeatedly	resigned	retractable	rickets	
repel	resilient	retreat	rickety	
repellant	resist	retrench	rickshaw	
repellent	resistance	retrenchment	ricochet	
repent	resistant	retrieval	rid	
repentance	resistor	retrieve	riddance	
repentant	resolve	retriever	ridden	
repetitive	resolved	return	riddle	
replace	resort	returnable	riddled	
replaceable	resound	returnee	ridge	
replacement	resounding	returner	ridged	
replenish	resource	reveal	ridicule	
replenishment	resourced	revealing	ridiculous	
replete	resourceful	reveille	ridiculously	
reply	respect	revenge	riff	
report	respectable	reverberate	riffle	
reportage	respected	reverberation	riff-raff	
reportedly	respecter	revere	rift	
reporter	respectful	reversal	rig	
reporting	respective	reverse	rigging	
repose	respectively	reversible	rigid	
repository	resplendent	reversion	rigmarole	
repress	respond	revert	rigor	
repressed	respondent	review	rigor mortis	
repression	response	reviewer	rigorous	
repressive	responsibility	revile	rigour	
reprieve	responsible	revise	rim	
reprisal	responsive	revision	rimless	
reprise	restorative	revisionism	rimmed	
reproach	restore	revisionist	ring	
reproachful	restorer	revival	ringer	
reproof	restrain	revivalism	ringing	
reprove	restrained	revivalist	ringleader	
reproving	restraint	revive	ringlet	
republic	restrict	revoke	ringmaster	
republican	restricted	revolt	ringside	
republicanism	restriction	revolting	ringworm	
repudiate	restrictive	revolve	rink	
repugnant	result	revolver	rinse	
repulse	resultant	revue	rip	
repulsion	resume	revulsion	ripcord	
repulsive	resurgence	reward	riposte	
repute	resurgent	rewarding	ripple	
reputed	resuscitate		riptide	
request	retain	**rhe:**	risen	
require	retainer	rhetorical	risible	

/raɪ/

risk
risky
risotto
risqué
rissole
ritual
ritualistic
ritualized
ritzy
riven
river
riverboat
riverfront
riverside
rivet
riveting
rivulet

wri:
wriggle
wring
wringer
wrinkle
wrinkly
wrist
wristwatch
writ
written

/raɪ/

rhi:
rhinestone
rhinitis
rhino
rhinoceros
rhizome

rhy:
rhyme

ri:
riboflavin
rice
ride
rider
riding
rife
rifle
rifleman
rile
rind
riot
riotous
ripe
ripen
rise
riser
rite
rival
rivalry

righ:
right
Right
righteous
rightful
rightist
righto
rightward

rt:
Rt Hon.

rye:
rye

wri:
write
writer
writhe
writing

wry:
wry

/rɒ/

re:
rendezvous

rho:
rhombus

ro:
rob
robber
robbery
robin
rock
rockabilly
rocker
rockery
rocket
rock'n'roll
rocky
rod
roger
rollicking
ROM
romp
roster
rostrum
rot
rotten
rotter
rottweiler
rowlock

wra:
wrath

wro:
wrong
wrongdoer

wrongdoing
wrongful

/roʊ/

rho:
rhododendron

ro:
robe
robot
robotic
robotics
robust
rode
rodent
rodeo
roe
rogue
roguish
role
roll
rollback
roller
rolling
roly-poly
Roman
Romanesque
romantic
romanticism
romanticize
Romany
Romeo
rope
ropey
rosary
rose
rosé
rosebud
rosehip
rosemary
rosette
rosewater
rosewood
rosy
rota
rotary
rotate
rotation
rote
rotor
rotund
rotunda
rove
roving

roa:
roach
road
roadblock
roadhog
roadhouse

/ruː/

roadie
roadshow
roadside
roadster
roadway
roadworks
roam
roan
roast
roasting

row:
row
rowan
rowboat
rower
row house
rowing

wro:
wrote

/rɔː/

rau:
raucous
raunchy

raw:
raw
rawhide

roar:
roar
roaring

wrough:
wrought

/rɔɪ/

roi:
roil

roy:
royal
royalist
royally
royalty

/rʊ/

roo:
rook
rookie

/ruː/

rheu:
rheumatic
rheumatism
rheumatoid
  arthritis
rheumatology
rheumy

/rʊə/ /sæ/

rhu:
rhubarb

ro:
Romanian

roo:
roof
roofed
roofer
roofing
roofless
rooftop
room
roomful
roommate
roomy
roost
rooster
root
rooted
rootless

rou:
rouble
rouge
roulette
route
routine
routinely

ru:
rubella
Rubicon
rubicund
ruble
rubric
ruby
ruched
rude
rudimentary
rudiments
ruin
ruination
ruined
ruinous
rule
ruler
ruling
Rumanian
ruminate
rumination
ruminative
rumor
rumour
rumoured
rune
rupee
ruse
rutabaga
ruthless

rue:
rue
rueful

/rʊə/

rur:
rural

/raʊ/

rou:
round
roundabout
rounded
roundel
rounders
roundly
roundup
roundworm
rouse
roust
roustabout
rout

row:
row
rowdy

/rʌ/

rou:
rough
roughage
roughen
roughneck
roughshod

ru:
rub
rubber
rubbery
rubbing
rubbish
rubbishy
rubble
ruck
rucksack
ruckus
ruction
rudder
rudderless
ruddy
ruff
ruffian
ruffle
ruffled
rug
rugby
rugged
rugger
rum
rumba

rumble
rumbling
rumbustious
rummage
rummy
rump
rumple
rumpled
rumpus
run
runabout
runaround
runaway
run-down
rung
runner
running
runny
runt
runway
rupture
rush
rusk
russet
Russian
rust
rustic
rusticity
rustle
rustler
rustling
rusty
rut
rutted
rutting

wru:
wrung

/rə/

ra:
rapacious
rapacity
ravine

re:
recherché

ro:
rococo
romance

/s/
/sæ/

sa:
sab
Sabbath
sabotage
saboteur
sac

saccharin
saccharine
sachet
sack
sackcloth
sackful
sacking
sacrament
sacramental
sacrifice
sacrificial
sacrilege
sacrilegious
sacristy
sacrosanct
sad
sadden
saddle
saddlebag
saddler
saddlery
saffron
sag
saggy
Sagittarius
salad
salamander
salaried
salary
salivate
sallow
sally
salmon
salmonella
salon
salsa
salutary
salutation
salvage
salvation
salve
salver
salvo
samba
samizdat
samovar
samurai
sanatorium
sanctify
sanctimonious
sanction
sanctity
sanctuary
sanctum
sand
sandal
sandalwood
sandbag
sandbank
sandbar

/seɪ/

sandbox
sander
sandpaper
sandpit
sandstone
sandstorm
sandwich
sandwiched
sandy
sang
sangria
sanguine
sanitarium
sanitary
sanitation
sanitize
sanity
sank
Sanskrit
Santa Claus
sap
sapiens
sapling
sapper
sapphire
sappy
sash
sashay
sassy
sat
SAT
satay
satchel
satellite
satin
satinwood
satire
satirist
satirize
satisfaction
satisfactory
satisfied
satisfy
satisfying
satsuma
saturate
saturated
saturation
Saturday
saturnine
satyr
savage
savagery
savant
savoir-faire
savvy
sax
Saxon
saxophone
saxophonist

/seɪ/

sa:
saber
sable
sabre
sacred
sadism
sado-masochism
sado-masochistic
safe
safeguard
safekeeping
safely
safety
sage
sago
sake
sale
saleable
saleroom
salesgirl
salesman
salesmanship
salesperson
saleswoman
salient
saline
same
sameness
sane
Satan
Satanism
sated
satiate
save
saver
saving
saviour
savour
savoury

sai:
sail
sailboat
sailcloth
sailing
sailor
sailplane
saint
sainthood
saintly

say:
say
saying

se:
seance

/sɑː/

psal:
psalm

sa:
saga
sahib
saké
sample
sampler

sar:
sarcasm
sarcastic
sarcoma
sarcophagus
sardine
sardonic
sarge
sari
sarnie
sartorial

ser:
sergeant

/se/

ce:
celebrant
celebrate
celebrated
celebration
celebratory
celery
celibacy
celibate
cell
cellar
cellmate
cellophane
cellphone
cellular
cellulite
celluloid
cellulose
Celsius
cemetery
cenotaph
censor
censorious
censorship
censure
census
cent
centaur
centenarian
centenary
centennial
center
centigrade
centilitre
centimetre
centipede
central
centralise
centralism
centralist
centralize
centre
centred
centrefold
centrepiece
centrifugal force
centrifuge
centrist
centurion
century
cerebral
ceremonial
ceremoniously
ceremony
cessation
cesspit
cesspool

sai:
said

say:
says

sce:
scent
scented
scepter
sceptre

se:
sec
secateurs
second
secondary
secondly
secretarial
secretariat
secretary
sect
sectarian
sectarianism
section
sectional
sector
secular
secularism
secularized
sedative
sedentary
sedge
sediment
sedimentary
segment
segmentation
segmented

/siː/

segregate
segregated
segregation
segregationist
segue
seldom
self
self-
self-aggrandizement
selfish
selfless
sell
seller
Sellotape
selves
semaphore
semblance
semi
semi-
semiconductor
seminal
seminar
seminarian
seminary
semiotics
semitone
semolina
Senate
senator
senatorial
send
sender
Senegalese
sensation
sensational
sensationalism
sensationalist
sensationalize
sense
senseless
sensibility
sensible
sensitive
sensitize
sensor
sensory
sensual
sensuous
sent
sentence
sentient
sentiment
sentimental
sentimentalist
sentimentalize
sentinel
sentry
separable
separate
separated

separately
separation
separatism
separatist
September
septic
septicaemia
septuagenarian
sepulchre
seraph
serenade
serendipitous
serendipity
serrated
serried
sesame
session
set
setback
sett
settee
setter
setting
settle
settled
settlement
settler
seven
seventeen
seventeenth
seventh
Seventh Day Adventist
seventieth
seventy
sever
several
severance
sex
sexism
sexist
sexless
sexologist
sextant
sextet
sexual
sexuality
sexy

/siː/

c:
C,c
CB
cc
CD
CD-ROM
CD-ROM drive
CFC
CIA
CID
C.O.
CPU
CSE
CV

ce:
cedar
cede

cea:
cease
ceasefire
ceaseless

cei:
ceiling

sce:
scene
scenery
scenic

se:
sebum
secrecy
secret
secretive
semen
senile
senior
seniority
sepia
sequel
sequence
sequencer
sequestrate
sequin
sequinned

sea:
sea
seabed
seabird
seaboard
seaborne
seafarer
seafaring
seafloor
seafood
seafront
seagoing
seagull
seahorse
seal
sealant
sealer
sealskin
seam
seaman
seamanship
seamless
seamstress

seamy
seaplane
seaport
seascape
seashell
seashore
seasick
seaside
season
seasonal
seasoned
seasoning
seat
seating
seaward
seaweed
seaworthy

see:
see
seed
seedbed
seedless
seedling
seedy
seek
seeker
seem
seeming
seemingly
seemly
seen
seep
seepage
seer
seesaw
seethe

sei:
seize
seizure

si:
Sikh
Sikhism

sie:
siege

/si/

si:
siesta

/sɜː/

cer:
cert
certain
certainly
certainty
certifiable
certify

/sɪə/

certitude
cervical
cervix

cir:
circa
circle
circuit
circuitry
circular
circulate
circulation
circulatory
circumcise
circumflex
circumlocution
circumnavigate
circumscribe
circumspect
circumspection
circumstance
circumstantial
circumvent
circus

sear:
search
searcher
searching
searchlight

ser:
Serbo-Croat
serf
serfdom
serge
sermon
serpent
serpentine
servant
serve
server
service
serviceable
serviceman
serviette
servile
serving
servitude

sir:
sir
sirloin

sur:
surcharge
surf
surface
surfboard
surfeit
surfing
surge

surgeon
surgery
surgical
surly
surname
surplice
surplus
surtax
survey

/sɪə/

cer:
cereal

sear:
sear
searing

ser:
serial
serialization
serialize
series
serious
seriously
serum

/sɪ/

cae:
Caesarean

ce:
cedilla
celeb
celebrity
celestial
cement
ceramic
cetacean

ci:
cicada
cigar
cigarette
ciggy
cinch
cinder block
Cinderella
cinders
cine
cinema
cinematic
cinematographer
cinematography
cinnamon
cirrhosis
cissy
cistern
citadel
citizen
citizenry

citizenship
citric acid
citrus
city
civic
civics
civil
civilian
civilisation
civilise
civility
civilization
civilize
civilized
civvies
civvy street

cy:
cyclamen
cyclic
cyclical
cygnet
cylinder
cylindrical
cymbal
cynic
cynical
cynically
cynicism
Cypriot
cyrillic
cyst
cystic fibrosis
cystitis

pse:
psephologist

sce:
scenario

sci:
scimitar
scintilla
scintillating
scissors

se:
secede
secession
secessionist
secluded
seclusion
second
secondment
secrete
secretion
secure
security
sedan
sedate
sedation

/sɪ/

sedition
seditious
seduce
seducer
seductive
seductress
select
selection
selective
semantic
semantics
semester
Semitic
sepulchral
sequential
sequester
sequestered
serene
severe

si:
sibilant
sibling
Sicilian
sick
sickbed
sicken
sickening
sickle
sickly
sickness
sickroom
sift
signal
signalman
signatory
signature
signet ring
significance
significant
signify
silhouette
silhouetted
silica
silicate
silicon
silicone
silk
silken
silkworm
silky
sill
silly
silt
silver
silvered
silversmith
silverware
silvery
simian

/saɪ/

similar
similarity
similarly
simile
simmer
simper
simple
simpleton
simplicity
simplification
simplify
simplistic
simply
simulate
simulation
simulator
simultaneous
sin
since
sincere
sincerely
sinecure
sine qua non
sinew
sinewy
sinful
sing
singalong
Singaporean
singe
singer
singing
single
single-
singlet
singly
singular
sinister
sink
sinker
sinking
sinuous
sip
sissy
sister
sisterhood
sisterly
sit
sitar
sitcom
sitter
sitting
situate
situated
situation
six
sixpence
sixteen
sixteenth
sixth

sixtieth
sixty
sizzle

sie:
sieve

sy:
sybaritic
sycamore
sycophancy
sycophant
sycophantic
syllable
syllabus
sylvan
symbiosis
symbiotic
symbol
symbolic
symbolise
symbolism
symbolize
symmetrical
symmetry
sympathetic
sympathize
sympathizer
sympathy
symphonic
symphony
symposium
symptom
symptomatic
synagogue
sync
synch
synchronize
syncopated
syncopation
syndicate
syndrome
synergy
synod
synonym
synonymous
synopsis
syntactic
syntax
synthesis
synthesize
synthesized
synthesizer
synthetic
synthetics
syphilis
Syrian
syringe
syrup
syrupy
system

systematic
systematize
systemic

/saɪ/

ci:
cider
cipher
citation
cite

cy:
cyanide
cybernetics
cyberpunk
cyberspace
cyborg
cycle
cycleway
cyclist
cyclone
cypher
cypress

psy:
psych
psyche
psychedelia
psychedelic
psychiatric
psychiatrist
psychiatry
psychic
psychical
psycho
psycho-
psychoactive
psychoanalyse
psychoanalysis
psychoanalyst
psychoanalytic
psychoanalyze
psychobabble
psychokinesis
psychological
psychologist
psychology
psychometric
psychopath
psychopathic
psychosis
psychosomatic
psychotherapist
psychotherapy
psychotic

sci:
sciatica
science
scientific
scientist

sci-fi
scion

scy:
scythe

sei:
seismic
seismograph
seismology

si:
Siamese cat
Siamese twin
side
sidearm
sideboard
sideburns
sidecar
sidekick
sidelight
sideline
sidelong
sideshow
sidestep
sideswipe
sidetrack
sidewalk
sideways
siding
sidle
silage
silence
silencer
silent
silo
Sino-
sinus
sinusitis
siphon
sisal
site
sizable
size
sizeable

sig:
sign
signboard
signer
signing
signpost
signposted

sigh:
sigh
sight
sighted
sighting
sightless
sight-read
sightseeing

/saɪə/   /suː/

sightseer

sʌɪ:
synapse
syphon

/ˈsaɪə/

sɪr:
sire
siren

/sɒ/

sa:
sang-froid

sau:
sausage

so:
sob
Soc.
soccer
sock
socket
sod
sodden
sodding
sodomy
soft
softback
softball
soften
softener
softie
software
softwood
softy
soggy
sojourn
solace
solemn
solid
solidarity
solitaire
solitary
solitude
solstice
soluble
solve
solvency
solvent
sombre
sombrero
somnolent
son et lumière
song
songbird
songster
songstress
songwriter
sonic

sonnet
sonorous
sop
sophistries
sophistry
sophomore
soporific
sopping
soppy
sorority
sorrel
sorrow
sorrowful
sorrows
sorry
sotto voce
sovereign
sovereignty

/soʊ/

sau:
sauté

sew:
sew
sewing
sewn

so:
so
sober
sobering
sobriquet
sociable
social
socialisation
socialise
socialism
socialist
socialistic
socialite
socialization
socialize
socio-
sociology
sociopath
soda
sodium
sofa
solar
solarium
solar plexus
sold
solder
soldier
soldierly
soldiery
sole
solely
solo
soloist

sonar
soubriquet
soul
soulful
soulless
Soviet
Sovietologist

soa:
soak
soaked
soaking
soap
soapbox
soapy

sow:
sow
sown

/sɔː/

sa:
salt
salty

sau:
sauce
saucepan
saucer
saucy
sauna
saunter

saw:
saw
sawdust
sawmill
sawn

soar:
soar
soaraway

sor:
sorbet
sorcerer
sorceress
sorcery
sordid
sore
sorely
sorghum
sort
sortie

sough:
sought

sour:
source

swor:
sword
swordfish

swordsman

/sɔɪ/

soi:
soil

soy:
soya
soya bean
soy sauce

/sʊ/

soo:
soot
sooty

/suː/

sew:
sewage
sewer
sewerage

soo:
soon
sooner
soothe
soothsayer

sou:
soufflé
souk
soup
soupy
souvenir

su:
sucrose
Sudanese
sue
suet
Sufi
suicidal
suicide
sui generis
sumo
super
super-
superannuated
superannuation
superb
supercharged
supercilious
supercomputer
superconductivity
superconductor
superficial
superfluity
superfluous
supergrass
supergroup
superheated

/saʊ/

superhero
superhighway
superhuman
superimpose
superintend
superintendent
superior
superiority
superlative
superman
supermarket
supermodel
supernatural
supernova
superpower
supersede
supersonic
superstar
superstate
superstition
superstitious
superstore
superstructure
supertanker
supervise
supervision
supervisor
supervisory
supine
supranational
supremacist
supremacy
supreme
supremo
sushi
suture

sui:
suit
suitable
suitably
suitcase
suited
suiting
suitor

/saʊ/

sau:
Saudi

sou:
sound
soundbite
sounding
soundless
soundly
soundproof
soundtrack
south
southbound
southward

sou'wester

sow:
sow

/saʊə/

sauer:
sauerkraut

sour:
sour

/sʌ/

so:
some
somebody
somehow
someone
someplace
somersault
something
sometime
sometimes
somewhat
somewhere
son
sonny

sou:
southerly
southern
southerner
southernmost

su:
sub
sub-
subaltern
subatomic
subcommittee
subconscious
subcontinent
subcontract
subcontractor
subculture
subcutaneous
subdivide
subdivision
subgroup
subheading
subhuman
subject
sub judice
subjugate
sublet
sublimate
subliminal
submarine
submariner
subnormal

subsection
subsequent
subset
subsidize
subsidy
subsoil
subsonic
substance
substation
substitute
substratum
subterfuge
subterranean
subtext
subtitle
subtitled
subtle
subtlety
subtotal
suburb
subway
succor
succour
succulent
such
suchlike
suck
sucker
suckle
suction
sudden
suddenly
suds
suffer
sufferance
sufferer
suffering
suffix
suffocate
suffrage
suffragette
sulfate
sulfide
sulfur
sulfuric acid
sulk
sulky
sullen
sully
sulphate
sulphide
sulphur
sulphuric acid
sulphurous
sultan
sultana
sultry
sum
summarize
summary

/sʌ/

summat
summation
summer
summery
summit
summon
summons
sump
sumptuous
sun
sunbathe
sunbeam
sunbed
sunblock
sunburn
sunburnt
sunburst
sundae
Sunday
sunder
sundial
sundown
sundries
sundry
sunflower
sung
sunglasses
sunk
sunken
sunless
sunlight
sunlit
sunny
sunrise
sunroof
sunscreen
sunset
sunshine
sunspot
sunstroke
suntan
suntanned
sup
supper
suppertime
supple
supplement
supplemental
supplementary
supplementation
supplicant
supplication
supposition
surreptitious
surrogacy
surrogate
suspect
suss
sussed
sustenance

/sjuː/   /sk/

/sjuː/

pseu:
pseud
pseudo-
pseudonym

/sə/

ce:
cerise
certificate
certificated

cir:
circuitous
circumference

pso:
psoriasis

sa:
sabbatical
sadistic
safari
sagacious
sagacity
saint
salaam
salacious
salami
saliva
salivary gland
saloon
salubrious
salute
Samaritan
sarong
satanic
satiric
satirical
savannah

so:
sobriety
societal
society
solicit
solicitation
solicitor
solicitous
solicitude
solidify
soliloquy
solution
some
sonata
sonority
sophisticate
sophisticated
sophistication
soprano

su:
subdue
subdued
subject
subjection
subjective
subjunctive
sublime
submerge
submerged
submersible
submission
submissive
submit
subordinate
subpoena
subscribe
subscriber
subscription
subservient
subside
subsidence
subsidiarity
subsidiary
subsist
subsistence
substantial
substantially
substantiate
substantive
subsume
subtract
suburban
suburbia
subversion
subversive
subvert
succeed
success
successful
succession
successive
successor
succinct
succumb
suffice
sufficiency
sufficient
suffuse
suggest
suggestible
suggestion
suggestive
supplant
supplied
supplier
supply
support
supporter
supporting

supportive
suppose
supposed
suppository
suppress
suppressant
suppressor
susceptibility
susceptible
suspect
suspend
suspender
suspense
suspenseful
suspension
suspicion
suspicious
suspiciously
sustain
sustainable

sur:
surmise
surmount
surpass
surprise
surprised
surprising
surreal
Surrealism
surrealist
surrealistic
surrender
surround
surroundings
surveillance
survey
surveyor
survival
survive
survivor

/sk/

sc:
scab
scabbard
scabby
scabies
scabrous
scaffold
scaffolding
scald
scalding
scale
scallion
scallop
scalloped
scallywag
scalp
scalpel

scalper
scaly
scam
scamp
scamper
scampi
scan
scandal
scandalize
scandalous
Scandinavian
scanner
scant
scanty
scapegoat
scapula
scar
scarce
scarcely
scarcity
scare
scarecrow
scared
scaremongering
scarf
scarlet
scarper
scarves
scary
scat
scathing
scatological
scatter
scatterbrained
scattered
scattering
scatty
scavenge
sceptic
sceptical
scepticism
sclerosis
scoff
scold
sconce
scone
scoop
scoot
scooter
scope
scorch
scorching
score
scoreboard
scorecard
scoreless
scoreline
scorer
scoresheet
scorn

/skw/

scornful
Scorpio
scorpion
Scot
Scotch
scotch
Scotsman
Scotswoman
Scottish
scoundrel
scour
scourge
scout
scoutmaster
scowl
scrabble
scraggy
scramble
scrambler
scrap
scrapbook
scrape
scraper
scrapheap
scrapings
scrappy
scrapyard
scratch
scratchy
scrawl
scrawny
scream
screamingly
scree
screech
screen
screenplay
screenwriter
screenwriting
screw
screwball
screwdriver
scribble
scribbler
scribe
scrimp
script
scripted
scriptural
scripture
scriptwriter
scroll
Scrooge
scrotum
scrounge
scrub
scrubber
scrubby
scrubland
scruff

scruffy
scrum
scrummage
scrumptious
scrumpy
scrunch
scruple
scrupulous
scrutineer
scrutinize
scrutiny
scuba diving
scud
scuff
scuffle
scuffling
scull
scullery
sculpt
sculptor
sculptural
sculpture
sculptured
scum
scumbag
scupper
scurrilous
scurry
scurvy
scuttle

sch:
schema
schematic
scheme
schemer
scherzo
schism
schizoid
schizophrenia
schizophrenic
scholar
scholarly
scholarship
scholastic
school
schoolbag
schoolboy
schoolchild
schooldays
schooled
schoolgirl
schoolhouse
schooling
schoolmaster
schoolmate
schoolmistress
schoolroom
schoolteacher
schoolwork

schoolyard
schooner

sk:
skate
skateboard
skateboarder
skateboarding
skein
skeletal
skeleton
skeptic
skeptical
skepticism
sketch
sketchbook
sketchpad
sketchy
skew
skewer
ski
skid
skid row
skiff
skilful
skill
skilled
skillet
skillful
skim
skimp
skimpy
skin
skinflint
skinhead
skinless
skinny
skint
skip
skipper
skirmish
skirt
skit
skitter
skittish
skittle
skive
skulduggery
skulk
skull
skunk
sky
skydiver
skydiving
skylark
skylight
skyrocket
skyscraper
skyward

/skw/

squ:
squabble
squad
squaddie
squadron
squalid
squall
squally
squalor
squander
square
squared
squarely
squash
squashy
squat
squatter
squaw
squawk
squeak
squeaky
squeal
squeamish
squeeze
squelch
squib
squid
squidgy
squiggle
squiggly
squint
squire
squirm
squirrel
squirt

/sf/

sph:
sphere
spherical
sphincter
sphinx

/sl/

sl:
slab
slack
slacken
slacker
slacks
slag
slain
slake
slalom
slam
slammer
slander
slanderous

/sm/

slang
slanging match
slangy
slant
slap
slapdash
slapstick
slash
slat
slate
slather
slatted
slattern
slaughter
slaughterhouse
Slav
slave
slaver
slavery
Slavic
slavish
Slavonic
slay
slaying
sleaze
sleazy
sled
sledge
sledgehammer
sleek
sleep
sleeper
sleeping
sleepless
sleepwalk
sleepy
sleet
sleeve
sleeveless
sleigh
sleight of hand
slender
slept
sleuth
sleuthing
slew
slice
sliced
slick
slicker
slide
slight
slightly
slim
slime
slimline
slimy
sling
slingshot
slink

slinky
slip
slippage
slipper
slippery
slipshod
slipstream
slipway
slit
slither
slithery
sliver
Sloane
slob
slobber
sloe
slog
slogan
sloganeering
sloop
slop
slope
sloppy
slosh
sloshed
slot
sloth
slothful
slouch
slough
slovenly
slow
slow-
slowdown
sludge
slug
slugger
sluggish
sluice
slum
slumber
slump
slung
slunk
slur
slurp
slurry
slush
slushy
slut
sly

/sm/

sm:
smack
small
smallholder
smallholding
smallish
smallpox

smalls
smalltown
smarmy
smart
smartarse
smarten
smartly
smash
smashed
smashing
smattering
smear
smeared
smell
smelly
smelt
smelter
smidgen
smile
smiley
smilingly
smirk
smite
smithereens
smithy
smitten
smock
smocked
smocking
smog
smoggy
smoke
smoked
smokeless
smokescreen
smokestack
smoking
smoky
smolder
smooch
smooth
smoothie
smorgasbord
smote
smother
smoulder
smudge
smudgy
smug
smuggle
smuggler
smut
smutty

/sn/

sn:
snack
snaffle
snag
snail

/sn/

snake
snakebite
snakeskin
snap
snapdragon
snapper
snappish
snappy
snapshot
snare
snarl
snatch
snazzy
sneak
sneaker
sneaking
sneaky
sneer
sneeringly
sneeze
snicker
snide
sniff
sniffle
sniffy
snifter
snigger
snip
snipe
sniper
snippet
snitch
snivel
snob
snobbery
snobbish
snobby
snog
snook
snooker
snoop
snooty
snooze
snore
snorkel
snort
snot
snotty
snout
snow
snowball
snowbound
snowdrift
snowdrop
snowfall
snowfield
snowflake
snowman
snowmobile
snowplough

/sp/

snowshoe
snowstorm
snowy
snub
snuck
snuff
snuffle
snug
snuggle

/sp/

sp:
spa
space
spacecraft
spaceman
spaceship
spacing
spacious
spade
spadework
spaghetti
spake
span
spangle
spangled
spangly
Spaniard
spaniel
Spanish
spank
spanking
spanner
spar
spare
sparing
spark
sparkle
sparkler
sparkling
sparkly
sparky
sparrow
sparse
spartan
spasm
spasmodic
spastic
spat
spate
spatial
spatter
spatula
spawn
spay
speak
speakeasy
speaker
speaking
spear

spearhead
spearmint
spec
special
specialise
specialism
specialist
speciality
specialize
specialized
specially
specialty
species
specific
specifically
specification
specifics
specify
specimen
specious
speck
speckled
specs
spectacle
spectacular
spectator
spectra
spectral
spectre
spectrum
speculate
speculative
speculator
sped
speech
speechifying
speechless
speechwriter
speed
speedboat
speedometer
speedway
speedy
spell
spellbinding
spellbound
speller
spelling
spelt
spend
spender
spendthrift
spent
sperm
spermatozoon
spermicidal
spermicide
spew
spice
spiced

spick and span
spicy
spider
spidery
spiffing
spigot
spike
spiked
spiky
spill
spillage
spillover
spilt
spin
spina bifida
spinach
spinal
spindle
spindly
spine
spineless
spinet
spinnaker
spinner
spinney
spinster
spiny
spiral
spire
spirit
spirited
spiritless
spiritual
spiritualism
spit
spite
spiteful
spittle
spiv
splash
splashdown
splat
splatter
splay
spleen
splendid
splendour
splenetic
splice
spliff
splint
splinter
split
splitting
splodge
splotch
splurge
splutter
spoil
spoilage

spoiler
spoilsport
spoilt
spoke
spoken
spokesman
spokesperson
spokeswoman
sponge
spongebag
sponger
spongy
sponsor
sponsored
sponsorship
spontaneity
spontaneous
spoof
spook
spooky
spool
spoon
spoonerism
spoonful
spoor
sporadic
spore
sporran
sport
sporting
sportsman
sportsmanship
sportswear
sportswoman
sporty
spot
spotless
spotlight
spotlit
spotted
spotter
spotty
spousal
spouse
spout
sprain
sprang
sprat
sprawl
sprawled
spray
sprayer
spread
spreadeagled
spreadsheet
spree
sprig
sprigged
sprightly
spring

/st/

springboard
springtime
springy
sprinkle
sprinkler
sprinkling
sprint
sprinter
sprite
spritzer
sprocket
sprout
spruce
sprung
spry
spud
spun
spunk
spunky
spur
spurious
spurn
spurt
sputter
sputum
spy
spymaster

/st/

st:
stab
stabbing
stability
stabilize
stabilizer
stable
stablemate
staccato
stack
stacked
stadium
staff
staffer
staffing
stag
stage
stagecoach
stagecraft
stagehand
stagflation
stagger
staggering
stagnant
stagnate
staid
stain
stainless steel
stair
staircase
stairway
stairwell
stake
stakeholder
stalactite
stalagmite
stale
stalemate
stalk
stalker
stall
stallholder
stallion
stalwart
stamen
stamina
stammer
stamp
stamped
stampede
stance
stanchion
stand
standard
standardize
standby
standing
standpipe
standpoint
standstill
stank
Stanley knife
stanza
staple
stapler
star
starboard
starburst
starch
starched
starchy
stardom
stare
starfish
stark
starlet
starlight
starling
starlit
starry
start
starter
startle
startling
starvation
starve
starving
stash
stasis
state
statehood
statehouse
stateless
statelet
stately
statement
stateroom
stateside
statesman
statesmanlike
statesmanship
statewide
static
station
stationary
stationer
stationery
stationmaster
statist
statistic
statistical
statistician
stats
statuary
statue
statuesque
statuette
stature
status
status quo
statute
statutory
staunch
stave
stay
stead
steadfast
steady
steak
steal
stealth
stealthy
steam
steamboat
steamer
steamroller
steamship
steamy
steed
steel
steelmaker
steelworker
steelworks
steely
steep
steeped
steeple
steeplechase
steer
steering
stellar
stem
stench
stencil
stenographer
stentorian
step
stepbrother
stepchild
stepdaughter
stepfather
stepladder
stepmother
stepparent
steppe
stepsister
stepson
stereo
stereotype
stereotypical
sterile
sterilize
sterling
stern
sternum
steroid
stethoscope
stetson
stew
steward
stewardess
stewardship
stick
sticker
stickleback
stickler
sticky
stiff
stiffen
stifle
stifling
stigma
stigmata
stigmatize
stile
stiletto
still
stillbirth
stillborn
stilt
stilted
stimulant
stimulate
stimulative
stimulus
sting
stingray
stingy
stink
stinker
stinking

287

/sv/

stinky
stint
stipend
stipendiary
stippled
stipulate
stir
stirrer
stirring
stirrup
stitch
stitching
stoat
stock
stockade
stockbroker
stockbroking
stockholder
stockholding
stocking
stockinged
stockist
stockpile
stockroom
stocktaking
stocky
stodgy
stoic
stoical
stoicism
stoke
stoker
stole
stolen
stolid
stomach
stomp
stone
stoned
stonemason
stonewall
stoneware
stonework
stony
stood
stooge
stool
stoop
stop
stopcock
stopgap
stoplight
stopover
stoppage
stopper
stopwatch
storage
store
storecard

storefront
storehouse
storekeeper
storeroom
storey
stork
storm
stormy
story
storybook
storyline
storyteller
storytelling
stout
stove
stow
stowage
stowaway
straddle
strafe
straggle
straggler
straggly
straight
straighten
straightforward
strain
strained
strainer
strait
straitened
straitjacket
strand
strange
strangely
stranger
strangle
strangled
stranglehold
strangulation
strap
strapless
strapped
strapping
strata
stratagem
strategic
strategist
strategy
stratification
stratified
stratosphere
stratospheric
stratum
straw
strawberry
stray
streak
streaker

streaky
stream
streamer
streamline
streamlined
street
streetcar
streetlamp
streetlight
streetwalker
streetwise
strength
strengthen
strenuous
stress
stressed
stressful
stretch
stretcher
stretchy
strew
strewn
stricken
strict
strictly
stricture
stride
stridency
strident
strife
strike
striker
striking
string
stringency
stringent
stringer
stringy
strip
stripe
striped
stripey
stripling
stripper
striptease
stripy
strive
strobe
strode
stroke
stroll
stroller
strong
stronghold
strongman
stroppy
strove
struck
structural

structuralism
structuralist
structure
struggle
strum
strung
strut
strychnine
stub
stubble
stubbly
stubborn
stubby
stucco
stuck
stud
studded
student
studied
studio
studious
studiously
study
stuff
stuffing
stuffy
stultify
stumble
stump
stumpy
stun
stung
stunk
stunner
stunning
stunt
stupefy
stupendous
stupid
stupor
sturdy
sturgeon
stutter
sty
stye
style
styling
stylised
stylish
stylist
stylistic
stylized
stylus
stymie
styrofoam

/sv/

sv:
svelte

/sw/

soi:
soignée
soiree

su:
suave
suede
suite

sw:
swab
swaddle
swag
swagger
swain
swallow
swam
swamp
swampland
swampy
swan
swank
swanky
swap
swarm
swarthy
swashbuckling
swastika
swat
swathe
SWAT team
sway
swear
sweat
sweater
sweatpants
sweatshirt
sweatshop
sweatsuit
sweaty
swede
Swede
Swedish
sweep
sweeper
sweeping
sweepstake
sweet
sweetbread
sweetcorn
sweeten
sweetener
sweetheart
sweetie
sweetish
sweetly
sweetmeat
sweetness
swell

swelling
swelter
sweltering
swept
swerve
swift
swig
swill
swim
swimmer
swimming
swimmingly
swimsuit
swimwear
swindle
swine
swing
swingeing
swinger
swinging
swipe
swirl
swish
Swiss
switch
switchback
switchblade
switchboard
swivel
swollen
swoon
swoop
swop
swore
sworn
swot
swum
swung

/ʒ/

/ʒɒ/

ge:
gendarme
genre

/ʒw/

joie:
joie de vivre

/ʃ/

sh:
sh
shh

/ʃæ/

cha:
chagrin
chagrined
chalet

chamois
champagne
champers
chandelier
chaperone
charabanc
chassis
château
chatelaine

sha:
shabby
shack
shackle
shadow
shadowy
shag
shaggy
shall
shallow
shallows
shalt
sham
shamble
shambolic
shampoo
shamrock
shandy
shank
shanty
shatter
shattered
shattering

/ʃeɪ/

chai:
chaise longue

sha:
shade
shaded
shading
shady
shaikh
shake
shaken
shaky
shale
shaman
shamanism
shame
shamefaced
shameful
shameless
shape
shaped
shapeless
shapely
shave
shaven
shaver

shaving

shei:
sheikh
sheikhdom

/ʃɑː/

char:
chargé d'affaires
charlatan

sha:
shaft
Shah
shan't

shar:
shard
shark
sharp
sharpen
sharpener
sharpish
sharpshooter

/ʃeə/

shar:
share
sharecropper
shareholder
shareware

/ʃe/

che:
chef
chevron

sche:
schedule

she:
shed
shelf
shell
shellfire
shellfish
shelter
sheltered
shelve
shelving
shepherd
shepherdess
sheriff
sherry

/ʃiː/

chi:
chic
chignon

she:
she
she'd

/ʃ3ː/

she'll
she's

shea:
sheaf
sheath
sheathe
sheaves

shee:
sheen
sheep
sheepdog
sheepish
sheepskin
sheet
sheeting

shie:
shield

/ʃ3ː/

sher:
sherbet

shir:
shirk
shirt
shirtsleeve
shirty

/ʃɪə/

shear:
shear

sheer:
sheer

/ʃɪ/

chi:
chicanery
chiffon
chivalric
chivalrous
chivalry

she:
shebang
shenanigans

shi:
shibboleth
shift
shifting
shiftless
shifty
shilling
shilly-shally
shimmer
shimmy
shin
shindig

shingle
Shinto
ship
shipboard
shipbuilder
shipbuilding
shipload
shipmate
shipment
shipowner
shipper
shipping
shipshape
shipwreck
shipwright
shipyard
shit
shitless
shitty
shiver
shivery

/ʃaɪ/

shi:
shine
shining
shiny
shite

shy:
shy
shyster

/ʃaɪə/

shire:
shire

/ʃɒ/

sho:
shock
shocker
shocking
shod
shoddy
shone
shop
shopaholic
shopkeeper
shoplift
shoplifting
shopping
shot
shotgun

/ʃoʊ/

chau:
chauffeur
chauvinism
chauvinistic

shoa:
shoal

shou:
shoulder

show:
show
showbiz
showcase
showdown
showgirl
showground
showman
showmanship
shown
showpiece
showroom
showtime
showy

/ʃɔː/

shaw:
shawl

shor:
shore
shoreline
shorn
short
shortage
shortbread
shortcake
shortcoming
shortcrust
shorten
shortening
shortfall
shorthand
shortish
shortlist
shortly

/ʃʊ/

shoo:
shook

shoul:
should
shouldn't
should've

shu:
shush

su:
sugar
sugary

/ʃuː/

chu:
chute

shoe:
shoe
shoehorn

shoelace
shoemaker
shoestring

shoo:
shoo
shoot
shooter
shooting

/ʃʊə/

sure:
sure
surely
surety

/ʃaʊ/

shou:
shout

/ʃaʊə/

shower:
shower
showery

/ʃʌ/

sho:
shove
shovel

shu:
shuck
shudder
shuffle
shun
shunt
shut
shutdown
shutter
shuttered
shuttle
shuttlecock

/ʃə/

cha:
charade

che:
chemise
chenille
cheroot

sha:
shall
shallot
shalt

she:
shellac

shou:
should

/ʃl/

schl:
schlep
schlock

/ʃm/

schm:
schmaltz
schmaltzy
schmooze

/ʃn/

schn:
schnapps

/ʃp/

sp:
spiel

/ʃr/

shr:
shrank
shrapnel
shred
shredder
shrew
shrewd
shriek
shrift
shrill
shrimp
shrine
shrink
shrinkage
shrivel
shroud
Shrove Tuesday
shrub
shrubbery
shrubby
shrug
shrunk
shrunken

/ʃw/

schw:
schwa

/t/
/tæ/

ta:
tab
Tabasco
tabby
tabernacle
tableau
tablet
tabloid
taboo
tabulate
tachograph
tacit
taciturn
tack
tackle
tacky
tact
tactful
tactic
tactical
tactician
tactile
tactless
tad
tadpole
taffeta
tag
talc
talcum powder
talent
talented
talisman
tallow
tally
Talmud
talon
tamarind
tamarisk
tambourine
tamp
tamper
tampon
tan
tandem
tandoori
tang
tangent
tangential
tangerine
tangible
tangle
tango
tangy
tank
tankard
tanker
tanner
tannin
Tannoy
tantalize
tantamount
tantrum
tap
tapas
tapestry
tapioca
taramasalata
tariff
Tarot
tarragon
tarry
tassel
tasselled
tat
ta-ta
tattered
tatters
tattle
tattoo
tatty
tavern
tax
taxable
taxation
taxi
taxicab
taxidermist
taxidermy
taxing
taxonomy
taxpayer

ti:
timbre

/teɪ/

ta:
table
tablecloth
tablespoon
tablespoonful
tableware
take
takeaway
taken
takeoff
takeout
takeover
taker
takings
tale
tame
tape
taper
tapeworm
taste
tasteful
tasteless
taster
tasting
tasty

tai:
tail
tailback
tailcoat
tailgate
tailor
tailored
tailpipe
tailwind
taint

/tɑ:/

ta:
ta
task
taskmaster

tar:
tar
tardy
target
tarmac
tarn
tarnish
tarpaulin
tarred
tarry
tart
tartan
tartar
tarty

/teə/

tear:
tear
tearaway

/te/

pte:
pterodactyl

te:
tech
techie
technical
technicality
technically
technician
Technicolor
technique
techno
techno-
technocracy
technocrat
technocratic
technological
technology
tectonic
tectonics
Ted
teddy
TEFL
Teflon
telecast
telecommunications
telecommuter
telecommuting

/tiː/

telegenic
telegram
telegraph
telepathic
telephone
telephoto lens
telescope
telescopic
televise
television
televisual
teleworker
teleworking
telex
tell
teller
telling
telly
temp
temper
temperament
temperamental
temperamentally
temperance
temperate
temperature
tempest
tempestuous
tempi
template
temple
tempo
temporal
temporary
temporize
tempt
temptation
tempted
tempting
temptress
ten
tenable
tenancy
tenant
tench
tend
tendency
tendentious
tender
tenderize
tendon
tendril
tenement
tenet
tenner
tennis
tenor
tense
tensile
tension

tent
tentacle
tentative
tented
tenterhooks
tenth
tenuous
tenure
tepid
terrace
terraced
terracing
terracotta
terra firma
terrapin
terrible
terrier
terrify
terrifying
territorial
territory
terror
terrorise
terrorism
terrorist
terrorize
terry
TESL
test
testament
tester
testicle
testify
testimonial
testimony
testing
testis
testosterone
testy
tetanus
tetchy
tether
text
textbook
textile
textual
texture
textured

/tiː/

t:
T,t
TB
TESOL
TM
TNT
TUC
TV

teː
tedious
tedium
tepee

teaː
tea
teacake
teach
teacher
teaching
teacup
teak
teal
team
teamster
teamwork
teapot
tease
teasel
teaser
teasing
teaspoon
teaspoonful
teat
teatime
teazel
teazle

teeː
tee
teem
teen
teenage
teenaged
teenager
teeny
teenybopper
teepee
teeter
teeth
teething
teetotal
teetotaller

/ti/

tiː
tiara

/tɜː/

terː
tercentenary
term
terminal
terminate
termini
terminology
terminus
termite
tern

terse
tertiary

turː
turban
turbine
turbo
turbot
turbulence
turbulent
turd
turf
turgid
Turk
turkey
Turkish
turmeric
turmoil
turn
turnabout
turnaround
turncoat
turning
turnip
turnout
turnover
turnpike
turnround
turnstile
turntable
turpentine
turpitude
turquoise
turtle
turtleneck

/tɪə/

tearː
tear
teardrop
tearful
tear gas
tear-jerker

tierː
tier

/tɪ/

teː
telepathy
telephonist
telephony
temerity
tenacious
tenacity
terrestrial

tiː
Tibetan
tibia
tic

/taɪ/

tick
ticker
ticket
ticketing
tickle
ticklish
tidbit
tiddler
tiddly
tiddlywink
tiff
tilde
till
tiller
tilt
timber
timbered
timid
timorous
timpani
tin
tincture
tinder
tinderbox
tinfoil
tinge
tinged
tingle
tingly
tinker
tinkle
tinned
tinny
tinpot
tinsel
Tinseltown
tint
tip
tipple
tipster
tipsy
tiptoe
tissue
tit
titbit
titillate
titter
tittle-tattle
titular
tizzy

ty:
typical
typically
typify
tyrannical
tyrannize
tyranny

/taɪ/

thai:
Thai

thy:
thyme

ti:
tidal
tide
tidings
tidy
tie
tied
tiger
tigress
tile
tiling
time
timekeeper
timekeeping
timeless
timely
timepiece
timer
timetable
timing
tine
tiny
tirade
titan
titanic
titanium
tithe
title
titled

tigh:
tight
tighten
tightrope
tights

ty:
tycoon
tyke
type
typecast
typeface
typescript
typewriter
typewritten
typhoid
typhoon
typhus
typing
typist
typographical
typography
typology
tyro

/taɪə/

tir:
tire
tired
tireless
tiresome
tiring

tyr:
tyrant
tyre

/tɒ/

to:
toddle
toddler
toddy
toff
toffee
tog
toggle
tolerable
tolerance
tolerant
tolerate
tom
tomahawk
tomboy
tomfoolery
tongs
tonic
tonsillitis
tonsils
top
topcoat
topic
topical
topknot
topless
topmost
topographical
topping
topple
topside
topsoil
topsy-turvy
torrent
torrid
toss
tot
totter
toxic
toxicology
toxin

/toʊ/

tau:
taupe

/tɔː/

to:
toga
token
tokenism
told
toll
tome
tonal
tonality
tone
toneless
toner
topaz
topiary
total
totalitarian
totalitarianism
totality
tote
totem

toa:
toad
toadstool
toady
toast
toaster
toastmaster

toe:
toe
toecap
TOEFL
toehold
toenail

tow:
tow
towpath
towrope

/tɔː/

tal:
talk
talkative
talker
talkie
tall

tau:
taunt
Taurus
taut
tauten
tautological
tautology

taugh:
taught

taw:
tawdry
tawny

/tɔː/

tor:
torch
torchlight
tore
torment
tormentor
torn
tornado
torpedo
torpid
torpor
torque
torsion
torso
tort
tortilla
tortoise
tortoiseshell
tortuous
torture
torturer
torturous
Tory

/tɔɪ/

toi:
toil
toilet
toiletries

toy:
toy
toyboy
toytown

/tʊ/

too:
took

/tuː/

to:
to
tomb
tombstone

too:
too
tool
toot
tooth
toothache
toothbrush
toothless
toothpaste
toothpick
toothy
tootle

tou:
toucan
touché

toupee

tu:
tutu

two:
two
twofold
twosome

/tʊə/

tour:
tour
tour de force
tourism
tourist
touristy
tournament
tourniquet

/taʊ/

tao:
Taoism

tou:
tousled
tout

tow:
towel
towelling
town
townie
townsfolk
township
townspeople

/taʊə/

tower:
tower
towering

/tʌ/

to:
ton
tongue
tonnage
tonne

tou:
touch
touchdown
touching
touchline
touchstone
touchy
touchy-feely
tough
toughen

tu:
tub
tubby

tuck
tuft
tufted
tug
tum
tumble
tumbledown
tumbler
tummy
tundra
tungsten
tunnel
tuppence
turret
tusk
tussle
tussock
tut
tuxedo

/tjuː/

teu:
Teutonic

tu:
tuba
tube
tuber
tubercular
tuberculosis
tubing
tubular
Tuesday
tulip
tulle
tumour
tumult
tumultuous
tuna
tune
tuneful
tuneless
tuner
tunic
Tunisian
tutelage
tutor
tutorial

/tjʊə/

tur:
tureen

/tə/

ta:
tarantula

te:
telemetry
terrain

terrific

to:
to
tobacco
tobacconist
toboggan
toccata
today
to-do
together
togetherness
tomato
tomorrow
tonight
topography
torrential
towards

/tr/

tr:
trace
traceable
trachea
track
tracker
tracksuit
tract
tractable
traction
tractor
trad
trade
trademark
trader
tradesman
tradespeople
tradition
traditional
traditionalism
traditionalist
traduce
traffic
trafficker
tragedy
tragic
tragi-comedy
tragi-comic
trail
trailblazer
trailer
train
trainee
trainer
training
traipse
trait
traitor
traitorous
trajectory

tram	transvestism	triad	trodden
tramline	transvestite	trial	troglodyte
tramp	trap	triangle	troika
trample	trapdoor	triangular	Trojan horse
trampoline	trapeze	triathlon	troll
tramway	trapped	tribal	trolley
trance	trapper	tribalism	trombone
tranche	trappings	tribe	trombonist
tranquil	trash	tribesman	troop
tranquillize	trashy	tribulation	trooper
tranquillizer	trattoria	tribunal	troopship
trans-	trauma	tributary	trophy
transact	traumatic	tribute	tropical
transaction	traumatize	trice	tropics
transatlantic	travail	triceps	trot
transcend	travel	trick	Trotskyist
transcendence	traveller	trickery	trotter
transcendent	travelling	trickle	troubadour
transcendental	travelogue	trickster	trouble
transcribe	traverse	tricky	troubled
transcript	travesty	tricolour	troublemaker
transcription	trawl	tricycle	troubleshooter
transept	trawler	tried	troubleshooting
transfer	tray	trier	troublesome
transferable	treacherous	trifle	trough
transference	treachery	trifling	trounce
transfigure	treacle	trigger	troupe
transfix	tread	trigonometry	trouper
transform	treadle	trike	trousers
transformer	treadmill	trilby	trousseau
transfusion	treason	trill	trout
transgress	treasonable	trillion	trove
transgressor	treasure	trilogy	trowel
transience	treasurer	trim	truancy
transient	treasury	trimaran	truant
transistor	treat	trimming	truce
transit	treatable	Trinity	truck
transition	treatise	trinket	trucker
transitional	treatment	trio	trucking
transitive	treaty	trip	truckload
transitivity	treble	tripartite	truculent
transitory	tree	tripe	trudge
translate	treeless	triple	true
translation	treetop	triplet	truffle
translator	trek	tripod	trug
translucent	trellis	tripper	truism
transmission	tremble	triptych	truly
transmit	tremendous	tripwire	trump
transmitter	tremolo	trite	trumpet
transmute	tremor	triumph	trumpeter
transparency	tremulous	triumphal	truncated
transparent	trench	triumphalism	truncheon
transpire	trenchant	triumphalist	trundle
transplant	trend	triumphant	trunk
transport	trendy	triumvirate	truss
transportation	trepidation	trivia	trust
transporter	trespass	trivial	trustee
transpose	tress	triviality	trusting
transsexual	trestle	trivialize	trustworthy
transverse	tri-	trod	trusty

/ts/

truth
truthful
try
trying
tryout
tryst

/ts/

ts:
tsetse fly

/tw/

tw:
twaddle
twang
twat
tweak
twee
tweed
tweedy
tweet
tweezers
twelfth
twelve
twentieth
twenty
twerp
twice
twiddle
twig
twilight
twill
twin
twine
twinge
twinkle
twinset
twirl
twist
twisted
twisty
twit
twitch
twitcher
twitchy
twitter

/θ/

/θæ/

tha:
thank
thankful
thankfully
thankless
thanksgiving
thankyou
thatch
thatched
thatcher
thatching

/θe/

the:
theft
therapeutic
therapist
therapy
thespian

/θi:/

the:
theatre
thematic
theme
themed
theocratic
theologian
theorem
theoretical
theoretically
theorist
theorize
thesis

thie:
thief
thieving

/θi/

the:
theatrical
theocracy
theology

/θɜ:/

ther:
therm
thermal
thermo
thermodynamics
thermonuclear
thermoplastic
Thermos
thermostat

thir:
third
thirdly
thirst
thirsty
thirteen
thirteenth
thirtieth
thirty

thur:
Thursday

/θɪə/

theor:
theoretician
theory

/θɪ/

the:
thesaurus

thi:
thick
thicken
thickener
thicket
thickset
thimble
thin
thing
thingummy
thingy
think
thinker
thinking
thistle

/θaɪ/

thigh:
thigh

thy:
thyroid

/θɒ/

tho:
thong

/θɔ:/

thor:
thoracic
thorax
thorn
thorny

though:
thought
thoughtful
thoughtless

/θaʊ/

thou:
thousand
thousandth

/θʌ/

tho:
thorough
thoroughbred
thoroughfare
thoroughgoing

thu:
thud
thug

thuggery
thumb
thumbnail
thumbscrew
thumbtack
thump
thumping
thunder
thunderbolt
thunderclap
thundercloud
thunderous
thunderstorm
thunderstruck
thundery

/θə/

tha:
thalidomide

ther:
thermometer

/θr/

thr:
thrall
thrash
thrashing
thread
threadbare
threat
threaten
threatened
threatening
three
threesome
thresh
threshold
threw
thrice
thrift
thrifty
thrill
thrilled
thriller
thrilling
thrive
throat
throaty
throb
throes
thrombosis
throne
throng
throttle
through
throughout
throughput
throw
throwaway

/θw/

throwback
thrown
thrum
thrush
thrust

/θw/

thw:
thwack
thwart

/ð/

/ðæ/

tha:
than
that
that's

/ðeɪ/

they:
they
they'd
they'll
they've

/ðeə/

their:
their
theirs

there:
there
thereabouts
thereafter
thereby
therefore
therein
thereof
thereon
thereupon

they're:
they're

/ðe/

the:
them
then
thence
thenceforth

/ði:/

the:
the
these

thee:
thee

/ðɪ/

the:
the

/ðɪ/

thi:
this
thither

/ðaɪ/

thi:
thine

thy:
thy
thyself

/ðoʊ/

tho:
those

though:
though

/ðaʊ/

thou:
thou

/ðʌ/

thu:
thus

/ðə/

tha:
than
that

the:
the
them
themself
themselves

/v/

/væ/

va:
vac
vaccinate
vaccine
vacillate
vacuity
vacuous
vacuum
vagabond
valance
valedictory
valentine
valet
valiant
valid
validate
Valium
valley
valour
valuable
valuables
valuation
value
valueless
valuer
valve
vamp
vampire
vampirism
van
vandal
vandalise
vandalism
vandalize
vanguard
vanish
vanity
vanquish
vapid
varicose vein
vascular
Vaseline
vassal
vat
Vatican
vatman

/veɪ/

va:
vacancy
vacant
vacate
vacationer
vagary
vagrancy
vagrant
vague
vaguely
vale
vane
vapor
vaporize
vapour

vai:
vain
vainglorious

vei:
veil
veiled
vein
veined

/vɑ:/

va:
vantage point
vase

vast
vastly

var:
varnish
varsity

/veə/

var:
variable
variance
variant
variation
varied
variegated
various
variously
vary

/ve/

ve:
vector
veg
vegeburger
vegetable
vegetarian
vegetarianism
vegetate
vegetated
vegetation
vegetative
veggie
velcro
veldt
vellum
velvet
velveteen
velvety
vendetta
vendor
venerable
venerate
vengeance
vengeful
venison
venom
venomous
vent
ventilate
ventilator
ventricle
ventriloquist
venture
venturesome
venue
verifiable
verify
verily
verisimilitude
veritable

/viː/

verity
very
vespers
vessel
vest
vestibule
vestige
vestigial
vestments
vestry
vet
vetch
veteran
veterinarian
veterinary
vex
vexation
vexed

/viː/

v:
V,v
VAT
VC
VCR
VD
VDU
VHF
VIP
VSO

ve:
vegan
vehement
vehicle
venal
venous
veto

vea:
veal

vi:
visa
vis-à-vis
vitro
viva

/vi/

vi:
viola

/vɜː/

ver:
verb
verbal
verbalize
verbiage
verbose
verdant

verdict
verdigris
verge
vermin
vermouth
versatile
verse
versed
version
versus
vertebra
vertebrate
vertical
vertiginous
vertigo
verve

vir:
virgin
virginal
Virgo
virtual
virtually
virtue
virtuosity
virtuoso
virtuous

/vɪə/

veer:
veer

/vɪ/

ve:
vehicular
velocity
veneer
venereal disease

vi:
vibrato
vicar
vicarage
vicarious
vicinity
vicious
vicissitudes
victim
victimize
victor
Victorian
Victoriana
victorious
victory
video
video conferencing
videophone
videotape
vigil
vigilant

vigilante
vignette
vigorous
vigour
vilify
villa
village
villager
villain
villainous
villainy
vinaigrette
vindicate
vindictive
vinegar
vinegary
vineyard
vintage
vintner
virile
virulence
virulent
visage
viscera
visceral
viscose
viscosity
viscous
visibility
visible
vision
visionary
visit
visitation
visitor
vista
visual
visualize
vitamin
vitiate
vitreous
vitriol
vitriolic
vituperation
vituperative
vivacious
vivacity
vivid
vivisection
vixen

/vaɪ/

vi:
via
viable
viaduct
vial
vibe
vibrant
vibraphone

vibrate
vibrator
vice
vice-
viceroy
vice versa
Viking
vile
vine
vinyl
viol
violate
violence
violent
violet
violin
violinist
viper
viscount
viscountess
vise
visor
vital
vitality
viva

vie:
vie

vy:
vying

/vaɪə/

vir:
viral
virus

/vɒ/

vo:
vocative
vodka
volatile
volcanic
volcano
volley
volleyball
volte-face
voluble
volume
voluntary
volunteer
vomit
vox pop

/vəʊ/

vo:
vocabulary
vocal
vocalist
vocalize

/vɔː/

vocals
vocation
vocational
vogue
vole
volt
voltage
vote
voter

/vɔː/

vau:
vaudeville
vault
vaunted

vor:
vortex

/vɔɪ/

voi:
voice
voiced
voiceless
void
voile

voy:
voyage

/vuː/

voo:
voodoo

/vaʊ/

vou:
vouch
voucher
vouchsafe

vow:
vow
vowel

/vʌ/

vu:
vulgar
vulnerable
vulture
vulva

/vjuː/

view:
view
viewfinder
viewpoint

/və/

va:
vacation
vagina

vaginal
validity
vanilla
variety
vasectomy

ve:
velour
Venetian blind
veracity
veranda

ver:
verbatim
vermilion
vernacular
verruca

vo:
vociferous
volition
voluminous
voluptuous
voracious

/vw/

voy:
voyeur
voyeurism
voyeuristic

/w/

/wæ/

wa:
wacko
wacky
wag
waggle
wagon
wagtail
wangle
wank
wanker
wax
waxen
waxwork
waxy

wha:
whack
whacking
whacky
wham
whammy

/weɪ/

wa:
wade
wader
wafer

wage
wager
wake
wakeful
waken
wane
wastage
waste
wastebasket
wasted
wasteful
wasteland
wasting
wastrel
wave
waveband
wavelength
wavelet
waver
wavy

wai:
waif
wail
waist
waistband
waistcoat
waistline
wait
waiter
waitress
waive
waiver

way:
way
waylay
wayside
wayward

weigh:
weigh
weight
weighted
weighting
weightless
weightlifter
weightlifting
weighty

wha:
whale
whaler
whaling

whey:
whey

/weə/

war:
ware
warehouse

warehousing
wary

wear:
wear
wearable
wear and tear
wearer
wearing

were:
werewolf

where:
where
whereabouts
whereas
whereby
wherefores
wherein
whereupon
wherever
wherewithal

/we/

wea:
wealth
wealthy
weapon
weaponry
weather
weatherman
weatherproof

we:
web
webbed
webbing
wed
wedded
wedding
wedge
wedlock
Wednesday
weft
welcome
welcoming
weld
welder
welfare
well
wellington
well-read
welly
Welsh
Welshman
welt
welter
wench
wend
went

/wiː/

wept
werewolf
west
westbound
westerly
western
westerner
westernization
westernized
westernmost
westward
wet
wetland

whe:
whelk
whelp
when
whence
whenever
whet
whether
whetstone

/wiː/

we:
we
we'd
we'll
we're
we've

wea:
weak
weaken
weakling
weakness
weal
wean
weasel
weave
weaver

wee:
wee
weed
weedkiller
weedy
week
weekday
weekend
weekender
weekly
weep
weepy
weevil

whea:
wheat
wheatgerm

whee:
wheedle
wheel
wheelbarrow
wheelbase
wheelchair
wheelhouse
wheelwright
wheeze
wheezy

wie:
wield

/wɪ/

we:
we'd
we'll
we've

whi:
which
whichever
whiff
Whig
whim
whimper
whimsical
whimsy
whinge
whinger
whinny
whip
whiplash
whippersnapper
whippet
whisk
whisker
whiskery
whiskey
whisky
whisper
whist
whistle
whit
whither
Whitsun
whittle
whizz

wi:
wick
wicked
wicker
wickerwork
wicket
widget
widow
widowed
widower
widowhood
width
wig
wiggle
wigwam
wildebeest
wilderness
wilful
will
willie
willing
will-o'-the-wisp
willow
willowy
willpower
willy
willy-nilly
wilt
wimp
wimpish
wimpy
win
wince
winch
wind
windbag
wind-blown
windbreak
windbreaker
windfall
wind farm
wind instrument
windlass
windless
windmill
window
windowpane
windowsill
windpipe
windscreen
windshield
windsurfer
windsurfing
windswept
wind tunnel
windward
windy
wing
winged
winger
wingspan
wink
winkle
winner
winning
winnings
winnow
winsome
winter
wintertime
wintry

wisdom
wish
wishbone
wishy-washy
wisp
wispy
wisteria
wistful
wit
witch
witchcraft
with
withdraw
withdrawal
withdrawn
withdrew
wither
withered
withering
withhold
within
without
withstand
witless
witness
witter
witticism
wittingly
witty
wizard
wizardry
wizened

wo:
women
womenfolk

/wɜː/

were:
were
weren't

whir:
whir
whirl
whirlpool
whirlwind
whirr

whor:
whorl

wor:
word
wording
wordless
wordplay
wordy
work
workable
workaday

/wɪə/

workaholic
workbench
workbook
workday
worker
workforce
workhorse
workhouse
working
workload
workman
workmanlike
workmanship
workmate
workout
workplace
workroom
worksheet
workshop
workstation
worktop
world
worldly
worldwide
worm
wormwood
worse
worsen
worship
worshipful
worst
worth
worthless
worthwhile
worthy

/wɪə/

wear:
wear
wearisome
weary

weir:
weir
weird
weirdo

we're:
we're

/waɪ/

whi:
while
whilst
whine
white
whiteboard
Whitehall
whiten
whitewash
whiting

whitish

why:
why

wi:
wide
widen
widespread
wife
wifely
wild
wildcat
wildfire
wildfowl
wildlife
wildly
wiles
wily
wind
wind-up
wine
winery
wino
wipe
wiper
wise
wisecrack
wisecracking
wives

y:
Y,y
YMCA
YWCA

/waɪə/

wir:
wire
wired
wireless
wiretap
wiring
wiry

/wɒ/

wa:
wad
wadding
waddle
wadi
waffle
waft
wallaby
wallet
wallop
wallow
wally
wan
wand
wander

wanderer
wandering
wanderings
wanderlust
wanna
wannabe
want
wanting
wanton
warrant
warranty
warren
warrior
was
wash
washable
washbasin
washcloth
washer
washing
washout
washroom
washstand
wasn't
wasp
waspish
watch
watchdog
watchful
watchman
watchtower
watchword
watt
wattage
wattle

wha:
what
whatever
whatnot
what's
whatshername
whatshisname
whatsit
whatsoever

who:
whopper
whopping

wo:
wobble
wobbly
wodge
wog
wok
wombat
wonky

/woʊ/

whoa:
whoa

wo:
woke
woken
wont
won't
wove
woven

woe:
woe
woebegone
woeful

/wɔ:/

wa:
wall
wallcovering
walled
wallflower
wallpaper
walnut
walrus
waltz
water
waterbed
watercolour
watercourse
watercress
waterfall
waterfowl
waterfront
waterline
waterlogged
watermark
watermelon
watermill
waterproof
watershed
waterside
watertight
waterway
waterworks
watery

wal:
walk
walkabout
walker
walkie-talkie
walking
Walkman
walkout
walkover
walkway

war:
war
warble
warbler
ward
warden

/wʊ/

warder
wardrobe
warfare
warhead
warhorse
warlike
warlord
warm
warmonger
warmth
warn
warning
warp
warpath
warplane
warring
warship
wart
warthog
wartime

whar:
wharf

wor:
wore
worn

/wʊ/

whoo:
whoopee
whoops
whoosh

wo:
wolf
wolfhound
wolves
woman
womanhood
womanizer
womanizing
womankind
womanly

woo:
wood
woodcock
woodcutter
wooded
wooden
woodland
woodlouse
woodpecker
woodpile
woodshed
woodwind
woodwork
woodworm
woody
woof

wool
woollen
woolly

wor:
worsted

woul:
would
wouldn't
would've

/wu:/

whoo:
whoop

wo:
womb

woo:
woo
woozy

wou:
wound

/waʊ/

wou:
wound
wound up

wow:
wow

/wʌ/

o:
once
one
one's
oneself
one-upmanship

wo:
won
wonder
wonderful
wonderland
wonderment
wondrous
worried
worrier
worrisome
worry
worrying

/wə/

wa:
was

were:
were

woul:
would

/j/

/jæ/

ya:
yak
yam
yank
Yankee
yap

/jeɪ/

yea:
yea

/jɑ:/

ya:
yahoo

yar:
yard
Yardie
yardstick
yarn

/je/

ye:
yeah
yell
yellow
yellowish
yellowy
yelp
Yemeni
yen
yes
yesterday
yesteryear
yet

/ji:/

ye:
ye

yea:
yeast
yeasty

/jɜ:/

year:
yearn
yearning

/jɪə/

year:
year
yearbook
yearly

yie:
yield
yielding

/jɪ/

yi:
Yiddish
yippee

/jɒ/

yach:
yacht
yachting
yachtsman
yachtswoman

yo:
yob
yobbo
yoghurt
yogurt
Yom Kippur
yon
yonder
yonks

/joʊ/

yeo:
yeoman

yo:
yodel
yoga
yogi
yoke
yokel
yolk
yo-yo

/jɔ:/

yaw:
yaw
yawn

yor:
yore
Yorkshire pudding

your:
your
you're
yours
yourself

/jʊ/

eur:
eureka

ur:
uranium
urinal

/jaʊ/

yow:
yowl

/jʌ/

/jʌ/

you:
young
youngish
youngster

yu:
yuk
yum
yummy
yuppie

/z/

/zæ/

za:
zap

/zeɪ/

za:
zany

/zɑː/

czar:
czar
czarina

czarist

tsar:
tsar
tsarina
tsarist

/ze/

xe:
xenophobia
xenophobic

z:
Z,z

ze:
zebra
Zen
zenith
zephyr
zest

zea:
zealot
zealous

/ziː/

zea:
zeal

/zɪə/

xer:
Xerox

zer:
zero

/zɪ/

zi:
zigzag
zilch
zillion
Zimmer frame
zinc
zing
zip
zipper
zit
zither

/zaɪ/

xy:
xylophone

zei:
zeitgeist
Zionism

Zionist

/zɒ/

zo:
zombie
zonked

/zoʊ/

zo:
zodiac
zone

/zuː/

zoo:
zoo
zoology
zoom

zu:
zucchini
Zulu

Other titles in The COBUILD Series

COBUILD English Grammar is an authoritative reference grammar specially designed for advanced students and teachers of English. It gives detailed treatments of the common grammatical patterns and parts of speech, along with thousands of real English examples, all chosen from The Bank of English.

COBUILD English Usage is a comprehensive reference book aimed at intermediate and advanced students and teachers of English. It presents the most important facts about modern English usage with detailed explanations of over 2000 usage points.

COBUILD English Guides provide extensive information on specific areas of today's English based on the evidence of The Bank of English. A unique series which is indispensable to students and teachers alike.

COBUILD Concordance Samplers provide corpus data taken direct from The Bank of English. Each sampler focuses on a particular area of English grammar or vocabulary. Suitable for learners of intermediate to advanced level, the material offers a fresh and different approach to language learning and reinforcement.